Oscar Wilde

Oscar Wilde as a child

OSCAR WILDE

♣ by Philippe Jullian ♣

TRANSLATED BY
VIOLET WYNDHAM

Readers Union · Constable
LONDON 1970

Translation © 1969 Constable & Co. Ltd.

This is one of a small edition made available to its members only by
Readers Union by arrangement with the original publishers Constable
& Company Limited.

Details of RU may be had from Readers Union Limited at 10–13
Bedford Street, London W.C.2 and at Letchworth Garden City, Herts.

The book was printed in Great Britain by
The Anchor Press Limited at Tiptree, Essex.

For Christian and Josiane Ayoub-Simano

Contents

Illustrations

LINE DRAWINGS IN TEXT

The front and back endpapers contain a facsimile of the letter written by Wilde to the publisher Leonard Smithers, in connection with the publication of *Salome*, quoted in full on page 373.

Oscar Wilde

Introduction

In an earlier work I have traced the development of Art Nouveau from its inception, through the man who was its most active propagator in France – Robert de Montesquiou. We can now follow through Oscar Wilde the heights and the depths of aestheticism. Wilde was no more an originator than Montesquiou, but he was the better propagandist and certainly the better writer. His insolent behaviour and the punishment it brought him have made him appear in turn a clown and a martyr. These contrasts in his destiny have inspired many books. This one has benefited from recent publications which have brought to light much material hitherto unpublished about Oscar Wilde and his era. First and foremost there is the admirable collection of *The Letters of Oscar Wilde* edited by Sir Rupert Hart-Davis: I have made use of the English edition that appeared in 1962. Then two works of Mr. Montgomery Hyde; *The Trials of Oscar Wilde* and *Oscar Wilde – The Aftermath*. Max Beerbohm's *Letters to Reggie Turner*, also edited and published by Sir Rupert Hart-Davis (1964), supply a lot of new material. A work such as that of Phyllis Grosskurth on John Addington Symonds tears away a part of the veil which covers the Victorian homosexual world. Furthermore, every year brings more revelations, England has lost her inhibitions and Oscar Wilde is no longer the only one of his kind; it has recently come to light that Samuel Butler was in love with a young Australian. Probably soon it will be the turn of Henry James, as some very compromising letters concerning him are circulating in London. Two books have been particularly useful to me, Monsieur Robert Merle's thesis (1943), important for the understanding of the psychology of Wilde, and Hesketh Pearson's extremely vivid biography which appeared in 1946 and includes the evidence of some of Wilde's contemporaries. In the bibliography can be found a list of the other works which have been consulted.

When writing about Montesquiou, I had a great deal of unpublished material and plenty of living witnesses; I have not been so lucky in this respect with Wilde. At best the Comtesse Gabriel de la Rochefoucault has been kind enough to tell me of a visit by the poet to her mother, the Princess of Monaco, and Christabel, Lady Aberconway remembers having been kissed by Oscar Wilde when out with her nurse in Chelsea. On the other hand, I have met many friends of Lord Alfred Douglas; two well-known writers, Mr. William Plomer and Mr. Angus Wilson, have confirmed my theories about Douglas being blackened in De Profundis and about the jealousy of Robert Ross. Ross, considered a saint by Wilde's biographers, behaved more like a wronged widow. Mr. William Plomer, a great specialist of the period, has been willing to research into the evidence about certain people in the book. Miss Nathalie Barney, with her good sense and her faithful memory, has helped me to find my way among the disciples of the poet.

I would like to thank Professor Mario Praz warmly, first for his excellent Romantic Agony to which I often had recourse, and also for having drawn my attention to articles on Wilde. His pupil, Mr. Tomaso d'Amico, has had the goodness to allow me to see his thesis on Wilde's aesthetic ideas, which was of great use. Like all biographers of Wilde, I have indulged in the sport of seeking in his works his sources, that which he borrowed and what he imitated. I have two small discoveries to my credit: *Intentions* descends in a direct line from Paul Bourget's *Dialogues Esthétiques*, and *Dorian Gray* owes much to Jean Lorrain. It also seems strange that the considerable influence of Gustave Moreau has so far not been recognised.

During a winter in Egypt, my friends Christian Ayoub, Desmond Stewart and Bent Mohn, all three writers, patiently agreed to talk about Wilde for hours on end. In London, George Painter, the biographer of Proust, and the poet Alberto de Lacerda, suggested useful books to read. George Painter even plunged into the inferno of the British Museum in order to find an erotic novel attributed to Wilde. In Paris, the Baignères told me about the meeting of Wilde and of Proust, which had been described to them by their grandfather. Mr. Philippe Barrès allowed me to see his father's correspondence. Mr. Yves Clojenson provided me with documents concerning Huysmans and Wilde. Mr. Vyvyan Holland showed me the very beautiful photograph of his mother with her first-born; Mr. Benjamin Sonnenberg the drawing by Greiffenhagen; and Madame Schnerb, born Pierre-Lièvre, the portrait of the Baronne Deslandes. I want also to thank Giraud-Badin, the booksellers, for having shown me an unpublished letter from Wilde on the subject of Beardsley.

Walks in Dublin with Mr. Desmond Guinness and Miss Shewan Lynann have given me a chance to discover the background to Wilde's youth, and Miss Lynann has given me the records on which the admirable actor Micheál MacLiámmóir makes the poet live again. I should, however, feel ungrateful were I to stop my thanks here. I owe a great deal to English friends and English houses, which it would take too long to enumerate. At the house of Mrs. Guy Wyndham, my admirable translator, and the daughter of Mrs. Leverson, I heard the echo of famous conversations and I also recognised the atmosphere of the comedies at Lady Aberconway's and at Lady Bonham-Carter's. After the war I knew two celebrated aesthetes of the 'twenties', Harold Acton and Brian Howard who appear, since Oxford days to have shared Oscar's domain, the former erudite and social, the latter debauched and paradoxical. Some settings appear scarcely to have changed in eighty years, week-ends at Oxford, tea-parties of old gentlemen in boudoirs which could almost be mistaken for chapels, and certainly the period spent in a house in Tite Street, near to that of Wilde, where I discovered the taste, the confusion, the air of panache and the indolence of that remote relation whom they still think of as 'Dear Oscar'.

I am particularly happy that the translation of this book has been entrusted to Mrs. Wyndham, who through her mother, has special knowledge of the Wilde epoch. It would take too long to enumerate all the additions and improvements that Mrs. Wyndham has made to my text, but among many others are the incidents connected with Mrs. Leverson, Ellen Terry, Gerald Campbell and the Hope-Nicholson family. I would like to thank most warmly my friend Felix Hope-Nicholson, who told me of the links between his mother's family and Wilde, and Mrs. Hope-Nicholson who has allowed us to include many passages from her mother's diary, some of which are unpublished. I would also like to thank Mr. Brian Reade for permission to quote his letter about *Teleny*.

I join with my translator in thanking Mrs. Elizabeth Wyndham for having taken so much trouble, in research, in tracing sources and in trying to ensure the correctness of the English version. My thanks are also due to the owners of the copyrights and to the authors from whom I have quoted, who have given me permission to do so.

1   The people of Dublin

A park-like countryside, a coastline that might have been painted by Turner, misty headlands, rocks foaming with spray, hundreds of views and beauty spots for tourists, picturesque villages and a colonnaded capital: Ireland, when it does not rain too much, can be enchanting. Yet, in the middle of the nineteenth century, through famine and emigration, this demi-paradise lost half its population. Potatoes being the staple diet of the people, it was a major calamity when the crops failed through exceptionally hard frosts followed by the potato pest, phylloxera. Between 1845 and 1850, more than two million people died of starvation and a few years later an even greater number emigrated to America in the hope of escaping this calamity.

The incapacity of the Administration, the cupidity of the large landowners who seldom set foot on their properties, the obstructions thrust upon Catholics by a Protestant Church, were finally revealed to Europe through a catastrophe which went far beyond anything already suffered; and there were certain civil servants who believed that the Irish question could only be answered by making matters worse. The problem dated from the savage tyrannies of Cromwell and William of Orange against a nation which looked for supporters of its Faith in France and Spain, the enemies of England. It came near to being solved in the second half of the eighteenth century when the island, then prosperous, was granted legislative independence, but the involvement of Irish patriots with revolutionary France gave England a good excuse to

B

put Ireland under a Viceroy and to dissolve its Parliament. The Irish aristocracy then left the country to be nearer the seat of power and many of the prolific Irish population crossed the channel to swell the ranks both of the soldiers and prostitutes in England. In 1848 the emergence of a French Republic spurred the starving inhabitants of the island to commit reckless murder and arson. The leaders were outstripped in violence by those they had aroused, and reprisals were of equal brutality: villages were set on fire and whole families expelled, while agitators were whipped or shot.

In spite of these former horrors, life in Dublin and its outskirts retained many delightful aspects. The eighteenth century lingered on in the form and style with which the capital had been constructed, though the rafters of Parliament no longer resounded to those orations in which Celtic charm had been enhanced by Latin quotations. Virtuosi of the highest class were no longer heard performing to impressed audiences under the chandeliers of the concert halls. Drawing-rooms covered in stucco had ceased to be the setting for balls and parties, and no more were coaches to be seen rolling round the squares of pilastered pink brick houses. On the river, very few boats dropped anchor before the Claude Lorrain customs house.

Power, money, and elegance might have disappeared, together with semi-liberty, but the spoken word – Ireland's greatest art – remained. What is affectionately called 'blarney' by Irish and non-Irish alike, is a mixture of fable and charm, the gift of beautifying truth (very much in need of it) for the benefit of the unimaginative. Having kept apart from the industrial revolution, Ireland retained an agricultural society which the Victorians failed to understand. Dublin was a hundred years behind London, and in its decaying drawing-rooms members of a hospitable, gossiping society entertained each other at interminable parties, and assembled under the pretext of weddings or of hunting, in the neighbouring castles. The Anglo-Irish, while retaining the prestige of a governing class, shared the Irish fantasies, just as the bulk of the families who came to Ireland in the course of the centuries had succumbed to its charm; in two generations charm overcame principles, but there remained good education, the possession of which easily excused eccentricity, and a love of sport which was respected by everyone. The Anglo-Irish were heavy drinkers, gamblers, womanisers, often unscrupulous, but generally brave and good company. Dublin knew beautiful adventuresses, like Lady Blessington, and brilliant politicians, such as O'Connell and Parnell; the former was to father bastards far and wide, and the latter, thirty years later, saw his career ruined by the scandal of a divorce case. They comprised landowners, many of whom had been impoverished by the great famine, lawyers and some doctors. They had remained Protestant because no official post would be given to a Catholic. They were called 'gentry' rather than 'middle-class' having aristocratic tastes in spite of precarious resources. The nobility who had left their Dublin houses were completely English, contenting themselves with the rents which were sent to them regularly by their bailiffs. Boredom had emptied the castles with the exception of those in the neighbourhood of Dublin, such as the Castle of Malahide, where the Talbots had settled since the twelfth century (its proximity to a bay entitled the owner to the hereditary title of Admiral of the Seven Seas) and also one belonging to Lord Dunsany, head of the Plunkett family.

Legend was soon to be associated with these houses of the preceding century, as, for example at Castletown, which the Connollys had embellished with triumphal arches and an obelisk, and to which the Devil paid a visit as recently as 1820; at the end of a day's hunting the subject of conversation at dinner chosen by a handsome unknown man (who had been made welcome as is anyone on a horse in a hunting community) shocked a bishop, himself a follower of the hunt; not able to contain himself any longer, the prelate asked to have the Bible brought to him, this he proceeded to fling at the blasphemous stranger who immediately disappeared in a clap of thunder, leaving behind him a strong smell of sulphur. The scorched traces in the woodwork of his departure are still pointed out to visitors.

Another legend concerns the coat of arms of the Fitzgerald family, of which the Duke of Leinster is the head. A monkey has been depicted on it ever since the day that a baby was snatched out of its cradle to safety during a fire by one of these animals. The third Duke was one of the noblemen who helped to relieve the miseries of the famine. His house near Merrion Square, then a palace, is now the Irish Parliament. The nobility and gentry alike loved horses, cards, brandy and conversation.

In this oppressed country intellectuals took refuge in delving into the distant past. To be able to claim former grandeur, the erudite exhumed that civilisation which between the fifth and eighth centuries produced the marvellous illuminated manuscripts and sculptured crosses covered with tracery whose influence could be seen reappearing at the end of the nineteenth century in Art Nouveau. They wrote wild and poetic legends from which Ossian drew his inspiration; they lived on in the ironic and disrespectful tradition of Swift and Sheridan. Thus the eccentrics who pullulated in Dublin could claim the right to the dandyism of Sheridan whose exploits were those of a legendary hero. Thanks to them, the magnificent, forsaken city seemed to an English stranger like 'a theatre delivered over to clowns'.

One could have met Charles Maturin (the extravagance of whose novels outdid those of Mrs. Radcliffe) looking like Don Quixote about to tilt at some new windmill; or that baronet who killed his greatest friend in a duel after having ruined him; or perhaps the young girl, an intimate friend of the Princess Dashkova, lady-in-waiting to Catherine the Great, who ran a home for old ladies and forced them to sing hymns composed by her closest friend. To an intrepid horseman, a man of wit, or a charming woman, everything was forgiven; money meant less in Dublin than well-born relations, and 'blarney' more than either scholarship or pretension.

Among the characters whose sayings, adventures and scandals provided food for the lively imaginations of the Dubliners of the nineteenth century, were a young doctor and a young poetess. They were remarkable by reason of their intellectual qualities; he, inquisitive, dissolute, ribald, a figure of the eighteenth century; she, with her enthusiasms and illusions, a pure romantic.

William Wilde was born in 1815, the son of a doctor whose family, originally of Anglo-Dutch origin, had been settled in Ireland since the seventeenth century. William's mother had been a Miss Emily Fynne, a descendant of the ancient chiefs of Connaught, a line which was not only lost in mythology but also particularly noted for mental instability. As William's paternal grandmother was an O'Flynn, he could boast of being three-quarters Irish. From the time that he left college, having passed his examinations with ease, William, small and odd-looking, attracted much attention in Dublin, and his malicious wit brought him many friends. Of these he was certainly in need, if only to support him through the embarrassments caused by his amorous misadventures. Near-dwarf though he was, William was irresistible to women: his first notable platonic conquest was the romantic novelist Maria Edgeworth. At twenty the first of his many natural children was born. The admirable side of his character, to be recognised later, was first shown when he distinguished himself during a cholera epidemic, and again when in Egypt, deeply shocked by the prevalence of trachoma and other diseases of the eye, he determined to start what was to be his life-long study of that subject.

Following the publication of a travel book and some articles on medicine, William was elected a member of the Irish Academy. His appointment as lecturer was apt, as no one enjoyed talking more than he did, and all Dublin went to listen. He visited Vienna for a short time to further his studies of the eye and ear, and returned to Ireland a specialist in the diseases of both.

Medicine, however, was not enough to satisfy William's insatiable craving for knowledge; archaeology became his next interest. He unearthed Celtic tumuli and published his discoveries in an album beautifully illustrated with lithographs, which linked his name with the Celtic revival. This preoccupation with the seventh century did not deter him from springing forward to the eighteenth where his study of the last years of Swift showed how the mind of this genius had been slowly destroyed by lethargy and madness. The famine of 1845 interrupted William's literary career. Disaster always brought out the best in him; he organised relief, visited those abandoned in deserted villages, treated typhoid fever cases and never seemed to give up hope even when faced by appalling catastrophes; he overcame exhaustion with an inner buoyancy of energy and spirit.

The responsibility of the English for the famine infuriated many young Irish patriots who went further than Daniel O'Connell and demanded complete independence. William secretly associated himself with the views of the most advanced of these, Gavan Duffy and Thomas Davis, founders of *The Nation*. In this newspaper some verses of an exalted patriotism appeared, signed 'Speranza', inciting the Irish to join the anti-monarchist revolt which was sweeping Europe at that time. William read in March 1848:

> 'No! soul answers soul, steel flashes on steel,
> And land wakens land with a grand thunder-peal.
> Shall we, oh! my Brothers, but weep, pray and groan,
> When France reads her rights by the flames of a Throne?
> Shall we fear and falter to join the grand chorus,
> When Europe has trod the dark pathway before us?'

Quite transported, and fired with admiration, William Wilde obtained an introduction to Speranza and found her in appearance to be a Junoesque figure, with a high forehead and straight nose, which deflected the attention from a rather weak chin. She was very large, and the fine effect she made was enhanced by a crown of dark hair; even though she was ten years his junior, her face was already showing signs of heaviness. Like William, she could claim much Irish blood. Her father was a solicitor from Wexford called Elgee, who had his daughter baptised Jane Francesca to stress a doubtful Italian ancestry. Elgee might be a corruption of Algiotti, or indeed a link, however apocryphal, with Dante Alighieri. In point of fact, she had a real uncle of whom she could boast: the Rev. Charles Maturin, a distinguished writer, the author of the 'black' or, as we might call it today, 'sick' novel, *Melmoth the Wanderer*, which had been greatly admired by Byron and Balzac; here and there this enormous book has something in common with the works of the Marquis de Sade, and jumps from the ludicrous to the tragic with a typically Irish confusion. Jane Francesca, as an infant prodigy, spoke French and Italian fluently. At the age of

twenty, she translated *Sidonia von Stork* from the German, a
story of sorcery which inspired a picture by Rossetti, and
wrote poems on almost every subject until her heart found
worthy inspiration in patriotism. On momentous occasions
she abandoned verse for proclamation. Her article 'Jacta
Alea Est', printed in *The Nation* of 29th July 1848, could
hardly fail to be read as a Call to Arms: 'Oh! for a hundred
thousand muskets glittering brightly in the light of
Heaven, and the monumental barricades stretching across
each of our noble streets made desolate by England –
circling round that doomed Castle, where the foreign tyrant
has held his council of treason and iniquity against our
people for seven hundred years. . . . One bold, one decisive
move, one instant to take breath, and then a rising; a rush,
a charge from the North, South, East and West upon the
English garrison and the land is ours!'

The courage of this girl did not stop at the written word;
The Nation was seized and at the trial of its editor, Gavan
Duffy, Speranza sensationally interrupted the counsel to
claim authorship of the inflammatory article attributed to
Duffy; the magistrates were no longer able to get a word in;
'I alone am the culprit, I wrote the offending article,' she
cried. Her imposing presence may have intimidated the
Court but her eloquence and beauty touched the hearts of
the jury; true Irishmen, they found it impossible to agree.

Speranza left the tribunal a national heroine. The little
Doctor, completely dazzled, flung himself at her feet and
later asked for and obtained her hand in marriage. The
wedding took place on 12th November 1851, and seldom
can there have been such an ill-assorted couple: the husband debauched and almost deformed, the wife idealistic
and statuesque. But whatever the future difficulties of their
marriage, because of their shared curiosity in people and
books and their love of conversation, it can be said that the

marriage was a success and that they were never bored in each other's company.

At first the Wildes installed themselves in a small way in Westland Row, Dublin, on the fringe of a better-class neighbourhood. They had no great expectations from their families, who had lost what little they had in the famine. In this house their two sons were born: Willie in 1852 and Oscar on 16th October 1854. On the latter occasion the young mother wrote to a friend: 'Joan of Arc was never meant for marriage, so here I am bound heart and soul to the home hearth. Behold me, Speranza, rocking a cradle at this present time of writing, in which lies my second son – a babe of one month old the sixteenth of this month, November, and as large and fine and handsome and healthy as if he were three months. He is to be called Oscar Fingal Wilde. Is that not grand, misty and Ossianic?' She forgot to mention his two other Christian names; O'Flaherty, after her ancestors, the ferocious O'Flahertys of Galway, and Wills. Oscar was the first name of the King of Sweden who, it was said, had asked to be godfather to the child because William had operated on him and cured him of cataract.

When speaking of their sons, Speranza would say: 'I am not anxious about Willie, he has a well-shaped head, but I expect simply extraordinary things of Oscar.' Rich patients and further journeys abroad spread the reputation of the Doctor, whom both Napoleon III and the Emperor Maximilian consulted. At last William was appointed Oculist to the Queen in Ireland – no hard task, as Queen Victoria's sight was excellent and, in ten years, she certainly did not spend more than a few days in that country. But, apart from his medical consultations, he never ceased to work, he finished a treatise on ear surgery and continued to publish works on Irish antiquities. As to Speranza, she undertook a translation from Dumas and published a book of poems,

Shadows from Life in the style of Tennyson, and also taught
herself Greek; there could seldom have existed a couple
more avid for culture than Mr. and Mrs. William Wilde.

William Wilde's prosperity enabled him to move
his family to Merrion Square, one of the most beautiful
localities in Dublin; the garden was surrounded by houses
identical behind their wrought-iron railings. Since the
nobility had abandoned the capital after the abolition of
Parliament, the Square was now inhabited by the middle-
classes. Oscar grew up in the background which Sheridan
chose for his comedies; the dramatist had been born a
hundred years before Oscar in Dorset Street, only a few steps
from Merrion Square. The School for Scandal could have been
staged on the vast flight of stairs with wrought-iron bani-
sters, or in the drawing-room of the Wilde's house which
was decorated with cameos on a mauve and pistachio-green
background. One could have visualised Joseph Surface leaning with his elbows on one of the marble-columned mantel-
pieces, or Lady Sneerwell's face reflected in the looking-
glasses flanked by dwarf palm-trees. But Irish confusion
soon prevailed over English elegance. The Wildes arrived
and with them was a grotesque train of servants – sluts to
do the cooking and cleaning and an urchin to run errands
and play the part of a footman. They brought masses of
books, plaster casts, hangings from Egypt, pictures richly
framed (no doubt gifts from grateful patients) and, as in all
Irish households, enormous salmon in glass cases which
had been caught by the master of the house.

Hardly were they settled in than Speranza started to entertain; the guests were as ill-assorted as the furniture, and the
young couple kept completely open house. They gave
concerts, they played charades, as in the eighteenth century,
and their life was generally somewhat reminiscent of the

novels of Smollett or even more of Diderot's *Le Neveu de Rameau*. Discussions or story-telling often lasted until dawn and it was sufficient to be a would-be good talker to be received with open arms at 1 Merrion Square. The youngish hostess, already of imposing size, her face heavily powdered, her looped hair parted in the middle, saw herself as an allegorical figure – sometimes with a crown of laurels on her head as Corinna, on other occasions, dressed all in white, with mistletoe twined in her glossy hair, as Norma. One ungrateful guest likened her to 'a tragedy queen at a suburban theatre'. This sibyl appeared to be trying to revive Sheridan's wit, and her sayings were repeated all over the town.

In contrast to the English custom, the little Wildes were always round their mother's skirts, and as soon as their table manners were suitable, they were present at meals. The widely assorted guests usually to be found at the table could have included officers from the garrison, or colleagues of the Doctor, literary and political bohemians, ladies with large hearts, or ladies who had been abandoned by husbands or lovers – Mrs. Wilde, like George Sand, liked to be surrounded by the victims of society: 'I soar above the miasmas of the commonplace,' she would say as she closed her eyes to the Doctor's affairs with one or other of his protégées.

English visitors were surprised at the looseness of the conversation. Among them was an astronomer, Sir William Hamilton, who kept up through a voluminous correspondence, a platonic passion for Speranza. Among the Irish table-companions were two remarkable men. One of these, Sheridan Le Fanu, was a journalist and a novelist, a master of the uncanny, and of horror. In *Uncle Silas* and *The House by the Churchyard* he created a style between a 'black' novel and a detective story. He was the nephew of Richard Brinsley Sheridan, and must surely have evoked in the presence of the young Oscar the career of the famous dramatist – a career with which Oscar's was to have many points in common: the success of their brilliant comedies, popularity with the fashionable world, a glamorous reputation for wit and, on the darker side, constant anxieties about money. No one has described better than Sheridan Le Fanu the horror that can overcome one in deserted houses, in gardens which have reverted to a wilderness, or before a face which looms up in a fog. Le Fanu died in 1873 from an overdose of laudanum taken to ward off his nightly nightmare of being buried alive.

The other remarkable guest at 1 Merrion Square was the Rev. John Pentland Mahaffy, a much younger man than Le Fanu. He was a distinguished Greek scholar, a wonderful conversationalist and very popular with the nobility; Oscar was to be his pupil at Trinity College. It is not certain whether a far greater man, who was also to influence Oscar, may not also have dined at Merrion Square. It is unlikely that Speranza would have allowed so distinguished a lion as Ruskin to escape her. He was in Dublin in 1868 to lecture and to supervise the building in Venetian-Byzantine style of a School of Engineering. He did not like the city and thought that it had 'the sadness of Modena and the morals of St. Giles'. (The latter was one of the worst neighbourhoods in London.)

The year 1864 saw the Wildes at the zenith of their glory and at the start of their very rapid decline. At the beginning of the year the Doctor received the Knighthood of St. Patrick at Dublin Castle, and the ceremony was performed with pseudo-mediaeval pomp. He thus became Sir William Wilde and the heroine of the Independence was forced thereby to accept the title of 'Lady'. She had recently given birth to a daughter called Isola Francesca; no doubt after Francesca di Rimini, made celebrated by 'Uncle' Dante. As honours accrued, money flowed in, and the Wildes built a country

Sir William and Lady Wilde

house on the borders of Lough Corrib in Co. Mayo. Blocks of granite emerged here and there against the sepia-coloured water; on one side a marsh bordered the lake, on the other were fields of brilliant green, separated by stone walls, with tufts of grass sodden with water like a sponge. The summer twilight lingers late over this peaceful landscape: a ghostly mist will suddenly rise, and behind a chain of black hills enormous swirling clouds are torn to shreds by the wind from the sea.

Sir William did not look happy. He drank more and washed less, and spiteful remarks about him, going further than mere back-biting, became increasingly common: 'Why has the Doctor got black nails?' 'Because he has been scratching himself.' He entrusted part of his practice to one of his bastards, Henry Wilson, left the care of the children to his wife and would often disappear for several days on end. He was worried, and not surprisingly, because for four years a young half-mad girl had been blackmailing him. Having been his mistress for a time, she was determined not to be deserted. Twice she had got enough money out of him to go to Australia; neither time had she gone further than Liverpool. More than money, she wanted the entire attention of the Doctor for herself; she interrupted his consultations and once arrived unexpectedly in the drawing-room of Merrion Square. Lady Wilde, to whom the situation was only too familiar, sent her away. Finally the girl bombarded everyone who counted in Dublin with scandalous anonymous letters. As no one paid any attention to them, this maenad printed pamphlets in the name of 'Speranza', which told how the Doctor had violated her, after having given her chloroform. The libel was distributed before the door of the Young Men's Christian Association on the day when the Doctor was to deliver a lecture there.

Lady Wilde, so as to be disturbed no longer by the visits

of the leech-like Miss Travers, of whom Sir William had made so disastrous a conquest, retired with her children to the seaside. But there, under the windows of the boarding-house, urchins were selling newspapers, crying 'Frightful Wilde Scandal', 'Rape of a young girl'. The mother was roused by that which the wife had ignored. She wrote to the father of Miss Travers, putting into focus the relations between 'this creature' and her husband. Armed with this letter, Miss Travers sued Lady Wilde for libel and Sir William 'in conformity' claiming £2,000 damages and costs. The case was indelicate and interminable and reported copiously in the Press. Miss Travers only obtained a symbolic penny for her virtue, but Sir William had to pay the costs of the case which amounted to several thousands of pounds. He got into debt, neglected his patients and spent more and more of his time in the country, leaving his wife in Merrion Square, where the house was thronged by an increasingly motley succession of guests.

2   Oscar – the hope of Speranza

Regretfully Speranza accepted separation from her sons when the time came for them to go to school. The inevitable choice, from motives of economy, was Portora Royal School, Enniskillen, which occupied a white-painted country house overlooking a lake in a large park. Its high reputation in Ireland derived as much from antiquity as from the level of its education – not that the Portora Old School Tie was ever a guarantee of class in the British Empire. Oscar, a child who for some time had been clothed in his mother's dresses (and what dresses!), must have suffered agonies of mind when, at the age of ten, he found himself in the midst of a crowd of rough and teasing boys: he knew himself to be the object of curiosity – the son of the Wildes, the details of whose case filled the newspapers; also he was tall for his age and awkward, and felt himself to be different from the others. He disliked games but, with a mercy that seems surprising, the masters soon gave up making him hold a cricket bat or play football. Years later he informed a stupefied schoolmaster: 'Football is all very well as a game for rough girls, but it is hardly suitable for delicate boys', and when watching a lacrosse match in America he said that he had refused to play cricket at school 'because the attitudes assumed were so indecent'.

Willie had already been at the school for a year and except for his laziness was thought to be the replica of his father. He was popular and impressed his schoolfellows both by the way he used his fists and by his gift for repartee: boys

20

who enjoyed a joke always took his part in disputes.

The young Oscar, on the contrary, was very much his mother's son; the chief thing that he had in common with Willie was the 'gift of the gab' and the art of repartee. Oscar rarely spoke of his father and the famous line in his play *The Importance of Being Earnest*: 'All women become like their mothers. That's their tragedy. No man does. That's his.' was perhaps his genuine belief. Like Speranza, Oscar's appetite for reading was immense; his memory was exceptionally good and he learned without difficulty. If Speranza was a Gargamella in the way she devoured books, he was a Gargantua. She had grounded the boy in Greek and Latin and it was not long before he overtook even his older schoolfellows in his knowledge of the classics. Having very little respect for his masters, Oscar much enjoyed asking questions that exposed their ignorance. Later, when he recalled the time spent at Portora he did so with no sentiment: in his works there are several epigrams against professors such as; 'Education is an admirable thing, but it is well to remember from time to time that nothing that is worth knowing can be taught.' However, the masters put up with this difficult pupil because his astonishing progress lent a certain prestige to the school. At the age of twelve he read both Homer and Virgil in the original, and – which seemed even more extraordinary – with passion. Books such as adventure stories and the novels of Dickens, dear to his schoolfellows, meant absolutely nothing to him. Despite Oscar's horror of games, and his taste in literature, the other boys were won over by his life-like imitations of the mannerisms of the masters, and by his power of turning quite ordinary incidents into fascinating stories. In the secluded paths of the gardens, and in the dormitories, the children crowded round this large boy who charmed them even at that early age, as he was to charm others all his life, by the rarest of gifts, being

c

able to give an extraordinary quality to the events of every-day life.

After having heard so much at home about law-suits, Oscar's interest was aroused, and he read carefully in the newspapers the chronicles of the law-courts, collecting facts which he wove into stories. One complicated case excited his curiosity so much that he immersed himself in the study of the Court of Arches and eventually declared that to be the hero of a famous law-suit and to go down to posterity as a defendant in a case of 'Regina v. Wilde' was his greatest ambition.

In view of John Addington Symonds' revelations of love-affairs and orgies at his public school, where the prettiest boys received feminine nick-names from the older boys who fought each other to obtain their favours, and where brutal bullying awaited those who refused them or who gave them imprudently, revelations that are borne out in *Tom Brown's Schooldays* with its account of relentless beatings of small boys by prefects, one cannot but ask whether Oscar had any sentimental or physical relationship with any of the boys at Portora. The answer to this is no, except for one sentimental episode reported by that often unreliable bio-grapher Frank Harris who, in this case, appears convincing. According to him, Oscar confided that he often went for walks with a boy a little younger than himself who listened agape to his improvisations: 'My friend had a wonderful gift for listening,' he said. When the time came for him to leave school for good, Oscar did not disguise his joy. 'You seem to be glad to go,' said the friend, asking if he could accompany Oscar to the railway station. On arrival there, the boy stayed in the compartment until the whistle sounded for the train to leave, whereupon he took Oscar's head in his hands and kissed him on the mouth. Oscar sat there in amazement. 'This is love: this is what he meant –

love. I was trembling all over. For a long while I sat, unable to think, all shaken with wonder and remorse.'

The Public School system is frequently blamed for the sexual imbalance of the British upper and upper-middle classes: be that as it may, it is true that some years before Oscar's school-days Swinburne discovered at Eton the pleasures of being beaten. For others brutality became an expression of passion. Unlike some of his companions and acquaintances in later life, Oscar was never to practice either of these perversions.

The admiration of his friends encouraged him to assume a theatrical attitude in contemplation of, say, a flower or a sunset. Certainly he genuinely reacted more deeply towards that kind of beauty than did others, but there was also something provocative about his manner of expressing these reactions.

Lady Wilde alone prevented the family from foundering in scandal and bankruptcy, not that she was practical or economical herself, but she forced others to be so. In Dublin it would be hard to press a debt on a woman who received bailiffs while reading Aeschylus aloud to her son; Speranza had a taste for the sublime. She had replied to the Magistrates: 'These things do not interest me,' and never would she reproach her husband for having dragged her into the disastrous case. Nor did she appear jealous of the mistresses whom he continued to welcome under her roof, for this dirty, drunken mannikin was attractive to women to the end of his life. Oscar later related as an instance of her noble serenity that 'before my father died in 1876, he lay ill in bed for many days. And every morning a woman dressed in black and closely veiled used to come to our house in Merrion Square and, unhindered by my mother or anyone else, used to walk straight upstairs to Sir William's bedroom and sit down at the head of the bed, and so sit there all day without ever speaking a word or once raising her veil. She took no notice of anyone in the room, and nobody payed any attention to her. Not one woman in a thousand would have tolerated her presence, but my mother allowed it because she knew that my father loved this woman, and felt it must be a joy and a comfort to have her there by his dying bed. And I am sure that she did right not to grudge that last happiness to a man who was about to die, and I am sure that my father understood her apparent indifference, understood that it was not because she did not love him that she permitted her rival's presence, but because she loved him very much, and died with his heart full of gratitude and affection for her.'

One can see that with the Wildes there was a great deal that was ridiculous, a certain pretentiousness, but nothing that was petty or typically middle-class. Fate offered Lady Wilde misfortunes worthy of her character: her daughter Isola died at the age of nine. Oscar, who adored his little sister, was heart-broken and he consecrated to her memory one of his first poems, not surprisingly an extremely sentimental one:

Requiescat

'Tread lightly, she is near, under the snow,
Speak gently, she can hear the daisies grow.
All her bright golden hair, tarnished with rust
She that was young and fair, Fallen to dust.'

Another drama caused less ink to flow. Two natural daughters of the Doctor, whom Speranza looked on as her own, were burnt alive; they were going to a ball when the crinoline of the elder one caught fire, and the younger one embraced her in an attempt to save her. These dramas and the consequences of the law-suit darkened the mood of the Doctor, who withdrew for long periods to Moytura by the lake. Willie and Oscar spent their holidays there, but their mother took them to England and to Germany when the atmosphere became too stifling, or the boredom too great. The chief distraction was fishing. In one of his first letters, Oscar tells of how the lake 'was full of large melancholy salmon, which lay at the bottom of the lake and paid no attention to our bait'.

Sometimes the children helped the Doctor to pick out the tracing on the crosses in the cemetery, and they also climbed the cylindrical belfries which rose higher than the trees. They dug up tumuli and listened to old people who still spoke Gaelic, and their stories took the Wildes back to the dawn of time, which in Ireland began the day before yesterday.

When the family passed by, the women curtseyed showing their red flannel petticoats, and the men took off their old top hats. This pastoral atmosphere is to be found in some of Oscar's stories. But a great sadness had fallen on the country; a greater part of the cottages had been deserted, the castles burned down, the fields had lain fallow since the famine and the consequent emigration. When rain prevented excursions, and there seemed no book left to read in the library, at least whiskey, the only solace, remained.

In the houses which were too big and suffocating, under trees which were never pruned, lived alcoholics or somnolent neighbours, out of politeness called eccentrics. Wilde often told the story of 'my poor Aunt Jane': 'Poor Aunt Jane was very old and very, very proud and she lived all alone in a splendid, desolate house in County Tipperary. No neighbours ever called on Aunt Jane and, had they done so, she would not have been pleased to see them. She would

not have liked them to see the grass-grown drives of the
demesne, the house with its faded chintzes and suites of
shuttered rooms, and herself, no longer a toast and a beauty,
no more a power in the countryside, but a lonely old
woman who had outlived her day.

'And from year to year she sat alone in her twilight,
knowing nothing of what passed in the world without. But
one winter . . . new people were coming to the new house
on the hill and were going to give a great Ball, the like of
which had never been seen. The Ryans were enormously
rich – "Ryans?", said Aunt Jane, "I don't know any Ryans.
Where do they come from?" Then the blow fell. The Ryans
come from nowhere in particular and were reported on
good authority to be "in business".

' "But," said Aunt Jane, "what are the poor people thinking of? Who will go to their Ball?" "Everybody will go,"
Aunt Jane was assured. "Everybody has accepted. It will be
a wonderful affair."

'When Aunt Jane fully realised this, her wrath was
terrible. This is what things had come to in the neighbourhood, then – and it was all her fault. It had been for her to
lead; she had brooded in her tent when she should have
been up and doing battle. And then Aunt Jane made her
great resolve. She would give a Ball – a Ball the like of which
had never been imagined: she would re-enter Society and
show how a "grande dame" of the old school could entertain . . . and instantly she set to work; the old house was
repainted, refurnished, the grounds replanted; the supper
and the band were ordered from London, and an army of
waiters engaged. Everything should be of the best – there
should be no question of cost. All should be paid for; Aunt
Jane would devote the rest of her life to the paying. But now
money was as nothing; she spent with both hands.

'At last the great night arrived. The demesne was lit for

two miles with coloured lamps, the hall and staircase were gorgeous with flowers, the dancing-floor smooth and shining as a mirror.

'The bandsmen were in their place and bowed deeply as Aunt Jane, in a splendid gown and blazing with diamonds, descended in state and stood at the ballroom door.

'There she waited, time went on . . . but no guests arrived. Eleven, twelve – half past twelve. Aunt Jane swept a deep curtsey to the band, "Pray go and have your supper," she said. "No one is coming". . . . And not for some considerable time after her death was it discovered that Aunt Jane had quite forgotten to send out any invitations.'

Away from school, Oscar had time to read. His mother guided him towards Keats and Shelley, the poets she loved more than the then fashionable Lake Poets. With Oscar's help, she translated the works of Dante and the French classics. It was then that he discovered Balzac, whose works he was to read and re-read always and from which he derived his interest in Parisian life, filling it in his imagination with reincarnations of Rastignac, of the Duchess of Langeais, of Esther. At the height of his own glory, Oscar was to declare 'the death of Lucien de Rubempré is the great drama of my life'. He told Vincent O'Sullivan that: 'A steady course of Balzac reduces our living friends to shadows and our acquaintances to the shadows of shades; who would care to go out to an evening party to meet Tomkins, the friend of one's boyhood, when one can sit at home with Lucien de Rubempré? It is pleasanter to have the entrée to Balzac's society than to receive cards from all the Duchesses in Mayfair.'

The name of Dickens evoked for Lady Wilde 'miasmas of the commonplace', whereas both mother and son were enthusiastic about the novels of Disraeli which, to Oscar, summoned up the great world and great ambitions. These

works, presenting as they did so many personalities interesting from a political point of view, seem today to be
overburdened with lavish descriptions. In the middle of
the nineteenth century, it is true, the English aristocracy
represented a life of opulence and grandeur: titles fascinated
everyone, especially such half-foreigners as Irishmen and
Jews. At the age of fifteen Oscar, through the works of the
novelist who became Prime Minister, explored a world that
he was later to conquer in the same way that Proust invented
the Guermantes after having been received in that Faubourg
Saint-Germain that he already knew from Balzac's pages.
The essence of Oscar's comedies, their social setting, even
their paradoxes are there, crushed under the weight of
Disraeli's oriental ornamentation. In *Endymion*, for example,
Lady Montford is the forerunner of Lady Bracknell of *The
Importance of Being Earnest*: 'Not go into Parliament! Why what
are men made for except to go into Parliament?' and in
Henrietta Temple, Lady Bellairs, an elderly hostess who talks
like the society ladies in *Lord Arthur Savile's Crime* or in *An
Ideal Husband*, says 'Ah! How I hate you! I could cut you up
in minced meat; that I could. Here I have been giving
parties every night, all for you and you have been in town
and never called on me. How is your wife? Oh, you are not
married. You should marry; I hate a ci-devant young man.'
This chatterbox is talking to Comte de Mirabel, modelled
on Alfred D'Orsay, the ideal dandy so reminiscent of Dorian
Gray. (It should not be forgotten that Disraeli's first novel,
published in 1826, was called *Vivian Gray*.) One also found
political tirades from that author's pen liberal enough to
please Speranza and her son. Especially the following exchange between Egremont and a stranger, in *Sybil*; ' "Well,
society may be in its infancy," said Egremont, slightly
smiling; "but say what you like, our Queen reigns over the
greatest nation that ever existed." "Which nation?" asked

the young stranger, "for she reigns over two." The stranger paused; Egremont was silent, but looked inquiringly. "Yes," resumed the younger stranger after a moment's interval. "Two nations; between whom there is no inter-course, and no sympathy; who are as ignorant of each other's habits, thoughts and feelings as if they were dwellers in different zones, or inhabitants of different planets; who are formed by a different breeding, are fed by a different food, are ordered by different manners, and are not governed by the same laws."

' "You speak of . . ." said Egremont, hesitatingly.

' "The Rich and the Poor." '

Disraeli's flamboyant dandyism – his gold chains and rings, his fur-lined coats and his black curls – aroused the admiration of the young Oscar who had nevertheless read the advice of Bulwer-Lytton (whom he also admired), that in dress the wearer should not stray too far from the general taste; for the world calls eccentricity in large things genius, but in small things folly.

In 1871, Oscar left school, having won an entrance scholarship at Trinity College, Dublin, and an exhibition from Portora. He was soon to win many prizes for classics, including a Foundation Scholarship and the Berkeley Gold Medal for Greek.

Trinity College, its old dark stones contrasting with its green lawns, its long oak-panelled library, containing that most precious of manuscripts, the Book of Kells, as well as the most important of the relics of Swift, was the domain of Mahaffy; he was the chief Hellenist of Ireland, and only thirty-two when Oscar started to attend his lectures. Most of the students thought of nothing but drinking and whoring, but Oscar was different and soon became the professor's favourite pupil and disciple. Thanks to the help of Mahaffy, Oscar won the Gold Medal for the best student in the Humanities; being made of heavy gold it was a useful decoration to possess, and, being Irish, it had a horse engraved on it. This medal was well known to the pawnbrokers.

Beneath his ecclesiastical charm, his pink cheeks, clear eyes and dark, well-cut clothes, the young Professor hid two passions: one for Greece ancient and modern, and the other for social life. It was said of Mahaffy that he only lifted his eyes from Homer in order to look at invitations from the nobility, but as in his book *Rambles and Studies in Greece*, he reveals great sensitivity to the beauty of the landscape, he must sometimes have lifted his eyes elsewhere. His talk was a model of courteous liveliness and discreet gossip; he well knew how to adapt Irish animation to English protocol; no one knew better than the professor how to keep the conversation going at the tables of the great when after a day in the hunting field, it was in danger of flagging. This erudite man, in his Pink coat (named after Mr. Pink who made the coats for those who had the right to wear them), would follow the hounds of the Duke of Leinster or of Lord Carew. He would play lawn tennis with the nobility or make a fourth at a dowager's card-table and was made much of in a world of which the Wildes could only catch a glimpse. Oscar was as thrilled by the stories he brought back from Dunsany Castle as by a dissertation of Demosthenes. Mahaffy had a house on the peninsula of Howth, at the gates of Dublin, but shrouded in mists and surrounded by gorse, to which he often invited his pupil; Oscar's phenomenal memory was of great use to Mahaffy in his work. Soon there was little else that the Professor could teach him about literature, but he encouraged him to ride, to play tennis and to use a gun. Oscar's conversation, at times impetuous and a little vulgar, became polished by practice with this supreme exponent of the art.

Meanwhile the Wildes persisted in entertaining the dregs of Dublin, and the family atmosphere became even more deplorable. At a debate on 'social evils' at which the Doctor presided, Willie threw himself into a passionate defence of prostitutes. Since Willie and his father shared both their names and their natures, this led from time to time to complications. Once, an unmarried expectant mother wrote to William Wilde putting the blame for her condition on him; the letter, meant for the son, was opened by the father, and the two had an argument as to which was the guilty one. Their Dublin was the drunken, garrulous city of James Joyce; they were the predecessors of the 'Dubliners', dirtying their frock-coats at the bars on the banks of the Liffy, but conversationally as scintillating before an audience of prostitutes and bookmakers as in Speranza's drawing-room; sometimes Oscar would accompany them. In College his rooms overlooked the quadrangle called 'Botany Bay', and drink and tobacco were to be found there on the rare occasions that he invited anyone. While at Trinity Oscar wrote poems and, needing an audience, he recited them aloud. Many of his contemporaries were moved by the romantic outpourings recited in his wonderfully sonorous voice, but on one occasion the ringleader of some toughs laughed sneeringly; Oscar's features contracted with fury and he slapped the sneerer's face; everyone trembled at the thought of the fate in store for the poet, but when the two men went outside to fight it out, it was Oscar who dealt the knock-out blow.

During his three years at Trinity, Oscar made no friends other than Mahaffy. (Later, when he ran into his fellow students, he fled from them, but on the day of his trial he was to meet one from whom he could not flee in the shape of Sir Edward Carson.) Oscar's only pleasures during

those three years at Trinity were his conversations with
Mahaffy and his mother; she always astonished him and
often made him laugh. One day he announced with a
certain solemnity, 'My mother and I have founded a Society
for the suppression of Virtue'. To hide the decline of her
beauty and the shabbiness of her furniture, Lady Wilde only
entertained with drawn curtains and in candle-light. One
visitor, Miss Corkran, described her thus: 'She must have
had two crinolines on, for as she advanced there was a
curious swaying, swelling motion like that of a vessel at
sea. Over the crimson silk were flounces of Limerick lace,
and round where there had been a waist was an Oriental
scarf. In her hands, always gloved in white, she carried a
bottle of scent, a lace handkerchief and a fan.' Beside this
figure who looked as if she had come out of a circus, the
Doctor, hirsute and stooping, looked more and more like
a monkey.

Dublin was far too small a theatre for Oscar; he gave
himself a little trouble, not much, and won a Demyship
worth £95 a year for four years at Magdalen College,
Oxford, where he took up residence at the age of twenty in
the year 1874.

3 Oxford

If Dublin had stood still since the eighteenth century, Oxford University, in most respects, had remained mediaeval and scorned the present. It was there that Wilde found contentment in idle strolls on velvet lawns under gigantic elms, lying reading a book at the bottom of a boat on the Isis, in conversation with attentive Dons and delightful friends. This was the happiness that for the rest of his life Oscar strove to rediscover.

Oxford seemed paradise to him after the general disorder of Dublin. He confided to Frank Harris many years later: 'Oxford is the capital of romance, in its own way as memorable as Athens, and to me it was more entrancing. In Oxford, as in Athens, the realities of sordid life were kept at a distance. No one seemed to know anything about money or care anything for it. Everywhere the aristocratic feeling: one must have money, but must not bother about it. And all the appurtenances of life were perfect; the food, the wine, the cigarettes; the common needs of life became artistic symbols, our clothes even won meaning and significance.'

Helped by the discipline of a regular everyday life, the studious spirits plunged into their studies (only to slumber in them when they became Dons). The more inflammable flung themselves into the religious quarrels which were raging in England at the time. Besides the various chapels and churches trying to attract the undergraduates, there were also clubs. Snobbishness played a larger part in these

than in the Church, although Anglicanism tainted with
Catholicism, was the most fashionable religion to profess.
Clubs trained their members for Parliamentary debate.
Already two undergraduates had gained distinction who
later were to become well known as proconsuls – Lord
Curzon and Lord Milner. To be a member of the Bullingdon
Club it was obligatory to be well-born or rich; a handsome
face could replace one of these conditions, but not both.
The members of this club, and of less exclusive ones, met on
the Cherwell and from the barges, like Gothicised house-
boats, furnished with tents and cushions, the undergraduates
watched the rowing races and gave tea to their sisters when
they came down to Oxford for the day. In winter an undergraduate would give breakfast parties in his rooms to
introduce special friends to his family: romances sometimes resulted from these meetings, and Oscar fell in love
with one or two of the sisters.

The University was torn apart by the intrigues and the
long-planned treacheries which tend to occur in enclosed
communities. The choice of College heads was often
influenced by family or religious considerations. It was the
Dons who formed and voiced opinion. The adjective
'donnish' came to suggest a lover of gossip who is also a
pedant, but when Mallarmé went to Oxford in 1893, he
saw them in a more poetic light: 'Today let us choose to
round off with an impression of beauty and what do we
find? The Fellows.'

The prestige of aristocracy was great; no one would have
thought of reproaching a future duke for not having
attended lectures. Old Etonians looked down on those from
other public schools and they, despised the Exhibitioners
who did not come from any. (Portora and Trinity were no
recommendation.) But here again, a strong arm for the scull
or a beautiful profile could wipe out many a social in-

equality. The great difference between the public schools and Oxford University was that in the former the athlete was the hero, but in the latter a brilliant man or a dandy was equally admired. The Colleges took pride in their oarsmen, and the Clubs in their orators.

There was a group of athletes who looked with jaundiced eyes on Oscar's eccentric clothes: it had reached their ears too that he boasted of spending all his allowance on collecting china; this incited them to organise a 'rag', one of the traditions of the University; sometimes it was the victim's books that were burned, sometimes the man himself was ducked in one of the fountains. This time the bullies decided to smash the incipient collection into small pieces. They were unlucky. Oscar seized the strongest of them and flung him on top of the rest of the gang who were on the stairs outside waiting for the signal to start the vandalism. 'And now,' said Oscar, 'give me the pleasure of tasting a bottle of excellent brandy.' The party ended at dawn with the athletes sitting at Oscar's feet listening to his stories, like the animals enchanted by the music of Orpheus.

When Wilde went to Oxford he was free from complexes, apart from his interest in and admiration for the nobility. His Irish optimism, added to his belief that he was more intelligent than anyone else, gave him perfect ease of manner. Sometimes this appeared to be a pose and came very near to insolence, because Oscar believed that the English accept sarcasm good-naturedly from people they consider to be their superiors. (Shaw was to profit by a similar insolence twenty years later.)

From the time of his arrival Wilde attracted attention by the unconcern with which he answered the examiners in theology. Once when it was his turn to read from Deuteronomy, he preferred the Song of Songs. He arrived late at his first examination and said to Canon Spooner who wanted to know the reason: 'You must excuse me, I have no experience of these pass examinations!' The examiners were so annoyed by his casual manner that one of them handed him a Bible and told him to copy out the 27th Chapter of the Acts of the Apostles. After he had been writing industriously for some time they relented and said that he had done enough, but observing half an hour later that he was still at it, they called him up: 'Didn't you hear us tell you Mr. Wilde that you needn't copy out any more?' Spooner asked. 'Oh yes, I heard you,' he answered, 'but I was so interested I couldn't leave off. It was all about a man named Paul who went on a voyage, and I was afraid he would be drowned. But do you know Mr. Spooner, he was saved; and when I found that he was saved I thought of coming to tell you.'

This false ingenuousness brought Spooner to the verge of apoplexy. The stories of these impertinences were repeated from College to College; Wilde's strange appearance alone made them unforgettable. This large pale youth changed his suits three times a day, from dark green tweed to brown velvet, and back again to violent checks. His contemporaries were often most impressed, not having discovered that discretion is the essence of real dandyism; the dandies themselves, preferring one well-cut suit to a whole improvised wardrobe, only smiled.

Oscar's rooms in Magdalen College included one large room whose Gothic windows looked out over the river. His high spirits attracted many who were not put off by his clothes. In this University, so taken up with religion, there were endless discussions on the subject. Sometimes, if the undergraduates were Magdalen men, they stayed listening until dawn; his rooms, naturally, were the last word in their decoration; full of the blue and white china made fashion-

able by the Pre-Raphaelites – and providentially saved
from annihilation by the hearties. Oscar admitted to a pride
in his collection: 'Oh! would that I could live up to my
blue china!' This remark was criticised and taken quite
seriously by the Vicar of St. Mary's, Oxford who 'opened his
sermon in this way', Oscar was to tell the Americans a few
years later: 'When a young man says, not in polished banter
but in sober earnestness, that he finds it difficult to live up
to the level of his blue china, there has crept into the cloistered shades a form of heathenism which it is our bounden
duty to fight against and to crush out if possible.'

This undergraduate who so irritated the authorities
found allies in two great men who counted among the sages
and philosophers of the age. Few writers have been so dissimilar as John Ruskin and Walter Pater; yet they had in
common a passionate love of beauty – the Middle Ages for
Ruskin, the Renaissance for Pater. Their private lives were
equally unsatisfied, Ruskin liking little girls and Pater
young men. When Wilde arrived at Oxford in 1878 Ruskin
was at the height of his fame. He had been Slade Professor
of Art since 1869, and occupied rooms at Corpus Christi
overlooking Christ Church meadows. He had brought part
of his collection with him, some Turners, a very fine portrait
by Titian, and some Renaissance furniture. In the evening
lighted tapers burned before the masterpieces. His library
was rich in illuminated manuscripts and portfolios of
precious drawings. Ruskin was a socialist with the vague
generosity of those who have always had enough money, a
little in the manner of Tolstoy. Strenuous work, a marriage
that he had been unable to consummate, and a passion for
a child who 'has the air of a young sister of Christ' had
exalted his ideas to a prophetic violence. His style is that of
the Old Testament, from which he took his description

D

of the City of the Future and his invective against the wicked
rich and against minds that are closed to beauty: Oscar
Browning, a Cambridge Don who had been an Eton master,
describes how the lecturer would gather his swinging robes
round him and chant a long-drawn dithyramb which held
his audience spellbound. Soon Ruskin was to be possessed
by a sacred delirium, mingled with obscene tirades, and
with mediumistic invocations to his beloved Rose La
Touche, dead at twenty-six. He then offered his resignation,
the better to express his ideas and vision in pamphlets: *Fors
Clavigera* or *The Sublime Borders on the Ridiculous*. He wished to
put into practice in the University his gospel of manual
labour: he said to the undergraduates 'that it seemed wrong
that all the best physique and strength of the young men in
England should be spent aimlessly on cricket ground or
river, without any result at all except that if one rowed well
one got a pewter pot, and if one made a good score, a cane-
handled bat. He thought, he said, that we should be working
at something by which we might show that in all labour
there is something noble.' And he found a method of
utilising the enthusiastic energies of his pupils: the construction of a road between two villages separated by a marsh.

Oscar, who still had a horror of sport, revered Ruskin. He
became one of the most fervent labourers and would not
allow anyone else to push the wheelbarrow of the Master:
'so out we went, day after day, and learned how to lay
levels and to break stones and to wheel barrows along a
plank – a very difficult thing to do. And Ruskin worked
with us in the mist and rain and mud of an Oxford winter,
and our friends and our enemies came out and mocked us
from the bank. We did not mind it much then, and we did
not mind it afterwards at all, but worked away at our road.
And what became of the road?' (Wilde was addressing an
American audience.) 'Well, like a bad lecture it ended in a

swamp – Ruskin left for Venice, when we came back for the next term there was no leader, and the "diggers", as they called us, fell asunder. And I felt that if there was enough spirit amongst the young men to go out to such work as road-making for the sake of a noble ideal of life, I would from them create an artistic movement that might change, as it has changed, the face of England.'

Side by side with the prophecies of Ruskin the disquieting voice of Walter Pater was steadily undermining consciences. Two hundred yards from the College where Ruskin magnificently drew out his disciples by instigating impassioned discussions, Pater gave tea parties to some unusual pupils in a small set of rooms furnished with a simplicity necessitated equally by the monastic architecture of Brasenose and his own limited means. But on the table, what perfection! The biscuits and fruit arranged as still life, the bunch of flowers recalling the foreground of an Annunciation. The subjects of conversation were as well chosen as the decoration, as we may learn from a parody of the aesthetic world (which was to inspire so many), that of W. H. Mallock; Mr. Rose, the character taken from Pater, says: 'To me, Mr. Herbert's whole metaphor seems misleading.' (Herbert is a character taken from Ruskin.) 'I rather look upon life as a chamber which we decorate as we would decorate the chamber of the woman or youth that we love, tinting the walls of it with symphonies of subdued colour, and filling it with works of fair form, and with flowers, and with strange scents, and with instruments of music.'

This was ten years before *A Rebours* and fifteen years before *Dorian Gray*.

But the master used to stammer when he spoke to a handsome undergraduate, and his lectures were delivered in little more than a whisper. After one of them, he enquired of a few friends: 'I hope you heard me?' Oscar replied: 'We

Walter Pater by William Rothenstein

overheard you.' Pater would only have been an ordinary-looking little man if an enormous moustache had not accentuated his ugliness. 'A lover of Circe changed into a mastiff', wrote Paul Bourget in an exceptionally happy phrase. Henry James is no warmer: '. . . how curiously negative and faintly grey he, after all telling, remains! I think he has had – will have had – the most exquisite literary future; i.e. to have taken it out at all, wholly, exclusively, with pen (the style, the genius) and absolutely not at all with the person. He is the mark without the face and there isn't in his total superfice a tiny point of vantage for the newspaper to flap his wings on.'

The pupil of Mahaffy soon proved his reputation; he was the best Hellenist of his generation, and he agreed with the best authorities in affirming that Walter Pater's *The Renaissance*

goes much further than the humanism of Matthew Arnold
or the digressions of Ruskin.

Oscar had all the attributes of an elected disciple: culture,
enthusiasm, and a prodigious vocabulary. Unfortunately,
he was very showy and Pater, who feared scandal like the
plague, only half opened his doors when, in July 1879,
Wilde brought him an article on an exhibition at the
Grosvenor Gallery consisting of the works of their favourite
painters. Nevertheless, there is an anecdote which admitted-
ʁsis only reported by the unreliable Frank Harris, who
lseyrts that it was told to him by Oscar ten years after
it had happened, about Pater and Wilde seated on a bench
in Parson's Pleasure watching undergraduates bathing.
Before the beauties, Greek of course, who emerged from the
water, Wilde with simple enthusiasm improvised on his
theme; 'the era of the new Beauty has arrived, it will
sweep away that Christianity which is founded upon
feebleness and ugliness. . . .' Oscar said: '. . . I really talked
as if inspired, and when I paused, Pater – the stiff, quiet,
silent Pater, suddenly slipped from his seat and knelt down
by me and kissed my hand. I cried, "You must not . . . what
would people think?" He sat up with a white, strained face:
"I had to, I had to – once", he muttered.'

Strange and beautiful stories were invented by
Oscar for his contemporaries, still so close to childhood.
The Irish imagination, in the grip of Homer and Shakespeare, created marvels, and style was easily born from these
improvisations. A pretty poem, Magdalen Walks, remains to
commemorate these strolls; 'Too beautiful,' Oscar often
repeated, his white hand on a shoulder, or while contemplating a boy lying on cushions, pink and fair in
white flannels; photographs preserve the looks of these
Oxford friends and they were, in fact, beautiful. There was

Reginald Harding, fair-haired and dark-eyed; Hunter-Blair,
very slim, most serious of them all, the heir to a baronetcy
and a large fortune; William Ward, the favourite, had a
turned-up nose and bright eyes. Each had his nickname,
Harding was Kitten; Hunter-Blair, Dunsky; Ward, Bouncer,
and Oscar was Hosky. They would invite each other to
interminable tea parties in their respective colleges, or go off
into fits of uncontrollable laughter at lectures and, in the
holidays, wrote slightly sentimental letters to each other on
matters concerning tennis, girls and hostesses. Flowers were
sent if one of them was ill, and on leaving Oxford rings
were exchanged. Oscar was watchful that Pater's ideal was
upheld and scolded Ward: 'How can you, an aesthetic youth,
dress yourself as a Chinaman and so exhibit yourself to
some girl you are fond of? You ought to go as Pico della
Mirandula with a Plato under your arm. . . .'

At the beginning of the Academic year Oscar wrote to
William Ward; 'the freshmen in it* are Gore, a great pal of
Tom Peyton's lot, Grey, a nice Eton boy – and we have all
suddenly woke to the idea that Wharton is charming.' Wilde
summed up these impressions in *Wasted Days*, one of his first
sonnets, in 1877:

> 'A fair, slim boy not made for this world's pain,
> With hair of gold thick clustering round his ears,
> And longing eyes half veiled by foolish tears.'

We will not find in those letters of Oscar's which were
preserved by Kitten and Bouncer, when they became respectable fathers of families, anything which could lead us to
believe there were feelings other than ordinary friendship,
exept that Oscar told Kitten that one evening Bouncer had
been 'most kind' and in his joy he engraved the name of

* Contemporary University slang; underlined in the original.

the young man on the window-pane of his room. One could have believed that the Oxford friendships did not go further than hand-holding and stolen kisses if one did not have the evidence of John Addington Symonds, an undergraduate at Oxford five years before Wilde. During the course of his years of study, this writer came near to causing a scandal by taking too much interest in the choir and by leaving about some imprudent letters for anyone to see. The friendships of this pioneer of aestheticism had nothing platonic about them. While at the University, Oscar became the centre of a small, perhaps unconsciously homosexual world, with its dramas, its gossip and its scandals. The temptations were of two kinds: on one side the athletes, the pride of the colleges, who gladly allowed themselves to be adored, on the other the choir boys. In some of the college chapels were choristers whose age varied from ten to seventeen. In their lace surplices over red cassocks they walked solemnly behind the cross, the smallest at the head; the dons glancing over their prayer-books, and the undergraduates kneeling solemnly in their black gowns, blushing when Tom or Harry passed. Oscar was interested when he surprised one of his fellow students in the company of a chorister in a box at a Music Hall: 'Myself I believe Todd is extremely moral and only mentally spoons the boy, but I think he is foolish to go about with one, if he is bringing this boy about with him.'

All his life Wilde was to search for faces which reminded him of Kitten or Bouncer. He was often to return to Oxford to find again the echo of his first successes. Perhaps it would have been better for him never to have left it, and after the brilliant results of his examinations to have continued the work of his masters, but to do that he would have had to have as much patience as respect for authority. The world of Oxford is too small for one who wishes to be in turn

Byron (he imitated *Childe Harold* in a long poem about Italy), and Goethe (to prepare for this rôle, he wrote a long essay, *The Rise of Historical Criticism*).

Oscar's last day at Oxford was a triumph. On 26th June 1878 he read his poem *Ravenna*, which won him the Newdigate Prize, in the Sheldonian before the entire University. In the first row sat the Masters of the Colleges in their black and red robes, then, squeezed into the back benches, were the undergraduates, some transported, others exasperated by the voice and appearance of the poet. In fact at twenty-four Wilde could have considered himself handsome, his features had taken on a nobility, his voice an assurance; he felt as an actor feels who reads aloud a long poem and receives his first ovation. When the laureate went to thank his masters, or rather to receive their praises, he remembered Pater's first words to him: 'And now, Mr. Wilde, you should try to write prose; it is, notwithstanding, much more difficult.'

4 Holidays

Oxford was the Anglican Rome of those days, where orthodoxy was represented by Benjamin Jowett, the remarkably clever but completely uncompromising Master of Balliol. His partisans were admirers of Matthew Arnold – a greater thinker than poet – another Goethe whose horror of the industrial age led him to dream of a Platonic city. He was profoundly religious and Oscar was only interested in him from afar. As opposed to this official religion, the Catholic Church, its prestige increased both with people of imagination and with those who merely sought a discipline, launched an offensive with Manning and Newman at its head. There were also Puritans who attacked the exorbitant privileges enjoyed by the Established Church. In university circles, religion was a more consuming interest than politics at that time.

Therefore the city whose influence was most felt in Oxford was no longer London, consecrated to business, not Paris, where people's minds were preoccupied by political revolutions, but Rome – the Rome of the Church humiliated in 1870. The flower of the intellectuals, with some exceptions, turned towards Catholicism. The poets Gerard Manley Hopkins and Coventry Patmore had recently been converted. It was fashion rather than Faith that urged Oscar into churches, even as far as to the confessional, though his flirtation with the 'Scarlet Woman' was not regularised until his death-bed. In his eyes the Catholic Church was like a beautiful Princess who, despite excesses and misfortunes,

lived in the pomp of another age, surrounded by masterpieces and willing to forgive anything. To him she was an
idealised Speranza. But that one side of his nature genuinely
craved a Faith is proved not only by his interest in the
dogmas of the Church but by his pursuit of Aestheticism.

The paths that led to Rome started from Oxford, and men
of standing in the University were tempted to follow them.
Newman had tried to convert Ruskin, Pater was enthusiastic
about the ceremonial. Oscar attended Mass in the Chapel of
St. Aloysius (which the Catholics had eventually been
allowed to build) and in London he went to the Church of
Our Lady of the Victories (which was used as pro-cathedral
until the consecration of Westminster Cathedral in 1903)
to listen to Cardinal Manning: 'He is more fascinating than
ever', Oscar wrote to William Ward in July 1876. The case
of Cardinal Newman interested him but he was not prepared
to share his heart-searchings; 'About Newman, I think that
his higher emotions revolted against Rome but that he was
swept on by Logic to accept it as the only rational form of
Christianity. His life is a terrible tragedy. I fear he is a very
unhappy man...' This in the same year to the same recipient.
Wilde had a horror of unhappiness.

The young poet explained his temptations, again in a
letter to William Ward, who was then in Rome: 'I now
breakfast with Father Parkinson, go to St. Aloysius, talk
sentimental religion to Dunlop and altogether am caught in
the fowler's snare, in the wiles of the Scarlet Woman – I may
go over in the vac. I have dreams of a visit to Newman, of
the holy sacrament in a new Church, and of a quiet and
peace afterwards in my soul. I need not say, though, that I
shift with every breath of thought and am weaker and more
self-deceiving than ever.

'If I could hope that the Church would wake in me some
earnestness and purity, I would go over as a luxury, if for no

better reasons. But I can hardly hope it would, and to go over to Rome would be to sacrifice and give up my two great Gods: "Money and Ambition".'

Rarely had Wilde seen so clearly into himself as in this letter written at the age of twenty-two; generally his sentimental and aesthetic effusions veiled his cynicism. Later Ward was to evoke a conversation on religion which went on until dawn: 'One dim morning, I remember well, in my rooms at Magdalen when he and I and Hunter-Blair, a new and eager convert to Roman Catholicism, a man of singular enthusiasms and vivacity, had talked through the short summer night till there was the sound of waking birds in the trees that fringed the Cherwell and Oscar had hung, poised in a paradox, between doubt and dogma – I remember that Hunter-Blair suddenly hit him on the head and exclaimed: "You will be damned, you will be damned, for you see the light and will not follow it". "And I?", I asked. "You will be saved by your invincible ignorance," was the reply.'

Debt kept Oscar chained to Oxford. However, David Hunter-Blair wished to get him to Rome where he himself was going. He had been converted to Roman Catholicism three years earlier and was determined to convert Oscar. Believing that the end justified the means, he sent a note from Monaco (while on his way to Rome) to Oscar at Magdalen to the effect that he, Dunskie, would be successful at the Casino if Heaven wished that Oscar should join him in Rome. Soon, Oscar received £60 from him. In April 1877 (not in 1876 as Hunter-Blair wrongly records in *Victorian Days*), Oscar set forth in company with Mahaffy, but when they reached Genoa the master insisted on carrying Oscar off to Greece. Their companions were William Joshua Goulding, later to be a director of many Irish companies, to succeed to a baronetcy in 1904 and to be made a Privy

Councillor in 1917, and George Macmillan, a member of
the publishing family, and one of the founders of the
Hellenic Society.

A more brilliant sun than that of Italy was to quicken
Oscar's imagination, the sun that shone on Greece. Thanks
to Mahaffy's insistence that he should visit Mycenae and
Athens, Oscar discovered the country that was to be the
nearest to his heart, a country whose literature the professor had already taught him to love. Oscar's religious
temptations, aroused during his first visit to Italy in 1875,
had irritated the agnostic priest Mahaffy who wished to
rescue his pupil from them, turn him into a pagan and, at
the same time, secure for himself an indefatigable companion who was not only always in a good temper, but
could recite and share his own relish for Sophocles at
Epidaurus and Homer at Mycenae. The friends travelled by
easy stages, skirting the Adriatic, stopping at both Venice
and Ravenna, the town which was to inspire in the following
year Oscar's Newdigate prize-winning poem; and at Corfu.
In those leisurely days it was quite usual to journey with a
trunkful of literature, containing the classics as well as guide-
books. They also had with them the works of poets who
had dreamed of Greece without having been there – such
as Swinburne, and Keats whose line *A thing of beauty is a
joy for ever* became the credo of aestheticism.

Since Byron, nobody had disturbed the English as deeply
as Swinburne. When his *Poems and Ballads* appeared in 1866,
undergraduates with linked hands recited the more
audacious couplets in the cloisters of Oxford; the poem
Dolores, full of descriptions of whips and daggers, did not
appeal to Oscar as much as did *Atlanta in Calydon*, conceived
as an ancient tragedy with choruses and high-flown orations
over the body of the beautiful Meleager. This was a more

vigorous Greece than Matthew Arnold's; more disturbing
than Robert Browning's Italy. Swinburne, a fervent Baude-
lairian, wished to become a pagan, to justify his highly
irregular life. Oscar had been able to catch a glimpse of
Swinburne's Greece from some pictures which hung on the
walls of Walter Pater's house, painted by a young Jew called
Simeon Solomon. He was as beautiful as a Greek statue, and
distracted the Pre-Raphaelites from their Gothic visions by
dancing naked, crowned with vine leaves, in the gardens of
Chelsea. Oscar, his head full of poetry and history, forgot
the complications of his life in England and gave himself
up to the happiness of being in Greece.

The full moon illuminated the white houses on the quayside of Piraeus as the four men stepped ashore, and
Mahaffy quoted Plato's evocative words: 'Haunts of sailors
where good manners are unknown'. Mahaffy described the
expedition in his book *Rambles and Studies in Greece* (published
1887 by Macmillan). A typical comment was that 'the
museum of the Acropolis should be provided with a better
set of casts of the figures which are now to be seen there.
They look very wretched and hastily prepared.' He regretted
that the colours had disappeared from the statues. Oscar
soon tried to remedy this by the constant use of the
adjectives purple and gold, with which he loaded Keats'
Greece. Brigands were camping on Hymettus, Athens was
a Turkish village at the foot of the Acropolis. The travellers
were quick to notice that the men were far handsomer and
vainer than the women, and that some of them wore stays.

The party must have had many picturesque adventures
and possibly also experiences bringing them a little nearer to
Plato's disciples. Despite his cult of the English nobility,
Mahaffy remained a fervent Irishman and reminded his
companions, when they were among the innumerable
Greek Islands, of those of Ireland; he compared the ruins of

Mycenae and the Parthenon with the burial places of Meath
and the Rock of Cashel. His comparisons could apply
equally well to the two peoples: imaginative, enthusiastic
about politics, childishly passionate after centuries of sub-
jection. The travellers helped in the discovery of the first
Tanagra terracottas; they braved brigands and bugs to reach
a lost temple; Mahaffy deciphered inscriptions and quoted
Aristophanes. It is not surprising that, when published, his
account of this journey should have won him much
praise, including that of Renan.

Mahaffy forgot his Chair of Philosophy in Dublin and
Oscar put his Oxford examinations out of his mind; this
forgetfulness was to cost Oscar dear when he eventually got
back as, because of it, he forfeited half his bursary. 'For
having been the first Oxonian to visit Olympia,' was his
philosophic observation when taking his gold medal to the
pawnbroker. The poems he wrote in Greece have an
ambiguity about them, as have those of Swinburne. In *The
Garden of Eros* – 'here are the flowers which mourning
Heracles strewed on the tomb of Hylas . . .', in the dramatic
poem *Charmides*, the story of a sailor loved by Diana who
caused his death through her jealousy, certain passages are
particularly touching, especially one that tells of a little girl
who surprises the sleeping hero: 'and when she saw the
white and gleaming arms, and all his manlihood with
longing eyes, whose passion mocked her sweet virginity . . .'
– the style of this poem is reminiscent of Keats' *Endymion*.
The story itself was taken from a work by Lucian where the
setting was Cnidos, and the main protagonist Venus.

Some of his poetry was essentially Victorian. Ifor Evans,
author of *English Poetry in the Later 19th Century*, expresses his
views of it thus: 'It is rather like a "beautified" room in
some over-expensive boarding-house with rococo decorations, classical statuary and objets d'art mingled in

elaborate profusion but with little taste.' In spite of the
lessons of Pater and Mahaffy, Oscar remained very much
the son of Speranza. He got from Greece ideas rather than
inspiration to write fine poetry, but above all it gave him
a new idea of himself. He decided to be the new Plato, to
lead generations towards the cult of Beauty. His was not to
be the Greece of the chiselled marbles of the fourth century,
but that of a Greece softened by the Orient as revealed in
the Alexandrian terracottas. The return to Oxford was
further delayed by Oscar's very natural desire to break that
journey in Rome to join Hunter-Blair; after all it was to
that young man's chivalrous and spirited plan to raise
money that Oscar owed his temporary liberation from debt
and the University.

Hunter-Blair was counting on the splendours of the
Vatican to bring about Oscar's conversion and lost no time
in getting him on his knees before Pope Pius IX. Afterwards,
Oscar, much moved, and with tears in his eyes, asked if he
could be driven past the Aurelian Wall on the way back
to the hotel, to the English cemetery where his tears and
genuflections were renewed before the grave of Keats. His
essay, The Tomb of Keats (to be found in Decorative Art in
America, published by Brentano of New York), was printed
in The Irish Monthly, a magazine of general literature, and was
presumably written in the Spring of 1877 after the above
experience. His hero-worship of the young poet is revealed
in these words: 'As I stood before the mean grave of this
divine boy, I thought of him as a Priest of Beauty slain
before his time, and the Vision of Guido's St. Sebastian came
before my eyes . . .'.

In Rome they made two friends, both of whom were
honorary Papal Chamberlains. Their names were Grissell
and Ogilvie Fairlie. The four became inseparable, riding in
the Campagna together, visiting princely palaces and the

English colony. One of the many blue-stockings who had been drawn to Rome from the British Isles was Constance Fletcher, who clearly made a great impression on Oscar as he dedicated *Ravenna* to her. She was to publish six novels under the name of George Fleming. She can only have been nineteen when they met. In the same year she wrote a three-volume novel called *Mirage* in which one of the minor characters, a young poet and aesthete called Claude Davenant, was based on Oscar: she describes him as looking like one of Holbein's portraits: 'A pale large-featured individual; a peculiar, an interesting countenance of singularly mild yet ardent expression; he spoke like a man who made a study of expression.' Here is an example of Claude Davenant's verse:

> 'A flowery fan for a white flower hand
> (White cranes flying across the moon) –
> A breath of wind from a windless land
> A breath in the breathless noon.'

But the most curious story of these holidays chronicled by Vyvyan Holland in his book *Son of Oscar Wilde* is the following: One day the handsome Hunter-Blair received a present from an unknown admirer in the shape of a fine diamond. Having renounced worldly vanities, he thought no more of wearing it than of trying to find out the donor, be it Princess or Cardinal. But instead he decided to use it to propitiate Heaven and further Oscar's conversion. He therefore entrusted the diamond to Ogilvie Fairlie, the Papal Chamberlain, who was to present it to the monks of St. Augustine when Oscar was finally converted. What followed is like one of Oscar's fables. The friends separated, each going his own way – Oscar's, needless to say, a worldly one, Hunter-Blair's priestly and the Chamberlain's matrimonial.

He felt justified in having the jewel mounted in his wife's tiara. However when, twenty-two years later, he heard that Oscar had gone over to Rome on his death-bed, he had the stone taken out of the tiara and offered it to the Madonna of St. Augustine. It is not known how the wife reacted to the loss of the diamond – or if admiration of her husband's integrity consoled her for its loss.

Catholicism appealed more to the theatrical than to the religious side of Oscar's nature. This was evident when six years later Oscar dramatically knelt before Hunter-Blair, by then a priest, begging his former fellow student to pray for him. This was all very fine, but in Dublin, Catholicism being the religion of the proletariat, Oscar's flirtation was looked upon with very different eyes. For example when Henry Wilson, the natural son of Sir William Wilde, died he left Oscar a little money which he would forfeit if he became a Roman Catholic and which would be transferred to Willie Wilde.

Oscar returned to Oxford loaded with pious images; portraits of the Pope and Cardinal Manning, for a time replaced the blue and white china on his shelves. An inclination towards Roman Catholicism was not unusual among English homosexuals at this time. Some, the sentimental ones, found that the Protestant religion left them too much alone with their consciences. They needed to be listened to and forgiven; several of Oscar's friends chose this road after having been disappointed in love. Some, frustrated by not being able to dress in silk and lace, wished at least to play a part in the ballet of the Mass or in the operatic services performed in the Cathedrals on the great Feast Days; this was the case much later with Ronald Firbank; the strange Frederick Rolfe, alias Baron Corvo, was another; and it is notable that in one of Disraeli's novels hostesses make much of a charming Cardinal, a hundred

E

years before Cardinal Pirelli turned the heads of Firbank's
frivolous heroines.

Holidays far less agreeable than those spent in Rome
or Greece brought Oscar back to Dublin twice during his
years at Oxford. In 1876, Sir William Wilde had died,
leaving a very reduced fortune. His two sons and their
illegitimate brother, Henry Wilson, each received £4,000
and Lady Wilde £7,000 – very little money for people used
to good living. A law-suit further depleted the inheritance
and Oscar feared he would have to leave Oxford to earn his
living. He wrote to William Ward: 'As for me I am ruined.
The law-suit is going against me and I am afraid I will have
to pay costs, which means leaving Oxford and doing some
horrid work to earn bread. The world is too much for me.
However, I have seen Greece and had some golden days of
youth. . . .'

Speranza, belying her self-given name, cultivated the
blackest pessimism. She took a dislike to Dublin; from the
moment that she could no longer entertain, everything
there seemed to her provincial and shabby. Lady Wilde
decided to make a fresh start and to throw herself into the
conquest of London. Her sons encouraged her to sell the
large house in Merrion Square – William because he preferred to become a journalist in London rather than a
lawyer in Dublin, and Oscar because he believed in
his mother's power to collect interesting people around
her.

It took two years to liquidate their Irish assets, which
involved Oscar in further gloomy visits to Dublin. Luckily,
to distract him, there was Mahaffy, and an old friend of his
mother's, Aubrey de Vere, a poet and a recent convert to
Catholicism. The latter encouraged the poetic attempts of
his young friend, whose first verses *Graffiti d'Italia* were pub-

lished in the September issue of the Irish Monthly in 1876 (and reprinted with slight revision and re-named Rome Unvisited in Poems in 1881), and the True Knowledge which also appeared in the September issue (reprinted in Lyra Hibernica Sacra in 1878 and in Poems in 1908). These poems, and above all the personality of the author, attracted the attention of Richard Monckton Milnes, Lord Houghton, a curious personage who often went to stay in Ireland and who knew everyone in the world of letters. As well as being a philanthropist, he had a library celebrated for its collection of erotica. After several evenings spent in his society, Oscar wrote to him urging that the ugly bas-relief of Keats' head, near his tomb, should be replaced by a really beautiful memorial. In the intervals between associating with men of business and men of letters, Oscar fell in love with a beautiful girl called Florence Balcombe. There were expeditions, balls and protestations: but she was poor and Oscar had no expectations, and no engagement followed. In 1878 she married Bram Stoker, creator of Count Dracula.

Oscar delighted in visiting his Oxford friends in their English country houses. He played croquet, went for walks with girls, and dined with the neighbours; this mode of life spurred him on to be at his best: he took trouble to please the country gentlemen and, brought up as he had been in a bohemian world, he found a certain charm in the diversions of the upper middle classes. He went to stay with Frank Miles, a handsome and gifted draughtsman, who had lovely sisters and amusing neighbours. Miles was the protégé of Lord Ronald Gower, a gifted amateur sculptor who was the younger son of the 2nd Duke of Sutherland. This was Oscar's first real encounter with the famous aristocracy of Disraeli's novels.

The Leveson-Gowers owned huge properties in Scotland. Stafford House, where they lived in London, was so magni-

ficent that, after a Ball, Queen Victoria said to the Duchess of
Sutherland: 'I leave your Palace for my house.' The walls of
the State Rooms were hung with Van Dykes and Murillos,
Lord Ronald's sisters had married into the great families of
England. The son of the eldest daughter, the Duchess of
Argyll, had recently become engaged to Queen Victoria's
daughter Louise; Constance was to be the future Duchess
of Westminster; the third was the wife of the Duke of
Leinster. The young Duchess of Sutherland was considered
to be the most beautiful woman of her generation. Lord
Ronald's uncles were the Dukes of Devonshire and Norfolk.
When the family were not in Scotland they lived at Cliveden,
more recently the home of the Astors. Lord Ronald divided
his time between visits to country houses, where he
searched for archaeological curiosities and ghost stories, and
Paris where he had a studio in the Boulevard de Mont-
parnasse. He was a friend of Sarah Bernhardt; the Empress
Eugénie and the Prince Imperial were devoted to him. His
circle of friends included such distinguished people as
Ruskin and Carlyle. To be within easy reach of Oxford,
Lord Ronald had rented a house at Windsor. This agreeable
man became easily bored, having always had everything he
could possibly want, yet Oscar succeeded in amusing him
for hours on end. Lord Ronald would often go to Wilde's
rooms in Magdalen and, when Oscar was in London, they
attended exhibitions together or went to listen to a popular
preacher, or to visit music-halls. Once Oscar met his sister
Constance when lunching with Lord Ronald and wrote of
her, '. . . the most fascinating, Circe-like brilliant woman
I have ever met in England; something too charming.' The
character of Lord Henry in the Portrait of Dorian Gray is siad
to be taken from Wilde himself, but with his paradoxes,
his melancholy induced by satiety, an intelligence that
allowed itself to be dissipated by a worldly life, he has more

than a little in common with Lord Ronald. In the house at
Windsor, Oscar discovered for the first time the total
luxury enjoyed by those who have always been accustomed
to riches. Tea was poured out in a garden planted with
peonies: 'Too beautiful'. 'Orange Pekoe or Lapsang Sou-
chong, Mr. Wilde?' A footman would remove the porcelain
plates, while a white peacock perched on a red-brick wall:
'Simply heavenly,' one could hear Oscar exclaim, 'with
rapidity, in a low voice, with peculiarly distinct enunciation',
as Claude Davenant, the character in *Mirage*, based on Oscar,
is described as speaking.

Oscar's meeting with Lord Ronald was Balzacian; it was
like Rastignac entering Mme. de Bauséant's drawing-room
or Lucien de Rubempré being introduced to duchesses by
Madame de Bargeton. Till now, Oscar had only heard of
such people through the friends he had made at Oxford, and
they had a position in England which it was only natural
for a romantic and ambitious young man to find glamorous.
Never had a relatively restricted society gathered together so
much money and so much political power; nor, be it said,
so much moral prestige; the high-born ladies at that time
were prone to imitate the Queen's virtues, except for the
dissipated camp-followers of the Prince of Wales. Even
Victor Hugo was impressed by the grandeur of the English
families and he took the trouble to study their curious titles
in *Debrett* before writing *L'Homme qui rit*. In this world where
there was no lack of physical beauty, only intellectual
qualities were lacking. The constant company of horses
made most people wary of intelligence, though there were
exceptions such as Wilfrid Blunt who bred Arab horses as
well as writing poetry, and George Wyndham, who besides
writing both poetry and prose was also an impassioned
rider to hounds. Erudition was tolerated in a Bishop, wit
in a diplomat, love of reading in a dowager and a certain

genius in a few cranks who squandered their fortunes on
eccentricities.

This world presented a front as strictly correct as the
carriages which were to be seen in Belgravia and Mayfair.
Families had to appear united, the young men, mostly
good-looking officers of the Brigade of Guards, won the
hearts of the richest heiresses who had been brought
up in the cloistered seclusion of their homes; ladies
busied themselves with good works; the men went to their
clubs, in some of which they played cards for high stakes.
A gentleman might have as many as forty servants in his
country house where he would entertain with a generosity
which was often extended to poor relations and spongers as
well as boon companions. Victorian society had something
patriarchal about it, in contrast to the licence which had
spread under the Regency. But every now and then an
appalling scandal would explode, sordid details of a divorce
case or of a swindle would fill the pages of the Press: Lady
Mordaunt accused by her husband of having had as a lover,
among others, the Prince of Wales; Lord Willoughby de
Eresby robbed his mistress of £30,000 before running away
with her maid; and Lord Hastings stole the fiancée of his
friend Henry Chaplin.

To save its face, Society closed its doors to the victims as
well as to the guilty and applied to the letter the evangelical
principle of rather the fault than the scandal. So when the
wife of Lord Henry Somerset, son of the Duke of Beaufort,
asked for a divorce because she had found her husband in
the arms of a footman, she was at once banned from
Society – a Lady should not know that such things take
place, and if she discovered them she should, like Speranza
ignore them. Lord Ronald knew the secrets of that world,
its alliances and its estrangements; he could afford to
sponsor this showily handsome Irishman, already known

for his successes at Oxford, and make the wild prophecy, somehow characteristic of the self-importance of the age, that 'he will be the new Byron'. The fear of intelligence which had begun to fade before the taste for celebrities, was to melt like snow in the sun before the charm of Oscar.

5 A glittering success

In the autumn of 1879, Oscar was installed in London; he shared rooms with Frank Miles in Salisbury Street, close to the Strand. It was between the theatres and St. James's, on the fringe of clubland. Gustave Doré has given in a volume of engravings a complete and poetic picture of London at that time, the London which was to play so large a part in Oscar's plays. He evokes the incredible confusion of omnibuses and cabs in the Strand and in Hyde Park, where impeccably dressed horsewomen, followed by their grooms, pass before the eyes of equally impeccably dressed gentlemen wearing whiskers, and highly polished top-hats. On the lawns of Kensington ladies are shown playing croquet, in the gardens of Mayfair striped awnings shield beautiful guests surrounding the young Princess of Wales, and on the terraces of Richmond elegant people are to be seen watching a regatta or a boat race. There are coaches brimming over with sportsmen, gaily popping champagne corks, looking down on char-à-bancs packed with coloured musicians, bookmakers and down-and-out rakes.

In contrast to the glittering side of London, Doré also depicted the darker side; docks bristling with cranes, coal barges floating up the Thames in the midst of steamers, endless streets where little girls danced to barrel-organs – all this shown by gas-light in a thick fog: 'At present people see fogs not because there are fogs, but because poets and painters have taught them the mysterious loveliness of such effects. There may have been fogs for centuries in London. I dare say there were. But no one saw them, so we did not know anything about them. They did not exist until Art invented them. Now, it must be admitted, fogs are carried to excess. They have become the mere mannerism of a clique and the exaggerated realism of their method gives people bronchitis', wrote Oscar in the Decay of Lying.

But he ignored the dangers and, it seems, the temptations, which are born of mysterious meetings. He was too pre-occupied with the conquest of London to think of guilty loves or even innocent ones; equipped with an address book instead of a heart, he walked, his head held high, between the ranks of footmen; these inspired a French visitor of that time, Madame de Pouliga, to write satirically in the Vie Parisienne, that 'to remind her of her wholesome traditions, England still has the calves of her footmen. So long as to wear silk stockings is the ambition of men of a certain class, the old England will not have lived in vain; and these calves are still very fine and much respected. One sees them on the thresholds of the great houses, one sees them also on the pavements, rolling out the carpet on which one can walk direct to the carriage, and on the days of the Queen's Drawing-Rooms, they can be seen braced, immobile, behind the carriages.'

In the company of Frank Miles, for whom the sisters and sisters-in-law of Lord Ronald took turns to pose, Oscar made his début at Grosvenor House, one of the most sumptuous of London's great houses and reigned over by Lord Ronald's sister. She would receive her guests either beneath the Rembrandts and Rubens in the ballroom or, at tea-time, under Gainsborough's picture of 'The Blue Boy'. Thus the young poet was initiated into a world where he was to find the setting of his plays and the inspiration for his best stories. For instance, it might have been a reception at

Grosvenor House that is described at the beginning of *Lord Arthur Savile's Crime*: 'It was Lady Windermere's last reception before Easter and Bentinck House was even more crowded than usual. Six Cabinet Ministers had come from the Speaker's Levée in their stars and ribands, all the pretty women wore their smartest dresses, and at the end of the picture-gallery stood Princess Sophia of Carlsrühe, a heavy Tartar-looking lady, with tiny black eyes and wonderful emeralds, talking bad French at the top of her voice, and laughing immoderately at everything that was said to her. It was certainly a wonderful medley of people. Gorgeous peeresses chatted affably to violent Radicals, popular preachers brushed coat-tails with eminent sceptics, a perfect bevy of Bishops kept following a stout prima-donna from room to room, on the staircase stood several Royal Academicians, disguised as artists, and it was said that at one time the supper-room was absolutely crammed with geniuses. . . .'

Oscar said elsewhere, 'No man has any real success in this world unless he has got women to back him, and women rule Society.' It was true enough that Queen Victoria ruled the Empire, and about a dozen women, whom Oscar determined to get to know, led the most imposing Society in Europe. These women were bored, surrounded by over-well-mannered husbands or lovers; they were bored by interminable Court functions and ever more magnificent dinner parties; they were bored at the Opera where for the twentieth time they had to listen to Patti; they were still more bored in the country, reduced to the company of the hunting-set and their dogs. Oscar had the power, with his gaiety and his imagination unhampered by the slightest modesty, to rescue people from their boredom and under a veneer of morality to lead them into a constant routine of amusement.

'To get into Society nowadays one has either to feed people

or shock people – that is all,' asserted Oscar, and the
method that he adopted was the latter – the feeding he
could not afford. His paradoxes and affectations for which
he had been well known at Oxford, now opened the doors
of drawing-rooms for him and, better still, those of country
houses. Augustus Hare, author of travel books and Journals,
was horrified by Wilde's nerve and exasperated by his
success. 'Mrs. M. L. had recently met this type of an aesthetic
age staying at a country house', he wrote, 'and described
him going out shooting in a black velvet suit with salmon-
coloured stockings and falling down when his gun went
off, yet captivating all the ladies by his pleasant talk. One
day he came down looking very pale. "I'm afraid you are ill,
Mr. Wilde," said one of the party. "No, not ill, only tired,"
he answered, "the fact is I picked a primrose in the wood
yesterday and it was so ill, I have been sitting up with it all
night." '

Augustus Hare, the old gentleman whose interminable
anecdotes are now seldom read, forgot that the English have
a weakness for nonsense, and that the social success of a
young man can frequently come from his complete lack of
reverence. Oscar did not defer to those great men who now
stand out like monuments, ruggedly, from a fragile age.
Oscar even dared to make fun of Carlyle, whose French
Revolution he still considered the work of a great artist, whatever its value as history.

Two generations earlier, Brummel had established his
reputation largely through insolence. Oscar was not ready
enough to bend the knee, to become as faultless an exquisite
as Brummel, nor had he the swagger of a d'Orsay, so he
invented a new line – the languid dandy. He would take a
cab in order to cross the street and would lean on the arm
of a friend to cross the room; the sight of a badly furnished
house took away his strength and he wondered if he was

strong enough to stand the sight of a masterpiece. One day, noticing his listlessness, a lady became quite anxious: 'That interesting boy must work too hard,' she said and Oscar agreed, explaining, 'I was working on the proof of one of my poems all the morning, and took out a comma. In the afternoon I put it back again.' And the lady went everywhere repeating the latest mot of 'that extraordinary Mr. Wilde'. Not everyone was taken in by the weakness which contradicted the Herculean build (a soft Hercules, it is true), and the hearty laughter. A young blue-stocking, Vernon Lee, recognised that in most of his foolishness he was making fun of himself and others, but this was not generally realised.

That a Society so sure of itself should have allowed an unknown Irishman to laugh at it was because he rendered it a service beyond price in rescuing it from boredom.

Among the 'Souls', the name given to a group of young people who included the more intelligent of the fashionable world, Oscar perfected a form of conversation which could be compared to a display of fireworks consisting entirely of set-pieces. It was necessary in order to attract attention to dazzle at all costs, to be disapproved of by serious people and quoted by the foolish.

Among the Souls, Oscar found the same kind of atmosphere as at the Oxford parties; with the skill of a craftsman he shaded the brilliance of his art, carefully calculating his surprises. He went in for murmuring disturbing confidences, which like Bengal lights illuminated for one or two intimate friends the corner of a winter garden, showing life in a soft and rather sad light, subtly changing the mood from the artless to the disturbing. On the other hand when in company already engaged in laughter and repartee, it was quite the contrary – he would dazzle by quick words, biting allusions, preposterous exclamations. Each was welcome to add his own spark to the effect of setting alight the most stolid dinner or supper table. Or rather, like an undulating rocket tracing its way in the night to explode, when the attention of the public reaches its highest point, in a dazzling shower of sparks, where in turn other showers of sparks gush forth in varied colours to set fire to the sky, so Oscar began his stories with deliberation, murmured memories from the deepest recesses of his mind, and pursued them through the silence with rare words and descriptions. The drawing-room audiences would hold their breath until the unexpected poetic conclusion, which they would greet with soulful praise: '. . . Too pretty to be true', '. . . Too beautiful!', 'Quite divine!', 'Dear Oscar'.

The virtuoso conversationalist took nearly as much care of his voice as did a singer, he studied diction in order to perfect his mastery. Women applauded his slightest word, asked his advice about dress, a lecture, or the arrangement of a room, but in general men were hostile towards him. However, after dinner when the ladies left the dining-room, Oscar would win over some of them. He would drop his languid manner and throw himself into the telling of some preposterous story, about Ireland perhaps, or about ghosts. Then he might be forgiven for his hair, which was much too long, and his trousers, which were much too narrow, and those black velvet breeches, only worn by others at Court functions, but which Oscar would wear on an ordinary evening, might be overlooked. At first received as an importunate lap-dog, he later won the respect of a number of serious people, either by reason of his erudition, or because he encouraged them to talk on their favourite subjects and frequently found his patience rewarded by reaping some sententious enormity. It was only the pedantic, whose pretensions he had seen through, who pulled long faces about Oscar's popularity, and compared the admiring

peeresses to the patrician ladies of the Byzantine Empire
who, according to Gibbon, preferred the titillations of
eunuchs to the ponderous compliments of senators.

Like Proust, Wilde enjoyed Society. Each found in it both
the satisfaction of his vanity and an inexhaustible source of
fatuity. Only the confidence that a certain position in the
social world can give, makes it possible for someone, who in
other surroundings would have been no more than ordinary,
to go as far as Oscar did without making himself ridiculous.
He took every opportunity to collect eccentrics who were
to provide him later with comic characters for his plays,
and he also cajoled the learned, already well-disposed
towards a prominent Oxford man. He renewed his acquaintance with Lord Houghton, at whose breakfasts he met writers and politicians. Houghton had anticipated the future
success of the young poet when he had met him in Dublin,
and made friends with him. Lord Lytton, a more charming
man, was a diplomat who liked to think to himself in some
ways as the new Byron, and wrote romantic novels and
verses. Perhaps he found an echo of his own romanticism in
Ravenna; in any case his approval was a passport to the most
serious circles where, as in Disraeli's novels, the fate of a
Government was decided between a hunt and a ball. Some
thought Oscar so marvellous a talker that he might make
a good orator. There was even a question of finding him
a constituency; but Wilde was not interested in politics, he
was only impressed by the pomp and the power that goes
with it.

The English upper classes at that time were more
sensitive to beauty than to wit; perhaps they judged human
beauty from the standpoint of breeding, as they did horses,
and therefore, in order to be accepted, an upstart had to
have the attributes of a thoroughbred. The fashionable

world, closed in general to the new rich, opened its doors to pretty women as well as to good horsemen and fine shots. Next to such divinities as the Duchess of Sutherland and Lady Brooke were to be found women who were popular only because of their looks. The Cockneys knew the fashionable beauties by sight, and photographs of them were on sale at the newspaper stalls, wearing Court dress or riding habit. Crowds would spend hours in front of a house whenever a ball was in progress, in the hope of catching a glimpse of a celebrity standing on the doorstep between hedges of footmen, while a linkman shouted 'The Duchess of Leeds' carriage', or 'Lady Dudley's carriage blocks the way'. One linkman of the time was called Piddlecock. It was he who, while ushering a dowager into a barouche with her five daughters, remarked compassionately: 'Taking them all home, M'Lady?'

The 'professional beauties', the title given rather acidly by those women whose photographs were not on sale, were usually rich or had rich admirers: they had well-dressed husbands, and well-run houses. Some ladies turned to intrigue and it was on them that Oscar later based such characters in his plays as Mrs. Cheveley and Mrs. Erlynne. *Vanity Fair*, the magazine which pandered to the interest taken by the general public in this select society, described their dresses and their parties. Lord Ronald Gower was one of its contributors, under the pseudonym of 'Talon Rouge', and his articles helped the public to decide between real and false elegance. Spy, the caricaturist, ratified individual success.

The most celebrated of these beauties was the daughter of a Jersey clergyman, married to a moderately rich Irishman, Mr. Langtry. When passing through London she was invited to an evening party at which the painter Millais, and several other men who set the fashion, were present.

As a result of their admiration she rapidly became the rage.
Her beauty was intoxicating; her profile and proportions
those of a Greek statue, her skin transparent and her hair
golden. In addition to these charms, she had gay and natural
manners, and was only twenty. The Archduke Rudolph
came hurrying from Vienna especially to see her, only to
find that the Prince of Wales was first in the field. Wilfrid
Blunt, the poet, anti-imperialist and diarist, was one of
her early admirers and is said to have given her one of his
beautiful Arab horses. Millais painted Mrs. Langtry with
lilies in her hand and henceforth she was called the Jersey
lily. The Queen took away the copy of this portrait that she
had found in the room of her son, the Duke of Albany; and
at the Court at which Mrs. Langtry was presented, it can be
imagined how curious Victoria must have been to see the
original. The eyes of the sovereign no doubt opened wide
when the exquisite head, adorned with the regulation three
ostrich feathers, bent before her; the fat little hand would
be extended dryly, and no doubt a rebuking frown took in
the theatrical gesture as Mrs. Langtry picked up her train
and joined the other ladies.

Naturally, Oscar was one of the first to meet Mrs. Langtry
and at once evinced a mad passion for her. Late passers-by
would see him night after night before the house of his
loved one. He was heard to order a florist to send every
flower in the shop to 18 Pont Street, by then a well-known
address. He declared that Mrs. Langtry '. . . owes it to
herself and to us to drive through Hyde Park in a black
Victoria drawn by black horses and with "Venus Anno-
domini" emblazoned on her black bonnet in dull sapphires.
But she won't.' The Press reported the dedication of his
poem The New Helen, first published in 1879 and reprinted in
1881, 'To Helen, formerly of Troy, now of London'. Oscar
was to be seen following Mrs. Langtry to the studios of

Watts and of Burne-Jones, both of whom were anxious to hitch their wagon to the star of the Lily. At a Private View Oscar introduced Ruskin the theoretician of beauty, to this ideal in the flesh. Last and most important, several times a week Mrs. Langtry would visit his little house in Salisbury Street, and pose for Frank Miles. Soon the Prince of Wales, benevolent, and already inclined to be short of breath, climbed the stairs to the studio which also served as a drawing-room. The panelling was painted white, and on either side of a large portrait of Lily by Edward Poynter were blue and white china pots filled with azaleas. At one end a long sofa, covered with many multi-coloured cushions, invited secret confidences.

Oscar was so delightful a person that with him an artificial love developed into a solid friendship; he took in hand what would nowadays be called public relations for Mrs. Langtry, and decided to make her the Gioconda of her century, but the task was not an easy one because the Lily was the least mysterious person in the world. To the pleasure of contemplating this perfection from so near and of meeting her illustrious admirers was added the amusement of living among laces and furs (for such a connoisseur of women's clothes as Oscar), and of watching the diverting situations in which a fashionable woman finds herself; Oscar the entertainer became the confidante, while Mrs. Langtry unfortunately encouraged his sartorial follies. When going out together, they matched or blended their colours, and Oscar could be seen in pearl-grey trousers, embroidered waistcoat and lavender gloves, following his beloved dressed in the colour of a pigeon's breast. One day, thus accoutred, he heard a passer-by cry, 'There goes that bloody fool Oscar Wilde', upon which he remarked to his companion, 'It's extraordinary how soon one gets known in London.'

F

The intimate friends of the Prince of Wales soon found their way to the studio. Among these was Lady Lonsdale, afterwards Lady de Grey (who took part in arranging for Diaghilev's Russian Ballet to be brought to England); Lord de Grey, whom she married after the death of Lord Lonsdale, was the best shot in England; Lady Warwick, who succeeded Lily Langtry in the Prince of Wales' affections; Lady Dorothy Nevill, famous for her reminiscences, and many others whose portraits could be found in the Book of Beauties.

Society women rubbed shoulders with actresses in Frank Miles' studio; this could not have happened in Paris, but in England the love of beauty, the passion for celebrities, overcame prejudices. Soon to be seen among them was the most celebrated star of all, Ellen Terry, to whom there is a strong likeness in many of the paintings of Burne-Jones: beautiful features, and a melancholy expression which inspired Wilde to write the celebrated lines:

'She stands with eyes marred by the mists of pain
Like some wan lily overdrenched with rain.'

written after seeing Ellen Terry as Henrietta Maria. 'That phrase, "wan lily", represents exactly what I tried to convey not only in this part, but in Ophelia', she wrote twenty years later. She further wrote that the most remarkable men she had ever met were Oscar Wilde and Whistler. Another of her notable rôles was that of Lady Macbeth. She was a friend full of gaiety and fun; an agitated emotional life spared her in real life from playing the part of a fashionable woman. It was she, above all, who enticed Oscar towards the theatre. Another actress of that time whose Polish chatter contributed an exotic note was Madame Modjeska. In the full flower of her second or even third youth, she was celebrated

for having been one of the ugliest *Dame aux Camélias* ever
seen on the stage and in spite of this handicap, for having
actually reduced the Prince of Wales to tears while playing
the part. Above all, there was Sarah Bernhardt whose
success in England was fantastic; had she not threatened
Paris that she would settle in England after her rows with
the Comédie Française? Wilde made a conquest of her by
arriving at Dover, his arms full of lilies, to await her boat;
and when it arrived, he called in a voice loud enough to
rise above the storm and to reach the ears of the porters,
'Long live Sarah, Long live the Goddess'. He gave a supper
in her honour and to pay for it once more pawned his
gold medal. Sarah Bernhardt indulged in all sorts of
eccentric behaviour, such as standing on the table in his
room in order to write her name on the ceiling. The following morning a friend woke Oscar, who was lying fully
clothed on a sofa surrounded by cushions and over-turned
furniture; he lit his first cigarette of the day nonchalantly
with one of the bills piled up in a basket by the fireplace.

All the gossip writers knew that the prettiest women in
the country were to be found at the rooms of the young
Irishman with long brown hair who walked down Piccadilly
a flower in his hand, often in danger of his life when, lost
in contemplation of a sunflower, he glided between hansom
cabs and four-wheelers. Charming as this popular conception of Wilde may be, and although not discouraged by
him, it was not a true one, as will shortly be seen.

Oscar was also frequently to be seen in his mother's
London drawing-room, which was always full to bursting.
Speranza had landed in England in 1880 with Willie, who
lost no time in forcing his way into journalism. (There
was something of the arrival of Lady Wilde on the trail of
her brilliant son that was, yet again, like an incident in
one of Balzac's novels.) She settled herself at first in a little

house near the Park – a good address but too high a rent –
then in Chelsea. Each Sunday she entertained and sent out
invitations to all those who had made the slightest name in
literature. It was known that she had published several
translations and some poems, and people went out of
curiosity, some never to return. Ruskin, for example, was
horrified by the general confusion, and by the appearance of
the mistress of the house; more powdered, more heavily
bedecked and plumed than ever, with the air of a lion-
tamer in the midst of the curious beasts whom she
introduced with whispered explanations of their characteristics. Lady Windermere evokes Speranza's receptions
when she says to Lord Arthur Savile, 'People are so annoying.
All my pianists look exactly like poets; and all my poets
look exactly like pianists; and I remember last season asking
a most dreadful conspirator to dinner, a man who had
blown up ever so many people, and always wore a coat of
mail, and carried a dagger up his shirt-sleeve: and do you
know that when he came he looked just like a nice old
clergyman, and cracked jokes all the evening? . . .'
Lady Wilde's parties were attended by such successful
lady novelists as Marie Corelli, but also by actresses without
parts, students newly disembarked from Dublin, and
Willie's doubtful conquests (since he was a café Don Juan in
the same style as his father). One day Martin Tupper could
be heard reciting a hymn in praise of John Brown, the
intimate servant of Queen Victoria: 'Simple pious honest
man . . . child of Heaven while son of earth . . .'. Oscar,
asked his opinion of the hymn, replied; 'Charming, I doubt
if I could have written portions of it myself, you should
have it set to music by Arthur Sullivan . . . and have it
sung by a choir of virgins standing round the Albert
Memorial on the anniversary of Mr. Brown's death.'
Sometimes Oscar brought his new friends to see Speranza,

as a young hunter brings his first prey to his native hut. His arrival with a professional beauty on his arm, or with a fashionable painter, brought a whiff of 'High Life' into the confusion of mediocrities and, half touched, half mocking, he accepted their compliments and praise. Soon Speranza was nicknamed the 'Récamier of Chelsea', though in view of her turban and her voluminous conversation and writings, Madame de Staël would have been a closer analogy.

6   The cult of the beautiful

About 1850 there was built a series of rather monotonous streets of small houses with white painted porches, between Cheyne Walk and the King's Road. Behind these there were still village lanes full of workshops where a swarming Irish population tried to earn its living. The beauty of the neighbourhood lay in the river and its mystery. On the opposite bank the trees of Battersea Park could be seen and, at low tide, the mud-banks so often painted by Whistler.

Oscar and Frank Miles moved from their chambers in Salisbury Street to a small house at the top end of Tite Street, which led fom Tedworth Square down to the Thames. At their new home, called Keats House, they transformed the top floor into a studio.

It was in Chelsea, at 24 Cheyne Row, that Carlyle wrote his violent historical books. And in the most beautiful house in Cheyne Walk, Dante Gabriel Rossetti, one of the originators of the Pre-Raphaelite movement, painted his models as prisoners in some strange mediaeval winter garden. His love of the exotic was such that he kept a zoo in his garden. For a time Swinburne shared this house with him: the latter, although a wonderful poet, also indulged in eccentric excesses which nearly cost him his life; for years they certainly cost him dear every time he was reminded of them by a local blackmailer called Howell. This sinister man, thought to be a Portuguese Jew, was physically very attractive, with a fair skin and dark eyelashes. His overt profession was that of a picture-dealer, but it was known that he was also an expert forger of masterpieces. The victims of his blackmailing activities once clubbed together and produced enough money for him to go to Australia, but taking it he replied: 'Who would go to Australia, if he had the money to go with?' George Eliot lived and died in 4 Cheyne Walk; Edward Burne-Jones, though he lived in West Kensington in a house with stained-glass windows and low-ceilinged rooms, belonged to Chelsea in spirit, as can be seen from the pale, misty, idealised figures that he painted. The Pre-Raphaelites lived in a perpetual twilight, amid uncomfortable furniture designed by William Morris. Chelsea also had a colony in Florence. This was the golden age of the boarding-house called more attractively by the Italian word *pensione*, where virgins of both sexes made emotional discoveries while following the cult of beauty. Some leaned towards Catholicism, others let themselves go in pursuit of tastes which were better not cultivated in England. The novelist Vernon Lee, whose real name was Violet Paget, reigned for forty years over Lesbians dressed as Botticelli pages. With her long face, flattened hair, her pince-nez and her dark tailor-made suits, Vernon Lee looked like an ecclesiastic. At the age of twenty-five she had already published two important essays: *Euphorion*, about love in the Middle Ages, and another in the form of a counter-blast to Ruskin's morality.

In Florence, as in Chelsea, Ruskin was respected. Ruskin, of whom Oscar by now considered himself a friend, was the author of *Sesame and Lilies* translated by Proust in many pages of whose *Time Regained* the combination of archaeology and poetry is recognisable; all the aesthetic socialism of the end of the century derived from Ruskin. Yet another exponent of this creed, William Morris, undertook to continue Ruskin's work. He believed that Art was a morality, the best source of

comradeship, and that lack of comradeship was death. This
morality is expounded in the stories and essays of Wilde,
where it is also, happily, enlivened by epigrams.

Many aspects of Victorian England owed their origins to
the influence of Ruskin. For example, at Oxford, buildings
such as the Union and the Museum bear traces of his form of
mysticism. In the Union, the frescoes were painted by
Dante Gabriel Rossetti and Burne-Jones in 1864. All this
was better in theory than in practice; it is not surprising
that after inclining towards Ruskin the aesthetes should
have come to adore Walter Pater. His influence was to last
longer than that of Ruskin, which was submerged along
with the Utopians of the nineteenth century, while Pater
and Baudelaire were the first of the modern critics; although
they did not know each other, they met often in thought;
for instance Baudelaire's 'Le beau est toujours bizarre',
approximated to Pater's 'a lovely strangeness'. 'Pater', wrote
Miss Enid Starkie, 'would have wished to make of English
prose what Flaubert made of French prose'. To Michelet
Pater owed his love of the paganism of the Renaissance
which he set against Ruskin's mediaeval morality. Pater
dreamed of a Platonic Academy on the banks of the Isis,
like that founded by Politian among the villas of Fiesole;
and the disciples of Pater were persecuted by Victorian
judges as those of Politian were by Savonarola.

From the time of his arrival at Oxford all this had enchanted Wilde, who was always to seek in his friends the
beauty which Pater admired in Leonardo and Giorgione.
And in De Profundis he refers to Pater's The Renaissance as '. . .
that book which has had such a strange influence over
my life'. Everywhere he declared that Pater's essays were
'the golden book of spirit and sense, the Holy Writ of
beauty. . . . I never travel anywhere without it. But it is the
very flower of decadence. The Last Trumpet should have

sounded the moment it was written.' 'But would you not have given us time to read it?' asked a prosaic member of his audience. 'Oh no, there would have been plenty of time after, in either world.'

Amongst these intellectuals, a provocative American launched himself with all the fervour of a present-day public relations campaign. But in the case of Whistler impudence always triumphed over self-interest. Through ill-temper in which, it must be admitted, vulgarity was never predominant, he would lose his best clients, among them Frederick Leyland the rich ship-owner, for whom he had designed and painted a *Peacock Room* (the favourite bird of the Art Nouveau style). After two years of growing dissension between them, in which money played a part, as an insult Whistler painted a cartoon of two peacocks at war – the rich peacock and the poor peacock – on the wall of Leyland's dining-room, and thus lost his patron.

To someone else who objected to the enormous price he asked for a canvas which it had taken only two days to cover, Whistler replied: 'But which is the result of a lifetime.' In that year, 1880, Whistler had received a great deal of publicity as a result of his law-suit against Ruskin. In 1877, the Grosvenor Gallery had exhibited several of Whistler's paintings called by such names as *Arrangement in Black and Brown*, *Nocturne in Gold and Black*, *Nocturne in Blue and Silver*. Before these crepuscular canvasses, Ruskin saw red; accustomed as he was to the detailed pictures of subjects chosen by the Pre-Raphaelites from the Middle Ages, he determined to avenge his friends in his little newspaper *Fors Clavigera*, and on the 2nd July 1877 he wrote, '. . . I have seen and heard much of Cockney impudence before now, but never expected to hear a coxcomb ask two hundred guineas for flinging a pot of paint in the public's face.' Poor Ruskin did not realise that he had trodden on a

viper's tail; Whistler had the susceptibility and latent
nervous energy of talent wishing to pass as genius. He
alleged that Ruskin's article was prejudicial to him
financially, and attacked the philosopher with venomous
zest. Whistler showed an insolence which Wilde was later
to copy in a far graver law-suit. He was brilliant enough to
win his case, although he had refused to have a lawyer, but
had to pay the costs which temporarily ruined him. Being
one of those people who are resourceful in defeat, he sold
his beautiful house, settled in Venice for a year and returned
to London more virulent than ever. As for the solemn
Ruskin, already ill, the serpent's venom hastened the loss
of his reason.

When he was thirty, Oscar said to a friend, 'My
name has two "O"s, two "F"s, and two "W"s. A name
which is destined to be in everyone's mouth must not be
too long. It comes too expensive in the advertisement.
When one is unknown a number of Christian names are
useful, perhaps needful. As one becomes famous one sheds
some of them, just as a balloonist, when rising higher, sheds
unnecessary ballast . . . All but two of my five names have
already been thrown overboard. Soon I shall discard another
and be known as "The Wilde" or "The Oscar".' Just how
well-known Oscar had become can be gauged by where he
is placed in a picture of the opening of an exhibition at the
Royal Academy. He is seen in the centre, his fine, pale face
raised towards a masterpiece, while he is pointing out its
beauties with a languid hand to the encircling ladies whose
soulful qualities are proclaimed by their dresses. Oscar
laughed at the pictures exhibited at the Royal Academy as did
Chelsea. It was unfortunate for him that he had arrived on the
artistic scene ten years too late; the great figures of the post-
romantic movement, who at one time had caused the

Victorians some anxiety, had now become inoffensive. Rossetti had lost his inspiration on the death of Elizabeth Siddal, and was consoling himself with alcohol and drugs; his new paintings had become like morbid caricatures of his early work. William Morris had retired to Kelmscott where he painted scenes from Arthurian legends, and wrote socialistic pamphlets. His simplicity protected him from loud and flashy people. Oscar had admired his work since boyhood and took trouble to propitiate him. This is shown in a letter from Oscar thanking Morris for the gift of his book: '. . . I have always felt that your work comes from the sheer delight of making beautiful things; that no alien motive ever interests you. . . . But I know you hate blowing of trumpets.' Swinburne, whose masochistic excesses had alarmed his friends, ruined his health and emptied his purse, was now living in seclusion in a little house in Putney, to the great regret of his admirers, with a solicitor who was also a novelist and poet called Theodore Watts-Dunton; he was to live on for another thirty years. Oscar only met Swinburne once, at Lord Houghton's, but few words were exchanged as Swinburne's mentor put a stop to a conversation which was too amusing. He was Oscar's favourite poet, had not Tennyson held his immorality to be disgraceful? Browning, also, had attacked the effemin-ate, carnal school, the credo of which was Swinburne's essay on Baudelaire. Like Swinburne, Oscar looked towards Greece and France, like him he had a vice to hide.

Luckily, there was Whistler, and when Oscar moved into Chelsea he found the modernists divided into two camps; in one was Ruskin and the older Pre-Raphaelites, in the other Whistler and the social world of London. Without a doubt Whistler's supporters were the more amusing. At the beginning of their acquaintance Whistler saw in Oscar a young admirer just down from Oxford and invited him to a breakfast party. To his amazement the young man knew the greater part of the guests and made it his business to make friends with the rest.

Oscar, charmed by the pleasant things said by this new friend and his amusing originality, decided to join Whistler in the war against bad taste, and it took at least a year before Whistler's astonishment turned to spite. Meanwhile, Oscar understood every shade of meaning, Oscar had read everything, Oscar made fun of everything so wonderfully and, for the time being, their friendship became firmly established.

In Whistler's world also, it was the women who made much of Oscar. Among these elegant ladies was one of bohemian tastes, to whom Oscar became attached, whose name was Lady Archibald Campbell. The original of Whistler's *Arrangement in Black*, she had two passions; spiritualism and the theatre. With the help of Godwin, the architect, she produced at Coombe Park, Kingston, Elizabethan pastoral plays – among others, *The Faithful Shepherdess* by Fletcher, and Shakespeare's *As You Like It* – in which, with her slender pliant figure, she liked to play the part of a page. Oscar loved these costume fêtes under the great trees of the Park. In a June twilight the pink and grey silhouettes of the characters formed a perfect Whistlerian composition. He adored the mercurial Lady Archie, whom Vernon Lee was to describe as imperious and a dreamer, always vague, dressed either as a Prince of the Arabian Nights or in the blue smock of the artist. Needless to say, Lady Archie also lived in Chelsea.

Between the years 1877 and 1884 Oscar showed signs of being susceptible to feminine beauty; he had been more or less in love with Lily Langtry, Ellen Terry, Sarah Bernhardt and Florence Balcombe, attracted to Constance Fletcher, to whom he dedicated *Ravenna*, and to Lady Archie

Campbell, and very much in love with Constance Lloyd. Before he decided to marry her, he had been interested in meeting desirable marriageable girls, a fact which is confirmed in the following hitherto unpublished information, for which I am indebted to the Hope-Nicholson family. A staid contemporary of Oscar's at Magdalen, called Cresswell-Cresswell, expressed a wish to meet Sarah Bernhardt. Oscar promised to introduce him if he would promise to bring his cousins, the Troubridge girls, and Oscar together. Luckily this was brought about because in Laura Troubridge's diary, published by John Murray in 1966 under the title, *Life Amongst the Troubridges* (edited by Jaqueline Hope-Nicholson), Laura's thoughts about Oscar over the years have come to light. She was the daughter of Colonel Sir Thomas Troubridge who had been A.D.C. to Queen Victoria. Laura and her sister met Oscar at the house of her cousin Charles (Tardy) Orde in June 1879 '... Met Oscar Wilde the poet, both fell awfully in love with him, thought him quite delightful.' And again she wrote: 'July 1879, to the National Gallery, saw Sarah Bernhardt there, had a good stare at her, met Tardy and went together to tea at Oscar Wilde's – great fun, lots of vague intense men, such duffers, who amused us awfully. The room was a mass of white lilies, photographs of Mrs. Langtry, peacock feather screens and coloured pots, pictures of various merit.' Oscar's name does not appear in the diary again for several years.

With the help of so remarkable a woman as Lady Archie, Oscar was able to embark with enthusiasm on a crusade for good taste. In the first place he was ardent and full of good-will and secondly he believed that his fame would be more widely spread as an evangelist than as a mere poet. In fact, this crusade had begun as early as 1860 when the Pre-Raphaelites had shown up the absurdities of the 'establishment' painters, though naturally many thought that the Pre-Raphaelites painted no better themselves.

William Morris wanted to save mankind from the threat of industrial civilisation by making them work with their hands: he advocated the art of weaving, of using vegetable dyes, of making rustic pottery; he turned towards mediaeval simplicity (an important aspect of Art Nouveau); he loathed upholstered furniture. Morris's great law was that a house should contain nothing that was neither useful nor beautiful, and many children of the time were indoctrinated with this idea. (Walter Crane the draughtsman, who later illustrated these new theories, tended to weaken them; he designed a corded velvet suit to be worn by workmen which was not unlike that designed by Oscar for himself.) Every effect was towards the simple, and Morris' disciples were rather like early colonists hacking their way through a jungle; they succeeded in making a little clearing in the jungle of Victorian bric-à-brac; but hot on their heels came Whistler, whom they considered to be an unscrupulous adventurer, but who decided to arrange the clearing in his own way and in that of his architect, Godwin. This clearing, so to speak, became the stage on which Oscar was to preach his version of good taste, directing his attacks both against those whom he regarded as Philistines, and also, in homage to Baudelaire, against what he considered bourgeois.

The Crusade for Beauty was, above all, a feminine concern; the professional beauties rallied to Oscar's banner. It was towards fashion in dress that the first efforts were directed; slim ladies with a tendency towards mysticism preferred the dress of the Middle Ages; Belles Dames Sans Merci and Demoiselles Elues materialised in Chelsea, and descended upon Piccadilly. Those who were not pale enough adopted the style of Kate Greenaway. The generously-built school, to which most of the professional beauties belonged, leaned towards antiquity, adapting the Grecian tunics and the ringlets of the models of Alma Tadema. 'What will Oscar think?', was the question they pondered after having rigged themselves out in peacock feathers as an up-to-date version of Psyche. For two Seasons, England, and London in particular, took part in a carnival. Like all who deliberately adopt a pose, the ladies of that time over-did their affectations, which were not overlooked by their critics. They went into ecstasies over the colour of a dead leaf, over a line of Pater, a word of Oscar's, 'Too utterly utter . . .'. They were caricatured in *Punch* by Georges Du Maurier, who invented a family for his cartoons called the Cimabue Browns. Dressed like figures in a Botticelli picture, Mrs. Brown and her friends swooned whenever the languid Mr. Gellaby Postlethwaite appeared, dressed in velvet, a lily in his hand, exuding a special air of insipidity. Another of Du Maurier's characters represented a far less pleasing image of Wilde, depicting him as a fat woman wearing pince-nez and uttering the following words: 'Ah, Madam, your son is of an accomplished beauty, there is nothing else to do in life than to be beautiful.' Following in the footsteps of *Punch*, a Gilbert and Sullivan opera was to make Oscar into a national figure. *The Mikado* had drawn its inspiration from Japan; now, in *Patience*, there followed some gentle mockery of the cult of aestheticism. Two aesthetes, Archibald Grosvenor, an apostle of simplicity, and Bunthorne, a follower of Swinburne, wittily rivalled the officers of the Dragoon Guards who up to then had had the undivided attention of their numerous female admirers. But how could the ladies bear the uniform of the Dragoons – red and yellow: primary colours: Shame! the aesthetes suggested that the military should adopt a uniform 'in spider-web grey velvet which, trimmed with Venetian leather and Spanish lace, topped by something Japanese,

would at least have the look of old England'. They made
fun of Ruskin's favourite adverb 'consummately'; of the
cult of the Primitive: 'How Fra Angelican!' The satire was
not cruel; Wilde was the first to laugh when he recognised
his favourite expressions; 'I am a very narcissus' . . . 'too all
but precious'. Gilbert had noticed that Wilde, like Bunthorne, 'was readier to laugh than the spectator believes'.
To be sure Oscar did not 'walk down Piccadilly with a
poppy or a lily in his mediaeval hand' as in the famous line
in *Patience*. 'Anyone could have done that,' said Wilde, 'the
great and the difficult thing was what I achieved – to make
the world *believe* that I had done it.'

It was due to the friends who were his constant
companions that Oscar got the reputation of being a rake.
On one occasion he only just avoided being involved in a
typical London scandal: his friend, Frank Miles, ignoring
Lord Ronald's avuncular advice, had set up a thirteen-year-
old nymph in his studio. Endless Academicians wanted to
paint the little marvel, and she did the honours at the tea-
table when the Prince of Wales came to see Oscar with Lily
Langtry. But the world was malicious and the police
suspicious; one morning a Superintendent knocked at the
door of Keats House; Oscar with his powerful build, held
the door against three policemen and by the time they got
into the studio, Frank had escaped by the roof.

Another friendship showed Oscar that his success could
not be achieved without getting a different sort of bad
reputation. During his last years at Oxford he had become
involved with an intelligent youth whose special charm lay
in his seriousness; they visited Touraine together and
Oscar encouraged him to write; the friends of Rennell Rodd
(who later became an Ambassador) disapproved of his
friendship with Oscar and also with Lord Ronald. In fact a

journalist, perhaps jealous of Lord Ronald, who, as we have
seen, wrote articles in the Press himself, had used the gutter
press to attack Lord Ronald's morals; the latter brought an
action which he won and the newspaper went bankrupt.
But even so it was better for young men interested in their
careers to give Lord Ronald the cold shoulder. A year later
Rennell Rodd broke with Oscar, who had taken great
trouble to get the young man's poems published, and had
only been able to induce a publisher in Philadelphia to take
them by promising to write a preface himself. Unfortunately Oscar also dedicated the book to himself thus:

To

Oscar Wilde

'Heart's Brother'

These few songs and many songs to come.

Rodd thought the dedication too affectionate, and complained that he did not wish to be identified with many
ideas in the preface with which he had no sympathy. Oscar
remarked haughtily – a shade too haughtily – 'What he says
is like a poor linnet's cry by the side of the road along
which my immeasurable ambition is sweeping forward.'

One can understand the jealousy which was aroused
by Wilde's success, resting as it did upon charm and
bluff. He had produced no masterpiece to justify it; and
when the first collection of his poems appeared in 1881,
very elegantly produced, although the author's reputation
enabled five editions to be sold very quickly, the critics
were severe.

When Oscar presented a copy to the Oxford Union, the
usual acceptance and vote of thanks being proposed, Oliver
Elton rose to object. 'It is not that these poems are thin –
and they are thin,' he said. 'It is not that they are immoral

G

– and they *are* immoral : it is not that they are this or that –
and they *are* all this and all that : it is that they are for the
most part not by their putative father at all, but by a
number of better-known and more deservedly reputed
authors. They are, in fact, by Philip Sidney, by John Donne,
by Lord Byron, by William Morris, by Algernon Swinburne
and by sixty more whose works have furnished the list of
passages which I hold at this moment. . . .' This severity,
even if one takes into account normal university jealousies,
is in great part justified. The most original poems are about
Oscar's memories of Oxford. Certain images are frankly
equivocal, like the line already quoted – 'A fair slim boy
not made for this world's pain'. There is always a large
public and a large sale, for this kind of poetry. A touch of
the 'keepsake' style pleased young ladies ; for example the
sonnets On *Approaching Italy* and *The Golden Room*, which recall
Verlaine – 'Her ivory hands on the ivory keys'. There are
many reminders of Hugo's *Châtiments* in Oscar's sonnet *On
the Massacre of the Christians in Bulgaria*. But Wilde had reservations about martyrdom :

> '. . . . and yet, and yet,
> These Christs that die upon the barricades,
> God knows it I am with them, in some ways.'
> (Sonnet *To Liberty*)

In Oscar's poem *Humanitad* there are verses which reveal
an ambiguity :

> 'Being ourselves the sowers and the seeds,
> The night that covers and the sights that fade,
> The spear that pierces, and the side that bleeds,
> The lips betraying and the life betrayed . . .'

Pater's beautiful prose is turned into verse on more than

one occasion, for example, 'To burn always with this hard gem-like flame', becomes in Oscar's *Panthea* 'This hard hot flame with which our bodies burn', and in *Humanitad* it is 'To burn with one clear flame'.

The poems brought in a little money, but not enough to enable Oscar to set himself up in the style he felt he deserved. It must have been due to Lord Ronald's help that Frank and he had been able to pay for their rent and their parties. When Frank left after a quarrel Oscar went to live with his mother. It was then that he decided to write for the theatre; he chose an up-to-date subject: nihilism. Wilde's *Vera* is interesting insomuch as the only female, the Vera of the title, cannot control her weakness for the very régime she wishes to overthrow. Between the scenes of melodrama, her disillusioned Prime Minister, Prince Paul happily appears, and sets the tone of the comedy. 'We speak the truth to one another here,' says the President of the nihilists, to which he replies, 'How misleading you must find it.' And again – 'Experience, the name men give to their mistakes.' But the intrigue is unworthy of Sardou, to whose play *Fedora* (one of Bernhardt's first triumphs) *Vera* owes much. Unfortunately, just as a management was thinking of putting on this play, about which naturally there had been much talk, the nihilists assassinated the Czar Alexander II. Futhermore, the Duchess of Edinburgh, the sister-in-law of the kindly Prince of Wales, was the Czar's daughter. In order not to upset an august acquaintance Oscar withdrew the play, as it indicated a certain sympathy with the assassins. Money became scarcer than ever.

In the autumn of 1882, the impresario Richard D'Oyley Carte suggested that Oscar should undertake a lecture tour in the United States of America. Necessity no less than the interesting bohemianism of the idea decided

Oscar to allow himself to be exhibited like a calf with two
heads. The lecturer was to receive two-thirds of the profits
with a guaranteed minimum of $200. On what subjects
should he speak? Well, on those that had already entertained artistic ladies and up-to-date young men in London:
he must entertain grown-up children with stories, flavouring
the truth with a dash of snobbery. It was certain that two
hundred Chicago ladies would throw away those hideous
embroideries with which they protected their armchairs
once he had told them, 'My divine friend the Duchess of
Westminster would never put up with antimacassars'.

In his crusade Oscar never stopped deploring the type of
decoration which resulted from the industrial revolution,
the effects of which had been felt as early as 1830, and the
products advertised by exhibitions throughout the world.
Papier-mâché furniture and wardrobes with looking-glasses
were objects of scorn to the aesthetes, whose horror also
contained traces of compassion, because these objects were
the result of frightful exploitation. Oscar was no economist,
but his reactions, Irish and aristocratic, were always in
opposition to capitalism.

Besides considering the rôle of the artist in society, which
one also finds in his essays, he neglected no detail – 'He
teaches the art of arranging a bouquet or an hors d'oeuvre.'
There was something of Mrs. Beeton in his lectures – 'Like
Lot's wife, English cooks should be turned into pillars of
salt for the use they make of it.' Bad painting inspired him
as much as bad cooking. Of the Royal Academicians whose
canvases ornamented the palaces of Fifth Avenue, he said:
'Varnishing is the only artistic process with which Royal
Academicians are thoroughly familiar.' 'Is it really all done
by hand?', he recalled having murmured as he stood in
front of Frith's 'Derby Day'.

In his lectures he elaborated the cult of the artificial which was to form the basis of *Intentions*, and he made fun of Nature with the whole-heartedness of Voltaire attacking the Church. His epigrams shook George Eliot's disciples, as well as those of Wordsworth. They would have replied severely to any attack upon morality, but the slightest word against Nature stupefied them. Wilde's lectures were for the readers of those magazines which teach 'gracious living'. Severely dressed in a Louis XV velvet suit, he was the centre of attraction when this section of the public foregathered in New York for the first time, and the illustrations of the hero of *Little Lord Fauntleroy* were modelled on this original. Both the ethics and the aesthetics of *Vogue* were combined in this frivolous gospel, preached though it was by eminently serious people. Oscar created a need for good taste among the immense Anglo-Saxon middle-classes: thanks to his tireless indolence, the over-elaborate taste of the wives of New York bankers and Manchester shop-keepers was pruned; luxury became an art.

On Christmas Eve, 1881, Oscar embarked, with his trunks full of clothes that were destined to astonish the United States in every latitude. He confessed to Whistler that he was afraid of being sea-sick, only to be advised that in that case he'd better 'disgorge all the Burne-Jones's'.

7 The land of the free

'A little bit too much is just enough for me': these words spoken by a Red Indian Chief during a banquet at the White House, sum up the enormous appetite of the United States in the eighties for every novelty and every kind of amusement. After the ordeal of the Civil War the world of the machine imposed itself upon the agricultural civilisation; and the cities became gigantic. In New York, and still more so in Boston and Philadelphia, this incredible activity would have submerged the small outposts of a more aristocratic era had the families of which they were composed not known how to keep up their moral and wordly prestige. Within easy reach of these three cities there were universities which have given the world such great thinkers as Emerson and William James; and other great writers had also originated there, of world fame. The 'museum' most frequented was Barnum's in New York, where bearded ladies and sea-serpents were the prize exhibits. The millionaires brought back from Europe products of the Salon in Paris and the Royal Academy in London, as well as marbles from Naples and china from Nüremberg.

The theatre of the United States, by contrast, was excellent; European stars were lured over but had to compete with very good actors in New York. In other towns and cities puritans regarded these distractions as dissolute, and looked instead to the preachers, some of whom were as celebrated as Patti, and brought millions of dollars to the sects they represented. Reporters bustled about everywhere, stimulating curiosity by inventing far-fetched rumours.

In this hurly-burly Oscar would have been completely lost without the women who were now coming to the fore in Society, whereas a generation earlier house-keeping had occupied the time and thoughts of all women except the very rich, and Calvinistic modesty had kept them to their family circle. At the time that Oscar arrived in the United States there was a great number of very rich people, and modesty by then was merely a barrier protecting the established social sphere of the new rich – the men, all of whom worked, left their wives alone far more than was usual in Europe. The women felt that it was their mission to civilise the inhabitants of the United States, and grouped themselves into philanthropic or artistic societies – *salons*, in the French meaning of the word, did not exist – and they bore witness to an appetite for culture and fashion as great as that of the Indian Chief for food. Up to the 1860's, elegance was the privilege of the Southern States only; after their defeat, the taste for luxury and idleness gained ground in the North. The very rich went to Europe for elegance, but in the next financial bracket there were many more who gratefully sought how to acquire it at home.

Richard D'Oyley Carte, when bringing over the Aesthete, advertised his exotic quality to amuse the men, as well as his cultural side to interest the women. Another element to further the success of the enterprise had more to do with patriotism than curiosity: the Irish colony would always welcome a compatriot with open arms. From the moment of his embarkation Oscar had resigned himself to being exhibited as a freak, since he had agreed to give his lectures wearing aesthetic dress. He was also ready to gratify all the curiosity of his female admirers. The visiting Irishman

reacted to their ridicule and to their questions with an
exquisite courtesy which made up for his youthful effrontery; his calm withstood the most uncomfortable journeys
and the most stormy meetings. In his emotional moments,
Oscar regarded himself as a missionary, a martyr to the
Beautiful, but most of the time he judged himself with the
detachment of a humorist – an amused observer of his
adventures. His burlesque cultural, circus tour of the thirty-
six states had many of the qualities of a series of cartoons:
the Aesthete confronting the Ocean, the Aesthete on Broadway, the Aesthete on the Prairie surrounded by buffaloes and
Indians, the Aesthete at the bottom of a mine or in a saloon
in the Far West – always impeccable, always polite, and in
the gravest circumstances hiding a yawn or a fit of laughter
behind a suède-gloved hand.

The *Arizona* arrived at New York on the 2nd
January 1882, and reporters hurried to the quay to cross-
question the hero of *Patience*. They expected a pale young
man dressed in silk, and found themselves face to face with
a giant huddled in a fur coat, from whom they could only
drag one sentence: 'I was disappointed in the Atlantic.' But
the remark went all over the United States, as did that which
he pronounced at the Customs a few minutes later: 'I have
nothing to declare, except my genius.' The reporters, disappointed at not having gathered more than two immortal
phrases, questioned the other passengers. Oscar must have
treated them haughtily, for they thought him affected and
repeated his remark: 'Decidedly, it is in the hold among
the immigrants that beauty is to be found.' Indeed,
according to one passenger he had much admired a
Roumanian gipsy girl. As Oscar got into the carriage with
the director of the D'Oyley Carte Bureau, Colonel Morse,
the reporters heard him say in a stage whisper: 'Bad

manners make a journalist.' They were not to forgive him for this remark.

In the streets, where buildings of fifteen and twenty storeys were being erected, the visitor was astonished by the hundreds of telephone wires linked from one office to another, but the news that, somewhere out of sight, Edison manufactured a thousand electric light bulbs a month left him cold. He stayed at the Grand Hotel on the corner of 31st Street and Broadway, where more journalists were waiting for him: 'What are your politics, Liberal or Conservative, Mr. Wilde?' 'Oh, do you know,' Oscar replied, 'those matters are of no interest to me. I only know two terms – civilisation and barbarism, and I am on the side of civilisation.' He glanced out of the window and what he saw might, strictly speaking, pass for respect for this civilisation, a reincarnation of the Château de Blois next door to a miniature Palazzo Vecchio. Between these palaces, the brownstone houses recalled the most depressing squares of Kensington. As to the passers-by, they inspired Oscar to make notes of the following kind: 'Everyone seems in a hurry to catch a train. This is a state of things which is not favourable to poetry or romance.' – 'It is the noisiest country that ever existed. Such continual turmoil must ultimately be destructive to the musical faculty.' – 'In America, life is one long expectoration.' – 'I believe a most serious problem for the American people to consider is the cultivation of better manners. It is the most noticeable, the most painful defect in American civilisation.'

Numbers of invitations awaited Oscar; on the evening that he went to dine with Mrs. Croly, better known as Jenny June, the writer, he noticed that the other guest of honour was Louisa May Alcott, the author of Little Women. The following day, he was taken in hand by a worldly man called Samuel Ward who knew the grander New York and

urged Oscar to avoid wasting his time in the houses of
people of small repute: his nickname was 'Uncle Sam'.
This opulent old gentleman and his sister Mrs. Julia Ward
Howe had a great many friends. His fortune came partly
from two rich marriages, and partly from trade, and he was
very influential in Washington. But it was in New York,
where he lived and entertained at 84 Clinton Place,
frequently serving his famous speciality – a Virginia ham
boiled in champagne with a wisp of fresh hay dropped in
at the crucial split second – that Oscar was to meet such
important people as the Vanderbilts, the Goelets, and the
Fishes. The first public appearance of the aesthete was on
6th January, at a performance of *Patience*, and the public was
able to compare the Bunthorne on the stage with the real
man on whom he was thought to be modelled. What they
may not have realised was that *Patience* was a satire on
aestheticism, and not on any particular aesthete. The frank
high spirits of Wilde won him sympathy, and his comment
put the situation in a nutshell: 'Caricature is the tribute
which mediocrity pays to genius.'

The first lecture took place at Chickering Hall on 9th
January, the same night as the 'Patriarchs' Dance' which was
held at Delmonicos. It was the peak of the season. The crowd
thronged to penetrate so heavily publicised a gathering, and
did not conceal its disappointment in the large, lazy young
man who contented himself with giving advice about
furniture in poetic terms: 'Let there be no flower in your
meadows that does not wreathe its tendrils round your
pillows, no curving spray of wild rose or briar that does
not live forever in carven arch or window of marble.'
(Already the stylisation of Art Nouveau was beginning to
show itself.) Women hoped that there would be a great deal
to be learned from these lectures where they mixed with the
'best people', and henceforth places were reserved at high

prices. Business must have been good, to judge from the following letter written on 15th January by Oscar to Mrs. George Lewis, the wife of the best solicitor in London. 'I am sure you have been pleased at my success! The hall had an audience larger and more wonderful than even Dickens had. I was recalled and applauded and am now treated like the Royal Boy. I have several Harry Tyrwhitts,* as secretaries. One writes my autographs all day for my admirers, the other receives the flowers that are left really every ten minutes. A third whose hair resembles mine is obliged to send off locks of his own hair to the myriad maidens of the city, and so is rapidly becoming bald.

'I stand at the top of the reception rooms when I go out, and for two hours they defile past for introduction. I bow graciously and sometimes honour them with a royal observation, which appears next day in all the newspapers. When I go to the theatre the manager bows me in with lighted candles and the audience rise. Yesterday I had to leave by a private door, the mob was so great. Loving virtuous obscurity as much as I do, you can judge how much I dislike this lionising, which is worse than that given to Sarah Bernhardt I hear. . . .'

In a letter of the same date to Norman Forbes-Robertson, Oscar writes: 'I am torn in bits by Society. Immense receptions, wonderful dinners, crowds wait for my carriage . . . girls very lovely, men simple and intellectual . . . I give sittings to artists, and generally behave as I have always behaved – dreadfully.'

Taking into account Irish exaggeration, it can nevertheless be believed that the mountebank did have a great success, and without taking much pains about it. Living caricatures of the Chelsea Demoiselles Elues then pullulated from Washington Square to Central Park, ready to swallow almost any

* Harry Tyrwhitt was an Equerry to the Prince of Wales.

folly. A lady who had known Oscar in England confessed to feeling embarrassed by his aesthetic conversation – 'Do you yearn?',* was Oscar's frequent conversational opening, and he would continue: 'What is the soul? It is the essence of a perfect Beauty. I would like to breathe it in like the scent of this perfect rose . . . and die of it if it had to be.'

In Boston, Oscar was to renew his acquaintance with the actress, Mary Anderson, and he suggested that she should play *Vera*. She was ready to commission an historical play in verse that he had already started, called *The Duchess of Padua*, a little in the style of Victor Hugo's dramas: but he had no time to think of such projects, being about to start his journey through the Northern States. Before his departure from New York he made the following note: 'Theodore Tilton brought me to see the old room where Poe wrote *The Raven*, on Friday, Nov. 10. An old wooden house over the Hudson, low rooms, fine chimney piece, very dull Corot day, clergyman with reminiscences of Poe, about chickens.' Other poetic expeditions broke the routine of the provincial lecture tour.

In Philadelphia, Wilde could hardly have failed to be impressed by Walt Whitman. Bearded, superb, and remote as Michelangelo's Moses, his struggle against bad health made him look more than his sixty-three years. The poet was considered immoral because he had written about Broadway prostitutes and pioneer democracy in the same volume, and his tastes were thought to be equivocal by those who read between the lines of his poem *Comrades*. He was living in a suburb, with relations, where the only distraction was to glimpse the coming and going of ships between factory chimneys. Wilde's visit was seen by the newspapers as the equivalent of the celebrated meeting between Emerson and Carlyle. Whitman distrusted any

* This became a catch phrase in San Francisco.

An American caricature

friend of Swinburne on the slender grounds that he might be like John Symonds, whose admiration became embarrassing through his constant allusions to Greek Love.* But the visit was a great success; Oscar, gay and simple, sat at the feet of the master, laughed at his jokes, conjured up the London litterati, light-heartedly caricaturing them: 'May I call you Oscar?' – 'With joy, dear Walt' – 'I should tell you Oscar that a fellow who makes a dead set at Beauty by itself is in a bad way. My idea is that Beauty is a result, not an abstraction' – 'Quite true: all Beauty comes from beautiful blood and a beautiful brain, and after all, I agree with you.' – The conversation lasted for two hours, interrupted by bumpers of punch. 'What a fine boy,' said the master to the journalist, 'I was glad to have him with me, for his youthful health and buoyancy are refreshing.'

In Washington, Wilde, ignored by the British Legation, was entertained by political circles. The newspapers were full of the trial of the assassin of President Garfield, but the *Washington Post* published a photograph of Wilde (with a satirical caption) by the side of one of a monkey, 'The Wild Man of Borneo who does not lecture however, and that much is to his credit.'

Oscar expected a great deal of his sojourn in Boston, the most cultivated city in the U.S.A., where a very great intellectual curiosity coincided with a protestant conscience. Having succeeded in their crusade against slavery the Bostonians were now in need of a new cause, and were preaching the suppression of tobacco. But thanks to the famous art collector, Mrs. Gardner, a passion for the arts was developing behind the puritan façade. The great man of the city was Emerson, and Wilde was not above re-hashing his aphorisms in a more pungent form. Emerson was too

* Some years later Whitman cruelly disappointed Symonds by denying ever having had the slightest pederastic thought.

old to be visited: 'He is fading, like a photograph', as Oliver Wendell Holmes observed. Longfellow was in no better state, but Oscar was determined to have an historic interview with him. He presented himself at the beautiful country house where the author of The Village Blacksmith was looked after by his two daughters, who refused to allow Oscar to see their dying father. Wilde, paying no attention to their protests, reached the poet's bedside, and the two men talked for a long time until Longfellow, exhausted, rang for his daughters. Already furious at Oscar's having penetrated to their father's room, they were even crosser to hear the conversation as they entered: 'How do you like Browning?', Wilde was asking. 'I like him well,' replied Longfellow gravely, 'what I can understand of him.' 'Capital, capital,' with a smile of condescension, 'I must remember that to repeat.' Soon after Longfellow died, Wilde's comment in the Press was: 'He was himself a beautiful poem, more beautiful than anything he ever wrote.'

The sister of the hospitable Mr. Ward of New York, Julia Ward Howe (author of The Battle Hymn of the Republic), gave a dinner in Boston in honour of Oscar where he met General Grant and Harriet Beecher Stowe, author of Uncle Tom's Cabin. Society thronged to Oscar's lectures, but the puritan Press was indignant, and the young men of Harvard decided to give a sharp lesson to the impertinent young man who thought he could teach them to be civilised. They took the first two rows in the hall and sixty of them arrived dressed as aesthetes, wearing fair wigs and with sunflowers in their hands. Oscar, warned in time, was in conventional evening dress, he glanced at the students and remarked, 'I am impelled for the first time to breathe a fervent prayer, save me from my disciples'; thus getting the laugh on his side. He added, 'I think it would be an ennobling influence to have in your gymnasium the statue of a Greek athlete. I do not see why you should not receive diplomas for painting a good picture as well as for gaining a knowledge of that dreadful record of crime known as history.' This flattery was applauded by the students themselves. Indignant at their behaviour, Dion Boucicault,* who was in Boston supervising the rehearsal of one of his plays, said, 'He is too simple and gentle in his nature to realise his position. He is the easy victim of those who expose him to ridicule.' Wilde's hostility towards journalists dated from his arrival in America: 'They force the public to judge a sculptor not by his sculptures, but by the way he treats his wife, a painter by his income, and a poet, like me, by his ties.' 'And how much are you paid for the stupid things you have said about me?', Oscar asked a young reporter. 'Six dollars,' he replied. 'Well, the rate for lying is not very high in America.'

There followed a short stay in New York, during which students from Yale tried to play the same joke as those of Harvard. It still fell flat although they numbered two hundred and were preceded by an enormous Negro, also wearing aesthetic dress. Oscar was sent by his agent to the Wild West, where he was more than ever the victim of journalists. He cheerfully submitted to this gruelling tour, but in the end it did not bring him in the money he had anticipated. The journey must have been a tedious one, in sleeping-cars stinking of cigar smoke, with ugly and pretentious cities at the end of the line. Often the audience was very small, as in Cincinatti, where a Mission held a revivalist meeting in the open air, and the hymn 'Oh wondrous bliss, oh joy sublime, I've Jesus with me all the time', drowned the poet's voice. On another occasion

* Dionysius George Boucicault (1822–1890), Irish dramatist and actor, had lived in America since 1870.

Oscar Wilde at Oxford

Oscar Wilde by Greiffenhagen

Barnum had engaged a famous preacher who, if the poster can be believed, had had 582 people arrested for misconduct and twenty-eight tons of immoral publications destroyed. Boxing matches proved to be formidable rival attractions. Happily Wilde had no trouble in finding compatriots to applaud him; in certain towns, if the Irish colony was large enough, Oscar renounced aestheticism to talk of his country and of the spirit of Speranza in terms worthy of his mother: 'When the heart of a nation breaks, it breaks in music.' In the midst of the applause, he went on to announce the Celtic revival: 'The Anglo-Saxons have taken our lands, have left them abandoned, we have taken their language and have added beauty unknown to it.' In Chicago, Oscar met a fine sculptor of Irish origin, John Donaghue, who had studied in Paris, and was living in poverty. Oscar praised sculpture in his lectures – 'Sculpture is the best method to end the mediaeval struggle between the body and the mind' – 'Do not forget that one production of Michelangelo is worth a hundred by Edison.' As a result Donaghue was launched and was later able to return to Europe, though, like many who attracted Wilde's attention, he had a tragic fate. Too poor to pay the freight of a gigantic work, which was consequently thrown into the water off New York, he committed suicide in 1913.

In San Francisco, Oscar put up at the famous Palace Hotel, the largest in the world, built round a winter garden where an orchestra played at tea-time. But this luxury did not overwhelm him – 'At the hotel I was obliged to drink my chocolate or coffee out of a cup an inch thick and I enjoyed getting down into the Chinese quarter and sitting in a pretty latticed balcony and drinking my tea out of a cup so dainty and delicate that a lady would handle it with care.' He would have liked to have spent all his evenings in Chinatown because the House of Flowers enchanted him, but he

H

had to frequent the artistic circles for which the city was already celebrated. One evening four artists invited him to their studio, which was decorated according to aesthetic principles; for a joke they had dressed up a dummy which they used for portraits, to save their subjects from the boredom of posing when only their clothes were being painted. She looked lifelike, her gloved hand holding a black feather fan. 'This is Miss Piffle, the most important lady of the town,' they told their guest who bowed to her and started a conversation or rather a monologue, and behaved as if he did not know that she was not real. To quote from *The Life of Oscar Wilde* by Hesketh Pearson:

'Isobel Field, who records the incident, must continue: "I think he was a little near-sighted, for he almost tumbled against her. Bowing, he apologised to the quiet lady sitting there so demurely, and made some casual remark. It may have been our watchful attitude that gave him an inkling of the situation, for without changing his voice he began a conversation with Miss Piffle that was a marvel of impromptu humour. He told her his opinion of San Francisco, and incidentally of the United States and its inhabitants; he replied to imaginary remarks of hers with surprise or approval so cleverly that it sounded as though Miss Piffle were actually talking to him. It was a superb performance, a masterpiece of sparkling wit and gaiety. Never before, or since, have I heard anything that compared to it. When he left we all felt we had met a truly great man."

'Before leaving, Oscar turned to his host and said: "What a charming lady – so cultivated. I can see straight away that San Francisco is the most civilised town in the United States. Thank you dear friends, thank you." '

From the coast, Oscar plunged into the 'gold rush' regions. He stopped off at Salt Lake City where he found the mormon ladies very ugly and the Tabernacle '. . . like a soup kettle'. Denver and Leadville were full of excitement over his arrival. The saloons were decorated with peacock feathers and the 'scarlet women', who were the usual attraction, dispensed with their ringlets, their low-cut dresses and their high-heeled boots and donned virginal headbands and the tunics of the *Demoiselles Elues*. To the stupefaction of their clients, they carried lilies in their hands, and the Sheriff stated that at this rate he would be obliged to plant sunflowers in the prison yard. The great man of the district was H. A. W. Tabor; his mine brought in $4,000,000 a year and his mistress, Baby Doe McCourt, was always festooned with pearls. He had had the opera house built, and it was in front of a bust of Mr. Tabor that Oscar spoke. But beside Leadville, Denver seemed a veritable Florence. Wilde arrived in a snowstorm, he visited a '. . . dancing saloon where I saw the most rational method of art criticism I have ever come across. On the piano was printed a notice "Please do not shoot the pianist: he is doing his best".'

Oscar brought back from these journeys stories that kept his audience on the edge of their seats. For instance, Edmond de Goncourt, who had not realised that Oscar was joking, noted that '. . . he told of the hall of the Casino, which, as it is the biggest room in the place, is used for the Assize Court and here they hang criminals on the stage after the performance. He told us that he had seen a man hanged from the scenery uprights while the audience fired their revolvers at him from their seats. . . . The theatre directors when they wanted someone to act the part of a criminal, get a real criminal. And for Lady Macbeth they engaged a woman who had just been released from prison for poisoning.'

Oscar crossed over into Canada in a raging blizzard. The

French-language newspapers were disappointed in him: 'He looks like a cross between a comic opera villain and a charlatan.' He, on the other hand, was disappointed by the Niagara Falls: 'Every American bride is taken there, and the sight of the stupendous waterfall must be one of the earliest, if not the keenest, disappointments of American married life.' Then he returned to the United States, travelling down to the South by easy stages. In New Orleans he found the atmosphere more congenial, in a society that lived its dream of pre-war splendour. In Dallas he went to see the tomb of Davy Crockett. In Galvaston his lecture was constantly interrupted by the people hurrying to and from the bar. In Savannah and Charleston the empty halls reverberated with his polished phrases on Botticelli. Eventually he finished up in Newport, home of the Goelets and the Astors, but no one paid much attention to him, as it had been announced that a more exciting star was arriving from England in the shape of Lily Langtry.

In order to meet his beautiful friend Oscar arose, incredibly, at 5 o'clock in the morning. When the Jersey Lily emerged, swathed in chinchilla, an orchestra played 'God Save the Queen', and Oscar flung sheaves of lilies at her feet. Arm-in-arm with his friend, Oscar regained some of his fame, but not for long; the Americans were scathing about Mrs. Langtry's talent. The Press commented unfavourably on her rich young lovers, and the drawing-rooms of New York closed their doors to the friend of the Prince of Wales. Oscar was no help to her; she was cold-shouldered. By then the poet realised that it was time for him to leave. On the 27th December he embarked on the *Bothnia*; the journalists whom he had spurned had posted sandwichmen on the quay displaying unkind comments. One reporter came up to him for a last word and Oscar said: 'They say that when good Americans die they go to Paris.

I would add that when bad Americans die, they stay in America.' Angry murmurs greeted this sally. Oscar, one foot on the gangway, surveyed the journalists: 'For you, Art has no marvel, Beauty no meaning, and the Past no message.' To the journalists who awaited him at Liverpool, Oscar remarked: 'The English and Americans have everything in common, except of course, their language.'

One would have thought that one visit would have been enough, but a year later Oscar returned to New York for a week, to see the first night of *Vera*. It was not a success.

8   Paris

Oscar was an admirable manager, but he did not conduct his life as wisely as he did his career. After the tour of the United States he only stopped in London for a few weeks, long enough however to realise that he must abandon his absurdities which had by now become vulgarised. Moreover, the literary and artistic worlds there had no more to offer him; after Chelsea and Mayfair and the United States he had to find new territories to conquer. Armed with the very few hundred pounds which remained from the tour, and the hope of several thousand dollars to come from Mary Anderson for his *Duchess of Padua*, the leader of aestheticism embarked for France.

Oscar had many causes for liking France. First literary reasons: he saw himself as a character from Balzac, he revered Baudelaire, he had heard of Mallarmé, and the academic poets Hérédia and Leconte de Lisle had immense prestige in his eyes. Decadent poets such as Verlaine had more talent than their English counterparts. There was Daudet, the old Goncourt and the young Bourget. The world of letters in France was organised, militant and concentrated, which pleased Oscar, a man of letters to his fingertips. Then there was the world of fashion, as always dominated by money, which the prophet of good taste wished to charm. Financiers reigned from the Madeleine to the Etoile, they rode in carriages even more ostentatious than those in London, where riches had less need of display. The decade of the 1880's saw the triumph of the Rothschilds and was to finish with Panama.* Orientated towards literature as much as fashion, the theatre also was more brilliant than in London. The divine Sarah dominated it – and her friendship with Oscar was one of the reasons for his visit. Perhaps she might interest herself in *Vera*, or better still in the *Duchess of Padua*, the verse drama that Mary Anderson had commissioned. The plays of the younger Dumas and of Sardou were acted by ravishing actresses, among whom were Jane Harding and the very young Réjane; Mounet-Sully and Coquelin played the classics with grandiloquence.

The world of painters was less amusing, but Whistler had assured Oscar that it was only in Paris that artists knew how to paint and the visitor paid tribute to the good taste of the French masters. 'Taste', backed by prodigious self-assurance was, in fact, all that Wilde had in his luggage, but it was excellent currency, as the French had begun to realise that their national stock of it was running low; established architects and painters carried on the mixture of history and exoticism that had been so fashionable under the Second Empire; the monuments and mansions were overburdened without arousing criticism – Paris had no Chelsea. Paris, for the English, had the prestige of debauchery; illicit love affairs were more open and brazen than in London, and this made them much less sinister. The great courtesans were quasi-official characters, the bordellos and private rooms at restaurants swarmed with picturesque figures who might have stepped out of a picture by Toulouse Lautrec, or Degas, or from the pages of Balzac. Yet that year, 1883, was one of the dullest of the Third Republic; the many anarchists became a problem, the ruins left by the Commune, still apparent, were reminders of the bad days.

* The stupendous French scheme for a Panama Canal, conceived by Vicomte Ferdinand de Lesseps, was started in 1881, and ended in a political financial scandal.

In literature, Renan brought out *Souvenirs d'enfance et de jeunesse*, and Alphonse Daudet *L'Evangéliste*. The previous year had been more interesting with Edmond de Goncourt's *La Faustin*, but the greatest successes of all had been Ludovic Halévy's *L'Abbé Constantin* and *Les Névroses* of Rollinat who was a disciple of Baudelaire. At the Salon *Alma Parens* by Bouguereau was admired by those who liked the sugary style, and *Amour au Village* of Bastien-Lepage by the lovers of realism.

Oscar landed in France in February 1883 and rashly rented an apartment in the Hôtel Voltaire, which was at least cheaper than the Right Bank. He promptly donned a dressing-gown of home-spun, a monkish garment, such as Balzac had worn, in which to sit up all night and write; he also bought a walking-stick with a turquoise knob – Balzac had used an identical one. Then he proceeded to order innumerable cups of coffee to be sent up, which he drank while re-reading *La Comédie Humaine*. Oscar's first visit was to the Greek marbles in the Louvre. He was so struck by his resemblance to the bust of the young Nero that he ordered a barber to cut off his long locks and to mass the curls that remained on his forehead. He explained to a friend: 'The Oscar of the first period is dead, we are now concerned with the Oscar of the second period, who has nothing in common with the gentleman who wore long hair and carried a sunflower down Piccadilly.'

After visiting the Louvre and purchasing the walking-stick, Oscar sent copies of his poems, elegantly bound, to all the best-known writers accompanied by a letter written in French modelled on the following to Edmond de Goncourt: 'Dear Sir, Please accept my poems as witness of my infinite admiration for the author of *La Faustin*. I would be very happy to think that my first poetic flowers may perhaps find a place near your Watteaus and your Bouchers, and the treasure in lacquer, ivory and bronze which you have immortalised forever in your *Maison d'un Artiste*.' Victor Hugo and Mallarmé, Catulle Mendés and Rollinat (whose poem *La Vâche au Taureau* Oscar particularly admired) all received the volume and soon he was the chief topic of conversation in the literary world. It had been a long time since any English writer had evinced so much curiosity about French literature, and furthermore he was known to be the apostle of a new taste for which a need was beginning to be felt – the official spokesman for the products of the House of Liberty and of Morris. He spoke French very well, in a sing-song manner which recalled the chant of Sarah. Un- luckily, his choice of clothes was less happy; his checked suits were reminiscent of a bookmaker and his affectations quickly revealed to the French a secret which had so far been fairly well concealed in England: Edmond de Gon- court had no illusions: 'Dined with the de Nittis with the English poet Oscar Wilde, an individual of doubtful sex who talks like a third-rate actor, and tells some tall stories, but gave us an amusing picture of a town in Texas.' These lines explain the immediate and superficial success of Oscar; French writers welcomed any discernible sign of eccentricity in foreigners; sometimes Oscar shone at the expense of one he admired, as, for example: 'This Swin- burne, whom he represents as boasting of vices in order to make his fellow-citizens believe in his pederasty and his bestiality, without having been in the slightest degree a pederast or bestial.' (This was written by de Goncourt, who frequently took Oscar too seriously and who later withdrew these allegations when Oscar accused him of misrepresent- ation.)

Wilde was soon invited by the Alphonse Daudets and talked at length of his ecstasies over the Venus de Milo, and

not enough about the works of his host which were too
near the style of Dickens for Oscar's taste. Léon Daudet
remembered meeting Oscar, and reported that 'Wilde
attracted and repelled; he told stories deliciously but his
conversation soon tired one. He emanated uneasiness.
Wilde belonged to that category of human beings to enjoy
whose company one needs to have two existences – one
normal, the other consecrated exclusively to them . . . his
voice was at once pallid and fat, the words came tumbling
out of his frightful slack mouth and when he had finished
he would roar with laughter like a fat, satisfied, gossipy
woman, and order an exotic drink. . . .'

In his desire for useful contacts, Wilde penetrated even as
far as Zola, and murmured as he left: 'Monsieur Zola is
determined to show that if he has not got genius, he can at
least be dull: and how well he succeeds!' Some years later
they met again with no more success; at the end of a
banquet, Zola proposed a toast in honour of the poet:
'Unfortunately Mr. Wilde will be obliged to reply in his
own barbarous tongue.' To which Oscar replied, in French:
'I am Irish by birth and English by race, and as Monsieur
Zola has said, condemned to speak the language of Shakespeare.' Sad to say, Wilde's visits to Mallarmé in the Rue de
Rome were not much more successful: the disciples preferred to listen to their Master or to Villiers de l'Isle Adam
rather than to this courteous Irishman. However, to Oscar
the Symbolists provided a treasure-house in which he could
delve for rare words; he was working at that moment on a
poem about the Sphinx and was inspired by a poem
René Ghil had dedicated to Mallarmé, 'father and lord of
gold, of precious stones and of poisons'.

On the other hand the cafés gave a rousing welcome to
the Aesthete. He was introduced to the poets who dined
regularly at La Côte d'Or, where Jean Moréas covered him

with flowers. At the Café Vachette, Oscar drank absinthe with Verlaine, but it must have been one of the poet's particularly difficult days as the experiment was not repeated. Moreover Verlaine was very ugly and therefore repugnant to Oscar who was to say: 'I consider ugliness a kind of malady, it is better to be beautiful than good, but it is better to be good than ugly.' Catulle Mendès, dressed in romantic old clothes he had picked up at the home of his father-in-law Théophile Gautier, had the prestige of having been blessed by Baudelaire's saying: 'I like this young man, he has all the vices!' Deplorable or sublime, poetry in Paris was a hundred times more alive than in London and then, of course, there was Jean Lorrain, the young colossus of the decadence, who gave promise at that time of becoming a genius, who repeated in the cafés the names of the artists who were to be the founders of the Art Nouveau movement; he knew everyone and distributed prints of Pre-Raphaelite pictures, as is indicated in the following letter to Maurice Barrès: '. . . it leaves me with among others 'The Golden Stairway', 'Mélisande at the feet of Pelleas', the two frescoes of the 'Sleeping Beauty' are also framed with appropriate verses. I send this to you at Charmes and beg you to keep as a souvenir a Burne-Jones and a Walter Crane.' Oscar discoursed on these prints to pretty women who, between amorous rendezvous, were beginning to notice that it was smart to have a soul.

In Paris, as in London, Oscar was most popular in the fashionable world. The *Gaulois* wrote: 'He scattered words about him as Buckingham at the Court of France had scattered jewels, which had been loosely sewn on to his glittering doublet.' Had he lost his sense of proportion in the United States? Had he ever had any? Or was he at this time one of those people who knew just how far too far he could go? Jean-Joseph Renaud, a French writer, who was later to translate Wilde's Intentions, fortunately left a record of an occasion when he met Oscar: Without listening to the names of the people who were being introduced to him he sat down and, with an air of exhaustion, begged his hostess to have the shutters of the dining-room closed, and the candles lit as he could not endure the light of day, also would she please alter the table decorations as mauve flowers were unlucky? His conversation was at first pretentious, he asked questions and did not wait for replies: 'You have never seen a ghost? No! Ah! Now you Madame . . . your eyes seem to have looked upon ghosts . . .' He went on afterwards to talk about French history and brought the past back to life by making it 'glitter under the light of his words . . . this Englishman who had appeared grotesque a few minutes earlier would suddenly attain . . . the expressive power of the most admirable odes to humanity. Many of us were moved to tears.' Oscar was frequently to be seen at the house of Madame Straus. It was there that he met the Princesse de Monaco, who was to become one of his most glamorous friends. A niece of the poet Heinrich Heine, it is said that she was the original of Proust's character, the Princesse de Luxembourg. There was Degas, of whom Whistler had often spoken; 'Ah! If only you knew how well-known you are in England,' said Oscar. 'Happily, less than you,' replied Degas boorishly. Oscar's methodical pursuit of the intelligentsia led him to Victor Hugo, but on the evening that they met, the grand old man was half asleep, so all conversation had to be carried on in whispers. He also met Anatole France, just beginning to be celebrated.

But perhaps the most charming family of all those who frequently entertained him were Charlotte and Arthur Baignères. Madame Baignères asked Jacques-Emile Blanche to bring Oscar to see her: Blanche was painting Mlle. Baignères, and so he undertook the introduction. They were cultivated and rich members of the upper middle class with relations in the Faubourg Saint Germain. Mlle. Baignères had two suitors: Paul Bourget and the future Maréchal Lyautey, but despite this early success, she remained unmarried. Everyone was infatuated with Jacques-Emile Blanche not only because of his amusing conversation but also because of his taste. His father was a clever doctor who ran a nursing home. Wilde often went to see him at his studio in Auteuil. It reminded him of Chelsea, and he wrote in French to the painter: 'I love your studio so much with its peacock blue door and the little green and gold room, because for me it is a cool oasis of beauty in the Louis XVI desert I find in Paris.'

Not all studios were as elegant as that of Blanche. But in the case of painters who took a pride in their modernity, the English influence had to compete with a clutter of antique bric-à-brac. Octave Mirbeau, in an article in the magazine Gil Blas, in 1886, described the surroundings of a fashionable painter in 1886: 'The studio of the painter is certainly the most curious of studios; one admires the old cabinets, three Botticellis, some studies by Rossetti and some works by Burne-Jones, Persian embroideries, Arabian steel work, a large quantity of Byzantine Madonnas and Italian pottery, china vases from Japan with swollen bulges and tapering necks, decorated with curious flowers and sacred beasts.' This painter talks the aesthetic jargon, interrupted by swoons, importations of Oscar's: 'He suffocates, he has the death rattle . . . will you have a glass of port? Thank you, no!' On another occasion Oscar, obviously talking nonsense, asked for the milk of a fisher-weasel. Was it in this semi-imaginary studio that Oscar met the diminutive Baroness Deslandes, ready to swallow all the affectations from across the channel, like her bronze toad which swallowed moonstones and beryls, tributes from Barrès, from Lorrain and from Montesquiou? Oscar, infatuated with the Baroness, persuaded Burne-Jones to paint her portrait, he spent hours stretched out on a bearskin at her feet and, it was said, from time to time was her lover. In the studios of the Impressionists, Oscar found he had been preceded by George Moore, who had lived in Paris for the last two years: there were many reasons to explain their profound antipathy; Moore was Irish, a writer and an interminable talker in a cloud of cigarette smoke; the plainness of his long, pale face and drooping fair moustache caused Oscar to describe him in 1899 in a letter to Reggie Turner as formless and obscene. Moore was a great lover of women, of whom Ada Leverson said 'he would kiss and tell and sometimes only tell'. Oscar failed to meet the great painters; those who fêted him were the de Nittis, and the Boldinis, fashionable young Italian painters. In their studios Oscar met John Sargent, a handsome Bostonian, the friend of Henry James and of Vernon Lee; Degas called him 'the shop-walker of painting'. Oscar and Sargent viewed each other with little sympathy because the latter was extremely conventional. The great revelation was Gustave Moreau's studio to which it may have been Jean Lorrain, a great friend of the painter, who took Oscar; there he found once more the themes that were popular with the Pre-Raphaelites, but treated in dazzling colours and expressed with a strange depth. He saw on the faces of Moreau's cruel princesses and beautiful martyrs the smile of the Gioconda so dear to Walter Pater.

Wilde was to find these characters again on the stage with Sarah Bernhardt. That Queen of Byzantine Paris, of which Moreau was the magician, had her tea-gowns cut in the style of the Empress Theodora and, every evening, having

risen from her quilted coffin she imparted a message of
strange beauty to the Boulevards. Too bad if the text was by
Sardou, the image and the voice were divine. Wilde, still
obsessed by his poem, sowed exotic words around the
Sphinx, as Sarah sewed stones (whose names alone were
precious) on her train. The great friendship, begun in London,
pursued its course, and he visited her in the studio where
she sculpted, sometimes in company with Lord Ronald
Gower. Oscar would arrive in a theatre box with armfuls of
lilies and compliments which she never heard. Her intimate
friends were irritated by such favour being shown him, in
fact the robust Jean Richepin wished to show the Englishman
the door. Oscar dreamed of seeing Sarah as the *Duchess of
Padua*, a character which had something in it both of
Lucrezia Borgia and the Cenci. When he described the
costumes everyone was sure it would be a masterpiece. But
he confided to a friend: 'Between them Hugo and Shakespeare have exhausted every subject. Originality is no longer
possible, even in sin. So there are no real emotions left, only
extraordinary adjectives.'

In the meantime Oscar lived on the thousand dollars that
Mary Anderson had given him on commissioning the play.
He lived very well, the Hôtel Voltaire was reasonable, but
restaurants such as Foyot where he lunched each day were
dear, as also were flowers and canes. After a sojourn of two
months, cash and advances had already been spent. The
play having been despatched to New York, Oscar cabled to
Mary Anderson to send him the $4,000 promised on
acceptance. But a telegram arrived refusing the play. Oscar
appeared completely unmoved: 'This is rather tedious,
Robert, I fear we shan't be able to dine with the Duchess
tonight,' he remarked to his new friend Robert Sherard, and
said no more about it.

During his continual pursuit of celebrities, Oscar had

met Coquelin; he made a note of his conversations with the actor: 'What is civilisation Mr. Wilde?' 'Love of beauty.' And what is beauty?' 'That which the middle classes call ugly.' 'And what do the middle classes call beauty?' 'It does not exist.' Intrigued by the paradoxes and flattered by compliments, Coquelin invited Wilde to visit him – 'I am always at home round about nine o'clock.' Wilde, stepping back and regarding the actor with amazed admiration, remarked, 'I am much more middle class than you, I am always in bed by four or five. I could never stay awake as late as that. Really you *are* a remarkable man.'

Wilde adored being behind the scenes; the costumes, the make-up, all the confusion of success; his vocation was of the Boulevards, he dreamed of the glory of the younger Dumas whose work *Francillon* was then being played, of Meilhac who wrote *Frou-Frou* for Sarah, the story of a young girl who dies of frivolity. He admired Pailleron's *Le Monde où l'on s'ennuie*, written two years earlier; its outstanding line was: 'Are not all children natural?' Yes, the theatre of Paris was much more interesting than that of London, where there were great actors, but no dramatists.

There was nothing frantic about Wilde's ambition, it was a comedy of the arts at which he was the first to be amused. All his absurdities brought him into the limelight and man of the theatre that he was, he could put himself across to the most unreceptive of audiences. But once the curtain was lowered he still needed to talk – solitude would have been suffocation. There had been Frank Miles in London, in Paris there was an Englishman, a few years his junior, Robert Sherard, who belonged to that species of generous parasite who are ready to do anything for the great man on whose intellect they live. What a difference there was between them! Sherard was a thin-lipped Puritanical bohemian who admired Robespierre (Oscar often addressed

Lady Archibald Campbell
('The Lady in the Yellow Buskin' by Whistler)

Oscar Wilde at a Private View

('Private View at the Royal Academy 1881' by William Powell Frith)

him as 'Citizen'), and disapproved of everything that makes life agreeable. At this first meeting Oscar described his ecstasies over the Venus de Milo, which he claimed brought him a sense of physical pleasure, Sherard burst out, 'I have never been to the Louvre. When that name is mentioned I always think of the Grands Magasins de Louvre, where I can get the cheapest ties in Paris.' 'I like that, that is very fine,' replied Oscar, who thought the answer was very sophisticated. Soon he was flattered to find that Sherard 'scientifically studied his style of posing'. For twenty-five years Sherard, incapable of rivalling the wit of Wilde, deliberately took the opposite view to Oscar, who would say to him, teasingly: 'One should rejoice in the success of others, it makes life gayer.' And Sherard, won over by frivolity, assumed the rôle of a faithful dog, which bares its teeth to strangers.

From that moment this untalented Boswell took notes which enabled him to write his books on Wilde. He reported that Wilde frequented the promenade of the Eden, '... when Priapus called to him'. There he met inexpensive prostitutes, to whom, nevertheless, he gave everything in his pockets. In Wilde's life the sinister was often not far removed from the amorous; for instance one of his meetings was with a woman who was later found with her throat cut by her ponce. Wilde as reported by Sherard, is never very amusing. One day when the confidant admired the view of the Seine from the hotel, Oscar said: 'That is altogether immaterial except to the proprietor, who of course, charges it in the bill. A gentleman never looks out of the window.' Passing by the ruins of the Tuileries, the disciple made a note of the following thought – 'there is not there one little blackened stone which is not to me a chapter in the Bible of democracy'. It might have been Speranza talking.

I

Sherard had very little money, and Oscar always invited him to the smartest restaurants: 'we owe that to the dignity of letters'. Zola had made various restaurants and cafés fashionable, and Huysmans had done the same for more squalid places such as the Château Rouge, the vast Café in Aubervilliers. One evening when he was with Oscar and two other Englishmen in a low haunt, Sherard thought that threatening looks were coming from a table near to them; he stood up, hit the table with his fist and said: 'The first man who dares to attack my friend Mr. Oscar Wilde, will have me to deal with.' – 'Robert,' said Oscar quietly, 'you are defending me at the risk of my life.'

Sherard, like all Puritans, was profoundly conventional and would not accept that a gentleman could sit on the terrace of a café in obviously low company. He understood nothing of Wilde's tendencies, and when Oscar gave some money to a dancer called 'Petit Louis', who was anxious to join the navy, Sherard put it down to an excess of philanthropy. Sherard was so easily influenced that when he thought of committing suicide, Oscar was able to dissuade him by saying: 'Suicide is the greatest compliment that one can pay to society.' But Sherard nearly died of shame when the poet Rollinat, whom Oscar had invited to the restaurant of his hotel, recited some of his morbid works which put the clients to flight. Oscar wrote the following phrases of Rollinat in a notebook: 'I do not believe in progress, but I believe in the stagnation of human stupidity – I admire Japanese chairs because they have not been made to sit upon.' He filled this notebook with notes which recall Flaubert's silliness: 'Art is disorder, said a waiter at the Hotel Voltaire.' 'The Old Masters are mummies – the keepers at the Louvre.'

At the end of the month of May, Oscar hadn't a penny left. He had given all but his last *louis* to Sherard to enable

him to return to England, and so he too had to leave.
Despite some exceptions he had been very warmly welcomed, and on every subsequent visit the Baroness Deslandes and Madame Baignères fêted him. In 1884 at
L'Epatant (the Club of the Artists' Union), Jacques-Emile
Blanche exhibited a picture entitled 'Les poésies d'Oscar
Wilde' representing a young girl in acid green, stretched
out on a chintz-covered sofa, reading the precious volume.
But Wilde's name was not appreciated everywhere and the
picture was relegated to a corridor. Robert de Montesquiou,
who was more than a little careful about his reputation,
crossed Wilde's path a hundred times but, having summed
him up as the 'Antinoüs of the Horrible', always succeeded
in avoiding him.

9   Aesthetic quarrels

In signing his canvasses with a small butterfly, Whistler may have wished to draw attention to the lightness of his touch, or, alternatively, to the subtle blending of his dusty, pastel colours. Or was it suggestive of his own appearance, round black eyes, bristly hair twisted into two tufts like antennae, a little hooked nose? Whichever it was, this human butterfly went from house to house saying horrid things about those who had reservations about his pictures. He was elegant in appearance, well set up, contemptuous and, deep-down, embittered. His mockery had driven Ruskin half-mad; his nasal, strident laugh chilled the blood of his colleagues at Exhibitions. With his small beard and pointed moustaches he appeared to his enemies more devil than butterfly.

Whistler's quarrel with Wilde was first and foremost a clash of temperaments, or rather of attitudes: his taste was ascetic, Wilde's was luxurious. Their ideas were not so different, in fact they were largely shared, but Oscar, enormous and always unconcerned, could not fail to exasperate this dry little man, who was incapable of remaining in one place at a time. It was like an elephant and a terrier: a white elephant covered in jewels from a bazaar, kindly, but with a mischievous eye, and a well-bred fox-terrier accustomed to hunting rats. After Oscar's return from America their relations steadily deteriorated – it was thought that Oscar had enriched himself by vulgarising Jimmy's ideas. Whistler, temporarily ruined by his law-suit, was unable to

continue living at the White House in Tite Street designed
for him by Godwin. It was the first really modern house,
not quite Art Nouveau, but, as it were, paving the way for it,
divested as it was of all the ornaments dear to the Victorians,
that is of all that was neither useful nor beautiful. Whistler,
closely linked with Morris and the Chelsea masters, had in
common with them only the cult of Art, his own in particular; he did not appreciate the Middle Ages, despised detail,
but painted superbly. The Pre-Raphaelites had more heart
than taste, Whistler had no heart but perfect taste. Wilde
had gone to Paris – as a kind of Ambassador of Chelsea –
and no sooner had he returned than he announced to the
Press his opinions on painting. Whistler met the new critic
(Oscar had been made Art critic of The World) by chance in
the street; Oscar was wearing a Polish cap and green over-
coat, frogged and lined with fur: 'Oscar, how dare you!'
lashed out the painter. 'What means this disguise? Restore
those things to Nathan's and never again let me find you
masquerading the streets of my Chelsea in the combined
costumes of Kossuth and Mr. Mantalini!' 'Too funny, dear
Jimmy,' replied Oscar. Chelsea expected sparks to fly at their
next meeting, but they each still had too much need to
shine and too much respect for each other's reputation in
the worlds of Art and Literature to permit a complete break.
Oscar continued to be genuinely amiable when he saw
Whistler, and the latter donned a mask of false cordiality,
but proffered the following advice: 'My dear fellow, you
must never say this painting is good or that bad. Good and
bad are not terms to be used by you. But you may say "I
like this" or "I don't like that", and you will be within your
rights. Now come and have a whisky: you're sure to like
that.' 'I wish I had said that,' replied Oscar. 'You will, Oscar,
you will,' retorted Whistler with his loud laugh. The Press
scented discord among the aesthetes, and Punch, in an issue

of November 1883, printed a fanciful conversation between Whistler and Oscar on Art and Life, upon which Wilde sent a telegram to Whistler saying: 'Punch too ridiculous. When you and I are together we never talk about anything but ourselves.' This was sent to The World by Whistler, as well as his reply which had also been sent by telegram: 'No, no Oscar, you forget. When you and I are together we never talk about anything except me.' He did not submit Wilde's answer: 'It is true Jimmy we were talking about you, but I was thinking of myself!'

Oscar enjoyed talking to Whistler, who inspired his wit, and Whistler, for his part, enjoyed making fun of Oscar. It is unfortunate that George Moore, Whistler's confidant, failed to record Whistler's sarcasms at Wilde's expense, but the very name of the aesthete was anathema to him. Had he not been told that Oscar had said of him: 'I know Moore so well, that I have not spoken to him for ten years.'

'The important thing is not to choose your friends, but your enemies,' remarked Oscar, when he saw Whistler coming into a drawing-room. 'I choose my friends for their good looks, my acquaintances for their good characters and my enemies for their good intellects. A man cannot be too careful in the choice of his enemies.'

But there was soon to be a truce; Oscar was in need of Whistler's advice regarding the arrangement of a house.

One of Oscar's idiosyncrasies was pretending that Queen Victoria took an impassioned interest in the slightest detail about him. If he left a house too hurriedly after luncheon, he excused himself by saying 'the Queen is in London and is dying to see me. I would not like to keep her waiting.' Everyone laughed, but in the end he himself almost believed in this fanciful friendship.

The newspapers were quoting Oscar more and more

often until Whistler, extremely annoyed, decided to take the floor. He hired the Prince's Hall, and on Friday, 20th February 1885, delivered a lecture at ten o'clock; since when it has been known as 'The Ten O'Clock Lecture'. Wilde described it in his review thus: '. . . the scene was in every way delightful: he stood there, a miniature Mephistopheles, mocking the majority! He was like a brilliant surgeon lecturing to a class composed of subjects destined ultimately for dissection, and solemnly assuring them how valuable to science their maladies were and how absolutely uninteresting the slightest symptoms of health on their part would be . . . nothing could have exceeded their enthusiasm when they were told by Mr. Whistler that no matter how vulgar their dresses were, or how hideous their surroundings at home, still it was possible that a great painter, if there was such a thing, could, by contemplating them in the twilight, and half closing his eyes, see them under really picturesque conditions which they were not to attempt to understand, much less dare to enjoy. . . .'

In his lecture Whistler denigrated the constant talk of Art: 'Yes, Art — that has of late become, as far as much discussion and writing can make it, a sort of common topic for the tea-table. Art is upon the Town! to be chucked under the chin by the passing gallants — to be enticed within the gates of the household — to be coaxed into compass, as a proof of culture and refinement.' Then the painter described his own canvases: 'And when the evening mist clothes the riverside with poetry, as with a veil, and the poor buildings lose themselves in the dim sky, and the tall chimneys become campanili, and the warehouses are palaces in the night, and the whole city hangs in the heavens, and fairy-land is before us. . . .' After some hits at Ruskin, it is clearly Wilde who is disparaged: '. . . the untaught ventures of thick-heeled Apollos — what! Will you up and follow the first pipes that lead you down Petticoat Lane, there on a sabbath to gather, for the week, from the dull rags of ages, wherewith to bedeck yourselves? That beneath your travestied awkwardness we have trouble to find your own dainty selves? Oh, fie! – Is the world then exhausted? and must we go back because the thumb of the mountebank jerks the way? Costume is not dress. . . . Haphazard from their shoulders hang the garments of the hawker – combining in their person the motley of many manners with the medley of the mummer's closet.'

One might well have taken these words as a declaration of war, but it was only a skirmish. Oscar replied in the *Pall Mall Gazette*: '. . . the poet is the supreme artist, for he is the master of colour and form, and the real musician besides, and he is lord over all life and all arts; and so to the poet above all others are these mysteries known: to Edgar Allan Poe and Baudelaire, not to Benjamin West and Paul Delaroche.' The following day Whistler wrote: 'Oscar I have read your exquisite article in the *Pall Mall*. Nothing is more delicate in the flattery of "the Poet" to "the Painter" than the naïveté of "the Poet" in the choice of his Painters – Benjamin West and Paul Delaroche! . . .' to which Oscar replied in *The World* – 'Dear Butterfly, By the aid of a biographical dictionary, I made the discovery that there were once two painters called Benjamin West and Paul Delaroche, who rashly lectured on Art. As of their works nothing at all remains, I conclude that they explained themselves away. Be warned in time, James, and remain, as I do, incomprehensible. To be great is to be misunderstood.' Oscar was too busy, he said to himself: 'the dogs bark and the caravan rolls on'. The controversy however had a good effect on his style, which gained in conciseness and pungency. From time to time Oscar would let slip a slightly treacherous remark such as: 'Whistler has opened the eyes of the blind and given great encouragement to the short-sighted.'

But Whistler was the first to overstep the mark when he said to the Committee of the National Art Exhibition: 'What has Oscar in common with Art? except that he dines at our tables and picks from our platters the plums for the pudding he peddles in the provinces? Oscar – the amiable, irresponsible, esurient Oscar – with no more sense of a picture than of the fit of a coat, has the courage of the opinions . . . of others?' Next day Wilde's reply could be read in The World: 'Atlas, this is very sad! With our James – vulgarity begins at home, and should be allowed to stay there.' Whistler's rejoinder to this sally was also printed in The World: ' "A poor thing" Oscar! "but", for once, I suppose, "your own".' The war had started with telegrams, was carried on by lectures and finished with columns. In a brilliant essay called The Decay of Lying, Oscar mocked the fog so dear to Whistler, that no one had noticed before. For the first time he stated dogmatically, if such a word can be used of so detached an utterance, that Nature imitates Art. In these lovely lines he expounds his views of the Impressionists: '. . . That white quivering sunlight that one sees now in France, with its strange blotches of mauve, and its restless violet shadows, is her latest fancy, and, on the whole, Nature reproduces it quite admirably. Where she used to give us Corots and Daubignys, she gives us now exquisite Monets and entrancing Pissaros.' The end of this essay exasperated Whistler, he saw in it an insult to his work, to his friends Degas and Manet (if the truth be told, Oscar was possibly thinking of painters at that time better-known, though now largely forgotten, such as Roll and Dagnan-Bouveret): '. . . As a method Realism is a complete failure, and the two things that every artist should avoid are modernity of form and modernity of subject-matter. To

us, who live in the nineteenth
century, any century is a suitable subject for art except our
own.'

Whistler blamed Wilde more
for the ideas borrowed from
him than for those of his own
which displeased him. The last
episode in this war, which
lasted for seven years, was a
letter addressed to *Truth*. The
painter revealed that Oscar had
asked him for ideas for a
lecture to students, and Whistler
finished his letter with the
words that 'the least any pla-
giarist can do is to say: "*Je
prends mon bien là où je le trouve.*"
You, Oscar, can go further, and
with fresh effrontery, that will
bring you the envy of all
criminal *confrères*, unblushingly
boast "*Moi, je prends son bien là
où je le trouve!*"' Oscar replied:
'. . . The definition of a disciple
as one who has the courage of
the opinions of his master is
really too old even for Mr.
Whistler to be allowed to claim
it, and as for borrowing Mr.
Whistler's ideas about art, the
only thoroughly original ideas I
have ever heard him express
have had reference to his own

Caricature of Whistler
by Aubrey Beardsley

superiority as a painter over painters greater than himself.

'It is a trouble for any gentleman to have to notice the lucubrations of so ill-bred and ignorant a person as Mr. Whistler, but your publication of his insolent letter left me no option in the matter.' Whistler replied quite amusingly: 'Oh! Truth! Cowed and humiliated, I acknowledge that our Oscar is at last original. At bay, and sublime in his agony, he certainly has, for once, borrowed from no living author, and comes out in his own true colours – as his own "gentleman".' The butterfly had alighted on a sensitive spot, because was dear Oscar a gentleman or not? He was delightful, generous, sometimes well-dressed, but incapable of conforming for long. But his affectation of worldliness led to his adopting the prejudices of Anglo-Irish Society. Whistler's stricture represents one point of view and seems to echo criticisms of Byron; it

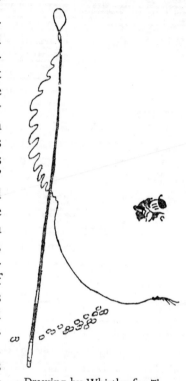

Drawing by Whistler for The
Gentle Art of Making Enemies

is relevant to quote here Wilde's views about Tennyson. He said to his friend Vincent O'Sullivan: 'How can a man be a great poet and lead the life of an English country-gentleman? Think of a man going down to breakfast at eight o'clock with the family, and writing Idylls of the King until lunch-time.'

The great quarrel had now run its course. Whistler published the record of their interchanges in a small volume *The Gentle Art of Making Enemies* which appeared in 1890, and then left for Paris where Mallarmé and Montesquiou were calling him. His influence remained considerable in England, but as Jacques-Emile Blanche remarked: 'It is the cult for Whistler and not his art which is important.' In this often ridiculous rivalry, something other than the clash of great minds or a specific difference of opinion can be detected. The Aesthete built his ivory tower with images, each memory of a portrait or of a sonata was a stone of the citadel; Whistler's pictures had greatly helped to erect Wilde's tower. But the aesthetic pleasure came from the work of art coinciding with the dream; it was an affair between the aesthete and the work of art and not between the aesthete and the artist. All was well when Botticelli provided the images, but it was otherwise when a Whistler came between the work and the idea. He then became as odious to the aesthete as the rationalist is to the mythomaniac whose lies he exposes. Whistler was as unbearable as a scene painter who, in the middle of a sublime play, interrupts the actor to tell him that the perspective is due to him. Wilde, the actor, was only at ease as long as no one came to tell him who had painted the scenery. When he went to prison it was the décor, if one can use such an unsuitable word in this connotation, which caused him to collapse all of a sudden, and *De Profundis* was an effort to re-create a poetic background out of the most horrible materials. This reaction of the aesthete coincided quite well with that of the man of the world, whose universe was not constructed of images either, but of conventions, ready-made maxims inherited from a specific circle, as fragile and as indispensable to the equilibrium of a situation as the pictures brought by the painters to the Ivory Tower. Thus, worldliness is often an annexe to this tower. Worldliness and aestheticism are the negation of the useful. The critique of the aesthete is only useful insofar as it urges the creator to use his imagination.

Whistler's critique is that of a marvellous technician, a friend both of Courbet and of the Impressionists. It is modern, because it puts the quality of the painting above all else, relegating imagination to second place. He was the first to proclaim the death of the subject, and forty years later, Paul Valéry's famous essay was to be the conclusion of the 'Ten O'Clock Lecture'. Wilde, on the contrary, preached representational painting because he liked literature above everything; thus he limited the choice of subjects to be attacked to the pictures at which he laughed in the Royal Academy and to the realists, because what he wanted above all was a fantastic art like that which he had discovered in Gustave Moreau's studio. Indeed, he evokes the visions of this painter in The Decay of Lying: '. . . And when that day dawns, or sunset reddens, how joyous we shall all be! Facts will be regarded as discreditable, Truth will be found mourning over her fetters. . . . The very aspect of the world will change to our startled eyes. Out of the sea will rise Behemoth and Leviathan, and sail round the high-pooped galleys, as they do on the delightful maps of those ages when books on geography were actually readable. Dragons will wander about the waste places, and the phoenix will soar from her nest of fire into the air. . . . Champing his gilded oats, the Hippogriff will stand in our stalls, and over our heads will float the Blue Bird singing of beautiful and impossible things, of things that are lovely and that never happen, of things that are not and that should be. . . .' He reproached religion for becoming

reasonable: '. . . The growth of common sense in the English
Church is a thing very much to be regretted. It is really a
degrading concession to a low form of realism. It is silly, too.
It springs from an entire ignorance of psychology. Man can
believe the impossible, but man can never believe the
improbable. . . .' One can understand that Pope Pius IX was
dear to Wilde for having pronounced the dogma of the
Immaculate Conception at the least happy moment of
his reign.

All the practitioners of Art Nouveau were to find formu-
lated in this text their need of the unreal . . . 'Art begins
with abstract decoration, with purely imaginative and
pleasurable work dealing with what is unreal and non-
existent. This is the first stage. Then Life becomes fascinated
with this new wonder, and asks to be admitted into the
charmed circle. Art takes life as part of her rough material,
recreates it, and refashions it in fresh forms, is absolutely
indifferent to fact, invents, imagines, dreams, and keeps
between herself and reality the impenetrable barrier of
beautiful style, of decorative or ideal treatment. . . .' It is
certain that Proust knew of the above passages written by
Ruskin's disciple, which so well defined his aestheticism,
the act of bringing imagination to a work of art; as Proust
knew the history of art better than Wilde, his commentary
on a church or on a picture is much more interesting, but
the attitude is the same: contemplation and imagination.
The English, who have not produced many plastic masterpieces, have nevertheless taught the world how to appreciate
them. It is noticeable that music was of no importance in
the aesthetic movement in England, unlike in France.
Wilde's remarks on the subject are worthy of *Punch*. 'I like
Wagner's music better than anybody's. It is so loud that
one can talk the whole time without other people hearing
what one says. Musical people are so absurdly unreason-

able. They always want one to be perfectly dumb at the very moment when one is longing to be absolutely deaf.' A little further on Wilde heralded the stylisation fashionable at the end of the century which he had already divined in William Morris, saying that the real school in which to learn art was not reality but art itself. This was excellent practical advice. Painters knew that they learned more by copying the masters than by drawing nudes and dishes of fruit. Wilde's ideas were those that triumphed around 1900, but not for long, because he was not able to find very great artists to illustrate them, only decorators who carried them out marvellously. He had expounded these ideas ever since his lectures in England in 1881. In the United States and then in the English provinces the effect of his lectures was enormous, because he had the gift of persuasion; he adopted the tone of a missionary spreading the evangelism of William Morris: 'Aestheticism is not a style but a principle.' (In fact, it was necessary to wait for Art Nouveau for a genuine new style, after the pastiches of the nineteenth century.) He expressed the principles that falsification should be avoided such as, for instance, painting wood to look like marble or marble to look like wood. No mirrors should be permitted as they falsify angles in a room . . . the school should be the most beautiful house in the village . . . and punishment to children should be not to go to school; these came from Oscar's lecture 'House Beautiful'. In another, delivered to art students of the Royal Academy in 1883 Oscar said: '. . . such an expression as English Art is a meaningless expression, one might just as well speak of English Mathematics'. In another lecture on 'Woman's Dress,' which was perhaps too theoretical, he advised dressmakers to contemplate Greek draperies. For ten years the Missionary of Beauty spread these ideas before they were collected in book form.

Wilde and Whistler at the Royal Academy—*Punch*, 1885

The taste for the fanciful, and for fables, can surely be attributed to Oscar's Irish origins; they are aspects of the Celtic revival of which his father had been a pioneer. The traceries which covered the large, Celtic stone crosses, and the margins of ancient Irish manuscripts, were the sources of the spirals which, in 1900, were to inspire the stylization that was to sweep away Victorian realism.

In Wilde's essay *The Critic as Artist*, he wrote: '. . . And though the mission of the aesthetic movement is to lure people to contemplate, not to lead them to create, yet, as the creative instinct is strong in the Celt, and it is the Celt who leads in Art, there is no reason why in future years this strange Renaissance should not become almost as mighty in its way as was that new birth of Art that woke many centuries ago in the cities of Italy.'

Speranza's drawing-room in London, with all its untidiness and enthusiasm, became an Irish Embassy eagerly sought out by young men in search of glory. The heroine received them with open arms; Oscar gave them advice, introduced them to publishers, wrote of them in his articles. Two of these protégés, younger than he by some years, became as famous. It was to Wilde that Bernard Shaw owed the technique of paradox that enabled him to insult the English without angering them; to Wilde too, Yeats owed his knowledge of Maeterlinck and also the impulse to give form to Irish legends. It was not easy for Oscar to get on with Shaw, who was quite insensible to his charm. He came from a needy middle-class background, he was contemptuous of the people who had come from Merrion Square, his puritanism was shocked by the easy-going, pseudo-aristocratic manner of the Wildes. His anti-snobbishness gave him a point of view as artificial as that engendered by Wilde's snobbishness; nor was the son of the house attracted by Shaw. In the first place because 'Shaw was not in those early days very attractive – dead white, and his face was pitted by some disease. The back of his neck was especially bleak – very long, untenanted, dead white. His hair was like seaweed.' He brought with him to Lady Wilde's, women who advertised their advanced ideas by neglecting their appearance. The pretensions as well as the appearance of the young Socialist annoyed the man of the world. One day Shaw explained interminably that he wished to start a magazine. Oscar listened carefully and eventually said: 'That has all been most interesting, Mr. Shaw; but there's one point you haven't mentioned, and an all-important one – you haven't told us the title of your magazine.' 'Oh, as

K

for that,' said Shaw, 'what I'd want to do would be to
impress my personality on the public – I'd call it *Shaw's
Magazine*.' 'Yes,' said Oscar, 'and how would you spell it?'
However, on one chance occasion the two Dubliners found
themselves together, and reduced each other to tears of
laughter with stories. When Shaw got up a petition to help
some anarchists who had been sentenced to death in
Chicago, Wilde was the only man of letters who signed it.
Asked what he thought of Shaw, Wilde replied: 'Shaw has
not an enemy in the world, and none of his friends like
him.' On the other hand, a friendship was born immediately
between Oscar and Speranza's other protégé, the poet Yeats.
He had just spent several years with the fishermen on the
Isles of Aran and had brought back wonderful stories and
Gaelic melodies, which Oscar made him sing later for his
children: 'My darlings, do not forget that you have listened
to Homer.' Wilde seemed to this young man a figure of the
Renaissance – humorous and cynical – a little like Pietro
Aretino. If it was Oscar's prestige that drew newcomers to
the drawing-room in Oakley Street, it was Willie's funniness
that made them stay well after Oscar had left to go to a
dinner party. 'Scratch Oscar and you will find Willie,' the
jealous were beginning to say. Like his father, the journalist
was much taken up with women, and his lack of scruples in
affairs of the heart was equally evident in affairs of any other
sort. Perhaps he was a little mad, or already unhinged by
drink, as the following episode seems to indicate. Willie
was on the point of becoming engaged to a rich widow
whose children adored him for being willing to play with
them for hours on end, pretending to be a tiger, or a Red
Indian. One day, telling them that he was a thief, he seized
their money-box and, before the children could catch him,
he ran away into the street; the widow never saw him again.
This charming character had some success with ladies of a

certain age; one of them paid him £300 a year in return for which he visited her three times a week and entertained her with his talk. Then he seduced the widow of an American newspaper proprietor, as much by his 'blarney' as by his talent as a journalist, and married her. He had, in fact, the gift of making believe that he had inside information, and his reports on the Parnell affair in particular gave him a brief hour of fame. Like his brother, Oscar suddenly decided to live an ordered life; he came to a decision, perhaps the most serious mistake that this charming man was to commit: he married.

10   A modern household

According to an entry in her diary Laura Troubridge's opinion of Oscar had changed since their first meeting a few years earlier when she had been so taken with him:

'July 1883 . . . went to a tea-party at Cressie's (Cresswell-Cresswell) to meet the great Oscar Wilde. He is grown enormously fat with a huge face and tight curls all over his head – not at all the aesthetic he used to look. He was very amusing and talked cleverly, but it was monologue and not conversation. He is vulgar, I think, and lolls about in, I suppose, poetic attitudes with crumpled shirt cuffs turned back over his coat sleeves.'

Oscar should have reflected on the epigram of his old hero Disraeli: 'A woman should always marry, a man never.' He too, like that great man, might have married a rich widow or, better still, a celebrated actress, or a young girl of the world with her eyes already opened, perhaps even one of the 'Souls'. The choice that he made could not have been a more unhappy one, at least as far as Constance was concerned. Her education had been insufficient in literature and excessive in morals and this twenty-six-year-old daughter of an eminent Cork barrister could hardly have been expected to share the interests of her husband, or to understand his digressions from normal behaviour. Constance had one of those upright characters which can easily become narrow; she was to suffer when love was no longer enough to keep her husband, but she had not the imagination to know how to divert him. From then on she was to be an exquisite shade in Wilde's life who followed from farther and farther away, resigned through the years to the ups and downs of his career.

The beauty of Constance thrilled the poet from their first meeting. She looked like a figure in a Burne-Jones' picture: childish, and a little sad. Her silences were disturbing: 'She never speaks and I am always wondering what her thoughts are like,' Oscar told a friend. He described her in a letter to Mrs. Langtry: '. . . I am going to be married to a beautiful girl called Constance Lloyd, a grave, slight, violet-eyed little Artemis, with great coils of heavy brown hair which make her flower-like head droop like a blossom, and wonderful ivory hands which draw music from the piano so sweet that the birds stop singing to listen to her. . . .'

They first met at a young people's party in 1881, and he fell in love with her at once. He then went to the United States and France, and on his return in 1883, when they re-met, he proposed and was accepted by return of post. Constance's father having died, and her mother having re-married, she lived with her grandfather. Oscar used to tell how his wife's grandfather, 'Lying on what threatened to be his death-bed, had no sooner joined our hands and given us his blessing than, for the very joy of the occasion, he suddenly blossomed out into new health and vigour.' Oscar was not at his ease among Constance's well off and much respected family, knowing full well that the Merrion Square scandals had not been forgotten. However, he soon charmed them, with the exception of one cousin who teased Constance for having fallen in love with a man like a third-rate actor after having sent three other suitors packing. Constance had expectations of about £1,000 a year from her grandfather after his death, but during his lifetime she had no more than a smallish income, and had Oscar decided to marry for money he could have done very much better.

For the moment, Oscar was madly in love and did not stop to think if his worldly life would suit this young provincial girl, nor, indeed, if he would have enough money to live as he intended. Oscar cannot be blamed for not having realised his real inclinations, because despite his passionate friendships at Oxford he did not think of himself as an invert. In aesthetic circles there were often marriages à la Pygmalion: a man who had had many love affairs, would find a very young and beautiful girl and mould her. This is what William Morris had done with great success; his wife became the ideal of the Pre-Raphaelites, and Watts, unhappily for him, had married the sixteen-year-old Ellen Terry who wasted no time in leaving him for the stage. The child-wife, irresponsible and caressing, like a pet animal, was one of the obsessions of the Victorians who attached great importance to innocence: the passion of Ruskin for Rose La Touche and the affection of Lewis Carroll for little girls were both of the same order. Oscar wanted to make Constance one of the most accomplished women of her time, but she had principles, no sense of humour and regarded the ideas most dear to her husband as hopelessly paradoxical. She was also gently obstinate – the woman who expects everything from the man she loves. One of her letters should have caused her husband some anxiety: '. . . When I have you for my husband, I will hold you fast with chains of love and devotion, so that you shall never leave me, or love anyone as long as I can love and comfort. . . .' She wrote again: '. . . I am afraid that you and I disagree in our opinion on art for I hold that there is no perfect art without perfect morality, whilst you say they are distinct and separable things.' However optimistic he may have been that he could make Constance forget her principles, at least he had been warned. The poet entered into the part of an engaged young man with ardour, wrote wonderful letters and sent her two telegrams a day, while he was on a lecture tour in the provinces. He wrote to an American friend: 'Her name is Constance and she is quite young, very grave and mystical, with wonderful eyes, and dark brown coils of hair; quite perfect except that she does not think Jimmy the only painter that ever really existed: she would like to bring Titian or somebody in by the back door: however, she knows I am the greatest poet, so in literature she is all right: and I have explained to her that you are the greatest sculptor: art instruction cannot go further.

'We are, of course, desperately in love. I have been obliged to be away nearly all the time since our engagement, civilising the provinces by my remarkable lectures, but we telegraph to each other twice a day, and the telegraph clerks have become quite romantic in consequence. I hand in my messages, however, very sternly, and try to look as if "love" was a cryptogram for "buy Grand Trunks" and "darling" a cypher for "sell out at par". I am sure it succeeds.'*

The wedding took place on 29th May 1884, at St. James's Church, Paddington, the parish where her grandfather lived. If the address was not elegant, the guests were hand-picked and were given numbered seat tickets. Whistler telegraphed: 'Fear I may not reach you in time for ceremony – don't wait.' 'We certainly shall not wait,' said Oscar, forcing a large carnation into his buttonhole, 'neither shall we wait for the dear Queen. In this fine weather I asked her to remain at Osborne.'

The Press made notes of the peeresses, the actresses, the novelists and, above all, the colours. They had been chosen by the arbiter of good taste, and sensible people pitied the

* This letter, dated 22nd January 1884 to Waldo Story (an American sculptor) was published in Letters of Oscar Wilde.

shy Constance for having to wear, instead of white tulle
trimmed with orange flowers: '. . . a rich creamy satin dress
of a delicate cowslip tint; the bodice cut square and somewhat low in front, was finished with a high Medici collar,
the ample sleeves were puffed; the skirt, made plain, was
gathered by a silver girdle of beautiful workmanship, the
gift of Mr. Oscar Wilde; the veil of saffron-coloured Indian
silk gauze was embroidered with pearls and worn in the
Marie Stuart fashion, a thick wreath of myrtle leaves,
through which gleamed a few white blossoms crowned her
brown frizzed hair; the dress was ornamented by clusters of
myrtle leaves; the large bouquet had as much green in it as
white.' Of the six bridesmaids, 'two dainty little figures that
seemed to have stepped out of a picture by Sir Joshua
Reynolds, led the way. They were dressed in quaintly-made
gowns of Surah silk, the colour of a ripe gooseberry; large
pale yellow sashes round their waists; the skirts falling
in straight folds to the ankles, displayed small bronze high-
heeled shoes. Large red silk Gainsborough hats decked with
red and yellow feathers shaded the damsels' golden hair;
amber necklaces, long yellow gloves, a cluster of yellow
roses at their throats, a bouquet of white lilies in their hands,
completed the attire of the tiny bridesmaids.' The four elder
bridesmaids were dressed differently: 'One of the ladies
present wore what was described as a "very aesthetic
costume". It was composed of an underdress of rich red silk
with a sleeveless smock of red plush, a hat of white lace
trimmed with clusters of red roses under the brim and
round the crown.' Lady Wilde provided a startling note of
red.*

The Hôtel Wagram, rue de Rivoli, in Paris, was chosen to
house the honeymoon couple. Robert Sherard, whom
Constance thought looked romantically like the famous

* *Life of Oscar Wilde*, by Hesketh Pearson.

portrait of Chatterton, breakfasted with Oscar on their first morning. Oscar was in an expansive mood and embarrassed Sherard by boasting of his prowess in love-making and telling him all the details of the wedding night. Then the two friends went out together, Oscar stopping, Sherard recorded, 'to rifle a flower stall of the loveliest blossoms and sent them, with a word of love on his card, to the bride whom he had quitted but a moment before'.

The Wildes went to a luncheon party given by Miss Reubell, an American friend of Henry James. Donaghue – the sculptor discovered and helped by Oscar in America – was there, and Constance admired his very handsome Roman face and Irish blue eyes. That morning Oscar had taken her to the Salon to admire Donaghue's sculpture of a young naked harpist.

The Wildes went to another luncheon party, given by Sargent, whose portraits were not admired by Oscar – in his eyes they lacked poetry – and yet they are representative of the characters found in Oscar's plays: opulent and dashing. Sargent had recently painted the French 'professional beauty' Madame Gautereau who, though born in New Orleans, was the most beautiful woman in the French official world between 1890 and 1900. Paul Bourget was also at the party. He thought Oscar's young wife was self-effacing and tender. After a week of theatres and dinners, the Wildes moved on to Dieppe, but not to hide their happiness, because there they found many friends gathered round Princess Pignatelli and her daughter Olga Alberta, who was reputed to be the daughter of the Prince of Wales. This might explain the great social success that she enjoyed in England after her marriage to Baron Adolph de Meyer, who became famous as a photographer and as a contributor to American *Vogue*. (In a way, Olga was a link between Wilde's world and that of Cecil Beaton.) There were also some amusing English people in Dieppe. The return to London was a cheerless one: the house was not ready, and they spent a few nights at the Brunswick Hotel in Jermyn Street, then moved to stay with relations, and then to Oscar's bachelor chambers. A great deal of money had been spent on the house, and Constance wildly contemplated the idea of becoming an actress, reporter or novelist in case of need. She was entranced by Les Misérables which Oscar had given her to read in order to occupy her thoughts.

Godwin had been entrusted with the decoration of No. 16 Tite Street, and he wanted to hand over to his young friends rooms that would be in perfect harmony with the simple brick front of the house which was a little in the Dutch style. One can imagine how Oscar relished the opportunity of displaying his taste in decoration. He threw himself into details like any editor of Homes and Gardens. He wrote to Godwin: 'and we find that a rose leaf can be laid on the ivory table without scratching it – at least a white one can'. Godwin designed some of the furniture, including a cabinet in the Japanese style made in the same wood as the wainscoting in the dining-room, with many shelves.

Whistler would often call to proffer advice about such things as the framing of pictures. He had presented the young couple with engravings of his Venetian studies; these, with others, formed a low dado on two walls of the drawing-room covered in old gold. Oscar did not consider Morris wall-papers to be a good background for pictures. but chose to cover some of his walls with material hanging in loose folds. He was pleased with his colour combinations and wrote proudly to a friend: '. . . I have, for instance, a dining-room done in different shades of white, with white curtains embroidered in yellow silk: the effect is absolutely

16 Tite Street

delightful, and the room is beautiful. . . . Some day, if you do us the pleasure of calling I will show you a little room with blue ceiling and frieze (distemper), yellow (oil) walls, and white woodwork and fittings, which is joyous and exquisite, the only piece of design being Morris blue and white curtains, and a white and yellow silk coverlet. . . .' Oscar did his writing in a small study downstairs facing the street, on a table which had once been Carlyle's, and which he hoped would be an incentive to work. Here the walls were buttercup yellow, the woodwork lacquered red; a cast of the Hermes of Praxiteles stood in a corner on a red stand; the pictures included a Monticelli, a drawing by Simeon Solomon, and a Japanese painting of children at play. The ceiling of the drawing-room was designed by Whistler, with two peacock feathers let into it. Wilde's taste, in spite of his concessions to Whistler's simplicity, was already Edwardian in his choice of red and gold walls in his book-room upstairs; beside it the Pre-Raphaelite decoration appeared monastic. Constance's bedroom was Victorian in style with its upholstered furniture, but Oscar had a Japanese "bed", which is surprising as one understood that the Japanese sleep on mats. (The decoration of Montes-quiou's flat in Paris was also influenced by the same Oriental style and he too slept in an Oriental bed.) On the top floor were nurseries, and in the basement the kitchen and 'usual offices'. To run this house properly it must have been necessary to employ a cook, a housemaid and a man-servant.

Oscar's house was to have a great influence as it was a living example of the subject of his lectures – Good Taste. The magazines were full of photographs and accounts of it. Adrian Hope described it thus in a letter to Laura Trou-bridge, his future wife.

'1885 – March 15. I have been lunching with the Oscar

Wildes, who both asked to be remembered to you and Amy (Laura's sister). Through a thick fog I found my way to Tite Street and looked for a white door – which being opened let me into a very ordinary Hall passage painted white. Going up a staircase, also white, and covered with a whitish sort of matting, I found the whole of the landing cut off by a dark curtain from the staircase, leaving just room to turn round if you were going higher. I, however, went through the curtain and found rooms to the right and left of the little ante-rooms thus formed. The little man-servant showed me into the room on the left looking out across Tite Street on to the garden of the Victoria Hospital for Children. No fire and a look as if the furniture had been cleared out for a dance for which the matting did not look inviting. The walls, all white, the ceiling like yours a little (old) but with two lovely dragons painted in the opposite corners of it. On either side of the fireplace, filling up the corners of the room were two three-cornered divans, very low, with cushions, one tiny round Chippendale table, one arm-chair and three stiff other chairs, also covered with a sort of white lacquer. The arm-chair was a sort of curule chair and very comfy to sit on. This is the summer parlour. Nothing on the walls so as not to break the lines. Certainly a cool-looking room and ought to be seen in the long dog days. Effect on the whole better than it sounds.

'All the white paint (as indeed all the paint used about the house) has a high polish like Japanese lacquer work, which has great charm for one who hates paper on walls as much as I do.

'The room at the back has a very distinctly Turkish note. No chairs at all. A divan on two sides of the room, very low, with those queer little Eastern inlaid tables in front. A dark dado, but of what colour I know not, as the window, looking on a slum, they have entirely covered with a wooden grating on the inside copied from a Cairo pattern which considerably reduced the little light there was today. A gorgeous ceiling and a fire quite made me fall in love with this room and I thought how lovely someone would look sitting on the divan with her legs crossed and with a faithful slave kissing her pretty bare feet. Here Oscar joined me and presently appeared Constance with her brother and his wife. Lunch was in the dining-room at the back on the ground floor. The room in front they have not as yet fitted up. A cream coloured room with what Oscar assured me, was the only sideboard in England, viz. a board running the whole length of the room and about nine inches wide at the height of the top of the wainscoting. Table of a dirty brown with a strange device: maroon napkins, like some rough bath towels, with deep fringes. Quaint glass and nice food made up a singularly picturesque table. Afterwards we went upstairs to see where the great Oscar sleeps. This room had nothing particular but hers was too delightful. You open the door only to find yourself about to walk through the opening in a wall apparently three feet thick. When you get into the room you find that on the one side of the door, forming a side of the doorway, is an ideal wardrobe with every kind of drawer and hanging cupboard for dresses. Next to this again and between it and the corner of the room is a book-case and a writing-table. All this is white and delightfully clean and fresh besides taking so little room. The writing-table is fixed to the book-case with knee-hole, solid part drawers. The bed looked very soft and nice. Upstairs again Oscar had knocked the garrets into one delightful book room for himself in which he had his bath as well. The doors and woodwork of this room were vermilion with a dado of gold leaves on a vermilion ground giving a delicious effect of colour which I revelled in. Here I sat talking till half-past six and listening to Oscar who, dressed in a grey velvet Norfolk shooting jacket and looking fatter than ever, harangued away in a most amusing way.'

In her answer Laura says: 'I was so interested in all you told me of the Wildes' house. Some of the new ideas I should think very pretty, I am sure, but I don't think we could live in a room without pictures and books – do you? and all white too and shiny, like living inside a jam-pot – without the jam! But I should like the Turkish room the best – for very idle times! Her room sounds charming and the whole thing is not nearly so fantastic and outré as one would expect, evidently. You do not say if Mrs. Oscar was dressed to live up to her husband's lectures or was she still swathed in a limp white muslin and lilies? But it must have been amusing altogether.'

No sooner were they installed than a carnival began for Constance which lasted as long as Oscar's interest in her. In compliment to Queen Victoria, her dress for her presentation was an exact copy of something that would have been right when Victoria succeeded to the throne: 'London became accustomed to seeing Mrs. Wilde at a Private View dressed as a shepherdess, as a Greek at a Garden party, as Queen Henrietta Maria at an evening party.'

An entry in Laura Troubridge's diary gives a description of Constance's appearance. Can it be an echo of a thwarted interest which makes her comments so acid? It will be remembered that when Miss Laura first saw Oscar she was quite in love with him. The date of the following entry was barely two months after Wilde's marriage:

'July 1884. Mr. and Mrs. Oscar Wilde to tea. She dressed for the part in limp white muslin with no bustle, saffron coloured silk swathed about her shoulders, a huge cartwheel Gainsborough hat, white and bright yellow stockings and shoes – she looked too hopeless and we thought her shy and dull. He was amusing of course.'

Almost dying of shyness Constance usually hung on Oscar's lips, waiting for a word of encouragement: 'I am proud of you – you are a dream my love, and now go and say How do you do to Lady Lonsdale . . .' and she courageously did her best to be a part of the social world which, basically, pitied her. The young couple were inseparable. They received their first visitors dressed in flowered kimonos at the breakfast table. One day when they were out shopping together in the King's Road in striking clothes, an urchin stared at them and shouted derisively: ' 'Amlet and Ophelia out for a walk I suppose.' Oscar replied: 'My little fellow, you are quite right, we are.' One day, while he was waiting for Constance outside Swan & Edgar's shop, a hard-eyed sinister young woman passed by, gazing at him, and went on with a mocking laugh; at least that is how he described the incident, adding, 'I felt as if an icy hand had clutched at my heart. But Constance emerged, and the sun shone again.' Among the motley of Chelsea Oscar, proud of having a pretty woman on his arm, condescended to walk about, taking off his hat to friends and acquaintances, like the lord of the manor in a village. It would have taken much to surprise the young ladies of Chelsea who did their shopping dressed as Primavera or Lady Hamilton; indeed, wasn't Ellen Terry to be seen for a whole season getting in and out of a cab opposite No. 16 Tite Street dressed as Lady Macbeth, in an apple-green mediaeval tunic, a silver crown on her long red-gold hair, to pose for Sargent? From his doorstep Oscar exclaimed: 'Really Ellen, how could you?' The actress, looking at his bronze waistcoat, replied: 'Really Oscar, how dare you?' Upon which he declared: 'The street that on a wet and dreary morning has vouch-safed the vision of Lady Macbeth in full regalia magnificently seated in a four-wheeler, can never again be as other streets, it must always be full of wonderful possibilities.'

The following hitherto unpublished entries from Laura's diary (she had by then become Mrs. Adrian Hope) are of value for their contemporary freshness and the spontaneity with which two young people discuss two other young people, of whom one rather awed the others, alternately impressing and slightly baffling them.

'1885. April 18. Adrian writes he is to lunch with Oscar on the 19th and take Charlie Orde. They met a brother and sister called Sickert – both hideous and very dull. Adrian wrote later: "The lunch was very entertaining and Charlie gushed in a way that made me feel quite surpassed." '

'April 23. Adrian met Oscar and went back to dine with him and stayed talking till 2 – discussing matrimony.'

Apropos of a book to be sold for Mrs. Amherst's Hospital at Hackney, Adrian suggested that Laura should do a drawing and says: 'I am going to try and squeeze out a poem from O.W.'

'May 9. Adrian to see O.W. who promised a poem on condition that Laura does a drawing for it.'

'May 19. Worked at the drawing for some verses of Oscar Wilde's for Mrs. Amherst's book – at last decided on the idea and got it. The verses are rubbish, and the size is tiny – two difficulties to overcome.'

'1886. May 12. Aunt Bache and Uncle Herbert (Mr. and Mrs. Herbert Jones) fascinated by Oscar Wilde whom they had met at Lady Dorothy Nevill's.'

'June 8. Adrian writes: "Did you see the Wildes have a boy, I rather pity the infant, don't you?"'

'June 9. I had not heard of the arrival of the infant Wilde – I agree that it is much to be pitied. Will it be swathed in artistic baby clothes? Sage green bibs and tuckers I suppose, and a peacock blue robe.'

'1887. March 29. Adrian writes: "O.W. was at the Lyric

L

Club, fat and greasy as ever and looking particularly revolting in huge white kid gloves." '

'April 8. (Adrian takes his sister to the Wilde's and she falls quite in love with the house. Adrian goes to the Owl Club, just started with Oscar Wilde on the Committee and says): "Some of the rooms are too beautifully done up – his taste, when he has been consulted, is excellent." '

'April 29. (Adrian writes in a letter): "Do you see that O.W. is to be the editor of a new magazine to be called *Woman's World*? I shall try to go and see him and suggest that you should be asked to draw for it, if I find there is any monied man behind the venture." '

Constance had hardly enough courage to invite anyone to the house. Oscar, on the other hand, having been brought up in an environment where the constant coming and going of guests was a commonplace, would have liked his wife to have a 'salon'. But this was not the custom in England where men preferred to see their friends in their clubs, rather than in their houses. 'At Homes' were fashionable, and ladies would have one particular day of the week or month which was known as their 'Day', when they received their friends, drank tea and ate cakes and cucumber sandwiches. People came to 16 Tite Street to see the house, and to listen to Oscar; the atmosphere, dull until his arrival, then became animated because, excellent host that he was, he inspired people with his own wit. 'Do come to my Wife's *jour*', he would say to anyone intelligent or of an attractive appearance. The receptions at Tite Street lured the stars away from Speranza's drawing-room, but she consoled herself by helping Oscar in an enterprise that should have made a great deal of money. Cassells the publishers had entrusted to the Prince of Aesthetes the editorship of a luxury magazine, *The Lady's World*, which was intended to enlighten the public on the latest refinements of fashion, and to offer the opinions of well-known ladies on many subjects. The cult of the nobility by the middle-classes was then at its zenith. When the portrait of a peeress appeared above the words: 'Thanks to Pond's Cold Cream I keep my schoolgirl complexion', the sale of this product was assured from Hong Kong to Toronto. Some were willing to lend their names to advertisements for substantial sums of money, but the custom was frowned upon by the purists and by the most exclusive, particularly when it emerged that one peeress who had enthused in print about a particular unguent had never once used it. It was a very different matter when ladies with great names were invited by Oscar to give their views about more serious subjects. Oscar knew who would be flattered by being asked to describe their house, as for example, Lady Constance Howard, who wrote about Kirby Hall. In 1888 the journal changed its name to *Woman's World*. In one issue Lady Archibald Campbell published a long article about the productions of her pastoral plays. According to the illustrations it appears that some of the male parts were played by women, and well-rounded ones at that. In this article are to be found various ideas of Gordon Craig, the natural son of Ellen Terry and Godwin, which were to revolutionise the theatre at the turn of the century. During Oscar's editorship he wrote to Queen Victoria to ask if she had any early verses of her own which he might publish in *Woman's World*. Wilde's letter has disappeared, but the Queen's minute has been preserved in the archives at Windsor; dated 1888, it runs: 'Really, what will people not say and invent. Never could the Queen in her whole life write one line of poetry serious or comic or make a rhyme ever. This is therefore all invention and myth.' Oscar was more fortunate with Princess Christian of Schleswig-Holstein who promised to write for his journal.

The Queen of Roumania, a blue-stocking who wrote under the pseudonym of Carmen Sylva, contributed her stories of the folk-lore of the Carpathians. The novelists whom Oscar had ridiculed the most, Ouida and Marie Corelli, were set to work on articles and Sarah Bernhardt contributed 'The History of my Tea-Gown'; later he was to ask her for an article on her tour in the United States, he was even ready to write it himself and suggested the following beginning: 'Americans, according to their own explanation, visit France in order to complete their education, and the French have to tolerate people who are so fascinatingly unreasonable as to attempt to finish in a foreign land what they never had the courage to begin in their own.' But Sarah was about to make another tour of the U.S.A. and refused to sign it. Lady Wilde, who had so often appeared in striking clothes, was aptly chosen to write on dress reform. Oscar chose the illustrations of the articles with great care and especially those on decoration. His taste was not very daring, but one of the first examples of the Art Nouveau line is to be seen in a *Woman's World* frontispiece, and he disseminated ideas which were very important to that style, already contained in Eastlake's *Hints of Household Taste* published in 1869. He also encouraged artistic work instead of crochet – ladies took to poker-work and weaving. Enamelling became the hobby of a few extremely artistic ladies and was taught by the best exponent of the art at that time – Alexander Fisher, whose work was much admired by Watts and Burne-Jones.

During the first months of his editorship, the poet went nearly every day to the office of the magazine. He would travel by underground from Sloane Square to Charing Cross, walk up the Strand and Fleet Street and arrive at the office in La Belle Sauvage Yard, Ludgate Hill. Sometimes, overwhelmed by letters needing answers, and probably needing comment he would ask himself – is this really important? When in a good mood he would reply to the more foolish of the correspondents with letters sparkling with wit and propagating ideas on subjects which ranged from cooking utensils to philosophy. Soon the good days became rarer and rarer and the letters piled up, and he would say: 'Is it necessary to settle anything today?' Once Wilde said to W. E. Henley: '. . . I have known men come to London full of bright prospects and seen them complete wrecks in a few months through the habit of answering letters.' Thereafter Wilde would leave his office without even sitting down at his desk. He contributed to the magazine some lightweight literary criticism. Two very pretty poems in the style of Verlaine with the French title of *Fantasies Décoratives* appeared in *The Lady's Pictorial* in 1887; they were just that, but the ideas of Art Nouveau were presented with grace in the stanza:

> 'Under the rose-tree's dancing shade
> There stands a little ivory girl
> Pulling the leaves of pink and pearl
> With pale green nails of polished jade.'

But the magazine was too literary. Oscar believed he had a mission to civilise society rather than to instil it with yet more wordly vanities, as did the rival magazine *Vanity Fair*. The proprietor became bored with Wilde's diminishing interest and finally sacked him in October 1889. The magazine died a year later.

Oscar spent money and got into debt. A few years earlier he had schemed to be nominated to an inspectorship of schools and wrote to Professor Mahaffy about this: '. . . I want you, if you would do it for me, to write to your

friend Lord Spencer, who is now Lord President of the
Council, to make a recommendation of me as a suitable
person to hold an Inspectorship of Schools. . . .' Nothing
came of this idea.

The literary criticism written by Oscar in the *Pall Mall
Gazette* was far superior to that written for *Woman's World*,
and was often anonymous, but he later collected it in his
work *Intentions*. The survey of embroidery was to be copied
in its entirety in one of the chapters of *Dorian Gray*. From
time to time a premonitory sentence appears in his works;
such as 'Prison has had an admirable effect on Mr. Wilfrid
Blunt as a poet . . .'. His journalistic work did not help much
with the costs of running the house. One day he was
accosted on his doorstep; 'I have called about the taxes, Sir.'
'Taxes? Why should I pay taxes?' said Oscar. 'But Sir, you
are the house-holder here, are you not? You live and sleep
here.' 'Ah, yes, but then you see I sleep so badly.'

Constance was worried; she came from the kind of people
who leave their capital intact except in a real emergency.
Her anxious looks became a reproach, and Oscar still found
her silences disturbing, though by then he knew what her
thoughts were. However he still loved her, and he was mad
with joy when his first son, Cyril, was born in June 1885,
and very pleased when Vyvyan was born in November 1886.
Visitors had the impression of a happy family and a bright
and elegant household. Yet Oscar was drawing away from
his wife, and this for two reasons; the aesthete, with his
hatred of all forms of ugliness, saw with horror the girl's
body deformed by pregnancy, he loathed the infirmities of
women and the illnesses of the children, and reserved his
pity for sublime adversity and for attractive paupers. The
other reason was more serious: Oscar had become bored
with a wife who could only bring him love. Constance, on
the other hand, was tired of fireworks. One day Constance

asked Oscar to meet some old Dublin friends of hers among whom was a clergyman, a meeting of no interest to him but desired by Constance. Robert Ross, who was there, reported, 'Oscar talked during lunch as I had never heard him talk before – divinely . . . Humour, tale, epigram, flowed from his lips and his listeners sat spell-bound under the influence. Suddenly in the midst of one of his most entrancing stories – his audience with wide eyes and parted mouths, their food untasted – his wife broke in: "Oh, Oscar, did you remember to call for Cyril's boots?" '

Constance consoled herself for having to lead a so-called brilliant life by the company of Margaret, Lady Sandhurst, who was a zealous worker for the Church. One day they spoke of missionaries. Oscar said: 'Missionaries! My dear, don't you realise that missionaries are the divinely provided food for destitute and underfed cannibals? Whenever they are on the brink of starvation, Heaven, in its infinite mercy, sends them a nice plump missionary.' A little later on, to play fair as it were, Oscar agreed to receive a missionary bishop who wished to ask for advice regarding the clothes he was about to send out to Kenya and Samoa. The arbiter of fashion with a straight face suggested the sort of material best suited to cover up the pagan nudities. Oscar was some-times affected by a nostalgic yearning for respectability, and it amused him to charm the very people who most liked to think of him as corrupt, and to shower blandish-ments upon the virtuous. But this hypocrisy was only a gesture; he was too afraid of boredom to keep it up. Constance became jealous of her husband's good humour when others were present and this crystallised into jealousy of the women with whom Oscar had been friends before his marriage and still continued to see. When she learned that Oscar sometimes spent an evening with a woman of doubt-ful reputation who received her admirers in a luxurious house, Constance made a terrible scene and her husband left the house slamming the front door. Then she suspected a love affair with an actress because Oscar was away from home at a time when the actress was performing in the provinces. On Monday morning, when he returned, the husband described in too detailed a manner what had taken place at the country house where he had supposedly been a guest; Constance interrupted him with the remark: 'And did she act well?' It is just possible, too, that Oscar may have found an interest not a hundred yards from his own house, because Adrian Hope had recently built a large house, vaguely Tudor in style, in Tite Street; Mrs. Hope was very pretty, Oscar saw her frequently.

In 1891 Laura did a portrait in pastels of Oscar's son Cyril, and in the same year, one of her daughter Jaqueline. Queen Victoria was so much struck by the portrait of Cyril shown her by one of her ladies-in-waiting, that she commissioned Laura to do the portraits of many members of the Royal Family. Now at last Oscar's assumption of the Queen's interest in him was to be realised – at one remove! Adrian Hope wrote to his wife: 'Have just met Oscar who was killing about the picture of Cyril for which he said he expected a knighthood.' Once when Adrian ran into Oscar in Tite Street the latter said: 'I know what you're thinking; there goes that horrid Mr. Wilde leaving Constance alone again.'*

After the birth of his first son Oscar would absent himself from home on the most futile of pretexts, and Constance knew so little about her husband that she believed him when he told her that he had been to play golf every afternoon: 'It will do him a great deal of good!', she would tell a friend, and she wrote to Clyde Fitch's mother that 'Oscar has become mad about golf and spends two or three hours

* Hope-Nicholson family papers, hitherto unpublished.

on the links every day and this is so good for him.' For his part, Oscar would say: 'The one charm of marriage is that it makes a life of deception absolutely necessary for both parties.' But Constance did not know how to lie; she sighed, the corners of her pretty mouth turned down, her violet eyes filled with tears, and Oscar could not bear it. Nothing is more painful to kind-hearted egoists – and he had a heart of gold – than the sight of people whom they have made unhappy. Nevertheless his work was to be strewn with epigrams on the subject of marriage:

'There's nothing in the world like the devotion of a married woman – it is a thing no married man knows anything about.'

'The only difference between a caprice and a lifelong passion, is that the caprice lasts a little longer.'

'The proper basis for marriage is a mutual misunderstanding.'

'Faithfulness is to the emotional life what consistency is to the life of the intellect – simply a confession of failure.'

'Women never know when the curtain has fallen. They always want a sixth act, and as soon as the interest of the play is entirely over they propose to continue it.'

'One should always be in love. That is the reason one should never marry.'

'When a man has once loved a woman, he will do anything for her, except continue to love her.'

11　The Evangelist of Chelsea

There was a noticeable slowing-down of Wilde's intellectual activity between 1884 and 1888; neither marriage nor work provided the sort of inspiration required for his genius. He needed freedom to sing, or failing that, a cage as vast and gilded as the fashionable world, with all its attendant hazards. The constraint that he imposed upon himself to lead a regular and respectable life made him at times believe that he really had become exemplary. He was to talk much of his soul during these decorous years, as he was later to speak of it during the dark periods of his life, the better to savour, as it were, the awful depths into which he had plunged it. It is difficult to take seriously his use of the word 'soul' which, more often than not, hides the vaguest of feelings, or at best a limited understanding, but in an era such as the Victorian one, so smugly religious and at the same time so material, the word indicated a touching wish to renounce the vulgarity of the age; but it was essentially little more than an expression of elegance. Oscar, sometimes accompanied by Constance, moved in a circle where the soul was worn with very good taste. This group abhorred the slightest vulgarity, and spoke in a polished style which contrasted sharply with the fashionable slang used by the Prince of Wales's set. Although they read a great deal, it did not prevent them from riding and playing cricket. They discovered the Bayreuth Festival and preferred Florence to Monte Carlo. Their interest in letters and half-contempt for trivial social amusements caused people with

158

different tastes to christen them ironically, the 'Souls', a title they resented, and individually disclaimed. The men frequently congregated at Crabbet Park, Wilfrid Blunt's house in Sussex, there to play the newly-invented game of lawn tennis and read poetry aloud. Some of them were members of the recently formed Crabbet Club, and in 1889 the politician George Wyndham added to it his own intellectual friends, many of whom were soon to become famous in the fields of politics and literature. His father's house, Clouds, in Wiltshire, had been built in 1885 by a colleague of William Morris, Philip Webb, and was considered to have been this architect's masterpiece. It contained a quantity of Morris designs, but the colours of the walls were light and beautiful as was also the old furniture which blended happily with the new.

The membership of this club was limited to twenty-one, of whom Oscar was one. Wilfrid Blunt wrote of him in his diary: '. . . he was, without exception, the most brilliant talker I have ever come across, the most ready, the most witty, the most audacious. Nobody could pretend to outshine him, or even to shine at all in his company . . .'. Blunt went on to record: 'The fine society of London, and especially the "Souls", ran after him because they knew he could always amuse them, and the pretty women allowed him great familiarities, although there was no question of love-making'; Blunt, poet, horseman and political rebel was older than the 'Souls', and had some influence on them in fighting against some of the prejudices of the time. His Diaries contain many fascinating insights into the period.

The cult of the beautiful which, as has already been pointed out, brought great ladies and actresses together in fashionable studios was, before Oscar's influence was felt, largely concerned with physical beauty. But from about 1885 intelligent young men straight from Oxford or

Cambridge, and young ladies, already bored with a purely
social life, extended the cult to things of the mind. They
were as interested in Liberal politics as in good literature
and good taste. Young men with a future and clever women,
were drawn to a very young girl, with more vitality than
beauty, Margot Tennant, the daughter of a Scottish millionaire. At eighteen her cleverness astonished Gladstone; at
twenty she had many enemies, but counted among her
intimate friends two future Prime Ministers, Herbert
Asquith, whom she married, and, perhaps the most brilliant
young man among the 'Souls', Arthur Balfour. Hellenist,
philosopher, music-lover, politician and tennis-player, he
looked aloofly at the rest of the world. Many ladies loved
him, as he was a consummate charmer. Perhaps he was clever
to remain a bachelor. Maurice Baring was the youngest of
this exquisite group: astonishly well-read, later a diplomat
and novelist, he too was much loved. Some of them also had
a social conscience, and Oscar had the gift and the good
nature to put both the helpers and the helped at their ease.
An instance of this had occurred a few years earlier when
the Thames had flooded its banks. With his friend Rennell
Rodd, Oscar had crossed the river to Lambeth to help the
homeless and had come upon a bed-ridden old Irishwoman.
He remained a long time attending to her wants and
laughing and joking with her, they exchanged stories of
their own country and she was so cheered up that she
prayed that the Lord would give him 'a bed in Glory'. As
he told Rodd afterwards, he was amply rewarded for his
efforts by her prayer, since a comfortable bed was her
highest aspiration.

Charity was more of a social duty than a religious virtue
to these intellectuals. Few of them had much respect for the
Established Church: ('There goes God's head-waiter,' said
one of them as a particularly pompous bishop passed),

and their attitude towards religion, by no means despicable, was summed up in the words of a friend to Margot Tennant: 'My child, believe in God, in spite of what they tell you in Church.'

Several interesting blue-stocking acquaintances of Oscar's, neither young nor stylish enough to be classed as 'Souls', nevertheless shared their ideals. There was that curious couple of aunt and niece, Katherine Bradley and Edith Cooper, who, under the name of Michael Field, published poems and verse-plays which never reached the stage; Miss Schuster, who lived at Wimbledon among flowers and books, and Vernon Lee, who would have been one of Oscar's friends had she not advertised so clearly her preference for the company of young ladies. Ouida was a best-selling novelist whose novels were an absurdly melo-dramatic (and non-political) version of Disraeli's. She was infatuated with riches and grandeur, and already seemed a little old-fashioned; Oscar called her the last of the lionesses.

Wilde's friendship with the 'Souls' dated from his arrival in London when he came down from Oxford. His life as father of a family and editor of a magazine had sobered him; most of his sparkle had been concentrated in the paradoxes. Yeats explains very well the technique used by Oscar to put over his thoughts: '. . . the impression of artificiality that I think all Wilde's listeners have recorded, came from the perfect rounding of the sentences and from the deliberation that made it possible. That very impression helped him, as the effect of metre, or of the antithetical prose of the seventeenth century, which is itself a true metre, helped its writers, for he could pass without incongruity from some unforeseen, swift stroke of wit to elaborate reverie.' Oscar described his own conversation in

The Picture of Dorian Gray: 'He played with the idea and grew wilful; tossed it into the air and transformed it, let it escape and recaptured it, made it iridescent with fancy, and winged it with paradox. . . . He was brilliant, fantastic, irresponsible. He charmed his listeners out of themselves and they followed his pipe laughing.' 'If only the Irish knew how to listen and the English knew how to talk,' sighed Oscar, one day in his mother's drawing-room. He retained his own preference for those who listened, especially if they were agreeable to look at, but also said paradoxically: 'One should never listen, to listen is a sign of indifference to one's hearers.' Young men straight from Oxford and Cambridge reminded him of the friendships in his twenties, and of his poem *Magdalen Walks*; he wanted to be to them not only what Pater and Ruskin had been to him, but also a friend who would make them laugh and share their pleasures. He set himself the task of freeing them from their prejudices – all this with a great deal of material and intellectual generosity. Wilde preached that everyone should extend himself to the limit of his capabilities, and should cultivate his personality without hindrance. Thus nice boys were urged into adventures which, in that Victorian society, could do them no good.

He himself needed a darker side to life, besides the spiritual and intellectual, and he took for granted that others shared this need; it existed among the masters of Aestheticism, and Chelsea hid some frightful secrets. To remind himself of the secrets – or rather pleasures – of others when under the conjugal roof, Oscar could look at a picture by Simeon Solomon which, according to Arthur Symons 'Shows the relations latent between pain and pleasure, the compromises of the good and the bad, of the alluring and the abominable.' The first of Oscar's questionable friends made his appearance two years after his marriage; he was called Henry Marillier.

He had been a classical scholar at Cambridge, and had lodged at Salisbury Street when Wilde was there. He later wrote for the *Pall Mall Gazette* and edited *The Early Work of Aubrey Beardsley*, and was also to write a book about Rossetti. Several passages in the letters written by Wilde to this young man set the tone of the friendship which was to follow: '... I would have liked to have gone to the National Gallery with you, and looked at Velasquez's pale evil King, at Titian's Bacchus with the velvet panthers, and at that strange heaven of Angelico's where everyone seems made of gold and purple and fire and which, for all that, looks to me ascetic – everyone dead and decorative! I wonder will it really be like that, But I wonder without caring. *Je trouve la terre aussi belle que le ciel, et le corps aussi beau que l'âme.* If I do live again I would like to be as a flower – no soul but perfectly beautiful. Perhaps for my sins I shall be made a red geranium!!

'And your paper on Browning? You must tell me of it. In our meeting again there was a touch of Browning – keen curiosity, wonder, delight ... I have never learned anything except from people younger than myself and you are infinitely young.'

This letter is an echo of a conversation; artistic advice enlivened by poetic nonsense and a sentimental note, perhaps a little ironical, after a visit to Cambridge. 'Does it all seem a dream, Harry? Ah! what is not a dream? To me it is, in a fashion, a memory of music. I remember bright young faces, and grey misty quadrangles, Greek forms passing through Gothic cloisters, life playing among ruins, and, what I love best in the world, Poetry and Paradox dancing together ...' '... you too have the love of the impossible ... (how do men name it?). Sometime you will find, even as I have found, that there is no such thing as a romantic experience; there are romantic memories, and there is the desire of romance – that is all. Our most fiery moments of ecstasy are merely shadows of what somewhere else we have felt, or of what we long some day to feel. So at least it seems to me. And, strangely enough, what comes of all this is a curious mixture of ardour and of indifference. I myself would sacrifice everything for a new experience, and I know there is no such thing as a new experience at all. . . . Only one thing remains infinitely fascinating to me, the mystery of moods. To be master of these moods is exquisite, to be mastered by them more exquisite still. Sometimes I think that the artistic life is a long and lovely suicide, and am not sorry that it is so. . . .'

Marillier disappeared from Oscar's life. At about this time the poet seems to have given up the idea of making Constance the ideal woman; the rôle of Pygmalion is an unrewarding one when the statue refuses to come alive. Plato suited Oscar better and he installed his Academy under the chandeliers of the Café Royal. The most loyal disciple, Robert Ross, appeared about 1886, and his engaging manner and loyalty caused his follies to be forgiven; Oscar first met him after a lecture at Cambridge. Robert Ross read History, but unfortunately he antagonised his tutors and fellow students alike; the former sent him down for having published an article making fun of them in a university review; the latter were so irritated by his aesthetic affectations that they ducked him in the King's College fountain.

In 1889, Ross, the son of a Canadian Attorney-General and grandson of the first Prime Minister of Upper Canada, was living on an allowance from his mother, and trying to earn his living as an art critic. He was never physically strong: all his life, which was not to be a long one, he remained a thin, lively, enthusiastic young man with a slightly turned-up nose and a lock of hair which concealed a convex forehead. In his youth his qualities touched the hearts of his elders, and his cleverness commanded their attention. Ross had a very receptive intelligence which owed its understanding to his chosen friends, whom he would inspire to shine and to be at their best. This fluctuating and insinuating person adapted himself to all surroundings. To one thing he held fast: Catholicism. Robert Ross was more theological than moral and his strictness did not interfere with his pleasures, except in the form of remorse.

Impressed by Oscar's physical presence and dazzled by his brilliance, Robert Ross could no more have resisted him than Ganymede could have Jupiter; throughout he was to keep Oscar's friendship – thanks to his powers of conversation. Many of the lines in Intentions are taken from remarks made by Robert Ross. Later the young man was to boast that he had been Oscar's first lover and the majority of his biographers, because this avowal is so courageous, have never doubted the truth of it. He may have been the first serious male friendship. Doubtless Lord Ronald Gower could have provided him with addresses of people of an inferior class had he asked for them. At that time a casual encounter, or a romantic attachment with a shepherd in Davos or a gondolier in Venice, did not appeal to him as it did to John Addington Symonds, who actually brought a gondolier to London with him. (This did not cause the sensation that it might have done, because Sargent had paved the way by already having a gondolier to look after his studio.) To Oscar then an intimate friendship with a cultivated young man was more agreeable. Soon he could not do without Robbie, who would come to luncheon in Tite Street two or three times a week and would spend the afternoon with Oscar in the smoking-room gossiping over endless cigarettes. Mrs. Wilde took a dislike to him because he prevented Oscar from working.

M

Not only Ross but other young men came, who were taken to the theatre and, above all, wasted a great deal of Oscar's time evoking Alcibiades or Sarah Bernhardt in an atmosphere heavy with Egyptian cigarettes. Graham Robertson (who was to be painted by Sargent and to write a successful play, Pinkie and the Fairies, as well as a charming autobiography, Time Was), small, delightful and a skilful draughtsman, had recently become a friend of the actress and he spent much of his time in Paris caught up in her toils; he was also intimately acquainted with Robert de Montesquiou and would report on the decorative discoveries of the poet, on his impudence and his neck-ties.

Robbie Ross had not sufficient breadth of personality to hope for complete possession, so became the accomplice of adventures which, in some cases, were anything but intellectual – complaisance being in this case another form of admiration. Robbie was not good-looking, nor did he have the creative element the Master required in an ideal disciple. Oscar believed he had found this in two very handsome poets. The first was called John Gray (if he had not been slightly snub-nosed, he would have been the ideal Greco-Oxonian). He was a serious and very cultivated young man, whom the poet and critic Richard Le Gallienne introduced to Oscar at a meeting of the Rhymers' Club. His poems sang the praises of young ladies of olden times, ancient musical instruments and flowers, although he was less talented than Le Gallienne, whose collection, London, The Accursed City, contains excellent poems in the style of Verlaine. A book of poems called Cyril and Lionel, by Gray's intimate friend André Raffalovich, presents a different aspect. These poems, some written in French and some in English, are absurd, and were typical of a pederastic school with religious tendencies which blossomed in the shadow of

Wilde. Raffalovich was the son of rich Russian Jews who had settled in Paris. His mother was beautiful and so deeply shocked at seeing the ugliness of her son that she entrusted him when a baby to an unmarried English lady called Miss Gribbel; his parents provided him with plenty of money. When he grew up he tried to establish a Salon; Wilde said that instead he ended up by running a saloon: – once, when arriving there for a party, Oscar impudently said to the servant who answered the door: 'A table for six please.' It was Pater, though, who really counted most in that house. When he went to luncheon there his glass was placed between two vases each containing one red rose. Oscar quarrelled with Raffalovich after having written an ironical criticism of a collection of his verses. The resentment of the author was aggravated by the jealousy of the lover. John Gray, whom Raffalovich loved, was on very good terms with Oscar and it was at the latter's expense that Silver Points, Gray's first book, was published, with illustrations by Ricketts. Gray wrote The Blackmailer – for which he had doubt-less found the subject in Wilde's circle – with Raffalovich, after which they led a tranquil life together. A Roman Catholic since boyhood, Gray took Holy Orders and Raffalovich had St. Peter's Church in Edinburgh built for him. Raffalovich, who did not practise forgiveness of one's enemies, pursued Oscar with his hate and waited until he was in prison to use material based on Oscar's life, for a thesis called Uranisme et Unisexualité.

Oscar's friendship with another poet was even less happy; Lionel Johnson was more talented than Gray but in his poems are to be found all the misty rhetoric of the English deca-dents with 'agonised hopes' and 'ashen flowers'. Wilde had heard Johnson spoken of by Walter Pater, of whom he was a favourite pupil, as one of those young men who wished to model their lives on Marius the Epicurean, (the last of the Master's books, less disturbing than Marcel Schwob's *Imaginary Lives* was to be, but capable of leading to an aesthetic Christianity). Oscar's curiosity about Johnson was excited by Pater, and he met the poet on a visit to Oxford. After which the young man wrote to a friend: '... I found him as delightful as Green is not. He discoursed, with infinite flippancy, of everyone: lauded the *Dial*: laughed at Pater: and consumed all my cigarettes. I am in love with him. ...' This letter shows the destructive side of Wilde's character, he became an accomplice by turning idols upside down, by taking nothing seriously. This friendship opened wider perspectives of emotions and amusements, which the pupil translated into a poem:

> 'All that he came to give,
> He gave, and went again.
> I have seen one man live,
> I have seen one man reign
> With all the graces in his train.
> With a light word, he took
> The hearts of men in thrall ...'

Richard Le Gallienne had already written a poem in the same vein after an outing with Oscar – he must indeed have had a magical charm. That there was also a cynical side to his character is shown in *A Few Maxims for the Instruction of the Over-Educated*: 'Even the disciple has his uses. He stands behind one's throne, and at the moment of one's triumph whispers in one's ear that, after all, one is immortal.' 'Friendship is far more tragic than love. It lasts longer.' 'Those whom the gods love grow young.'

A charming story is recorded by Yeats, of Wilde saying 'I have been inventing a Christian heresy', and he told

a detailed fable, in the style of some Early Father, of how
Christ recovered after the Crucifixion and, escaping from
the tomb, lived on for many years – the one man upon
earth who knew the falsehood of Christianity. Once St. Paul
visited his town and He alone in the carpenter's quarter did
not go to hear him preach. Henceforth the other carpenters
noticed that, for some reason, He kept His hands covered.
Ricketts recounts another fable characteristic of the mixture
of paganism and religion. He writes: 'I wish you could have
heard this fantasy spoken by him, it was one of his best.'

THE LADY OF SORROWS

By the silver marge of the Sicilian Sea, once stood a little shrine,
dedicated to Our Lady of Sorrows. And the fisherfolk of that place
worshipped her, bringing gilded apples on gilded shells, that their
fishing might be prosperous, for her image was very ancient, and
often wrought miracles. One Midsummer Eve the setting sun smote
the face of the Goddess and she, opening her eyes, stretched forth her
hands to unfasten the clasp of her mantle, whereupon seven daggers of
the seven griefs, which once had pierced her heart, were wrought.
Then, from her brow, she removed her veil and, white and naked, she
arose and left her shrine. When behold, as she passed the silver marge
of the sea, naïads appeared among the waves, and eager tritons blew
upon their polished conches to greet Her who had once arisen from
the foam. From forests and fields came dryads and hooved fawns,
from the caverned hills leapt shaggy centaurs bearing gifts. And Eros,
her son, with scarlet wings aflame, flew to embrace his mother, and
all rejoiced that beauty had once more returned unto the waiting
earth. All night long there was high revelry. The sea-nymphs sang
and the centaurs danced until dawn, when the cock crew thrice. Then
the Goddess waxed very pale and, breaking from her worshippers,
she moved towards the little shrine which stood on the margin of the
sea. In vain the fawns and dryads entreated her to stay, she heeded
them not, but wrapped the mantle of grief about her marble limbs.
The centaurs wept and the tritons wept, but she heeded not their tears,

and placed the veil of mourning on her brow. And when Eros be-
sought her not to leave him she bent to him and said 'I must again
return to the place from whence I come, for know I have another son
who has suffered greatly!

In Wilde's more serious works, his Christ closely resembled Him of whom Renan wrote, 'What distinguishes
Him from the agitators of His time and of every century
is His perfect idealism. Jesus, in some respects, was an
anarchist because He had no sense of civic government . . .
to Him, magistrates appeared to be the enemies of the
people and of God . . . He wanted to do away with riches
and power; not, however, to use them Himself.'

Fables provided Wilde with as many themes as did the
Scriptures. The most famous is that of Narcissus who loved
the river because he saw himself reflected in its waters. In
Oscar's version it was the river who also loved Narcissus
in whose eyes it saw its ripples reflected. But these fables
lost much of their charm when he wrote them down; they
lacked the richness of his voice, the pauses, in fact all the
effects that only an incomparable actor can produce. In
reality 'actor' is not the word to use for Oscar, the spontaneity of his manner of expressing himself, his deep enjoyment of his own stories, and the stimulating expertise of
his performance were instinctive – not acquired, as in the
case of a professional actor. His gospel according to Mary
Magdalen has an atmosphere of rare scents and loving
caresses; his Christ is the Christ of Leonardo da Vinci, the
disciples resemble the ethereal athletes of Burne-Jones's
pictures. Wilde presents an incredible array of souls: one
character will sell his soul, another will lose it and then find
it again and festoon it with noble virtues as a mistress is
hung with jewels. The word 'Soul' was so beautiful in
Oscar's ears that he could not resist continually repeating it,

but so much soul ended by being slightly nauseating, meaningless even, especially when used by someone who took such trouble to feed and adorn and give pleasure to his fourteen stones of flesh. This excessive harping on the soul together with a style which was carefully tailored to suit the drawing-room, gave to the fables when written down an antiquated and somewhat musty flavour, although when spoken aloud they were usually saved by the ingeni-ousness of their invention as well as by the perfect delivery. They are like rich brocade which has been exposed to the sun, whose design can still be admired although the gold has darkened and the purple faded; but these stories now have no more than a period charm. Those who heard them maintained that the speaker spoiled the effect by adding purple passages, like a famous actor inclined to use too much make-up. The use of the Biblical 'thee' and 'thou', the images taken from the Song of Solomon, were like rouge and eye-black in sacred productions which were to become more and more bizarre and jarring. In the fables the disciple is St. John the Baptist, and Oscar himself the Master of Wisdom. M. Edouard Roditi has pointed out that this mixture of neo-classicism and orientalism recalls a pre-descessor of Wilde's, von Platen, who summed up the fate of aesthetes in a line: 'He who has looked at Beauty face to face, pledges himself to death.'

12 The ivory tower

The teaching of a master, however charming he may be, is bound to be dogmatic to some extent. Wilde, who had started with examples, stories and fables arrived, in about 1887, at theory. This theory was Art for Art's Sake. He did not invent it, but he made it available for women and young artists without vulgarising it. It can be seen in his articles, which were in fact 'pot-boilers' but which helped to form his style. Like his conversation, and like some of Whistler's essays, they were rich in alliteration: '. . . the union of the personality and perfection', and in puns, as in the heavily humorous criticism of a mock-heroic poem called The Chronicle of Mites, about the inhabitants of a decaying cheese; Oscar wrote: 'This cheese epic is a rather unsavoury production and the style is at all times so monstrous and so realistic that the author should be called the Gorgon-Zola of literature.'

Already in his Oxford days Oscar had tried his hand at a long essay, as well as a long poem, but The Rise of Historical Criticism, which has only recently come to light, did not have the success of Ravenna. It is an extremely serious essay, as was only to be expected from a young man enthusiastic about a new science, and Oscar had wide knowledge. In it he analyses as had Herodotus and, even more so, Polybius how legend becomes history. He quotes abundantly from Herbert Spencer, Montesquieu, Victor Cousin and Tocqueville, and then heightens the solemnity with short quotations in French (which may have been his own inventions) such as 'Only Art must be asked of Art, only the Past of the Past.'

In these pages Wilde is nearer to Renan, of whom he knew through Mahaffy, than to 'dear wonderful Ruskin' – much admired but seldom listened to. Thus he wrote: 'The only spirit which is entirely removed from us is the Mediaeval; the Greek spirit is essentially modern.'

This arbitrary expression of his views was at least justified by his style, which was better suited to evoke the solid beauties of flesh or of bronze than to follow languidly the Botticellian contours representing souls. Thus the fables, and, as we shall see, the stories, brimming over with soul, are less well written than the essays, the tone of which is not unlike Fontenelle's elegant conversations on scientific subjects. This is not surprising in someone whose taste had been moulded at Trinity College by the classically-minded Mahaffy. As to the inspiration, it derived from Pater, who had written in his *Renaissance*: 'What is important, then, is not that the critic should possess a correct abstract distinction of beauty for the intellect, but a certain kind of tempera-ment, the power of being deeply moved by the presence of beautiful objects.' Like Goethe, Wilde was to speak of Beauty in concrete terms. What he wished for was that Greek or mediaeval thought should be revived with the addition of the acuteness of modern life. He soon abandoned the idea of modernity, which had made such a good effect in his lectures on decorative art, for a criticism more subjective and poetic, that of Baudelaire or Proust, owing more to con-templation than to fashion. Wilde's poetic vision allowed him to collect in one essay, itself a work of art, his impres-sions of disparate works of art; memories of lectures on subjects ranging from Plotinus to Kant and Schiller. He was never boring because his dogmatism was less that of a professional pedant than the insolence of a dandy intro-ducing a waistcoat of a new cut. His doubt was not meta-physical but irreverent. By mockery he attacked the values of an era which was very sure of itself; but eventually this irony was to be as much frowned upon as a heresy. Fundamentally, he preferred to instil doubts into the minds of his disciples in order that they should acquire self-knowledge, rather than to unravel the truth for them.

The volume published under the name *Intentions* in May 1891 was composed of four essays: *The Decay of Lying*; *The Critic as Artist*; *Pen, Pencil and Poison* and *The Truth of Masks*. The first two, written in 1889 and 1890, are the most important and contain the fruits of a hundred conversations in studies and in smoking-rooms.

Determined to hide the serious side of these essays under a flowery prose, the new Plato chose the form of a dialogue between master and disciple (Robbie Ross disguised as a young man of fashion) in the setting of a comedy; a library in a great house, a drawing-room looking out on to the Green Park with decorative objects scattered about; a piano on which to play Chopin, a supper enlivened by Chambertin – as if to justify Wilde's remark: 'The future belongs to the Dandy.'

Oscar succeeded in irritating serious people by the content of his essays. In the longest one, *The Critic as Artist*, the speakers pay each other a number of compliments: 'Ernest, you are quite delightful.' 'A charming doctrine, Gilbert', and make such remarks as 'that the desire to do good to others produces a plentiful supply of prigs is the least of the evils of which it is the cause'. 'We watch ourselves, and the mere wonder of the spectacle enthralls us.' 'I am the only person in the world I should like to know thoroughly, but I don't see any chance of it just at the present.' Frivolity in aesthetics appeared an inadmissible buffoonery. Moralistic novelists, sentimental painters and serious university professors were horrified to read that: 'We are born in an age when only the dull are taken seriously, and I live in terror of not being misunderstood.' 'It is always with the best intentions that the worst work is done.' 'Anybody can write a three-volumed novel. It merely requires a complete ignorance of both life and literature.'

Wilde's enemies were boredom and pretentiousness, and he had a particular hatred for journalists who, he thought, vulgarised this boredom: 'By giving us the opinions of the uneducated, it keeps us in touch with the ignorance of the community. By carefully chronicling the current events of contemporary life, it shows us of what very little importance such events really are. By invariably discussing the un-necessary, it makes us understand what things are requisite for culture and what are not.' Thus he generously provided anyone who wished to attack him with weapons. And the best of it was that he wrote this at the time when Gordon had died conquering the Sudan and was still a national hero, and everywhere in the world thousands of soldiers, missionaries and business men were waving the Union Jack. In any case, no one could be taken seriously who wrote: 'When a man acts he is a puppet. When he describes he is a poet.' 'Action is limited and relative. Unlimited and absolute is the vision of him who sits at ease and watches, who walks in loneliness and dreams.' In this one can recognise the influence of the Chinese sage Chuang Tzŭ-Sen, on whom he wrote an article in The Speaker, pointing out his creed of inaction and showing the uselessness of useful things. Another oriental influence can probably be attributed to that strange woman Madame Blavatsky, founder of the Theo-sophical Society in New York: 'Don't talk about action. It is a blind thing dependent on external influences, and moved by an impulse of whose nature it is unconscious. It is a thing incomplete in its essence, because limited by accident, and ignorant of its direction, because always at variance

with its aim. Its basis is the lack of imagination. It is the
last resource of those who know not how to dream.'

These verbal clouds hid reality as, in a Chinese picture,
the mist blurs the trees and rocks, and they surrounded the
Ivory Tower, the refuge of the artist – Pater's 'Palace of the
Arts'. If there was not enough mist, the sharp outlines had
to be blurred by vague ideas and sentences flexible as a
riband. Then, in a flash of lightning, the poet looks out
through a gap in the battlements and lets fly a few arrows
at reality (that is to say, at contemporaries who had kept
their feet more firmly on the ground). Luckily, in Wilde's
tower, laughter and good living were enjoyed, but the
ethereal and slightly scornful manner of the Master set its
stamp on a whole generation of would-be aesthetes around
1900; the best example of these is Legrandin, the social-
climbing aesthete of *A la recherche du temps perdu*. If one has
the courage to throw oneself into the works of Jean Lahor,
the writer on whom the character of Legrandin is partly
based, one would understand that only Wilde's insolence
made his aesthetic pose acceptable. It is tempting to write
'Humbug' in the margin of a sentence which trails on as
does the following: 'The longer I study, Ernest, the more
clearly I see that the beauty of the visible arts is, as the
beauty of music, impressive primarily, and that it may be
marred, and indeed often is so, by any excess of intellectual
intention on the part of the artist.' Many passages in these
essays are recipes from Swinburne or from Baudelaire, re-
written by the Mrs. Beeton of the Ivory Tower: take two
lines of Baudelaire, a reproduction of Leonardo . . . certain
passages are frankly pagan and were borrowed from the
Gautier of *Mademoiselle de Maupin*: 'My rebellious body does
not want to recognise the supremacy of the soul and my
flesh does not agree to being mortified. I find the earth as
beautiful as the sky. . . .' One recognises, as seasoning, the

apologia of Fatal Beauty, and Pater's 'exquisite passions'. All this delighted the aesthetes, because their Ivory Tower was very comfortable and not like the cells for guilty monks offered by the romantics. What reassuring phrases: 'What is termed Sin is an essential element of progress . . . by its curiosity Sin increases the experience of the race.' Wilde was to confess later: 'Paradox was for me in thought what perversion was in passion.' That is to say, an effort to escape from the tyranny of facts. Wilde's essays are much read abroad (At last an aesthetic work which does not appear to be translated from the German!). But university professors, whose aridity the author had emphasised, were avenged in a book called *Degeneration*, written by a German critic Max Nordau,* which was often to be quoted after the collapse of the Ivory Tower: 'the ego-mania of decadence, its love of the artificial, its aversion to nature, and to all forms of activity and movement, its megalomaniacal contempt for men and its exaggeration of the importance of art, have found this English representation among the aesthetes, the chief of whom is Oscar Wilde.

'Wilde has done more by his personal eccentricity than by his works. Like Barbey d'Aurevilly, whose rose-coloured silk hats and gold lace cravats are well known, like his disciple Joséphin Péladan, who walks about in lace frills and satin doublet, Wilde dresses in queer costumes which recall partly the fashions of the Middle Ages, partly the rococo modes . . . the predilection for strange costume is a pathological aberration of a racial instinct . . .

'When, therefore, an Oscar Wilde goes about in "aesthetic costume" among gazing Philistines, exciting either their ridicule or their wrath, it is no indication of independence of character, but rather for a purely anti-socialistic, egomaniacal recklessness and hysterical longing to make a

* Translated from the German in 1895.

sensation; justified by no exalted aim; nor is it from a strong
desire for beauty but from a malevolent mania for contradiction . . . the doctrine of the Aesthete affirms with the
Parnassians that the work of art is its own aim; with the
Diabolists that it need not be moral – nay, were better to
be immoral; with the Decadents that it is to avoid, and be
diametrically opposed to, the natural and the true; and with
all these schools of the ego-mania of degeneration, that art
is the highest of all human functions.'

The Decay of Lying, published in the January 1889 edition
of The Nineteenth Century, spread the influence of the lectures.
It has been shown how the quarrel with Whistler had
excited much argument on this theme – an important one
for the art of the time. The philosopher in his essay encouraged artists to break away from the realism which twenty
years earlier had nearly nipped the development of romantic
art in England. He pointed out that salvation lay in an
imaginary world, that of Burne-Jones or Gustave Moreau,
but his lessons only had an important effect on the decorative arts. The art historians saw Wilde as the master of the
first phase of Art Nouveau; they called it the 'Studio Style'
from the name of the magazine, which was imitated in
Germany by Pan or Jugend which disseminated throughout middle-class circles the Chelsea taste – the Arts and
Crafts style. Oscar himself was slightly Victorian in his
weakness for the picturesque; the real Art Nouveau was
more sparse. But he defined the decoration of the Ivory
Tower and of so many other buildings which were to be
the answer to Brussels or to Vienna, when he expressed his
conviction that art is at the same time surface and creed.
'The simple colour which does not spoil any meaning
independent of a definite form, speaks to the soul in a
thousand ways. The harmony that a delicate proportion of
line can give is reflected in the mind.' Wilde was too much

of a humanist to turn his back on the masterpieces of the
past; he did not make a clean sweep; but he chose that
which appealed most to the imagination, and above all he
wanted to draw wonderful curtains, the floral design of
which would cut him off from the world of Zola or of
Dickens swarming at the foot of the Tower. Artists were to
paint their visions on the curtains while waiting until the
windows could be opened to see the Blue Bird fly past.

These dreams did not prevent a certain wisdom from
emerging, as for example in the following passage in The
Critic as Artist: 'For, when the ideal is realised, it is robbed of
its wonder and its mystery, and becomes simply a new
starting-point for an ideal that is other than itself. This is
the reason why music is the perfect type of art. Music can
never reveal its ultimate secret.' Being not in the least degree
musical, Wilde was to write: 'Music is the most expensive
of all noises.' Like his contemporary Gauguin, before Hugo
von Hofmannsthal and after Baudelaire, he hoped for a link
between the plastic arts and music. Was it not the period
when Whistler called his pictures Nocturnes and Symphonies? It is certain that Rodin read Intentions, as many of
its ideas can be recognised in his conversations on art. In
Imaginary Lives the symbolist Marcel Schwob wrote like
Wilde: 'Art is opposed to general ideas, it describes only
the individual, wishes only for the unique. . . . It does not
classify; it declassifies. . . .'

Wilde is also important because he popularised William
Blake, already dear to the Pre-Raphaelites, whose flowing
line was so much a feature of Art Nouveau. He quoted Blake
the visionary: 'The imagination is the only real and eternal
world, of which our vegetable world is but a pale shadow.'
He inserts another line of Blake's in the sentence so typical
of the year 1900 which ends The Decay of Lying: '. . . And now
let us go out on to the terrace, where "droops the milk-

white peacock like a ghost", while the evening star "washes the dusk with silver". At twilight nature becomes a wonderfully suggestive effect, and is not without loveliness, though perhaps its chief use is to illustrate quotations from the poets.'

The Ivory Tower was founded on a library; the books were the bastions behind which the inhabitants were entrenched and from there, when necessary, the artist would launch some conclusive and irrefutable argument. Certain Towers, that of Pater for example, were made of books with not even the smallest window giving on to the world. The writers of the last century, Flaubert and Hugo, had immense libraries behind them. However for Wilde, so much learning must be justified by a masterpiece – hence the following: 'And who does not feel that the chief glory of Piranesi's book on Vases is that it gave Keats the suggestion for his *Ode on a Grecian Urn*?' Oscar himself burrowed among his books like an epicure descending into his cellar to bring up a rare and dusty bottle. From 1885 he had lent his knowledge to Godwin the architect and Lady Archie Campbell, who, it will be recalled, had produced *As You Like It* with costumes so authentic that the actual materials used for them were raw hide and wool. They were right, Oscar maintained, against the opinion of his friend Lord Lytton who had thought that the dresses needed only to be beautiful and more or less in period. Be that as it may, it is curious to find the champion of the imagination insisting on the importance of the smallest historical detail, and repeatedly referring to Shakespeare's own directions. The most learned of dons could not have produced a more convincing thesis than *The Truth of Masks*, but he would not have ended up by admitting with the incorrigible Oscar: 'Not that I agree with everything that I have said in this essay. There is much with which I entirely disagree. The essay simply represents an artistic standpoint, and in aesthetic criticism attitude is everything.'

Still on the subject of Shakespeare, Wilde invented one of his best tales, *The Portrait of Mr. W.H.*, which was to be published among the stories, but its style, a conversation between two close friends, resembled that of *The Decay of Lying*. It is suffused with the platonic atmosphere which, according to Wilde, prevailed at the time of Elizabeth I, sanctioning the love of a poet for a young actor, and which he maintained still prevailed at Oxford. Some of the most cultivated men, including Arthur Balfour, were convinced when Oscar expounded to them his theory about the sonnets: 'Had Mr. W.H. not made Shakespeare suffer, we should not possess the *Sonnets*, and England would be glad.' Wilde played down his erudition with frivolity, and with his graceful easy manner taught a lesson to the pedants who did not agree with his brilliant explanation. For Oscar to take an interest in his hero, it was absolutely necessary that he should be handsome and that the story should end unhappily. A portrait of Mr. W.H. was actually painted in the manner of Clouet by Oscar's friend Charles Ricketts. The half-serious essay was one of the imaginary portraits that the aesthetes, disheartened by reality, hung on the walls of the Ivory Tower; there were those of Pater, and there were to be those of Marcel Schwob. In *The Portrait of Mr. W.H.*, Oscar identified himself with the author of the *Sonnets*.

In another essay called *Pen, Pencil and Poison – a Study in Green*, he analysed in depth a much less brilliant person – a criminal whom, nonetheless, he succeeds in making amusing, because in the murderer he saw himself reflected, or rather, he made of him the St. John the Baptist of that typically Wildeian legend on which he was beginning to work – Thomas Griffiths Wainewright, Byronian aesthete, murderer of his wife's mother, his sister-in-law and his uncle,

N

but also a passable art critic, had, sixty years before Wilde's essay was written, astonished London by his wit and his follies.

Pen, Pencil and Poison is a plea in his defence; although Oscar would never have hurt a fly, his tastes gave him a lively sense of guilt. Wilde deals lightly with the crimes and seriously with Wainewright's writings; for the first time he clearly defines in this essay his theories on life: 'This young dandy sought to be somebody, rather than to do something. He recognised that Life itself is an art, and has its modes of style no less than the arts that seek to express it.' How much he had in common with Wilde: 'He loves Greek gems, and Persian carpets, and Elizabethan translations . . . and book-bindings, and early editions, and wide-margined proofs. He is keenly sensitive to the value of beautiful surroundings, and never wearies of describing to us the rooms in which he lived or would have liked to live. He had that curious love of green, which in individuals is always the sign of a subtle artistic temperament, and in nations is said to denote a laxity, if not a decadence of morals. Like Baudelaire he was extremely fond of cats, and with Gautier, he was fascinated by that "sweet marble monster", of both sexes [the Hermaphrodite], that we can still see at Florence and in the Louvre.' This sympathy for a murderer reveals Oscar's sense of guilt towards society: 'Janus Weathercock, Egomet Bonmot and Van Vinkvooms, were some of the grotesque masks under which he chose to hide his seriousness or to reveal his levity. A mask tells us more than a face. These disguises intensified his personality', wrote the author of The Truth of Masks. Masks were much worn in the Symbolist movement, and Schwob and Lorrain frequently gave them to their heroes. Aesthetes often need them when they slip out-side the Ivory Towers to find beauties of flesh and bone. The styles of the poet and of the murderer were related; Wainewright was 'the pioneer of Asiatic prose, and delighted in pictorial epithets and pompous exaggerations'. Even his humour is Wildeian; when reproached for having murdered one of his relatives, he said: 'Yes; it was a dreadful thing to do, but she had very thick ankles.' Oscar admired the audacity of the murderer who had insured his sister-in-law's life for £18,000, before he killed her. The insurance company had suspected something and refused to pay, whereupon Wainewright sued them and lost the case. Later he was arrested for forgery and deported to Australia: 'this sentence . . . was to a man of his culture a form of death', said the future prisoner of Reading Gaol, and continued: 'There is, however, something dramatic in the fact that this heavy punishment was inflicted on him for what, if we remember his fatal influence on the prose of modern journalism, was certainly not the worst of all his sins.'

Ever since these dialogues had appeared, Wilde felt himself to be threatened by everything that was most boring in England; it was only a step to being taken for a Socrates. To floor his enemies he wrote The Soul of Man under Socialism, and it appeared in February 1891 in The Fortnightly Review. Perhaps he was tempted to play the part of a Tolstoy – the 'soul' was then very much in fashion in Russia. In any case, he suppressed the Egyptian cigarettes and the 'oh, my dears' in this important essay, he was much more dogmatic, and showed himself very much the son of the revolutionary Speranza; the fervent reader of Victor Hugo's Les Châtiments retained a romantic idea about agitators. Had he not gone bail for John Barlas, a poet whom Oscar had met at New College, a Scot and anarchist who had fired a shot at the Houses of Parliament? He wanted to do away with the property and marriage laws, and all that atrophies the personality; nevertheless, strongly though he expressed his horror of the capitalistic world, it was more because it offended his sensibilities than from feelings of charity. As is known, he had a kind heart, and it was with verve rather than resentment that he denounced the stupidity of the propertied classes regardless of those who entertained him: 'The true perfection of man lies not in what man has, but in what man is.' Even Oscar the reformer could not prevent himself from being amusing: 'Property not merely has duties, but has so many duties that its possession to any large extent is a bore. . . . If property had simply pleasures, we could stand it, but its duties make it unbearable. In the interest of the rich we must get rid of it.' He could be as severe about power as about money. '. . . all authority is quite degrading. It degrades those who exercise it, and degrades those over whom it is exercised. When it is violently, grossly, and cruelly used, it produces a good effect, by creating, or at any rate bringing out, the spirit of revolt and Individualism that is to kill it. When it is used with a certain amount of kindness, and is accompanied by prizes and rewards, it is dreadfully demoralising.' In this he leaned towards nihilism.

These paradoxes did not amuse the Prince of Wales and his millionaire friends, but philanthropists and young Socialists such as Bernard Shaw were none too pleased either when they read: 'There is only one class in the community that thinks more about money than the rich, and that is the poor. The poor can think of nothing else. That is the misery of being poor.' 'To recommend thrift to the poor is both grotesque and insulting. It is like advising a man who is starving to eat less.' The writer is much nearer to the generosity of Prince Peter Kropotkin who had made such a great impression on him when they met at William Morris' house; this Russian author and anarchist was imprisoned for his political views and actions, and Oscar wrote: 'Two of the most perfect lives I have come across . . . are . . .

Verlaine and Prince Kropotkin.' A Wilde of today would have spoken of 'alienation' – (that is to say, he would have chosen another word) – to express Wilde's dictum: 'Man is made for something better than disturbing dust.' He stated that machines should be for the service of workers and not in competition with them. Perhaps he envisaged an Ivory Tower when he wrote that, 'enjoying cultivated leisure . . . and not labour, is the aim of man . . .'. Here again he levelled his attacks at journalists, coming back to the adjective 'unhealthy' which had been applied to his works by the newspapers: 'An unhealthy work of art, on the other hand, is a work whose style obvious, old-fashioned and common, and whose subject is deliberately chosen, not because the artist has any pleasure in it, but because he thinks that the public will pay him for it.' Literature played a large part in this essay, and, he affirmed, would save the world. This point of view was one of the reasons that the work was not taken seriously by the disciples of Karl Marx; the other reason was the attitude so well summed up by Tomaso d'Amico: 'In Wilde's lectures, as in the teachings of Ruskin and Morris, Art has an important social function; it helps to make life agreeable. In this essay, the method is reversed. It is life which should be reorganised in order to procure the best conditions for the development of Art.' The essay resulted in Wilde's being taken for a revolutionary writer in Russia, but that was many years before the Revolution.

After having set the fashion in decoration, Wilde wanted to set the fashion in thought while, of course, remaining charming. His disciples saw him now as Christ, now as Plato, but he was really more of a Scheherazade, ceaselessly weaving a marvellous tapestry of stories and thoughts, to stave off for yet another day that miniature form of death known as boredom.

13 Scheherazade in the country

A drawing-room with windows overlooking the Parc Monceau was the forcing-house of the French novelist, a large park surrounding a country house was that in which the English novel was cultivated. The French system was rapid, the length of an afternoon call, the English method longer, it took a week-end. Certainly Zola and Dickens escaped these conventions, but then they did not keep the same company as Paul Bourget and Henry James. Oscar did not like the country; 'I am afraid I play no outdoor games except . . . yes . . . except dominoes. I have sometimes played dominoes outside French cafés.' He did not venture his grey spats beyond the terrace at tea-time; while the men hunted or shot and the women went for walks with their admirers, he would shut himself in the library to appear at five o'clock, deliciously urban in his grey morning coat. He might have paid compliments such as: 'What a divine tea-gown, Lady Lonsdale, promise to give me some of the material so that I can have a waistcoat made out of it'; 'Dear, Miss Mary, there is something about your complexion that tells me you have returned from the walk nearly engaged.' One hour before dinner, every one disappeared, to return in fullest finery. The professional beauty never failed to make an entrance that would dazzle the country neighbours. Oscar would whisper to the lady he was escorting in the procession to the dining-room: 'There has not been a scandal in the neighbourhood since the time of Queen Elizabeth and consequently they all fall asleep after dinner. They get up early because they have so much to do, and go to bed early because they have so little to think about.' When Oscar was present it can be imagined how stupefied the male guests must have been when he pronounced his famous definition of hunting: 'The English country gentleman galloping after a fox – the unspeakable in pursuit of the uneatable.' Oscar's shining hour was after dinner, it was then that 'he sang for his supper', as it were, with the most brilliant conversational flights. It is not known how many country houses he visited because, after the scandal, many of the writers of memoirs deliberately forgot the name of one who had been a magnet to attract fashionable women, when cards were sent with the words 'To meet Mr. Oscar Wilde'. He was often the guest of the Duchess of Westminster at Eaton Hall, the enormous Neo-Gothic palace where parties of forty guests would be entertained, each with valet or ladies' maid. He is known to have visited other great houses, such as Warwick Castle, where the burly frame of the Prince of Wales would be shaken by Olympian laughter at such sallies as, 'It is only by not paying one's bills that one can hope to live in the memory of the commercial classes.' 'You said something wonderful about morality this morning.' 'Thank you Sir. Morality is simply the attitude we adopt towards people whom we personally dislike. I am sure Your Royal Highness will agree when I add that the English have a miraculous power of turning wine into water.' 'Excellent! my dear Wilde, excellent, really remarkable,' would comment the Prince of Wales, rolling his r's, and no doubt reflecting that he had often had his pleasures hampered by the puritanism of his future subjects.

Wilde succeeded in the difficult feat of talking scandal without being spiteful; thus he invented the story about Lady St. Helier who gave dinner parties to all who had the slightest claim to celebrity: 'An explorer lost his way in the middle of Africa and fell into the hands of a fierce tribe who were about to eat him' – at this point Oscar added a long and picturesque description of the ingredients that were being prepared – 'the Chief appeared in order to judge the weight of the joint, but the moment he saw the explorer he cried, "But I have already had the pleasure of meeting you at Lady St. Helier's, will you dine with me and take pot luck, the cook seems to be almost ready".'

He was also brilliant at literary games, such as one recalled by Lady Desborough, in which the players had 'to compose an imaginary letter from a woman thanking a man for flowers when she wasn't quite certain whether he had sent them or not'. For forty-eight hours, therefore, Oscar was the most marvellous entertainment that could be offered to a surfeited public, but this entailed a certain effort. Laurence Housman in *Echos de Paris* recalls being told by Wilde of how he had spent a week-end at a ducal country house, enter-taining the guests and how, missing an early train on Mon-day morning, he had been compelled to return for a time before another was due: 'The exhibition hours of the Duke were over,' said Wilde, 'and it was a charnel house – the bones of its skeleton rattled; the ghosts gibbered and moaned. Time remained motionless. I was haunted. I could never go there again. I had seen what man is never meant to see – the sweeping up of the dust on which the footfall of departing pleasure has left its print. There, for two days I had been creating my public . . . the breath of life I had so laboriously breathed into their nostrils, they were getting rid of again, returning to native clay. . . .' Although this was a perfectly truthful picture, the incident was also described to Laurence Housman by one of the family. 'Oscar missed his train and had to come back and wait for the next – and it was he who was the extinct volcano with all the fire gone out of him. He could no longer talk, he was played out; his powers of performance were over.'

When Oscar was invited to a great country house, it was not so much from snobbishness nor from a taste for luxury that he derived pleasure but because he found in those surroundings inspiration for many of his stories, and he was sensitive to an atmosphere which had remained unchanged, perhaps for two hundred years. In England it is difficult to differentiate between legend and history, each portrait suggests a ghost, and the Irishman was determined to believe everything he was told. He encouraged the neighbours to talk, he listened to the dowagers like a good child listening to a long fairy story. The immense riches of the English nobility gave rise to a whole mythology of eccentricity. For example, when Oscar visited Deepdene, which belonged to Mr. Henry Thomas Hope, whose grandson became the eighth Duke of Newcastle, he might have been shown the famous Hope Diamond, which was reputed to bring disaster on its owner, and at Welbeck Abbey he heard that the Duke of Portland had not only built himself a subterranean palace but was said to have led the life of a small grocer during the week and that of a great landowner only from Saturday to Monday. Yet another duke's eccentricities were so marked that he was suspected of being the untraced murderer, Jack the Ripper.

Side by side with the fantastic, there was much that was ludicrous in a society which used its wealth principally to alleviate boredom; the memoirs of the period abound with descriptions of preposterous episodes, which must have enchanted Oscar. Apart from the usual pastimes of cards, playing the piano and gossip, there were also practical jokes to bring a little of the unexpected into otherwise well-ordered lives. Augustus Hare, an habitual country house guest, tells in his book *For My Solitary Life*, of one

of these: 'Lord Devon's only son, Lord Courtenay, is seldom
here but when he is he amuses everyone. One evening
Mademoiselle Bekker arrived late at Powderham, coming in
the hope of enlisting a chairman for a meeting which was
going to be held at Exeter in favour of Rights for Women.
There was a distinguished party which included the Bishop
of Winchester, Lord Halifax, and the American Minister
etc., and they each, while refusing, made a speech in answer
to hers, which was most eloquent. Eventually Mademoiselle
Bekker declared herself so indignant as to be led to un-sex
herself – she was Lord Courtenay.'

One can well imagine the use to which Oscar would put
such absurdities! Very different was the atmosphere of
Babbacombe, the house of Lady Mount Temple overlooking
Torbay. There the fantastic had a quality of poetry about it.
Lady Mount Temple was a charming old lady, widow of a
politician, and confidante of Ruskin in his love for Rose
La Touche. She was a distant cousin of Constance, but the real
bond between the two women was spiritualism. Both were
followers of Madame Blavatsky, and conversed familiarly
with 'the other world'. The house had been built at the
height of the Pre-Raphaelite enthusiasm, and had something magical about it; over the door of each bedroom was
the name of the flower which decorated its William Morris
wallpaper, and the drawing-room, hung with Rossetti's masterpiece, 'Beata Beatrix', and many of Burne-Jones' pictures,
was called Wonderland. The park ran down to the beach,
which pleased Wilde who was as good a swimmer as he
was a bad walker. One could also put to sea with the fishermen of Torquay. At Babbacombe, Oscar showed himself an
attentive husband and a charming father. It was an ideal 'Ivory
Tower' atmosphere, and it should have inspired him to write.

Ever since their publication, Wilde's sentimental

stories have never ceased to sell to a wide public, perhaps because they offer in a soothing form ideas which appealed to the decadents, and also because grown-up people sometimes like to be treated as if they are children. Children, on the other hand, did not like them much because the miracles always conveyed a moral. Pater's influence pervades the stories, as a lily will flower in strange colours if transplanted to a soil containing phosphorus. In Pater's works and in those of Wilde the equivocal and the sacrilegious were always veiled; the foot of the devil could only be glimpsed disappearing down the colonnade of the cloister.

The first collection of stories, *The Happy Prince and Other Tales* (which included *The Nightingale and the Rose*, *The Selfish Giant*, *The Devoted Friend* and *The Remarkable Rocket*) was published in 1888. *The House of Pomegranates* containing *The Birthday of the Infanta*, *The Fisherman and His Soul*, *The Star Child*, was published in 1891. The heroes of the stories derived their appearance, their palaces, and their jewels from the paintings of Watts and Burne-Jones. In these, Botticelli's Florence merged with Memling's Bruges; mediaeval graces adorned antiquities whose models were more likely to be found on the Thames embankment than on the banks of the Nile. The stories abound with the characters so dear to the Pre-Raphaelites – magicians, young knights in silver armour, beautiful beggars and golden-haired pages. Each story is an imaginary portrait, a poetic commentary in the margin of a legend. As an actor chooses armour or a fan from a vast wardrobe, so Oscar delved into his literary memories for Dante's hood or Shakespeare's ruff. To illustrate his tales the poet chose Charles Ricketts and Charles Shannon, young men whose lineal compositions were already entirely Art Nouveau.

The touching climaxes in these stories appear a little insipid today, but they gave pleasure to a romantic

generation. Poetic charity in the style of St. Francis of
Assisi was acceptable to English readers lulled in the com-
forts of the Established Church, but it was as artificial as the
perversities of the end of the century. It was a Christmas
message tinged with Socialism for the benefit of future boy
scouts. The Young King who renounced his wonderful
ornaments because so many poor working men had toiled
to produce them, Wilde's favourite story, tended towards
an aesthetic anarchism. But the plots of the fables came from
sources very different from the Oxford idea of the Middle
Ages or the Byzantium of Montmartre. Rather, they came
from the most guileless of sources – Hans Andersen, and it
was a Wildeian flight of fancy to deck The Little Mermaid with
Sarah Bernhardt's jewels. He had not only imitated Andersen's famous stories, but he had also parodied Flaubert's
St. Julien l'hospitalier in The Star Child; and he borrowed from
Adalbert de Chamisso the idea of a man being separated
from his shadow, in The Fisherman and His Soul. The Birthday of
the Infanta came from Hugo's La Légende des Siècles. But Wilde,
the story-teller, was to be no less copied in his turn by a
host of minor French imitators.

Their moral, always without illusions, was that of the
discouraging proverb: 'Virtue is its own reward'. In The
Happy Prince, the swallow who took the jewels to the poor,
died of cold, and the statue melted; the nightingale's
sacrifice of its life-blood in order to stain the rose red was
useless because the young girl made fun of the boy. If good
triumphs, it is not for long – Death soon prevails. But
Death always brought with it a serene beauty, as in The Star
Child which, like Dorian Gray, represents destructive beauty.
In these symbolical works Love is always like a fairy sister
to the Fata Morgana celebrated by Swinburne and painted by
Rossetti; voluptuous and fatal, crowned with poppies, she
represents a nostalgia for paganism in the same way that all

allusions to St. Francis of Assisi come from a yearning for Catholicism.

These stories were written and first invented for fashionable ladies with beautiful houses and souls; they were in fact dedicated to Princess Alice of Monaco, to Margot Tennant, who became Mrs. Asquith, and to Mrs. William Grenfell, later Lady Desborough. But his favourite, The Young King, he offered to a woman whose lot had been particularly romantic. Margaret, Lady Brooke, the Ranee of Sarawak, and wife of the only English rajah, was a great friend of Constance; she was also an ardent admirer of Gustave Moreau, whom she frequently visited in Paris. It would not be difficult to portray this story in the style of a picture by Moreau; the half-naked adolescent amongst all the gold and incense of a ceremony – a distant memory of the Oxford choir-boys. Because of his admiration of the dresses of his great friends, Wilde introduced notes of high fashion into literature. The Birthday of the Infanta, conceived in 'Black and Silver' he complained when translated into French 'had come out Pink and Blue'.

If the dialogues and prose poems were conceived after luncheons at the Café Royal, the stories were evolved in the evenings in the country. In the library after dinner with a dozen or so guests grouped around him, here and there a piece of armour or a mirror or a curious picture catching the light of the oil-lamp, the writer, whose wit had animated the dinner, would give a recital, like some celebrated but friendly pianist moving over to the piano. Indeed, some of Oscar's stories are actually reminiscent of Chopin, his favourite composer.

Like the good improviser he was, Wilde used tricks dear to the story-tellers of old. He put words into the mouths of animals, but instead of rustic metamorphoses he made the

farm-yard talk in the style of the drawing-room. His geese
had the intelligence of dowagers, dogs the profundity of
diplomats, and the hen's repartees were worthy of Sheridan.
Thus the *Remarkable Rocket* experiences all the adventures
of a pretentious débutante.

In the second volume two long short stories – *Lord Arthur
Savile's Crime* and *The Canterville Ghost* – retain a sophisticated
style, but lack the moralising of the first stories. Oscar, as
has been said, found his inspiration during his visits to
country houses. He wanted to believe in all ghosts, but his
superstition rapidly gave way to his sense of fun. This
aspect of Wilde is far superior to the sentimental one:
when laughter penetrates the aesthetic fog, the style pruned
of purple passages loses its ridiculousness and, better still,
there is no question of a soul. Essentially worldly, the characters of these stories have emblems which also pleased
Oscar – crowns and diadems. Snobbery gaily took the place
of sentimentality. Wilde envisaged bejewelled dowagers as
animated Carabosses, the beautiful friends of the Prince of
Wales as fairies and the debonair royal Prince himself
as Prince Charming. He fell just as easily into comedy when
writing *Lord Arthur Savile's Crime* – and half a century later
this same humour, half black and half rose-coloured
humour, was to be found in the film *Kind Hearts and Coronets*.
The charming Edwardian humorist Saki was indebted to
these stories for the idea of the practical joke, and for the
paradoxes which appeared in them for the first time and
were later to be found in the plays: 'The world is a stage,
but the play is badly cast.' *The Canterville Ghost* (published in
Court and Society Review in 1887) is the origin of René Clair's
film *Fantôme à vendre*. It is written in the tradition of the
popular *Ingoldsby Legends* and is a parody of the black novels
of 1820. When a collection of stories was published in
1891, it included *The Sphinx without a Secret*.

Oscar had a strong feeling about Sphinxes. He had worked on a poem called *The Sphinx* ever since Oxford and soon he was to have a real Sphinx in his life; as so often happens, fiction created reality. To tell of this it will be necessary to anticipate a little. At a party in 1892 he met a young woman who hid intelligence and a tender heart under a frivolous manner; Oscar adored her at once and called her The Sphinx. Mrs. Ernest Leverson is a link with the world of Proust: her sister and brother-in-law, Violet and Sidney Schiff (who wrote under the name of Stephen Hudson) were great friends of Proust. After the death of C. M. Scott-Moncrieff, Sidney Schiff completed the English translation of *A la recherche du temps perdu*. Mrs. Leverson belonged by birth and marriage to the elegant Jewish cosmopolitan and cultivated society of the time and could be compared to Madame Straus in Paris, in whose *salon* Proust started his social career. Her wit conditioned her ideally to respond to Wilde's light-heartedness, his particular form of gaiety illuminated by genius. Her eyes were blue-grey, her nose aquiline and her skin pale; she wore her fair hair in a fringe and many saw in her a likeness both to Ellen Terry and Sarah Bernhardt. Oscar discovered that some sketches and parodies appearing anonymously in *Punch* were by Ada. Later, in July 1893, he wrote: 'Your sketch is brilliant as your work always is. It is quite tragic for me to think how completely *Dorian Gray* has been understood on all sides! Why don't you collect your wonderful witty, delightful sketches – so slight, so suggestive, so full, of *esprit* and intellectual sympathy? You are one of those who, in art, are always, by intuition, behind the scenes, so you see how natural art is.'

She was to write of him, 'I had been told that he was rather like a giant with the wings of a Brazilian butterfly and was not disappointed. But I thought him far more like a Roman Emperor who should have lived at the Pavilion at Brighton with George IV.'

The Green Carnation, published anonymously in September 1894, was a novel in which the two principal characters were recognisable portraits of Oscar and Lord Alfred Douglas. Many suspected Ada Leverson of being the author, but before long it was discovered that it had been written by Robert Hichens. In a letter from Worthing, Oscar wrote to her, '. . . of course you have been deeply wronged. But there are many bits in The Green Carnation not unworthy of your brilliant pen, and treachery is inseparable from faith. I often betray myself with a kiss . . .' After another parody he wrote: '. . . No other voice but yours is musical enough to echo my music . . .'. Her parodies became famous, and the following one of Henry James, (in which she may have used some of his own words from memory) is an excellent example. She had long wished to meet him and when at last she found herself sitting next to the great novelist she spoke to him of his books; something in the way she did so must have struck him as, turning to her, he said: 'Can it be – it must be – that you are that embodiment of the incorporeal, that elusive yet ineluctable being to whom through the generations novelists have so unavailingly made invocation; in short, the Gentle Reader? I have often wondered in what guise you would appear or, as it were, what incarnation you would assume.' This is quoted by Osbert Sitwell in Noble Essences.

Oscar and Ada Leverson constantly sent telegrams to each other which must have astonished the post offices. 'The author of The Sphinx will on Wednesday at two eat pomegranates with the Sphinx of Modern Life.' Bouquets arrived at the Leversons' house accompanied by no less flowery notes: 'Your dialogue is brilliant and dangerous. I am quite charmed with it. What the Comtesse Gyp (the pen-name of

the Comtesse de Martel de Janville) has done in France for
Life you have done in England for Art. No one admires your
clever witty subtle style more than I do. Nothing pains me
except stupidity and morality.' The new friends were
observed to be much in each other's company at first nights;
the young disciples doted on Mrs. Leverson and made her
a confidante in their interests. Sometimes she and Oscar
were invited for a Friday to Monday visit. They both hated
the country, apart from the seaside and beautiful landscapes,
but in country houses Oscar found wonderful audiences.

Little Robert Hichens, a great traveller, had made the
acquaintance of Lord Alfred Douglas in Luxor, and later
met Oscar once or twice in London. With the slight material
these meetings provided, he wrote The Green Carnation, of
which the dialogue is supposed to be that of Oscar, Alfred
Douglas and Ada Leverson. Most of it is a clever, vulgarised
imitation of the real thing, but one or two remarks have
the authentic touch and Hichens may well have heard these:
'the train has been punctual for once in its life. How shocked
the directors would be if they knew it, but of course it will
be kept from them', and 'thank Heaven there are no
nightingales to ruin the beauty of the stillness with their
well-meant but ill-produced voices'. What Ada and Oscar
really talked about is recalled in her memoir The Importance
of Being Oscar: 'margin in every sense was in demand, and I
remember looking at the poems of John Gray (considered
the incomparable poet of the age) and when I saw the
tiniest rivulet of text meandering through the very large
meadow of margin, I suggested to Oscar Wilde that he
should publish a book, all margin, full of beautiful unwritten thoughts, and have this blank volume bound in
some Nile-green skin powdered with gilt Nenuphars and
smoothed with hard ivory, decorated with gold by Ricketts,
if not Shannon, and printed on Japanese paper, and each

o

volume must be a collector's piece, a numbered one of a limited "first" (and last) edition: "very rare". He approved and suggested "It should be dedicated to you, and the unwritten text illustrated by Aubrey Beardsley. There must be five hundred signed copies for particular friends, six for the general public and one for America." '

They would have been sitting on wicker chairs on a velvet lawn, she shaded by a parasol, its colour reflected becomingly on her skin, and smiling mouth. Ada Leverson may have sighed when she said, 'Nothing spoils a romance more than a sense of humour in a woman and the lack of it in a man.' Wilde was to use this in his play *A Woman of No Importance*, written in Norfolk a few months after they met, and several of the epigrams in it were inspired in conversations with her. She records (in *The Importance of Being Oscar*) that he was quicker in repartee and conversation than in his writing, and afterwards constantly made use in his work of things he had improvised. Once, in conversation with Ada Leverson, he observed: 'One can't go on abusing Heliogabalus, censuring Caesar Borgia and scolding Nero. These figures have passed into the sphere of Art.' He little knew how applicable this observation was to be to him in the future. Mrs. Leverson was soon to be Oscar's best audience, she understood all his jokes and her laughter made every extravagance acceptable.

Oscar's poem *The Sphinx* was not published until two years after their first meeting. Ada Leverson was quick to recognise the silliness of parts of the poem, particularly in the following lines:

> 'Lift up your large black satin eyes which are like
>   cushions where one sinks!
> Fawn at my feet, fantastic Sphinx! and sing me all
>   your memories!'

Her parody of this poem was illustrated by a caricature by Edward Tennyson Reed of Ricketts' cover design. The skit ended with the following dialogue: 'Poet: In my opinion you are not a Sphinx at all. Sphinx: (indignantly) What am I then? Poet: A Minx.'

At once Oscar wrote to Ada: '20 July 1894 . . . Punch is delightful and the drawing a masterpiece of clever caricature. I am afraid she really was a minx after all. You are the only Sphinx.'

14 Arrangement in black and white

These Sphinxes have indeed caused us to anticipate a little in the story of their tamer's career, and it is necessary to go back five or six years. Around 1886 Oscar returned to his bachelor way of life; he had given up the idea of making Constance into a brilliant or fashionable woman of the world: he felt young, and ready to begin a thrilling life in which love was still to play a large part. He was thirty-two, and could still think of himself as handsome, with his regular features and broad, high brow, a nose almost classical, the mouth full but well-shaped, although the lower lip was a little heavy when it was not stretched in a smile; it was more of a sensual mouth than a greedy one. The lower part of the face was both thick and weak, the chin, a little receding, rested on a starched collar which hid a fat neck and held up jowls ending in double-chins. The look of intelligence and beauty stopped at the mouth, the rest had something unfinished about it, even brutish. Bernard Shaw believed that this monstrous side came from a thyroid deficiency. Wilde's appearance embarrassed all who were not beguiled by his intelligence. Lady Colin Campbell called him: 'That great white caterpillar.' (She may have heard Oscar's remark on the novel she wrote after her divorce case when, following a cruel cross examination, she had succeeded in clearing herself: 'Lady Colin has exhausted all her powers of imagination in the witness box.') His hands were too large, too well cared for, and on one finger he always wore a scarab ring which had been found in a tomb; he was always fascinated by Egypt. His powerful yet soft body, like that of an Indian Bacchus, was encased in clothes made by an excellent tailor. He held himself very straight and carried his head imposingly high. The poet had given up wearing his hair in the Neronian manner ever since he went to the Prince of Wales' barber, but he always refused to mar the marble of his countenance with a moustache. At that time actors, men-servants and Henry James (and perhaps one should add John Gray, Robbie Ross, Lord Alfred Douglas and Sherard) were among the few men who were always clean-shaven. Shimmering neck-ties, walking-sticks with knobs set with semi-precious stones, were the only remaining traces of the flamboyant period, but his contemporaries still thought of him as 'Babylonian'. English biographers of Wilde have used the words – 'self-indulgence' and 'self-pity' in regard to him. The first they apply to his epicurean selfishness when it is a question of the London Oscar; the second they make much use of when writing of his misfortunes. Wilde's care of his body was like that of a mother whose child stood a good chance of winning a baby competition. There were just not enough accessories to enhance his elegance, not enough scents to waft the news of his transit. The rarest viands, and in large quantities, were necessary to the functioning of his frame, and he was an epicure as well as a glutton. A good housekeeper might have held him in Tite Street, but Constance, instead of supervising the kitchen range, sought consolation for her solitude in spiritualism. Once, when her husband had invited some guests, a chicken was put before him, Oscar took up the carvers and tried to carve a wing. He laid them down again wearily, 'Constance,' he said, 'why do you give me these pedestrians to eat?'

After the failure of his marriage Oscar's homosexual

tendencies increased. He called those of his disciples who
allowed themselves to be seduced by women 'mulierasts', a
word used by him and his friends meaning heterosexual.
Bored by having to present to society a conventional
façade, when he could have reigned unimpeded over the
homosexual world, he started the pederastic propaganda
which prejudiced so many against him and which justified
some of the severity of his judges. Thus he would often
visit a bookseller who specialised in yellow-backed French
novels, next to books by Rachilde and Huysmans, designated
in the catalogue as 'Socratic'.

There have been different theories as to the authorship of
a pederastic novel called Teleny.* Mr. Montgomery Hyde
does not hesitate to attribute this work to Oscar Wilde. It is
true that there are to be found in it the strange mythologies
that Wilde invented to glorify his morals, which in themselves were fairly common: Christ and Antinous, twin gods,
each dying for their master, and the magic menagerie to
which he added a Theseus sodomised by the Minotaur.

The story is about a young man who made the acquaintance of Teleny, an Hungarian pianist; he was very vain and
had had great experience of women. Teleny took his new
rich friend to a low haunt: 'Some frowsy curtains at the
windows, a few old armchairs, and a long battered, and
much-stained divan completed the furniture of this room,
which had a mixed stench of musk and onions, but, as I
was just then gifted with a rather strong imagination, I at
times detected – or thought I did – a smell of carbolic acid
and of iodine; albeit the loathsome smell of musk over-
powered other odours.

'In this den, several – what shall I call them? sirens? no,
harpies! crouched or lolled about.

'Although I tried to put on a most indifferent blasé look,
* See Appendix, p. 409.

still my face must have expressed all the horror I felt. This is then, said I to myself, one of those delightful houses of pleasure, of which I have heard so many glowing tales?

'These painted-up Jezebels, cadaverous or bloated, are the Paphian maids, the splendid votaresses of Venus, whose magic charms make the senses thrill with delight, the houris on whose breasts you swoon away and are ravished into Paradise. . . .'

Disgusted by these ghouls the two young men fell into each other's arms, and experienced the enjoyments so lengthily described in which the author intersperses the most recherché words, but Nature's possibilities are more restricted than those of the vocabulary. The young man suspects Teleny of having a mistress and surprises him in an equivocal situation with the rich young man's mother. Teleny, in despair, commits suicide.

The descriptions in *Teleny* can be said to herald those of *Dorian Gray*: 'A thousand lamps of varied form filled the room with a strong yet hazy light. There were wax tapers upheld by Japanese cranes, or glowing in massive bronze or silver candlesticks, the plunder of Spanish altars; star-shaped or octagonal lamps from Moorish mosques or Eastern synagogues, curiously wrought iron crosses of tortured and fantastic designs, chandeliers of numerous iridescent glasswork reflected in Dutch gilt, or Castel-Durante majolica sconces.' This description could have come straight out of Huysmans' *A Rebours* and those brilliantly illuminated scenes could already be guessed at in Jean Lorrain's *Modernités*; and there is no doubt that Wilde was greatly influenced and inspired by both these writers. The author, whoever he was, avoids the monotony inherent in this type of story by some comic scenes which do suggest Oscar when he was not preaching the Chelsea gospel. Here and there a truculent vulgarity, mixed with preciousness,

transforms the horror into comedy. The great art of the
seducer is to make his victims laugh at everything which up
till then they had found improper or even repulsive. What
is most interesting in *Teleny* is the relationship between the
narrator and his mother whom he cannot help but admire
even when he sees her treated in cavalier manner by her
lover. It is not necessary to be very well informed about
psychoanalysis to recognise in these pages the unfurling of
the Oedipus complex. Speranza, sublime though she had
been, had strongly influenced the erotic evolution of her
second son; hatred for a scandalous father had strengthened
the influence of a dominating mother. Clearly poor Constance did not have a strong enough personality to eradicate
the influence of her mother-in-law.

Oscar lunched and dined less and less at home, but
he did not go to his club like most English husbands, since
the rights of privacy in clubs oppressed him. Sometimes he
would have luncheon at the Savoy, when it opened in
August 1889, and he often had supper at Willis's Rooms in
King Street, St. James. Ladies were ready to risk their
reputations by being seen in this recherché restaurant, until
the day when Skittles, the famous courtesan, was allowed in.
There in a private room the Prince of Wales entertained
those Americans whose social careers entirely depended on
being admitted to the Royal Enclosure at Ascot, or on
receiving an invitation to Marlborough House. When Oscar
was short of money he would content himself with a meal
at one of those flashy restaurants or public houses full of
waxed oak and polished copper in the Strand, frequented by
the theatrical profession. But his headquarters was the Café
Royal; founded by a Frenchman, it was (and still is) Second
Empire in style, with looking-glasses framed by caryatids,
chandeliers of Bohemian glass, red plush upholstery,

and with nude figures painted on the ceiling between masses of gilding. In those days there would have been houris sitting alone, and the brisk tapping sound of dominoes on marble tables could be heard. Of the poets, sipping away at their absinthe in imitation of Verlaine, the most remarkable was Richard Le Gallienne who, if one can judge by his photograph, looked like a *demi-mondaine* in cycling costume. And dandies, such as Harry Melvill (a relentless raconteur immortalised by Osbert Sitwell in his story *The Machine Breaks Down*) who was in constant need of champagne to stand up to his own loquacity. The Café Royal was well situated, between Mayfair and Soho, with drawing-rooms in one direction, music-halls in the other. Neighbourhoods frankly consecrated to amorous adventure are always less amusing than those where respectable people 'let their hair down' to meet a *demi-monde* which on the surface does not give the impression of making pleasure its business. Among would-be *femmes fatales*, actors playing noblemen on the town (a little less convincingly than on the stage), noblemen longing to be mistaken for jockeys, stockbrokers imitating the Prince of Wales (the German accent was a help), Oscar was as happy as a fish in water, a water that sparkled like champagne, on which he floated like a benevolent whale surrounded by Bohemian writers and painters: to one he would give advice, perhaps an introduction, to others dinners, or a favourite book slipped into a pocket. To all he distributed the treasure of his stories and his aphorisms:

'A well tied tie is the first serious step in life.'

'More women grow old nowadays through the faithfulness of their admirers than through anything else.'

'Anybody can sympathise with the sufferings of a friend, but it requires a very fine nature – it requires, in fact, the nature of a true individualist–to sympathise with a friend's success.'

'No modern literary work of any worth has been produced in the English language by an English author . . . except of course Bradshaw.'

To annoy his friends he would pretend that his favourite reading was the Railway Guide: 'I would sooner lose a train by the A.B.C. than catch it by Bradshaw.' Sherard recalls that one day in the Café Royal he noticed a man sitting alone and asked who he was. 'That is Frederick Sandys,' said Wilde, adding sorrowfully that he had been dead for some years. 'In his lifetime he was a great painter, a true artist. Then he died, but came back afterwards, and now he sits in the Café Royal all day and most of the night, drinking little glasses of brandy. What a pity it is that dead men will come back and persist in showing themselves, just to pretend that they are alive, when everybody knows the contrary!' And to an unknown young man who greeted him warmly, he replied: 'I don't know your face, but your manner is familiar.'

In this most continental of districts, the Master acted the part of Balzac and explained the underground doings of Society – 'Dear boy, since the Prince has met Lady Brooke, how do you imagine that Lord Charles Beresford could become First Lord of the Admiralty?' – He would charm a creditor, scribble an article on a corner of a table, and play the parts of a whole series of characters out of Balzac's novels.

In 1888, Oscar met Frank Harris, someone even more Balzacian, who lived his life in a truculent and precarious style. He was a thick-set, swarthy little man, with a large moustache; rings shone on his hairy hands, and a doubtful diamond drew attention to an opulent-looking neck-tie. He was so much like a music-hall version of a swindler that it was impossible to believe that he was in reality dishonest. Nevertheless he happily went in for swindling, pure and simple, for blackmailing and, when required, for pandering.

His enterprise and the number of his successes with women convinced him that he was a Casanova. He was a good talker, and Max Beerbohm described his voice thus: 'He has a marvellous speaking voice, like the organ at Westminster Abbey, and with infallible footwork.' A ceaseless power of invention made up for what he lacked in true culture, yet he had a uniquely thorough knowledge of the works of Shakespeare. He believed that he could make anyone swallow his lies, and he was a bully. At the same time he was a theorist in the art of living – of living well. But by a flaw in this astonishing blending of characteristics, he lost all that they might have brought him.

Harris passed his youth in America, arriving in London in 1882 where he was quick to make a name for himself in Fleet Street thanks to his American methods, becoming editor of the *Evening News*, then of the *Fortnightly Review*. He married a rich widow who gave him a house in Park Lane where he entertained indiscriminately. Once when Harris spoke too often of his own social success and of all the grand houses he had visited, Oscar remarked: 'Yes dear Frank, we believe you – you have dined in every house in London, *once*.' Harris much amused Oscar's friend the Princess of Monaco, and he often stayed with her in the Principality. Indiscretions told by him in a voice of thunder caused the clients of the Café Royal to hold their breath: 'Really Frank, you will never learn how far too far you can go', Oscar would protest.

Oscar thought he knew how far *he* could go and had the audacity to go very far indeed. Beneath the yellow light of the gas-lamps in Leicester Square, a constant dejected procession of boys, enlivened by the scarlet tunics of guardsmen and the white bibs of sailors, jostled feather-hatted prostitutes off the pavement. Ageless youths and sexless old

men crowded bars where furtive glances were reflected in
the engraved looking-glasses. Members of the upper-class
frequently rubbed shoulders with soldiers and gigolos, with
a passion for low company perhaps induced by the boredom
of the drawing-rooms. Oscar's white shirt-front was soon to
be a familiar sight in the streets of Soho when, looking
more distinguished than the most distinguished of men, he
alighted from a cab after the theatre, and his voice could be
recognised above the raucous sound of a barrel organ
saying, 'Fundamentally, dear boy, what is called the vice of
the upper-classes is really the pastime of the working
classes.' Wilde adored the smells and sounds of the great
city whose beauty he had learned from Whistler's canvases.
He was moved by the misery and fascinated by the hide-
and-seek of vice. The dark glamour of the 'modern Babylon'
had horrified Dostoievsky twenty years earlier when he
described, not without complaisance, the traffic in little
girls in the Strand. In 1840, Paul Feval, in *Mystères de Londres*,
had recognised the romantic possibilities of the capital
where vice and robbery were infinitely better organised than
in Paris: London, the city encrusted with soot, lost in fogs,
where Doctor Jekyll could suddenly be transformed into
Mr. Hyde, and where Sherlock Holmes was soon to brave
equally alarming adventures.

The contrast between black and gold was to be the theme
of *Dorian Gray* and of a masterpiece unspoilt by long descriptions and profound thoughts – *Lord Arthur Savile's Crime*. The
account of the walk taken by the young man who has to
commit a crime, is one of the finest in Wilde's work, and
since it is not for once an imitation there can be a genuine
comparison with certain passages of Thomas de Quincey or
to the reveries of Gérard de Nerval in Paris. His walk takes
him down Oxford Street where the prostitutes made fun of
him, into 'narrow, shameful alleys', and dark courtyards,

on and on until dawn when he finds himself surrounded by flowers in Covent Garden. On the Thames embankment realism is shown at grips with symbolist ornamentation: 'The moon peered through a mane of tawny clouds, as if it were a lion's eye, and innumerable stars spangled the hollow vault, like gold dust powdered on a purple dome. Now and then a barge swung out into the turbid stream, and floated away with the tide, and the railway signals changed from green to scarlet as the trains ran shrieking across the bridge. After some time, twelve o'clock boomed from the tall tower at Westminster, and at each stroke of the sonorous bell the night seemed to tremble. Then the railway lights went out, one solitary lamp left gleaming like a large ruby on a giant mast, and the roar of the city became fainter.'

The dangers which threatened good society in London were less imaginary than those invented by Balzac in L'Histoire des Treize. A whole class of swindlers, some of whom had links with that society, exploited their victims by means of blackmail – a weapon which in France was only used in political circles. Certainly France of the nineteenth century was indulgent towards adultery, and its laws ignored deviations which were criminal in England. Since the slightest breath of scandal could destroy a political or indeed any worldly career, hundreds lived on the ransoms they extracted from those whom they had encouraged or surprised in some weakness. In a city where debauchery was easy, temptations became ever stranger, every taste that money could buy developed in a way that amazed even the least prudish of Frenchmen. Paris gloated over the accounts of houses where whipping took place and the age of consent was brutally ignored, and of the traffic in soldiers and youths given by the journalist W. T. Stead. From time to time a suicide, an exile on the Continent, left an empty place in society; 'Poor dear' was said of the victims by those who had had the tact to escape the scandal, and they were no longer talked of.

Writers astray in this London frequently disguised the dangers in remorse, thus passing from the sordid to the tragic, as for example did John Addington Symonds after having followed a soldier in the Park in *The Valley of Vain Desires*, as Wilde was to do in *Dorian Gray*; the Victorians knew how to transform scandalous news items into mystical experiences. Oscar's casuistry produced a happy formula for avoiding remorse without renouncing morality. His strange distorted idea of chastity was the body being in harmony with the soul: disharmony between them was the only debauch.

One day, Oscar, looking through the misted plate glass of the window of the Café Royal, turned to Vincent O'Sullivan and said: 'There is a dreadful youth waiting for me in Regent Street. He is pacing up and down before the door like a wonderful black panther. I think he must be there yet. Do go and see; if he is I shall go out by the side door.' O'Sullivan did as he was told and noticed a fellow hanging about who did not look anything like a black panther and was only too pleased to accept a half a crown to go away.

Other ghosts would cross the threshold of the Café, emerging from some garret or other in Soho. There was Simeon Solomon, who lived from hand to mouth on the proceeds of blackmail or the sale of pornographic drawings. Ernest Dowson, the charming poet, and his friend the artist Conder, who kept harking back to old stories of Montmartre. There were the failures on whom Max Beerbohm based the pathetic, imaginary character Enoch Soames, who epitomised all the deliquescences of the end of the century, gone astray like Pater's disciples who, not having been protected by the Ivory Tower of Oxford, believed that 'morality was an intolerable affectation of style'. They exhausted themselves in trying to determine an ultimate, exquisite form, to stabilise it lightly, to be a disembodied voice, but nevertheless the voice of a soul. These poets were quick to look to Catholicism and to Socialism for that support which aestheticism could not give them, but in spite of all they often died of hunger. Sometimes at a bar Oscar would get into conversation with a poor wretch who would warm himself before the coals of a roast chestnut stall; his eyes dilated with hunger and with opium, he was dressed in an old caped box-coat. It was the poet Francis Thompson, who slept among the down-and-outs under the arches of Charing Cross Station, and in *A Captain of Song* we find an echo of sufferings of this kind:

> 'And pace the places infamous to tell,
> Where God wipes not the tears from any eyes.'

Alice Meynell writes in her book on Francis Thompson, that after hearing *Sister Songs* read aloud Oscar said: 'Why can't I write poetry like that? That is what I've wanted to do all my life.'

He well knew that compared to these works, and those of Verlaine, his poems were no more than literary exercises. Even *The Harlot's House* is too reminiscent of Baudelaire revised by Rops, in spite of the great originality of his gruesome ballad rhythm.

The risks that Oscar would have run in Paris were either that he would be slandered or, leading as he did a social life, that he could become an Academician – but in England there was no Academy. Perhaps feeling apart from one's social element is the greatest pleasure of vice. Oscar, in a majestic incognito, would go as far as the opium-dens of Whitechapel, would lie in wait for an actor at the stage-door of a music-hall in the suburbs, or throw a gold coin to a pianist in order to hear a favourite tune, *The Man Who Broke the Bank at Monte Carlo*. He liked the Cockney singers Marie Loyd, Albert Chevalier and May Belfort. He liked the promenade where people exchanged curious looks, and the uproar behind the scenes. Sometimes he would be accompanied by Walter Sickert, the painter of admirable pictures of overgilded and dusty music-halls. The stupidity of the couplets and even the ugliness of the costumes delighted him. Aesthetes often have a taste quite opposite to their love of the precious, an artistic masochistic streak which is excited by vulgarity.

The poet took his disciples on his expeditions, and described these to the least suitable audiences, adding details of strange perversions: 'I don't believe those people who do these things get half as much pleasure out of them, as I do in talking about them . . .'. He told too much when, during a fit of laughing, he confided: 'I am like the great Sappho with urchins who have the eyes of lesbians.' Oscar was a great boaster of vices, and this was shown in his article, mentioned above, about the poisoner Wainewright.

15 Dorian Gray

The teeming, mysterious city, where danger was so near to pleasure, provided Wilde with the background for his most celebrated works. On the other hand Lord Arthur Savile's Crime and Mr. W.H. prepared the way for Dorian Gray. Was the model on whom he based this story taken from one of Oscar's disciples? Certainly the habitual young visitors to Tite Street had well-cut suits and plenty of intelligence, but they lacked the glamour of luxury and birth, therefore none of these 'dear boys' could boast of personifying the hero in full.

As well as the poets, there were artists too among the disciples. John Sargent was a little too much linked to 'the establishment' to be of interest to his neighbour. But, still in Chelsea, Wilde was constantly in the company of two painters who worked together: Ricketts and Shannon. The former, half French, wore a pointed beard, while Shannon was fair, with a snub nose; they strove to simplify the figures in the pictures of Burne-Jones and William Morris ever since they had visited the studio of Puvis de Chavannes. They were young, they had taste – their studio was furnished with greco-florentine bric-à-brac enlivened by chinoiserie in the best romantic tradition. Oscar amused himself by suggesting marvellous subjects for pictures which no one would ever paint, and in trying to see again the colours he had so much admired in Gustave Moreau's studio, 'divinely false, this green', 'pistachio dressed as emerald'. He would decipher an inscription on a Greek vase that the two painters

P

had just unearthed. He brought them clients, made the models laugh by taking off Whistler's mannerisms, and left prodigiously late for some grand dinner party. There, one evening, stretched out on a cushioned divan, watching the spirals made by the smoke of his cigarette, he told them his original idea of *The Picture of Dorian Gray*; what he later wrote was but one episode in the much more complex story, which was to have taken place in the eighteenth century and would have comprised some of his favourite tales; there was one about an actress who lost her talent when she fell in love, which inspired the character of Sibyl Vane. Other episodes were to have included the story of a crucifix invented by the Inquisition, which suffocated in its iron arms the sinner who, repenting too late, embraced it. Religion was to play a large part in this curious 'legend of the centuries', at the end of which the body of Christ was to be found in a grotto at the foot of Golgotha. Laziness caused Oscar to abandon this medley, but he used the décor of Ricketts' studio for the setting of the first chapter of *Dorian Gray*.

The Picture of Dorian Gray was published in June 1890. About six years previously, Oscar had visited the studio of a painter called Basil Ward, for whom a very handsome young man was sitting; Oscar often dropped in after this first visit and kept the sitter entertained. When the portrait was finished, Wilde happened to say, 'What a pity that such a glorious creature should ever grow old'. The artist agreed, adding, 'How delightful it would be if he could remain exactly as he is, while the portrait aged and withered in his stead.' It was this experience that inspired the story of Dorian Gray and the character of Lord Henry Wotton was based on Oscar himself, with, perhaps, the addition of Lord Ronald Gower's complete cynicism. Wilde expressed his obligation by calling the painter in the story Basil Hallward.

Lord Henry Wotton talks in maxims, as do the characters in Oscar's plays, yet, in spite of the care with which he cultivates artificiality, he is the only consistent person in the novel. Perhaps the melancholy of this ageing seducer represented the feelings of Oscar Wilde, who at thirty-five was already surrounded by much younger men.

The person of that time most like Dorian Gray in his tastes, his neck-ties and his good looks, alas, so soon to pass, was Robert de Montesquiou who, as we have seen, took good care never to meet Oscar. As to the portrait itself, one can imagine it to be like Sargent's challenging portrait of Graham Robertson.

Much was borrowed in this story, but what is original is that it is a real romance of London, in the same way that Zola's Nana and Daudet's L'Immortel are novels of Paris. The reader is led from the Park to Whitechapel, from an artist's studio to a Duchess's drawing-room; Wilde is very much at home and opens all the doors, displays the treasures and the floral decorations, and from time to time actually allows the reader a glimpse behind the scenes. One of the reasons for the success of this book is that it is redolent of great luxury, a real luxury not that of Ouida's novels. Lord Henry and Dorian have their suits cut at Pooles, scent their baths with Floris bath salts, Fortnum and Mason deliver to their houses the rarest teas, the most exquisite jams; one knows that they belong to exclusive clubs and invite their friends to shoot, they have hot-houses, and yachts. They were the demi-gods watched by the crowds in Hyde Park as they rode their horses worth several hundred guineas each, whom the new-rich pointed out in the Duchess of Sutherland's box at the Opera. Like Le Côté de Guermantes, The Picture of Dorian Gray glorifies the aristocracy, even as far as its vices and its ridiculousness. It is also one of the last pictures of

that world by a great writer because from the moment the
nobility dismounted from their horses to get into motor-
cars, when they received at the Ritz rather than in their own
houses, when they preferred night-clubs to the Opera, their
aesthetic glamour vanished. The scene and the style was that
of the Society in which for the last ten years Oscar had
been entertained in the evenings, but he wanted to give his
heroes one more luxury – his wit. It is Oscar who often
speaks through Dorian, and always through Lord Henry.
That life of walks and conversations is a little reminiscent
of Oxford, but an Oxford where the college is a great house
in Belgrave Square or Park Lane, where the gentlemen
cultivate 'exquisite passions'. In this world, as at Oxford,
women had very little place; they come, as it were, from
the outside. It is conversation that plays the chief part, and
which is idealised as the supreme art.

The Picture of Dorian Gray has been said to be a succession
of parodies, almost a compilation: material borrowed from
Balzac (Le Peau de Chagrin, Splendeurs et misères), from Gautier
(Mademoiselle de Maupin), from Stevenson (The Strange Case of
Dr. Jekyll and Mr. Hyde). And from William Wilson in which
Edgar Allan Poe tells the story of a young criminal haunted
by a man who looks exactly like him; he finishes by killing
him and he sees in a mirror 'his own image, but with
features all pale and dabbled in blood', but it was his
antagonist whom he saw and who said, 'You have con-
quered and I yield. Yet, henceforth art thou also dead –
dead to the World, to Heaven and to Hope. In me didst thou
exist – and, in my death, see by this image, which is thine
own, how utterly thou hast murdered thyself.' There is also
to be found something of the terrifying stories of Sheridan
Le Fanu which had made such an impression on Oscar in
his youth in Dublin; also an affinity with Conan Doyle

(Sherlock Holmes and Dorian Gray might easily have met in a London fog on one of their respective searches for crime and pleasure). When Doyle travelled to London from Southampton one day for a luncheon given him by *Lippincott's* magazine, Oscar was one of the fellow guests. They were both commissioned to write tales of mystery for the magazine and a few months later there arrived *The Picture of Dorian Gray* and the *Sign of Four* in which Sherlock Holmes made his second appearance. Oscar's debt to Pater was immense, Dorian and Sibyl are like the young lovers in *Imaginary Portraits* – and often the style is melancholy in the same way, despite the purple passages threaded with gold.

It is obvious that many of the jewels and perfumes in *Dorian Gray* are taken straight out of *A Rebours*, 'the poisonous book' in a yellow cover that Lord Henry makes Dorian read. Wilde himself recognised this debt: 'The book in Dorian Gray is one of the many books I have never written, but it is partly suggested by Huysmans' *A Rebours*, which you will get at any French booksellers. It is a fantastic variation on Huysmans' over-realistic study of the artistic temperament in our inartistic age.' The Duc Floressas des Esseintes is really the father of Dorian Gray, but one can find many cousins in Byzantium and decadent Paris. The taste for trinkets and low company was very *fin de siècle* and had been exploited since 1885 by Jean Lorrain. This love of low life was very French, so much so that the French expression 'nostalgie de la boue' has become almost colloquial in the English language, but it was Oscar who introduced it into the aesthetic domain. 'Ugliness was the one reality. The coarse brawl, the loathsome den, the crude violence of disordered life, the very vileness of thief and outcast, were more vivid in their intense actuality of impression than all the gracious shapes of Art, the dreamy shadows of Song.' Like Huysmans and Lorrain, Wilde leads his heroes to hovels, but, like a child given the run of a pastry-cook's shop, he then proceeds to gorge himself with rare words, and with quotations drawn from The Cabala and little-known Elizabethan authors.

Part of the novel is in dialogue, which anticipates the comedies. The dinner at Lady Narborough's after the crime is a completely theatrical scene, and the contrast between the social event and the murder is typically Wildean. The idea of a novel in dialogue originated in France; in 1885 the first works of Gyp appeared in La Vie Parisienne in this form; another Frenchwoman from whom Wilde had borrowed, very different from the author of Le Mariage de Chiffon was Rachilde,* author of Monsieur Vénus. This novel was a catalogue of different forms of elegance and perversity. With the same appetite as he showed for curiosities, Oscar also filled his pages with peeresses; there is a Duchess in every two chapters, this iridescence of rare words and great names was necessary to encourage so indolent an author to write his novel. But with what simplicity of style he tells of the metamorphosis and discovery of Dorian Gray's body! There is not one word too many, and no emotion – just the bare facts.

This book could only have been written by Wilde; impressions graven on his heart since the gardens of Oxford are to be found in it: '. . . Dorian Gray burying his face in the great cool lilac-blossoms, feverishly drinking in their perfume as if it had been wine.' Oscar reveals himself as an admirable florist and an expert jeweller. The descriptions should be read in the insinuating and at the same time precise voice of a tempter who displays his treasures, and transforms flowers into precious stones. 'In a month there will be purple stars on the clematis, and year after year the green night of its leaves will hold its purple stars.' As to ivy:

* A young girl who wrote, very badly, scandalous novels and who married the editor-in-chief of the Mercure de France.

'. . . its leaves are like green lacquer', and at Covent Garden
there are '. . . the huge jade-green piles of vegetables', and
as he is equally himself in the amusing passages, his
laughter can be imagined in the following description of a
woman 'looking like a bird of paradise that had been out
all night in the rain, she flitted out of the room, leaving a
faint odour of frangipani'. All Lord Henry's ridicule of
marriage is Wilde himself venting his irritation at his own
mistakes. In Proust's *Sodome et Gomorrhe*, there is the same
combination of vice and comedy – one strengthens the
other. But as Wilde was good-hearted he was malicious
without going as far as Proust's ferocity. For him 'sin' alone
was awful, for Marcel the awfulness was in human beings.

Like his creator, Dorian knew the attractions of Catholicism: 'The daily sacrifice, more awful really than all the
sacrifices of the antique world, stirred him as much by its
superb rejection of the evidence of the senses as by the
primitive simplicity of its elements and the eternal pathos
of the human tragedy that it sought to symbolise. . . . The
fuming censers, that the grave boys, in their lace and
scarlet, tossed into the air like great gilt flowers, had their
subtle fascination for him.' Oscar's two great friends, Gray
and Ross, both yielded to this charm, but his reply to them
was that: '. . . he never fell into the error of arresting his
intellectual development by any formal acceptance of creed
or system, or of mistaking, for a house in which to live, an
inn that is but suitable for the sojourn of a night, or for a
few hours of a night in which there are no stars and the
moon is in travail'. Wilde was never more superficial than
when he took himself seriously. He could be excessively
pretentious in the rôles of Plato or of Christ, as in the
commandments which serve as a preface to the novel and
which appear to have been dictated from the top of a
would-be aesthetic Sinai.

Also typical of him is the narcissism which is the real subject of the novel; Wilde worshipped the superhuman proportions of his body and of his intelligence. If it is easy, with hindsight, to analyse the extraneous elements used by Wilde in this book which of all his works has been re-issued the most, the Victorian public and critics were well able to recognise Oscar himself in every page when *Dorian Gray* appeared as a serial in *Lippincott's* magazine in June 1890 and in book-form in April of the following year. The novel, when examined in detail by prosecuting counsel at his trials, was to be used in evidence against him.

The bitter philosophy of these delightful pages is also Wildean, but this is not to be found so much in the para-doxes or in the elaborate reflections as in the melancholy which emerges from the story. A life dedicated to Beauty, so much luxury and so many works of Art, only hide deception and decomposition, and here again one is re-minded of Charlus. It seems as if Oscar had had a pre-monition of his own ruin, inevitable although delayed by success, in the way he shows Dorian's beauty suddenly crumbling into decay. The clash between the life he led, his material pleasures, and the life he dreamed of, could only lead to catastrophe.

The critics could have recognised extracts from Flaubert's correspondence in the aphorisms of the preface, and indeed his work is one of the many sources of the novel itself. Had they done so, it would have been less serious than to bring Wilde's own nature into the limelight, as they did. After Oscar, the Prince of Elegance, the public was now being treated to Oscar, the arbiter of vice. Chauvinism ran riot, thus the *Daily Chronicle*: 'It is a tale spawned from the leprous literature of the French decadent'; the critic of *Punch* was very insulting, and the adjectives 'morbid' and 'un-

healthy' came from every pen. They said that Dorian had all
the vices, an expression which, in reality, designated only
one. For the first time the question of the law was brought
up, by the *Scots Observer*: 'The story – which deals with
matters only fitted for the Criminal Investigation Depart-
ment or a hearing in *camera* – is discreditable alike to author
and editor. Mr. Wilde has brains, and art, and style; but if
he can write for none but outlawed noblemen and perverted
telegraph-boys, the sooner he takes to tailoring (or some
other decent trade) the better for his own reputation and
the public morals.' For once Oscar became anxious; had he
gone too far? No, it was the journalists who understood
nothing and he took the trouble to reply to them at length.
He compared himself to Flaubert. In a letter to the editor of
the *Scots Observer* of 13th August 1890: 'You may ask me, sir,
why I should care to have the ethical beauty of my story
recognised. I answer, simply because it exists, because the
thing is there. The chief merit of *Madame Bovary* is not the
moral lesson that can be found in it, any more than the
chief merit of *Salambô* is its archaeology, but Flaubert
was perfectly right in exposing the ignorance of those who
called the one immoral and the other inaccurate ... the critic
has to educate the public, the artist has to educate the critic.'

No one was convinced, and the Victorians were horrified
because *Dorian Gray* was the first overt pederastic novel written
since the *Satyricon*. The painter frankly admits his love for
Dorian; Lord Henry lures him away: the intimate relationships between Dorian and the young men, all of whom
come to a bad end, can be guessed. Women are deliberately
sacrificed, like Sibyl Vane, flouted, like Lord Henry's wife,
reduced to the status of dolls, like the young Duchess who
appears in the last chapters; not once is it suggested that
Dorian feels for them any more than a certain curiosity
which soon turns to contempt.

Mr. Robert Merle has rightly compared Wilde to Byron (who also occasionally practised homosexuality): 'The poet saw very clearly the artistic potential of this sin which is never named, or this perversion symbolised by a continual paradox. By instinct he recognised the attitude of Byron, who allows the shadow of a terrible sin to hover over Manfred without specifying its nature.' Dorian is the Don Juan of the decadence, and not for twenty years, with *Death in Venice* by Thomas Mann, was a good book which is as completely homosexual, to be written. Even Gide was more discreet. Proust, much more indiscreet in some ways, repudiated his characters by caricaturing them. In Julian Green's *Journal* he underlines the divergence between the qualities and the faults of *Dorian Gray* by saying that, 'the story itself is admirable, as rich, as profound as a Greek myth but the action is of the most feeble, in the hands of those brilliant talkers who are the characters. All is false, but to such a degree that this falsity ends by attaining to a sort of bitter and cruel truth.' Wilde has put all homosexual literature under a tragic sign, perhaps because he looked upon his pleasures if not as sins then at least as offences against society. The verve of the *Satyricon* and the caricatures by Proust are much nearer to the reality.

Walter Pater, who saw in Dorian Gray the brother of his heroes, was the only one of all the critics to like the book and to mitigate the scandal: In the *Bookman* he pointed out that the gay and natural taste for life and the charming meetings between people did much to diminish anything in the paradox that might shock. But Pater was near to death, and did not want to see bad in anything. He is a Presbyterian Verlaine, said Oscar. Friends were no more consoling than the Press, and many of them looked upon *Dorian Gray* with disgust, as did the young and brilliant American art historian Bernard Berenson, who wrote in his book *Sunset and Twilight*: 'On the morning of its publication, Oscar came to my room in North Street, Westminster and handed me a copy, saying it was the first from the Press. I took it with appreciation of the gift. The next day Oscar came to lunch, and I did not hesitate to tell him how loathsome, how horrible the book seemed to me. He did not make the slightest attempt to defend it, but explained that he being hard up, the publisher had given him a hundred pounds for a story. . . .' In contrast, Mallarmé's letter was a fine consolation: 'I have finished the book, one of the few which can move one. Its deep fantasy and very strange atmosphere took me by storm. To make it so poignant and human with such astonishing intellectual refinement, and at the same time to keep the perverse beauty is a miracle that you have worked through the use of all the arts of the writer . . . This disturbing, full-length portrait of a Dorian Gray will haunt me, as writing, having become the book itself.'

After *Dorian Gray* the name of Wilde became a synonym for all that was most unhealthy. Oscar realised this but instead of becoming prudent he became provocative, parading a cynicism which was more dangerous than the lack of deference to public opinion that he had displayed in his youth. He had provoked public opinion after having scoffed at it, and he was already dedicated to courting disaster. For example, having dined one evening with Robert Ross at the Hogarth Club, once they had adjourned to the smoking-room, a member ostentatiously left the room. Other members rose to follow, but Oscar sized up the situation quickly, strode over to one of those about to leave and haughtily addressed him: 'How dare you insult a member of your own club! I am Mr. Ross's guest. An insult to me is an insult to him. I insist on your apologising to Mr. Ross.' The member was driven to pretend that no insult had been intended, and they all returned to their seats.

16 Lord Alfred

A limited edition of *Dorian Gray* was published on the 1st July 1891. In the same month Oscar met a youth who had both the beauty and the rank of his hero. For a great artist, Nemesis works to an impeccable time-table, with no wavering, no unpunctuality, no hesitation. The catastrophe came in the shape so often conjured up by the poet in his stories, and the affair unfolded beyond the control of the people concerned. From the first day, Oscar-Hamlet seemed to be an observer of his tragedy rather than the protagonist. The performance owed nothing to chance. It was inevitable that the most colourful undergraduate at Oxford should meet the most famous writer in London. Oscar strove to act the play in surroundings suitable for princes, and thirty years later fresh dramas were still to re-echo the circumstances. The protagonists were aware of being destined for superb misfortune, and they acted as their tragedy directed, though to their friends they appeared merely foolish or blind. They had already entered into the realms of legend, while the public still thought of them as personalities in the gossip columns.

Lionel Johnson, with the imprudence of a modest person who lacked confidence in his own charm but was anxious to be valued by his friends, had for some time spoken to Oscar of Lord Alfred Douglas. They had been at Winchester together and had met again at Oxford. Lord Alfred was cherished by Dr. (later Sir Herbert) Warren, the President of Magdalen, who was susceptible to a great name and a

beautiful face. Lord Alfred was not the only one in Oxford
to combine these two attributes, but Johnson added that he
was very intelligent, and a gifted poet. The young man's
poems were inspired principally by Fitzgerald's translation
of Omar Khayyám. He was also an excellent athlete, winning
the school steeplechase at Winchester and nearly winning a
half-Blue for running at Oxford. Intellectuals and sportsmen
raved about him; his special friend at Winchester had been
Lord Encombe, who later occupied Oscar's old rooms at
Magdalen over-looking the river. Johnson was a mystic and
the manner in which he spoke of his friend to Oscar can
be imagined after reading his sonnet in Latin in praise of
Dorian Gray and its author, *Benedictus sis, Oscare*. Lord Alfred
spent part of his vacations with his mother, Lady Queensberry, in Cadogan Place. One day, Johnson collected him in
a hansom-cab to take him to Tite Street, past the Pre-
Raphaelites doing their marketing, up to the red brick of
No. 16, with its white varnished balconies and dormer
windows. The little manservant ushered the visitors into
the red and yellow study; a minute later Oscar arrived,
wearing a frock-coat and a big button-hole. There, before
him, stood Dorian Gray. He may have put his hand to
his heart before offering it to his visitor, for he knew
then that the play had started . . . Oxford, Athens, Sarah
Bernhardt, Shakespeare, these were perhaps the subjects of
conversation at that first encounter, which doubtless consisted chiefly of a brilliant monologue interrupted by fits of
laughter. The mixture of the sublime and the ridiculous
fascinated Douglas, who at first had been disconcerted by
the appearance of the great writer, but who laughed when
he should and replied without shyness, with obvious admiration shining in his still child-like blue eyes.

After Wilde had invited Lord Alfred to dine with him at
the Albemarle Club a few days later, he took him upstairs

to be introduced to Constance. Doubtless she liked him at
first sight more than her husband's other young friends,
his illustrious name being an added attraction to his good
manners, looks and style.

Oscar would not have had to consult the *Peerage* to know
that Lord Alfred's family took up several pages. The name
Douglas derives from the Gaelic word 'dark water'; its
belligerent history includes the Black Douglas who, on Palm
Sunday, 1307, led a ruthless raid against the English; this
was followed, down the centuries, by a succession of duels,
murder plots and adulteries. The chiefs of the clan were
known by their nick-names: Douglas the Hardy, Douglas
the Grim, Douglas the Gross. Each added to their estates
either by marriage or by violence or treachery. The younger
sons founded illustrious families such as those of the Dukes
of Buccleuch and Queensberry and the Earls of Home,
Morton and Wemyss. The first Earl of Queensberry got his
title from Charles I, the second supported his monarch in
the civil war, to be mulcted of a quarter of a million pounds
by Cromwell. Several monarchs added further titles. The
last representative of the ducal branch, known as 'Old Q'
(alleged to have been the original of the Marquess of Steyne,
the wicked nobleman in Thackeray's *Vanity Fair*), was said
to have led the sons of George III in their debts and
intrigues. The marquisate then passed to Old Q's cousin,
Charles, friend of Byron and a great boxer and sportsman.
He was succeeded by his brother John, whose son was a
gambler. His grandson, John Sholto Douglas, 8th Marquess
of Queensberry, succeeded at the age of fourteen in 1858;
he had been in the navy for two years when his father was
found dead beside his gun. He was to be the dark figure of
our hero's tragedy, one moment sinister, the next a Shakes-
pearean buffoon, mad rather than bad. Small, alert, with an
aquiline nose, curly red hair, his skin weather-beaten and

reddened through drink, he divided his time between the race-course and the prize-ring: there he was looked upon as a king, having laid down the fourteen rules of boxing still known as the Queensberry Rules. These, together with a number of incredibly insulting letters and, rather surprisingly, a few passable poems, were the only literary efforts of the Marquess. His other great glory was that he frequently rode in the Grand National. Queensberry was at his ease among boxers and jockeys as his ancestors had been among troopers. He was a man from another age, with no Victorian scruples but with a lively sense of honour, as might have been found in the entourage of Black Douglas.

Unhappily, he married at the age of twenty-one a lovely creature who belonged to a far more sophisticated background than he. Sybil, daughter of Alfred Montgomery. Her mother was a Wyndham, daughter of the first Lord Leconfield. His bride was not only a famous beauty but a highly talented, carefully educated young woman, who spoke French and Italian and was well and widely read. The Montgomery family were popular in Court circles, the Queensberrys were not. Lord Queensberry's inherited semi-madness was apparent when the vicious sadism of his character began to reveal itself. Alfred was born in October 1870, and ten years later Queensberry and his wife separated. Lady Queensberry did not console herself with love affairs nor did she ever turn the children against their father, but rather encouraged them to think of him as a hero. Dorian Gray too had an exquisite mother and a terrible forefather. When Oscar was introduced to Lady Queensberry he found her utterly delightful, and she was equally pleased with Constance, thanks to the freemasonry of unappreciated wives. Thus this sinister adventure began with tea parties and country house visits, as in a novel by Gyp.

Oscar discovered that the Douglas's had a great deal in
common with his own Lord Arthur Savile; there was the
young uncle who was killed whilst climbing the Matter-
horn, there were Lord Queensberry's strange sisters, Lady
Gertrude, a convert first to Catholicism, then, after having
married a baker, to Socialism; and Lady Florence who had
just been the heroine of a thrilling headline; she had been
walking in her garden near Windsor when two ruffians disguised as women precipitated themselves upon her with
the intention of stabbing her; the whalebone of her stays
deflected the knife and a Saint Bernard dog chased the men
away; the Queen asked for a photograph of the heroic dog,
and meanwhile questions were asked in the House of
Commons which shook the Government. What were the
police doing? Were the criminals Irishmen or anarchists?
'. . . Too wonderful!' exclaimed Oscar, doubled up with
laughter in his armchair, when Lord Alfred confided under
the seal of secrecy that the whole affair had been invented
by his schizophrenic aunt who, until then, had been content
to express her delusions in poems. Her husband, Sir Beaumont Dixie, another eccentric, was devoted to another
member of the family, Lord James Douglas. When the latter
died Sir Beaumont's behaviour was odd in the extreme; with
loud sobs, and tears running down his cheeks, he threw
himself down by the grave, gasping, 'My God, how I loved
that man; we were like a pair of apes!'*

Alfred Douglas was ten years old when Queensberry
decided to leave Kinmont. He did so because he resented
the large sum of money it cost him to keep up the house,
but as the rent roll of the estate brought him in £40,000
a year he was in no hurry to sell and did not do so until
1896. He shut up the house and took rooms for himself in
Buckingham Gate, rented a house in Cromwell Road, and

* From *Without Apology* by Lord Alfred Douglas.

Oscar Wilde

Oscar Wilde and Lord Alfred Douglas

subsequently one in Cadogan Place, for his family. Lady
Queensberry owned a property in the country near Bracknell :
on one occasion the Marquess arrived there just before Ascot
week, announcing that his mistress, a notorious woman,
was coming to stay for the meeting. Lady Queensberry concealed her displeasure at this news, but immediately sent
telegrams to put off the friends she had invited. The following year Queensberry went too far; he proposed to come
back to live with his wife and family, but bringing his
mistress with him. Lady Queensberry petitioned for a
divorce and the proceedings took no more than fifteen
minutes. From then on she was regarded as a saint who
only concerned herself with her children.

Alfred had been a beautiful child and his mother's
favourite. As a baby she had called him Boysie, which he
turned into Bosie, and this name stuck with him all his life.
For the first ten years of his life he had every attention that
is bestowed on the child of rich parents in the country. He
never enjoyed riding and preferred to hang about the stables
listening to the grooms hissing through their teeth as they
rubbed down the horses, or gossiping about the race in
which his father was about to ride. Bosie's first school was
Lambrook, to which Queen Victoria's grandsons were sent
– but its reputation declined and he was taken away. A short
spell at Wixenford followed and then, when just under
fourteen, he went to Winchester. His popularity at school
came as much from his prowess as a runner as for his gaiety
and good looks. Bosie spent most of his holidays under his
mother's roof, where he would hear of his father's latest
exploit, and unfortunately Bosie had inherited his taste for
gambling.

Queensberry seemed to thrive on scandals, as if he had
exhausted the possibilities of those to be found in bad
company, and he became the champion of Free Thought

Q

against what he called 'Christian Hypocrisy'. Like his father and grandfather before him he had been elected one of the sixteen Representative Peers of Scotland. In 1881 Queensberry chose to call the Oath of Allegiance to the Crown 'Christian tomfoolery' and was described as a follower of Bradlaugh. Queensberry's combativeness, atheism and love of publicity had been aroused by this – he became violently unpopular among his fellow peers and indeed among everyone else. This went to his head, and he set out to court opprobrium wherever he could. At a performance of Tennyson's unsuccessful play, The Promise of May, Queensberry, having been told that in it atheism would be held up to derision, hissed the play off the stage and flung a bunch of vegetables at the cast. This attitude on the part of the champion of Free Thought had a strange political repercussion and eventually was to influence the drama of Wilde's life.

Queensberry's eldest son, Lord Drumlanrig, a very pleasant and able young man, was private secretary to Lord Rosebery who recommended him for an English peerage; knowing that his father had failed to be re-elected to the House of Lords, Drumlanrig was unwilling to accept, as if he was in the Lords while his father was not, Queensberry would be infuriated. However, the Marquess surprised everyone by saying he was delighted with the honour offered to his son, and Drumlanrig became Lord Kelhead. Within a month Queensberry began sending insulting letters to Rosebery, for whom he felt an implacable hatred, and also to Gladstone and the Queen. Lord Rosebery was taking the waters at Bad Homburg whither he was followed by Queensberry, who stalked him for several days, armed with a horse-whip; he was only induced to abandon his project by the personal intervention of the Prince of Wales. Mr. Montgomery, too, had tried to deflect his son-in-law's ravings, and in turn received his share of insults of which Bosie, who each year spent part of his holidays with his grandfather, missed nothing.

With an heredity so full of opposing influences, an agitated childhood and a boyhood with divided loyalties to his parents, it is no wonder that Bosie was unbalanced. His good looks won him everything with a smile, and this he took as his right. Alfred Douglas's impatience was that of a demi-god amongst men; he had to have everything, and the slightest contradiction was to him almost a sacrilege. He was generous, capricious, ready to give all one day and take it back the next, irresistible yet a flirt, with no self-control but without pettiness, with charm and arrogance and great physical energy; all this had led to his development as it was in his seventeenth year. He was incapable of putting himself in someone else's place and was easily irritated by the sorrows that came his way; he saw himself as a flame, and it was just too bad for the butterflies who burned their wings. Solitude frightened him, perhaps he felt madness lying in wait, but when surrounded by people he could hold his own in brilliant conversation as he had great intelligence; he learned by heart easily, and there is no doubt that he was a poet. Tired of being liked for his good looks, Alfred wanted to be loved for his mind and talents. Impulsive, generous, exquisite but brutal – like an Elizabethan figure, he no more belonged to the Victorian age than did Wilde, though the latter would have been more at home in the eighteenth century than the sixteenth.

After his last year at Winchester, following the tradition of the nobility, Alfred Douglas was sent off to Europe on a Grand Tour with a tutor, Gerald Campbell, the nephew of Bosie's great-aunt Mrs. Percy Wyndham. The young man still preferred race-courses and casinos to museums, and he already knew some of the fashionable watering-places, so he soon led his tutor to the Hôtel de Paris in Monte Carlo.

There he met a cousin of Gerald Campbell, a celebrated beauty, Maria Emma Georgina Preston. She married the Earl of Desart in 1871, was divorced by him in 1878 and married the co-respondent Charles Sugden, an actor who subsequently deserted her. Oscar had met her twelve years previously and recorded his impression in a letter to Reginald Harding, '. . . I found him (Frank Miles) sketching the most lovely and dangerous woman in London, Lady Desart. She is very fascinating indeed.' This siren enticed Bosie into her bedroom. The mentor, Gerald Campbell, discovered the affair and went to rescue his ewe-lamb; he knocked on the door and soon the ewe-lamb appeared in tears of rage at being interrupted, dressed in one of Lady Desart's much be-ribboned nightgowns (one wonders whether this was a resourceful gesture, or whether it was inspired by the lady's sense of humour). All this to the accompaniment of the loud barking of her Pomeranian. Bosie was sent back to England in disgrace while Gerald Campbell presumably remained with his seductive cousin. Everyone cried out against the lady for seducing the innocent, which infuriated Bosie who thought it impugned his manhood. Bosie's mother was dismayed that her darling was going to follow in the footsteps of his father. Were she to have guessed the adventures in store for Bosie at Oxford and after, the saintly Lady Queensberry would not have been so worried over this incident. For the sons of the well-born, only horses, cards and bad women were to be feared – no other dangers were acknowledged.

Bosie looked very much like his mother, which infuriated his father from whom he had only inherited an aquiline nose, a little too large at the end, in his otherwise perfect face. The young man, finding his allowance insufficient, was deeply grateful to his mother for occasionally paying his debts.

Lionel Johnson, the instrument of their destiny, faded for the time being from the lives of Oscar and Bosie, whose friendship for each other soon turned to infatuation; Bosie wrote in his autobiography: 'The truth is that I really adored him ... there is nothing I would not have done for him. He did succeed in weaving spells – one sat and listened to him enthralled.' Evidently the charming Johnson was a dim figure compared to the magician. A few months later he wrote a poem, presumably dedicated to Oscar, called The Destroyer of a Soul; it began with the words 'I hate you with a necessary hate'.

After the first meeting, Oscar and Bosie met again before separating, Lord Alfred to join his grandfather in Bad Homburg, and Oscar to make a short visit to Windermere, perhaps to pay his respects to his old master, Ruskin, who was reputed to spend his time admiring the shapes of clouds, and playing with the village children. Oscar sought a brief period of solitude to enable him to return to that art which had always tempted him and which could be so lucrative – the theatre. During the winter he made the acquaintance of a young employee of Elkin Matthews and John Lane, called Edward Shelley, whose head was quite turned by Oscar's invitations and compliments. This adventure had no more importance for Oscar (although it was to be disastrous for Shelley who lost his job and became a neurotic because of it) than real life has to actors waiting in the wings. One can imagine the voice of the stage manager calling 'Principals on stage for the second act' when Oscar hurried to Oxford where Bosie was sharing rooms with Lord Encombe in the High Street.

And how well it started, the second act. The extent of Oscar's youthfulness was quite alarming; he sported an outfit of corduroy velvet, wore a long scarf in the colours of his former college, and accepted invitations to luncheons,

tea parties and dinners with Lord Alfred Douglas. To Dr.
Warren Oscar announced: 'I am thinking of presenting a
statue of myself to the College . . . yes, to stand here in the
Quad . . . a colossal equestrian statue.' They visited Pater to
whom Oscar wished to exhibit his new friend, but Pater
scarcely opened his mouth and had no desire to dwell on a
happiness which had never been his.

A future Oxford acquaintance of Bosie's who was to
become a friend of Oscar's, Max Beerbohm, was the brother
of the famous actor, Herbert Beerbohm Tree, and was as
skilful with his pen as with his pencil; he admired, but was
never dazzled by his clever contemporaries. His round head,
a little like a Japanese doll except that his eyes were enormous, always remained firmly set on his shoulders. He was
a great dandy. In June of 1893, Max sent an article to the
magazine edited by Bosie, The Spirit Lamp, the first he had
ever published, called The incomparable beauty of modern dress.
The following was his word picture of Oscar which resulted
in the famous caricatures: 'Luxury – gold-tipped matches –
hair curled – Assyrian-wax statue – huge rings – fat white
hands – not soignée – feather bed – pointed fingers – ample
scarf – Louis Quinze cane – vast Malmaison – cat-like
tread – heavy shoulders – enormous dowager – or schoolboy – way of laughing with hand over mouth – stroking
chin – looking up sideways – jollity overdone – But real
vitality . . . Effeminate, but vitality of twenty men, magnetism
– authority. Deeper than repute or wit, Hypnotic.'* He had
met Oscar at rehearsals of A Woman of No Importance in 1893.

Oscar and Bosie as a couple rather shocked Max; he was
not homosexual unlike many of his friends.† Oscar said

* Max by David Cecil.
† Translator's addition.
  At the time of Oscar's tragedy Max Beerbohm went to the Court to
lend comfort and visited him between trials, but before that he had

that the Gods had bestowed on Max the gift of perpetual
old age, and once asked Ada Leverson, 'When you are alone
with him, Sphinx, does he take off his face and reveal his
mask?'

---

advised Reggie Turner to keep away from the sordid affair and wrote
to Robbie Ross asking him not to see too much of the impressionable
Reggie, who was the illegitimate son of the first Lord Burnham,
proprietor of the *Daily Telegraph*, who was born Edward Levy and
assumed the name of Lawson in 1875. Reggie was given plenty of
money by his half-brother Frank Lawson.

17 Byzantine interlude

During the winter of the first year of his friendship with Bosie, Oscar went to Paris in December, 1891. Wilde, ambassador of Chelsea at the time of his first visit to Paris, was ten years later, the ambassador of Sodom. He held his sessions at the house of the Baroness Deslandes, who was so well described by Goncourt: 'A little woman, with a large, curved nose betraying her Jewish origin, but with a slim waist, a supple body and an animal elasticity. She wears a black dress, the top of the bodice and the bottom of the skirt at the back is embroidered with gold beads enhanced by small imitation turquoises. She talks of her white boudoir, all white, of her love of Dresden china, then of the boaster Oscar Wilde whom she declares is the most witty Englishman she has ever met. Upon the "Oh! Oh!'s" that this remark brings forth, she laughingly says that it is perhaps because he has the charm of talking to only one person and that it is always she whom he chooses. "But," says Lorrain, "no one repeats himself so much as he."'

Goncourt had his knife into Wilde because his *Journal* of 1883 had just been published and contained the terrible things that he claimed Wilde had said about Swinburne, which had brought him a fairly disagreeable reply from Wilde in *L'Echo de Paris*, repudiating these remarks. As a result Goncourt collected everything disagreeable about the visitor that he heard.

'30 April 1893: At the name of Oscar Wilde, Henri de Régnier smiled. Ah! you don't know . . . besides he does not hide it. It was he who said one day, "I have been married three times in my life, once to a woman and twice to a man". Lorrain, seeing that the wind had changed, was very haughty with Wilde, but he was unlucky. One day they met at Mallarmé's and Lorrain refused to shake hands with Wilde, saying: "You are not one of my friends." "Ah! my dear Jean, you are right, when one leads the life that you and I lead one no longer has friends – one only has lovers." '

This phrase was to be used again by Oscar to Pierre Louÿs* a young poet and writer who interested him very much, to whom he wrote in French in November 1891 : 'I hope that the young poets of France will one day like me, as much as I at the moment like them.' As *Dorian Gray* was the fruit of London friendships and pleasures, *Salome* was to be the flower of the Modern Style which was just coming into bloom during Oscar's stay in Paris, and he confided his project to Louÿs. Nice-looking at twenty-one, with a cat-like face, velvet ties and a bristling moustache, he dressed in the style of de Musset and knew Greek as well as Oscar. Louÿs had already visited London, invited by Raffalovitch and John Gray, and had returned delighted : 'The young men are most charming. You cannot imagine the elegance of their manners. They are steeped in poetry in a way we cannot imagine.' Charmed but not converted, Louÿs' friends regarded Wilde with the curiosity and suspicion of school-boys being entertained by a famous actor, their enthusiasm interspersed with alternate fits of laughter and embarrassment. Among them, Wilde noticed a tall youth with long hair, 'The face of the young evangelist was slightly Chinese looking, masked by a large beauty-spot, and his slit eyes of

* Pierre Louÿs (1870–1929) married the daughter of Hérédia, French poet and writer, whose most famous works, Les Chansons de Bilitis and Aphrodite, equivocally evoke the ancient Greeks.

haematite glittered as they fixed you with a predatory gaze.'
This is Jacques-Emile Blanche's description of the timid
André Gide,* whom Pierre Louÿs took with him to the
salons. He had a horror of the literary set to be found at
Hérédia's house – forward young women and languorous
blue-stockings. He asked himself what on earth he was
doing in the house of Princess Ouroussoff, who gave large
dinner parties in her flat in the Boulevard Haussman when
she was not in Doctor Blanche's clinic restoring her artistic
emotions. Wilde and Gide met in that November of 1891
at the Baignères or at Hérédia's house. Wilde's intelligence
and wit captivated Gide, and he told, among others, his
famous story of Narcissus. Admiring but pitiless, the young
man demanded of Scheherazade more stories, more inventions. Wilde was charmed: 'You listen with your eyes . . .
I don't like your lips, they are straight like those of someone
who has never lied . . .', he said after telling several wonderful
tall stories during a dinner on the 2nd of December at
Drouant's with Marcel Schwob.

Gide had never met with such intelligence, never had he
been more entertained than by this magician who opened
up such a fantastic and disturbing world: had not Princess
Ouroussoff declared after listening to one of his fables that
she clearly saw an aura around his head? His influence was
so strong, so unsettling, that Gide destroyed several pages of
his Journal for November and December of 1891 because
'he is always trying to instil into you a sanction for evil'.
But a letter he wrote to Paul Valéry, who was also thrilled
by the theme of Narcissus, also bears witness to his fervour:
'. . . the aesthete Oscar Wilde, oh, an admirable man,
admirable'.

Valéry: '. . . to pursue with the Oscar Wildes of this world

---

* His Si le grain ne meurt contains stories about Oscar and Bosie. Oscar
said of him, 'He is an egoist without an ego.'

a dream, whose fugitive appearance will have made you feel that you had the secret of the new beauty at your finger-tips. . . .'

Gide: '. . . Wilde is religiously contriving to kill what remains of my soul, because he says that in order to know an essence, one must eliminate it: he wants me to lose my soul, and to miss it. The measure of a thing is the effort made to destroy it. Each thing is made up only of its emptiness. . . .'

Valéry: '. . . Apropos of the insights of Wilde (in your letter I see him as a symbolic mouth à la Redon,* swallowing a mouthful and mechanically transforming it at once into a satanic aphorism).'

Gide: '. . . since Wilde, I hardly exist any more . . .'.

André Gide left Paris to escape temptation. He pretended not to know the nature of the peril, which might have been genuine puritanical ignorance had not one of his closest friends been so salacious a man as Pierre Louÿs, who would certainly have enlightened him about Wilde's morals. The danger from which Gide fled as far as Uzès must certainly have been something more pernicious than a paradox, although the illness of his grandmother gave him the excuse he needed.

Pierre Louÿs remained and Wilde asked him to check the proofs of the biblical drama which he had just written in French. Many other friends were to be consulted, and among them none could have been more intelligent or more faithful than Marcel Schwob. He had just dedicated a story to Wilde which appeared in a collection called The King with the Golden Mask; it was in the manner of Maeterlinck and was about a little beggar-girl who lived in a world of

* Odilon Redon (1840–1916). Self-Portraits, the Gide/Valéry Letters. Edited by Robert Malet, abridged and translated by June Guicharnaud. University of Chicago Press.

her own imagination. The story which gave its name to the work was nearer to the style of Wilde. A court of masks surrounds a masked king who forces his courtiers to un-mask, which reveals that the laughing masks of clowns conceal miserable faces and the tragic masks of priests cover faces bloated with self-satisfaction. The king leaves the court, meets a beggar-woman who tells him that he is leprous but that he will attain beauty through sacrifice. This is the same story as that of *The Young King* and also a little like the legend of King Cophetua, illustrated by Burne-Jones. In the news-paper *L'Echo de Paris* and in his diary, Schwob gave a pen-portrait of Wilde: 'Large, smooth, fat of face, highly-coloured cheeks, an ironic eye, bad and prominent teeth, a vicious child's mouth, lips as if soft with milk and ready to suck again. The arch of his eyebrows and his upper lip is misleading, the indifference affected. He has a long brown frock-coat, a curious waistcoat, a long cane with a golden knob. While eating – very little – he ceaselessly half-smokes Egyptian cigarettes mixed with opium, and is a terrible drinker of absinthe, which gives him visions of red and yellow tulips flowering on the parquet of the Café Royal in London, under the feet of a melancholy boy who waters them in figures of eight like a gardener. . . . He has the art of lying. . . . He stops in the street in front of a house in the course of construction on which brick-layers are at work and says: "As soon as I see people who are doing something useful (laughing) at once it seems to me that they are doing something quite useless. . . ." "I don't know what to do any more", he said to me while lunching at Durand's, "Ideas come to me in French, very short ones, hardly two lines. I can't charge a guinea for two lines." ' Marcel Schwob was so loyal a friend that he even gave Jules Renard the impression that he placed Wilde in the same category as Shakespeare. Renard made the following note: '1st Decem-

ber 1891. Gide is in love with Oscar Wilde, the photograph
of whom is on the mantlepiece [Schwob's]. A fat, fleshy
gentleman, very distinguished, beardless, who has recently
been discovered.' '6th April 1892. Oscar Wilde had luncheon next to me, he does not offer you a cigarette, he
chooses one for you himself. He does not go round the
table, he disarranges the table. His face is covered with
broken veins, he has long decayed teeth. He is very large
and carries an enormous walking stick. . . .'

Madame Arman de Caillavet's reaction to the newcomer
was as follows, 'Mr. Wilde is a cross between Apollo and
Albert Wolff' [the dramatic critic of Le Figaro – an enormous,
corsetted, made-up homosexual]. It was Jacques-Emile
Blanche who brought Wilde and Proust together at
Madame Baignères'. Wilde was very touched by the enthusiasm for English literature evinced by Proust, by the intelligence revealed by his questions about Ruskin and George
Eliot, and willingly accepted Marcel's invitation to dinner
at the Boulevard Haussman. On the evening of the dinner,
Proust, who had been held up at Madame Lemaire's, arrived
very out of breath two minutes late. He asked the servant,
'Is the English gentleman here?' 'Yes, sir, he arrived five
minutes ago; hardly had he gone into the drawing-room
than he asked for the bath-room, and has not come out of
it.' Marcel ran to the end of the passage. 'Mr. Wilde, are
you ill?' 'Ah, there you are Mr. Proust,' Wilde appeared
majestically, 'No, I am not in the least ill. I thought I was
to have the pleasure of dining with you alone, but they
showed me into the drawing-room. I looked at the drawing-
room and at the end of it were your parents, my courage
left me. Goodbye, dear Monsieur Proust, goodbye. . . .'*
Proust was told how Wilde had made disagreeable com-

* This story was told to the author by the two grandsons of Madame
Arthur Baignères.

ments on the furnishing of the drawing-room saying, like
Robert de Montesquiou and the Baron de Charlus: 'How
ugly your house is.'

Formerly Oscar had probably stayed in the British
Embassy in the Faubourg Saint-Honoré, because the
Ambassador, Lord Lytton, was his friend. However, just
before this visit Lord Lytton had died; Oscar was the only
person other than his family whom Lytton would have near
him in his last days.

The British Embassy is in the house which belonged to
Pauline Borghese, the sister of Napoleon. The story that is
told of a British Ambassador remarking in the course of
conversation, 'It is really magnificent here, you know I sleep
in Pauline's bed,' to an austere Minister who replied, 'The
private life of your Excellency is no concern of mine,'
might well be one of Wilde's happy inventions.

At that time a junior Secretary on the staff of the British
Embassy was Reginald Lister, the most Parisian of Englishmen, an intimate friend of Sarah Bernhardt and of most of
the inhabitants of the Faubourg Saint-Germain. His brother,
Lord Ribblesdale, was the subject of one of Sargent's most
famous portraits, and Lister's zeal in furthering the *entente
cordiale*, as well as his tastes, earned for him the nick-name
'*La Tante Cordiale*'.

At the Embassy, Wilde met an unofficial artist who had
recently painted Queen Victoria's portrait. The Queen had
asked to see it; painter and canvas duly arrived at Windsor,
waited an hour in a glacial ante-room, when at last Her
Majesty arrived, glanced at the picture and remarked, 'We
are redder than that.' Oscar was entranced by the story: 'Dear
wonderful Queen, she is so pleased that I have come here
to put right the little differences with France.' While in Paris
he met two friends; Lady de Grey was there to follow the

opera season of the Polish tenor Jean de Reszke, who was
so much the fashion that his name was given to a brand of
cigarette. The Princess of Monaco asked him to stay in her
palace. The Princess was both beautiful and intimidating.
To this day her daughter, the Comtesse Gabriel de la
Rochefoucault, remembers Oscar very well: 'My brother
and I called him the slug, and we couldn't bear him because
each morning he asked us to recite a poem in English and
invariably he said to my mother: "Alice, your children's
accent is atrocious", and our governess punished us. I did
not much like Queen Victoria either because they put my
hair in curlers when she came to have tea at the Palace,
looking peevish, and followed by a submissive daughter.'

The poet moved gracefully from one world to
another, from that of Sargent's models to the Byzantine
Bohemia which paved the way to Art Nouveau, and to the
Montmartre of Toulouse-Lautrec. Soon Oscar was as well-
known on the Boulevards as in Soho. One evening he
appeared at a bar after an evening party, his tail-coat showing
below a short overcoat, his top-hat perched forward revealing a centre-parting which extended to the nape of his neck.
It is thus that he is portrayed by Lautrec in front of the stall
of La Goulue. Another model of Lautrec's was Charles
Conder,* a tall, fair young artist who was to be seen in
other pictures in the Moulin de la Galette. This giant painted
exquisite water colours on fans in which crinolined ladies
pursued the Blue Bird – all these in the then new colours of
lavender and rose. He was penniless, so the kind-hearted
Oscar brought him clients, and then sighed: 'Dear Conder,
with what exquisite subtlety he goes about persuading
someone to give him a hundred francs for a fan, for which
he was fully prepared to pay three hundred.' Conder's work

* Charles Conder (1868–1909), English artist.

inspired Oscar to write a fantasy in French on the style of Verlaine, called *Le Panneau*. Conder often drank too much absinthe before dinner, 'the interminable green hour'. Once, when drunk, he bared his arm and plunged a pin up to the head in a muscle, repeating the performance on his leg, without evincing any concern. 'How interested Baudelaire would have been,' was Oscar's only comment.

William Rothenstein,* a young Jewish artist from Bradford almost hidden behind enormous spectacles, was also there. He was an Oxford friend of Max Beerbohm, and had painted many well-known people. He and Conder had shared an exhibition and, at one time, a studio. Another English bohemian was Phil May who contributed sketches of the flower-sellers of Pigalle and of Piccadilly to the magazine *Pick Me Up*.

On the terrace outside a café, Oscar would preside over a table to which other tables would soon be drawn up, telling wonderful stories, throwing a gold coin to a flower seller in order to replace the faded carnation in his button-hole with a bunch of Parma violets. When he was in funds he would invite everyone to a restaurant.

Oscar's visit to Paris lasted until the end of the year, and it was a comparitively calm interlude in the drama of his life. Although they wrote to each other, no letters between Oscar and Bosie of that period survive, and as Oscar himself wrote, the friendship only started in May 1892. The poet's thoughts were all of enriching French literature with a strange work. Wilfrid Blunt noted in his diary; '27 October 1891. I breakfasted with him (George Curzon), Oscar Wilde and Willie Peel on which occasion Oscar told us he was writing a play in French to be acted at the Français. He is ambitious of being a French Academician. We promised to go to the first representation, George Curzon as Prime Minister.'

* Sir William Rothenstein (1872–1945).

Ada Leverson, 'The Sphinx'

Mrs. Wilde with her son Cyril

18 The Orient

The work to which Wilde dedicated himself when in Paris was to pass through many hands before it reached the publishers. Wilfrid Blunt's note proves that the author had arrived in France with at least the idea of the subject in his head. The letters to Pierre Louÿs mark the progress of the work; he tried out the effect of some of the speeches and scenes on his young friends before deciding to write them down; one day, after having once more told the marvellous story of Salome in greater detail than usual, he returned to his lodgings at 29 Boulevard des Capucines and, as a new note book happened to be lying on the table, he thought he might as well use it up by writing what he had just been speaking. 'If the blank book had not been there on the table I should never have dreamed of doing it. I should not have sent out to buy one,' he stated. He wrote with his usual speed and concentration and suddenly became aware that it was between ten and eleven at night. He went out to get some food at the Grand Café nearby and asked the leader of the orchestra to play something in harmony with his thoughts which were centred on 'a woman dancing with her bare feet in the blood of a man she has craved for and slain'. The leader rose to the occasion and, according to Wilde, played such terrifying music that the conversation in the restaurant dried up and the listeners 'looked at each other with blanched faces'.* One evening, soon after the above episode, the poet went to Montmartre

* From *Aspects of Wilde* by Vincent O'Sullivan.

R

with Stuart Merrill,* an American symbolist poet who wrote in French. They visited the Moulin Rouge, then went on to see a gypsy who danced on her hands: 'I want to meet that woman,' said Oscar, 'because the daughter of Herodias walked on her hands. . . . Yes, it would be marvellous.' But the gypsy was less attractive in a more natural position. Stuart Merrill was long-suffering, 'bulging eyes behind his spectacles, a military moustache, he exuded good health and generosity' is the description of him by a contemporary. He cannot have enjoyed the low haunts, but through Wilde he was to glimpse horrors of which he had never dreamed.

When *Salome* was nearly finished, Wilde showed it to Stuart Merrill and to another symbolist poet, Alfred Retté, who, between them, took out the anglicisms and cut out the over-long lists. Perhaps because these two friends were so censorious, the manuscript was then sent to Pierre Louÿs with the following letter in French: 'Here is the drama of *Salome*. It is not yet finished nor corrected, but it gives an idea of the *construction*, of the theme and of the action of the drama. Here and there there are lacunae, but the idea of the drama is clear. I am still suffering from a cold and do not feel well. But I shall be perfectly well by Monday and shall be waiting for you at one o'clock at Mignon's for lunch . . .'

In spite of his apparent confusion and unconcern, Wilde instinctively knew what the public was going to want. To a London society which was bored with the Victorian era, he was to offer comedies echoing some aspects of the eighteenth century. To the threatened and artificial world of inverts he had offered *Dorian Gray*; for the Art Nouveau

---

* Stuart Fitzrandolph Merrill (1863–1915). In November 1895 he drew up a petition to Queen Victoria begging for Wilde's release from prison but it came to nothing as hardly any French literary figures would sign it.

Europe he wrote *Salome*, one of the most famous and one of the worst of his works. He wrote it in the symbolist idiom, in slightly childish language, a little Biblical, put into form by Maeterlinck. In choosing to write in the French language, the poet joined an international *avant-garde*, but he was also in the tradition of the aristocratic authors such as Hamilton with his *Vie du Chevalier de Gramont*, and Beckford with *Vathek*, and later, an English woman called Pauline Tarn who wrote sapphic poems under the name of Renée Vivien, and, today, Samuel Beckett. Oscar wrote a flowery French in which the anglicisms were acceptable as they gave a real ingenuousness to the babbling of Salome and a strange majesty to Herod's speeches. In order that certain words should stand out as the author intended, Salome has to be acted with an English accent.

The subject had been in the air since Flaubert's story, and the famous pages in Huysmans' *A Rebours*. Art Nouveau owed much to the following description of Salome: 'Here she was, a true harlot, obedient to her passionate and cruel female temperament; here she came to life, more refined yet more savage, more hateful yet more exquisite than before; here she roused the sleeping senses of the male more powerfully, subjugated his will more surely with her charms – the charms of a great venereal flower, grown in a bed of sacrilege, reared in a hot-house of impiety.'* Already in 1887 Jules Laforgue had written of a most modern Salome: 'There on a cushion, amongst the fragments of the ebony lyre, sparkling with a coating of phosphorus, washed, painted, curled, grinning at the twenty-four million heavenly bodies . . . Salome kissed this mouth mercifully and closely and sealed this mouth with her corrosive stamp.' (*Moralités Légendaires.*) Professor Mario

* From *Against Nature*, translated by Robert Baldick.

Praz, who has studied all the pre-1900 Salomes, pointed out that their common ancestor was that invented by Heinrich Heine in his poem *Atta Troll*. In this it is Herodias who is enamoured of St. John, she appears overwhelmed with sorrow, juggling with the head of her loved one. There is also Mallarmé's *Herodias* which was not published until 1898, although copies of it were circulated in symbolist circles. Massenet's *Hérodiade* must not be forgotten.

The theme was in the air at the end of the century, glowing in a lurid mist, but what was genuinely Wildean was the outrageous idea of the little Salome being in love with the prophet. The fulfilment of this monstrous passion was in accordance with the demand of that time for the highly spiced and, furthermore, the poet needed a perversion to interest himself in the drama. But one can also find the sources of Salome in Wilde himself, since he brought together all the themes of the decadence in the poem *The Sphinx*, and in his stories, of which the moral is repeated in a much finer poem, '. . . each man kills the thing he loves'. Certainly the décor is by Gustave Moreau but, of all the writers of his time, the Oriental Oscar is the only one perfectly at his ease in temples reminiscent of Benares and of Justinian's *Hagia Sofia*, on the terraces covered with precious rugs where Salammbô and Herodias satisfy their caprices by the light of a mauve moon. Oscar mixes all the treasures of the antique Orient; 'I have jewels hidden in this place – jewels that your mother even has never seen; jewels that are marvellous. I have a collar of pearls, set in four rows. They are like unto moons chained with rays of silver. They are like fifty moons caught in a golden net. On the ivory of her breast a queen has worn it. . . . I have topazes, yellow as are the eyes of tigers, and topazes that are pink as the eyes of a wood-pigeon, and green topazes that are as the eyes of cats. I have opals that burn always with an ice-like

flame, opals that make sad men's minds, and are fearful of
the shadows. . . . I have sapphires big like eggs, and as blue
as blue flowers. The sea wanders within them and the moon
comes never to trouble the blue of their waves. I have
chrysolites and beryls and chrysoprases and rubies. I have
sardonyx and hyacinth stones and stones of chalcedony, and
I will give them all to you, all, and other things will I add
to them. . . . I have a crystal, into which it is not lawful for a
woman to look, nor may young men behold it until they
have been beaten with rods.' It was almost a parody, which
explains the success of *Salome* ten years later when all these
jewels had rolled out of their symbolist jewel-cases on the
stages of central Europe. Then Freud gave weight to the
décor by revealing the secret ways of passion which before
would no doubt have appeared ludicrous to the general public.

Twelve years later the sublime vulgarity of this
depraved Orient was to be interpreted in the music of
Strauss with his echoes not only of the Persian Market but
also of Wagner. The delirious obsession of the dance of the
seven veils, at once sacred and lascivious, would have
enchanted Wilde. The same opulence of decoration and of
feeling was to be found in Reinhardt's stage setting of *The
Tragedy of Salome* which Ida Rubenstein commissioned from
Florent Schmitt much later. Jewish, androgynous and
covered with real jewels, she was incomparable in the part.
Salome and the other works of this sort show how un-
English Wilde was. Where was the humour, the reserve or
even the sentimentality? In these dramas there is some
strange atavism, the disturbing blood of a pirate or a
merchant stranded in Ireland and transmitted through his
mother. The costumes of the dramas betrayed something of
Speranza's taste. With her necklaces and veils, she set her
stamp on the production.

Three years later Wilde once more took up the subject of lust in opposition to saintliness in *La Sainte Courtisane, or The Woman Covered with Jewels*. The passion of this princess of the Byzantine Empire could only have been expressed by Wilde, in spite of the fact that it is very near to *The Temptation of St. Anthony* and still nearer to Anatole France's *Thaïs*: 'Sometimes I sit in the circus and the gladiators fight beneath me. Once a Thracian who was my lover was caught in the net. I gave the signal for him to die and the whole theatre applauded. Sometimes I pass through the gymnasium and watch the young men wrestling or in the race. Their bodies are bright with oil and their brows are wreathed with willow sprays and with myrtle. . . . He at whom I smile leaves his companions and follows me to my home. At other times I go down to the harbour and watch the merchants unloading their vessels . . . when they see me coming they stand on the prows of their ships and call to me, but I do not answer them. I go to the little taverns where the sailors lie all day long drinking black wine and playing with dice and I sit down with them . . . I made the Prince my slave, and his slave who was a Tyrian I made my Lord for the space of a moon. . . .'

It is not Byzantine or Alexandrian ladies who express themselves through Oscar's mouth so much as rich homosexuals, always brimming over but always frustrated, who, in the Victorian age, keep their nostalgia for their secret fatherland. It is an Orient where everything is permitted, where men draped in silken garments dispose of marvellous slaves and weave terrible plots. Oscar was really the Prince-Magician of this imaginary country, the capital of which was Sodom. With rare words and haunting rhythms, he had worked for many years on the litanies of a Black Mass. *The Sphinx* is the most curious, the most decadent of his poems. Mr. Robert Merle has pointed out: 'The *Sphinx* is a poem that does not end, a gigantic python crawling in the dark, a haunting memory of a thought endlessly repeated.' Oscar had started it at Oxford, under the influence of Baudelaire's Les Chats and of Poe (the arrival of the Sphinx in the room of the student is reminiscent of The Raven). Then he took up the subject during his first visit to Paris, asking his friends for rhymes for Catafalque (he had to be content with 'Amenalk, the God of Heliopolis') and to 'Nenuphar'. Marriage, The Woman's World and the stories made Oscar forget the poem until he again returned to it when Robbie discovered the manuscript under a pile of papers in 1889. It was Robbie who persuaded his friend to finish and to polish the work. 'Sing to me of that odorous green eve when crouching by the marge/You heard from Adrian's gilded barge the laughter of Antinous.' (How near the poet comes to Scheherazade in the exoticism of the names he chooses, such as Hippogriffs and Basilisks. The outrageousness of this poem makes it better than the insipid stories. Christ certainly appears in the last stanza, but without adding any pungency to the mythological lechery of which one is a little weary after so many stanzas.) Professors of comparative literature enjoy finding in The Sphinx (the French prefer to attribute the feminine sex to it, although in the description of its pleasures it is shown to be an hermaphrodite) the sister of Swinburne's Dolores and of his Cleopatra. It has the Gioconda's fatal smile: '. . . and with your curved archaic smile you watched his passion come and go', and in Keats' manner cries out: 'away to Egypt', but there is more than literature in it. Egypt was the spiritual country of the man who wore a sacred scarab on his finger; the corrupt Egypt of the Ptolemies – which began to inspire Cavafy around 1900 – the land of miracles and mysteries – the neo-platonists and the Thousand and One Nights. Leaving Persia with its delicate miniatures to Fitzgerald, the magician turned to the world of Gustave Moreau.

Salome and the Sphinx, therefore, have Moreau's jewels
and palaces, they also have the bored caprices of Helen who
lets her brocade trail in the blood of handsome young men.
Thus the Tyrian warrior in love with Salome kills himself
only in order to bring a red stain to the picture. Quasi-
androgynous, Salome heralded the St. Sebastian which
d'Annunzio was to write twenty years later; and there is
much in common between these two works, both written in
French by foreigners.

Oddly enough, the only actress who could take the
part of the little girl, and for whom Wilde had written the
part, was nearing her fiftieth year. The soft, undulating lines
of her body were more those of a vase by Gallé than a
Tanagra, but she had brought to life all the exciting exoticism of Phèdre and Gismonda. It was again Moreau who,
through Sarah Bernhardt, inspired Wilde. Already in 1889
Lorrain had announced: 'Sarah is there, standing before me,
with her delicate and irritating profile, her eyes as glittering
and cold as precious stones. To see her thus undulating and
dying under the glint of her metal belt, I dream that she is
as much of the family of the old King David as of the young
archangel with a woman's face. Yes, she is surely the daughter
of Gustave Moreau, the enigmatic Sarah, sister of the Muses,
who carried decapitated chiefs, of Orpheus and of those
Salomes, willowy and bloody, the Salome of the famous
water-colour, the Salome of the Apparition, whose trium-
phant and coruscating costume she wore even in Theodora....'

She had no sooner read the play than she decided to make
a splendid production of it.* One can imagine the extrava-

---

* Wilde had already wanted to write a play about Queen Elizabeth for
the great actress in which during the whole of one act, she would be
disguised as a page, having gone to ascertain the beauty of her rival,
Mary Stuart.

gant costumes covered in peacock's feathers and pearls. Graham Robertson was asked to design them. He had just designed the costume of the Empress Theodora and so splendid was it that Sarah wanted Burne-Jones to paint her in it, at any cost. However all the gold and glory put off the artist and the portrait never materialised. To be sure the stage settings for Salome were not to be in half tones, the pastel shades and mists were left behind with Maeterlinck, and the colours to be found in the aquarelles of Gustave Moreau were chosen in preference.

Graham Robertson tells the following story in his autobiography, *Time Was*: ' "I should like," said Oscar throwing off the notion at random, "I should like everyone on the stage to be in yellow." It was a good idea and I saw it's possibilities at once – every costume in some shade of yellow from the clearest lemon to deep orange, with here and there just a hint of black – you must have that – and all upon a pale ivory terrace against a great empty sky of deepest violet. "A violet sky," repeated Oscar slowly, "yes, I never thought of that. Certainly a violet sky, and then, in place of an orchestra, braziers of perfume. Think – the scented clouds rising and partly veiling the stage from time to time – a new perfume for each new emotion." '

Yet Wilde was not quite sure about Graham Robertson's taste. (He was just becoming known as an illustrator of children's books.) Oscar talked over his project with Ricketts and asked this more serious artist to design the décor for the production of *Salome* in France. Ricketts had interpreted the equivocal melancholy of Oscar's stories very well, and for this play he proposed a black floor 'upon which Salome's feet could move like white doves. . . . The sky was to be a rich turquoise blue, cut by the perpendicular fall of gilded strips of Japanese matting forming an aerial tent above the terraces. Herod and Herodias to be in blood-red.'

Ricketts wanted a Salome in gold or silver, Wilde wanted her 'green, like a poisonous lizard'. Curiously enough, these designs went beyond Art Nouveau, and heralded those of the Russian Ballet.*

Sarah wished to play Salome in London, where she was as celebrated as in Paris, and at once started rehearsals. But she kept her head, the costumes for Cleopatra had cost her a lot of money and they would do perfectly well for Salome. The dresses were made of brocade trimmed with large stones, with a triple crown of gold on the blue-powdered wig. Over all this was to be flung Theodora's cope to remind the audience of the priestly rank of a Princess of Judea. 'By the way,' said Graham Robertson to Sarah, 'the Dance of the Seven Veils, what about it? I suppose you will get a walker-on to go through with it, won't you? – veiled of course and with your blue hair?' 'Not at all,' said Sarah, 'I am going to dance myself.' She had already studied the words and envisaged the performance as static, as in an oratorio. 'It is heraldic, like a fresco, and the words should drop like a pearl in a crystal bowl. That is right, no rapid movements, and stylised gestures.' Oscar was in the seventh heaven.

A theatre was hired (The Palace), actors were engaged and at last they had the bright idea of sending it to the Lord Chamberlain. The answer was not what they had expected. There was no question of presenting Biblical characters on the stage anywhere in the United Kingdom. It was useless to tell him that Salome had constantly figured in mystery plays, he was unbending. Sarah, furious, saw a superb part and a lot of capital already invested in it escaping her. The author in despair spoke of leaving England and becoming

---

* They were not realised until 1906. Ricketts said that Wilde wanted as realistic a setting as possible and that both of them had sought inspiration in Gustave Moreau.

a French citizen. 'But Oscar, you would have to do your military service.' 'Well my dear, that requires a lot of thought.' Punch published a caricature of him as an infantry-man, a bayonet replacing the usual sunflower. Furthermore, everything went wrong with Salome: Louÿs failed to thank the master for having dedicated the work to him: 'You alone, whose name I have written in gold on purple.' Later this young man attempted a reconciliation with Wilde, but Wilde replied, 'You thought I had friends, I have nothing but lovers . . .'.* To the great amusement of his friends, the poet published exasperated interviews. To Bernard Shaw, who alone upheld him, he wrote: '23 Feb. 1893. My dear Shaw, You have written well and wisely and with sound wit on the ridiculous institution of a stage-censor-ship . . . England is the land of intellectual fogs but you have done much to clear the air: we are both Celtic, and I like to think that we are friends: for these and many other reasons Salome presents herself to you in purple raiment. . . .' The French language edition was 'in Tyrian purple and tired silver' (Oscar's words) and was published simul-taneously in France and England.

Works of art become legendary when they inspire other painters and musicians on a sufficient scale: Wilde's Salome so well represented his period that even without Bernhardt it still had a tremendous success in book form. By asking a young man of twenty-two to illustrate the English-language edition, John Lane, the publisher, launched the work that precipitated Art Nouveau.

Around 1890 a very thin young man with a large beaky nose, impeccably elegant in the manner of Brummel, showed Whistler his first drawings: his name was Aubrey

* This was Louÿs' version. Wilde maintained that he had said 'I wanted you as a friend, now I shall only have lovers'. – Translator's note.

Beardsley. The master was critical of Beardsley's hair, saying
that he had too much on his head and that he even covered
the paper with it. It is true that the first drawings were not
his best: young angular warriors copied from Mantegna,
stiff-necked *Demoiselles Elues* wandering about the margins
of novels of the Round Table, and everywhere plant-like
arabesques which stretched
and twined and untwined
themselves among the in-
terlacings of a kind that
had not been seen since
the early Irish manuscripts.
And then, of course, pea-
cocks everywhere, herald-
ing with their piercing cry
an art form of which their
sinuous necks and irides-
cent tails became the hall-
mark. Beardsley had drawn
his inspiration from Japanese albums where ladies
who are literally held together by four pins con-
struct complicated effects
with flowers, and also
from the elongated Biblical
figures and scroll-like designs of William Blake.
He had also copied trop-

Self-portrait by Aubrey Beardsley

ical botany and the architecture of Nineveh. A year after
his visit to Whistler, Beardsley took his drawings to show
to John Lane. The great publisher of the *Mauve Decade* did not
share the peculiarities of his authors, and was described by
one of them, Frederick Rolfe (Baron Corvo), as 'a sort of

little stout fighting cock, with the look as if he had been
brought up on bad beer'.

Beardsley expressed his perfidious spirit in meander-
ings but he was also thirty years ahead of his time in
inventing the straight line. Thus Salome does her hair in
front of a 1925 table with Beardsley's own favourite books
on the shelves: Nana, The Golden Ass and the works of the
Marquis de Sade. He is prodigal with roses and garnets,
he portrays satyrs with the breasts of old women by the
light of ithyphallic candles. Dwarfs and slaves brandish
whips, of which the lash, drawn with a cruel and sure
line, comes from an edition of Vogue produced in Hell by
the Marquis de Sade and Sacher von Masoch; it tears the
shoulders of the slaves into black lace. Beardsley adorns
Salome's cloak with Whistler's peacock feathers; from
Utamaro he takes the princess's coil of hair and cape, and
the faces of the young men, though derived from Botticelli,
reflect a disillusioned lubricity. Here and there, rhythm is
provided by large black marks followed by constellations
of miniscule dots outlining mysterious palaces and forests.
When shown these designs, Wilde was furious: 'They are
all too Japanese, while my play is Byzantine. My Herod is
like the Herod of Gustave Moreau – wrapped in jewels and
sorrows. My Salome is a mystic, the sister of Salammbô,
a Sainte Thérèse who worships the moon; dear Aubrey's
designs are like the naughty scribbles a precocious schoolboy
makes on the margins of his copybook. . . .'*

But the personality of the draughtsman was astonishing.
This young man was, in fact, one of the rare people who
could return the ball to the marvellous conversationalist,
and as the English-language edition had a great success, the
poet ended by having a certain esteem for the illustrator.
Wilde wanted to charm Beardsley by pretending to believe

* Quoted by Ricketts in Recollections of Oscar Wilde.

that he was a monster of perversity, but the young man always had the last word: ' "Absinthe", said Oscar, "is to all other drinks what Aubrey's drawings are to other pictures; it stands alone, it is like nothing else; it shimmers like southern twilight in opalescent colouring; it has about it the seduction of strange sins. It is stronger than any other spirit, and brings out the subconscious self in man. It is just like your drawings, Aubrey: it gets on one's nerves and is cruel. Baudelaire called his poems *Fleurs du Mal*, I shall call your drawings *Fleurs du Peché* – flowers of sin. When I have before me one of your drawings I want to drink absinthe, which changes colour like jade in sunlight and makes the senses thrall, and then I can live myself back in imperial Rome, in the Rome of the later Caesars." "Don't forget the simple pleasures of that life, Oscar," said Aubrey, "Nero set Christians on fire, like large tallow candles; the only light Christians have ever been known to give," he added in a languid, gentle voice,' though he was to end his short life a conscience-stricken Roman Catholic.

In France, Beardsley exhibited his drawings at Bing's and at the Salon of 1892, where they were particularly admired by Puvis de Chavanne. It would appear to be a far cry from Sainte Geneviève to Salome, but the cold Puvis was a forerunner of Art Nouveau just as much as the mysterious Moreau. Beardsley liked monsters: Lautrec, grotesque and lubricious, fascinated him and they became friends. They were said to smoke opium together, and were to be seen on the terraces of cafés by revellers ambling from the Chat-Noir to the Moulin-Rouge. Neither had many more years to live.

Despite the fact that Beardsley and Oscar got on well in conversation, Beardsley could be as much irritated by him as were his fiercest enemies, as is revealed in the following conversation between Beardsley and Vincent O'Sullivan, recorded in the latter's *Aspects of Wilde*. O'Sullivan said that

Oscar had given him a discourse on Carlyle's *French Revolution* beginning with the flight of the 'unclean thing', Madame du Barry. 'What unclean thing?' said Beardsley, 'How was she unclean? She was perfectly charming. That kind of twaddle makes me seasick, and it is so like Oscar.' But Wilde was simply representing the Puritan Carlyle, and had not really adopted his opinion about Madame du Barry. In fact, he explained some of Carlyle's prejudices – and it must be admitted that Carlyle would have been an unsatisfactory lover for Madame du Barry.

19   In the limelight

We left Oscar in Paris in December 1891 correcting
the proofs of the French edition of *Salome*. He returned to
London in 1892 to supervise the rehearsals of his comedy
Lady Windermere's Fan. To Wilde, the aesthete, man-about-
town and, when necessary, prophet, was added another
personality – the dramatist. In three and a half years there
was to be a spectacular accumulation of theatrical triumphs,
close relationships often ending in rows, and innumerable
adventures: Wilde lived more fully in that short time than
in the rest of his life, but it was the artificial life of those
who are continually on show. The excitement, the squander-
ing of money and of time must have suited him, as he
produced the four comedies which people of taste agree are
the best of his works, containing as they do perfect dialogue,
few ideas, funny situations and conventional sentiments.
Not only in *Vera*, but in the dialogues of *Intentions* and in
certain chapters of *Dorian Gray*, Wilde had already prepared
himself for the theatre. *Lord Arthur Savile's Crime* is the outline
of a burlesque drama where the characters who reappear
in every play first make their appearance; the irresistible,
but slightly sentimental young man; the young girl, up-to-
date, but always chaste; the great lady, virtuous but
tempted; the dowager, witty but eccentric; and eventually –
the mysterious stranger, magician in the stories, intriguer
in the plays. For the stage Wilde added the devoted man-
servant, the rationalising and cynical friends, the fashionable
ladies whose gossip represents a frivolous chorus which

260

neatly breaks up the action of the play.

This world was as limited as that of Marivaux, because Wilde on the stage was a man of the eighteenth century, thanks to that gift for adaptation which enabled him to be Byzantine in Paris and Athenian at Oxford. All the more reason, therefore, that he should be of the century which preceded his own, rather than of those he had assimilated through literature. We have seen how Dublin stood apart from the nineteenth century – Industry and Victorian morality had not penetrated, conversation was brilliant, adventure easy. Sheridan had lived a stone's throw from Merrion Square, and his nephew had been a friend of Dr. Wilde.

Lady Windermere's Fan was the first good comedy to be produced in London since The School for Scandal of a century earlier. The tone is that of a leisured society, the wit that of Wilde because his characters always spoke with his own carefully recorded words. This play and those that followed, took place in eighteenth-century drawing-rooms, filled with aspidistras, Victorian lamp-shades, and needless to say, behind screens, on those pieces of furniture called love-seats, in the scenes where vows are exchanged. All this is the opposite of the setting, so artistic and so modern, of Salome. The Ritz Hotel somehow has retained the atmosphere with its glass screens, its little tables and the constant coming and going of men-servants. There is nothing in the least aesthetic in Wilde's comedies, no purple passages, not the slightest evangelical ingenuousness. As in the works of Madame de Ségur, Les Malheurs de Sophie for example, virtue is in proportion to rank, and only the schemers are without titles – an amusing example of worldly Manichaeism.

Without in any way imitating them, the style is as alive as that of Sheridan or Beaumarchais. Each character presents Oscar himself in various moods; nonchalance enhanced by

s

epigrams in the dandy, arrogance underlined by maxims
in the Duchess, worrying allusions in the intriguers; only
the good women talk like Constance. Wilde's plays owe
much to those he had applauded in Paris, their buoyancy is
as well maintained as in Pailleron's *Le Monde où l'on s'ennuie* or
in Dumas' *La Francillon*.* The social sphere is the same, the
character of the Duchess of Réville in the former play, the
famous scene about the salad in the second, are not unlike
Wilde. But after all Wilde and Dumas lived in the same
circles. That the Irishman ingenuously admired his French
rival is not in doubt, as these lines written in prison confirm:
'When I was actually engaged in writing, and penning
comedies that were to beat Congreve for brilliancy and
Dumas fils for philosophy, and I suppose everyone else for
every other quality . . .'. Yet when he set himself to work,
he agreed that his plays were pot-boilers which enabled
him to continue his artistic researches free from worries;
with what gay flippancy he spoke to Gide,† and to George
Alexander when he handed him *Lady Windermere's Fan*, of 'one
of those modern drawing-room plays with pink lamp
shades'.

Later, in 1900, Wilde as a playwright was to receive
perceptive attention from Max Beerbohm in *The Saturday
Review*: 'His work was distinct from that of most other play-
wrights in that he was a man who had achieved success outside the theatre. He was not a mere maker of plays. Taking
up dramaturgy when he was no longer a young man, taking
it up as a kind of afterthought, he brought to it a knowledge
of the world which the life-long playwright seldom possesses.

---

* In a very interesting thesis on the French influence on Wilde, a
Swedish author, Hartly, has shown how scenes and even words were
borrowed from Dumas fils, and their meanings reversed. He has not
however been able to explain why Dumas is now unplayable while
Wilde remains enchanting.

† Translator's addition.

But this was only one point in his advantage. He came as a thinker, a weaver of ideas, and as a wit, and as the master of literary style. It was, I think, in respect of literary style that his plays were most remarkable. . . .'

Oscar by Max Beerbohm

All this was new to the English, without being artistic or
very advanced. Oscar addressed himself to worldly people
as a man of the world himself. The fashionable recognised
themselves and applauded, the others, introduced into a
sphere about which they had before only speculated, were
delighted. Oscar forgot artistic poses and aesthetic messages,
the scene was a drawing-room and, as in all drawing-rooms
to which he was invited, he had only to amuse. But
irreverence was allowed, and from the first scene of *Lady
Windermere's Fan* the audience realised that they were going
to laugh at principles, as if they were all intimate friends.
When Lord Darlington says: 'Oh, nowadays so many conceited people go about Society pretending to be good, that
I think it shows rather a sweet and modest disposition to
pretend to be bad. Besides, there is this to be said. If you
pretend to be good, the world takes you very seriously. If
you pretend to be bad, it doesn't. . . .' Lady Windermere,
letting fall her fan at the entrance of the disquieting Mrs.
Erlynne, appears now to symbolise Victorian society,
powerless before the new world of money which was to
triumph in the Edwardian era: she represents British virtue
affronted by international luxury, the old order asserting
itself against the new dissipation.

It was furthermore a play in which some of the characters
were taken from life, where allusion was made to the fortune
lent by the Rothschilds to Disraeli at the time of the Suez
Canal for the shares bought by Britain. The Baron Arnhem,
who traffics in State secrets, is based on two friends of the
Prince of Wales, the financiers Baron Hirsch and Sir Ernest
Cassell. The latter was not very popular in Society despite
his generous hospitality. At one ball the Prince of Wales
asked a very pretty woman with whom he had been dancing
'And now, what does Lady Salome want?' 'The head of
Sir Ernest, sir.' The Prince turned his back upon her. When

The Importance of Being Earnest was being played, the Prince asked a friend if he had seen it. 'Not yet, sir, but every day I see the importance of being Sir Ernest! . . .' The Prince of Wales enjoyed Wilde's plays, he would even go a second time, taking his friends, and he twice went to a rehearsal. Clapping his large be-ringed hands, he led the applause himself, and his laugh endorsed the laughter of the audience at all the audacities.

The first night of Lady Windermere's Fan was a triumph. Up to the end the tussle between virtue and immorality held the audience breathless, because Wilde very skilfully made the characters change attitudes; in the first act Mrs. Erlynne plays at blackmail, in the last, at generosity. The sentimental scene in which she asks for the portrait of her daughter is a gift to tender hearts. But if virtue carries the day, it is through blindness, and cynicism has the last word, for the scheming woman makes a splendid marriage. The curtain fell to an ovation, with cries of 'Author!' After the bows of the actors, Oscar walked on to the stage as if into a drawing-room, a cigarette in his hand, smiling pleasantly to right and left and said: 'Ladies and Gentlemen, I have enjoyed this evening immensely. The actors have given us a charming rendering of a delightful play, and your appreciation has been most intelligent. I congratulate you on the great success of your performance, which persuades me that you think almost as highly of the play as I do myself.' This insolence maddened the critics but doubled the applause.

The value that Oscar now set on his genius (which the audience's applause confirmed each day) gave him the right to ignore the critics and to look upon the actors not as artists but as instruments. Before, Oscar had been courtesy itself, now he became proud and ironical. Backstage his words were repeated with venom: 'I never write plays for anyone. I write plays to amuse myself. If people want to act in them I sometimes allow them to do so.' An interviewer asked him: 'Do you regard the actor as a creative artist?' 'Certainly, terribly creative, terribly creative.' Although Oscar said he despised the critics, he was not unaware of them: he wrote to the *Daily Telegraph*: '. . . the frame we call the stage was "peopled with either living actors or moving puppets" . . . the actor's aim is, or should be, to convert his own accidental personality into the real and essential personality of the character he is called upon to impersonate. . . . There are many advantages in puppets. They never argue. They have no crude views about art. They have no private lives. We are never bothered by accounts of their virtues, or bored by recitals of their vices; and when they are out of an engagement they never do good in public or save people from drowning; nor do they speak more than is set down for them. . . .'

Wilde was a little too haughty in his treatment of actors, who were distinguished social figures in London, careful of their reputations, with an eye on an eventual knighthood. Thus Herbert Beerbohm Tree, who produced *A Woman of No Importance* at the Haymarket Theatre, of which he was manager, is said to have been extremely annoyed when in Bond Street he met one of his actors wearing a bowler and not a top-hat. Sir Herbert and Lady Tree and Irene Vanburgh were invited to Marlborough House and were completely at their ease when surrounded by the smart set, many of whom were their friends in real life. Ellen Terry, the most beautiful and outstanding actress in England, Oscar's friend for fifteen years, never acted in his plays, but her sister Marion, however, had a great success as Mrs. Erlynne. So prudish were the stars of the theatre that when Marion Terry had her hair henna'd and wore bronze make-up it created a sensation of shocked disapproval. Charles Brookfield, the actor, was one of Wilde's most vindictive enemies at the time of his troubles because he had once been rebuked by Oscar for wearing the wrong kind of suit off the stage. As Brookfield's parents moved in court circles he was furious at being given lessons in propriety from someone whom he probably considered an Irish upstart.*

Oscar's behaviour was frequently impossible: he made scenes about the slightest word skipped, over the shade of a tie or even a button-hole, even insisting on one occasion that the actor who played the part of Cecil Graham should wear a green carnation. Just before the first night of *Lady Windermere's Fan* the following conversation took place between Oscar and Graham Robertson: 'You have your place for the première?' 'That's right.' 'Now I want you to do something. Go to such-and-such a shop and get a green carnation button-hole for tomorrow night. No, I know there's no such thing, but they arrange them somehow at that shop, dye them I suppose. I want a good many men to wear them tomorrow, it will annoy the public.' 'But why annoy the public?' 'It likes to be annoyed: a young man on stage will wear a green carnation, people will stare at it and wonder. Then they will look round the house and see everywhere, here and there, more specks of mystic green. "That will be a secret symbol" they will say, "What on earth can it mean?"' 'And what does it mean?' I asked, 'Nothing whatsoever,' said Oscar, 'But that is just what no one will guess.'†

Even the most celebrated actors who saw Oscar continuously — he never missed a rehearsal — ended by unconsciously imitating him. Herbert Beerbohm Tree played the part of Lord Illingworth in *A Woman of No Importance* and he identified more and more with the part. Oscar noticed this and said, 'Ah, every day dear Herbert becomes *de plus en*

* Translator's addition.
† From *Time Was* by Graham Robertson.

plus Oscarisé. It is a wonderful case of Nature imitating Art.'
But Oscar's good humour frequently put an end to the
spite caused by his vanity. Very generously, instead of
insisting upon a great number of complimentary seats for
his first nights, he bought out of his own pocket several
rows of stalls.

First nights amused Oscar enormously, and he
arranged the house with the greatest care, placing peeresses
next to poets, dowagers next to young men, a box for
Royalty (incidentally, at the first night of *A Woman of No
Importance* the Prince of Wales refused to share a box with
Mrs. Langtry). A box for Mrs. Leverson who, moreover,
seldom missed a dress rehearsal, often accompanied by
Lord Alfred who doted upon her. And Constance? She also
had her box where Oscar and Alfred would join her. She
must have recognised herself in the part of Lady Windermere and sighed at the brilliant remarks on marriage.
The applause, the life of a prima donna, lived between
the theatre and grand restaurants, went to Wilde's head.
This was what he had been waiting for all his life; as he
said to a journalist: 'I am not nervous on the night that I
am producing a new play. I am exquisitely indifferent. My
nervousness ends at the last dress rehearsal. I know then
what effect my play, as presented on the stage, has produced
upon me. My interest in the play ends there, and I feel
curiously envious of the public – they have such wonderfully fresh emotions in store for them. . . . It is the public,
not the play, that I desire to make a success. . . . The public
makes a success when it realises that a play is a work of art.
On the three first nights I have had in London the public
has been most successful, and, had the dimensions of the
stage admitted of it, I would have called them before the
curtain. . . . The artist is always the munificent patron of

the public. I am very fond of the public and, personally, I always patronise the public very much. . . .'

This dazzling success was accompanied by another. According to Lord Alfred, Oscar became his lover. He had laid siege cleverly and patiently with not a few other distractions to occupy him in the meantime; one night, after a performance of *Lady Windermere's Fan* and supper, he brought back his loved one to Tite Street at two o'clock in the morning. Mrs. Wilde was at the sea-side with her children. Again according to Lord Alfred, such familiarities as took place were of the same kind as practised at Winchester – 'of the sin which takes its name from one of the Cities of the Plain there was never the slightest question,' says Bosie in his autobiography, although admitting that the love affair did have some sexual expression. Life for Wilde with Bosie at his side was an extension of his plays. At the Savoy and other restaurants it was as if he was on a stage, giving an admirable performance without those boring intermediaries, the actors. In his wake there followed, as in his plays, compliments, scandals and absurdities. Only too often a chorus of boys took the place of fashionable women. The disciples of Plato had become the followers of a disturbing star. Their chatter annoyed people of good sense and could only give rise to scandal. And gradually Oscar's sensibilities became blunted, his figure became gross, he frequently drank too much, and became less and less delightful. Increasingly, too, he put into his play 'The Life of Oscar Wilde' more passion than into those he offered to the public.

There was a considerable element of Irish devil-may-care about this love so carelessly displayed in theatres and restaurants. There was also the deep need to proclaim that which must not be mentioned, the intoxication of a scandal

that must at all costs be avoided. His too-brilliant friends
and his shady connections represented much more than
pleasure – they represented the attraction of danger. Wilde
could not resist flirting with this danger even in his plays,
in which irresistible young men, Lord Goring, Algernon
Moncrieff, Gerald Arbuthnot, appeared. But scorched by
the scandal caused by his novel, Wilde offered only innocent
plays to the public, in which the adultery is always in the
past. In the play *A Woman of No Importance*, dedicated to Lady
de Grey, which followed *Lady Windermere's Fan*, a member of
the audience today might well think that Lord Illingworth,
so like Lord Henry in *The Picture of Dorian Gray*, is interested in
Gerald for his personal charm: indeed, many political
careers have started in this way. The play, apart from comic
characters such as The Venerable Archdeacon who speaks of
his wife's ailments and the despotic Lady Caroline Pontefract,
is spoilt by a plot about a natural child (which might have
come from the pen of Dumas) and by over-contrived co-
incidences, which, unlike those in *The Importance of Being
Earnest*, are not saved by glorious absurdity.

At the beginning of the latter play, it might well be
thought that John and Algernon talk exactly like Oscar's
'dear boys'. Certainly the irresistible Lord Goring of *An
Ideal Husband* had been Mrs. Cheveley's lover and pays court
to Mabel, but with detachment because for him a woman
was only an extra ornament to make his entrance successful,
like that carnation round which Wilde weaves a whole
theory of frivolity. And then, those who had heard him
recount the absurdities of Lady Dorothy Nevill could
recognise the pervert showing the tip of his powdered nose
in the characters of Lady Bracknell and Lady Markby, who
could easily be played with the wry comedy of transvestites.
Oscar leaves to the brides and fiancées the important place
that they occupy in real life, but the brides in his plays

underline all that is narrow-minded in virtue by their over-moralising attitudes, and the fiancées are only pretty puppets who, by an ingenious but astonishing mechanism, utter Wilde's paradoxes as to the manner born.

Decorum was so well observed that only someone like André Gide could have asked himself whether Wilde's plays contained some secret; Gide wrote: '29 June 1913. Ransome's book on Wilde strikes me as good ... on the other hand he fails to show to what a degree the plays *An Ideal Husband* and *A Woman of No Importance* are revelatory – and I was about to say, confidential – despite their apparent objectivity. Later on I hope to return to the subject and relate everything that I didn't dare tell at first. I should like too, to explain Wilde's work in my own way, and especially his drama – of which the greatest interest lies between the lines.'

'1st October 1927. I believe ... that this affected aestheticism was for him merely an ingenious cloak to hide, whilst half revealing, what he could not let be seen openly; to excuse, to provide a text, and even apparently motivate, but that very motivation is a pretence. Here, as almost always, and often without the artist's even knowing it, it is the secret of the depths of his flesh that prompts, inspires and decides.

'Lighted in this way and, as it were, from beneath, Wilde's plays reveal, beside the surface witticisms, sparkling like false jewels, many oddly revelatory sentences of great psychological interest. And it is for them that Wilde wrote the whole play – let there be no doubt about it.

'Try to let some understand what one has an interest in hiding from all. Always he managed in such a way that the informed reader could raise the mask and glimpse under it the true visage (which Wilde had such good reason to hide). This artistic hypocrisy was imposed upon him by respect, which was very keen in him, for the proprieties and by the need of self-protection. . . .'

More than these semi-betrayals of his tastes, Oscar in his plays unconsciously gave away his deepest fear, that of scandal. The decisive scene is always that where the central character admits to a secret failing: Sir Robert Chiltern admits that he has sold a Cabinet secret, Mrs. Arbuthnot that she has a natural son, Mrs. Erlynne that she is the mother of Lady Windermere and, lastly but in burlesque fashion, John Worthing admits to Lady Bracknell that he was found in a handbag at Victoria Station. All have a secret, all flirt with scandal. Over-confident though it was, nothing was more dreaded in that Society than scandal; there had been many among the entourage of the Prince of Wales, who himself had been cited in two divorce cases and recently had had to appear in the case against his friend Sir William Gordon Cumming, who had been accused of cheating at baccarat. The career of an eminent politician, Sir Charles Dilke, had been shattered by the accusations of his mother-in-law that he had forced his wife to associate with prostitutes. Lord Randolph Churchill found it expedient to go to Ireland, because the Prince of Wales had challenged him to a duel;* and there was a row with Lord Charles Beresford because of the Prince's social boycott of Lady Charles. Mrs. Cheveley speaks for all the victims of a scandal: '. . . . Suppose that when I leave this house I drive down to some newspaper office, and give them this scandal and the proofs of it. Think of their loathsome joy, of the delight they would have in dragging you down, of the mud and mire they would

* Translator's addition.
Lord Randolph's brother, Lord Blandford, had had an affair with the wife of a great friend of the Prince, who consequently pronounced him a social outcast. Lord Randolph let it be known that if the ban were not withdrawn he would publish an account of the Prince's own love affair with the same lady (Lady Aylesford).

plunge you in. Think of the hypocrite with his greasy smile penning his leading article, and arranging the foulness of the public placard.'

What matters most to Wilde's characters is their position in the world, whether they are protecting their careers, like Sir Robert Chiltern, the unscrupulous civil servant, or like Lord Windermere protecting the dignity of his wife, who must not be known to be the daughter of a disgraced woman. When the situation is lost it must be recovered at all costs, which is what the two splendid adventuresses, Mrs. Cheveley and Mrs. Erlynne, tried to do. In *A Woman of No Importance* it only concerns a provincial virtue and this makes it the least successful of his plays, and finally in *The Importance of Being Earnest*, where masks fall and are automatically exchanged, it is the poor governess, Miss Prism, who sees her incompetence publicly denounced. But in a scene which George Alexander cut out (not without difficulty because Oscar was loath to sacrifice one line), Algernon is arrested for debt and the solicitor pronounces words which were soon to have a tragic echo: 'Time presses, Mr. Moncrieff, we must present ourselves at Holloway Gaol at four o'clock. After that it is difficult to obtain admission.' This obsession with scandal came as much from that which he feared as from that which had agitated his childhood.

Wilde's worldly position was both a treasure and a burden to him. His career was that of an acrobat balancing on a rope tightly drawn over the abyss of scandal, as he juggled with the flowers of aestheticism and the masks of comedy; would he finish the course, would he become Sir Oscar the favourite author of the future King, the most magnificent character in London? Or would he slip? Perhaps the acrobat, already feeling the first strands of the rope giving way, adjusted all the more firmly the insolent painted mask of a successful man who can do no wrong. But a false step or a slip of the tongue involuntarily betrayed what he wished to hide. Yet another secret, in *A Woman of No Importance*, was guessed by Robert Merle, who found that an Oedipus complex had been unconsciously revealed. The author who, for three acts, has identified himself with Lord Illingworth the amusing man of the world, suddenly identifies himself with Gerald at the dénouement; Lord Illingworth, the father, becomes odious and is practically chased off the stage; the father is eliminated, the mother and the son love each other more than ever.

Living as he did in the confusion of a perpetual charade and in the intoxication of perpetual applause, Oscar finally and inevitably lost his head. To a remark of Bernard Berenson, he replied: 'Bernard, you forget that in every way I want to imitate my Maker and, like Him, I want nothing but praise.'* These were the last words exchanged between them. If the public was delighted with the acrobat's feats, the critics were exasperated by the apparent simplicity of his technique, the 'nothing in my hands, nothing up my sleeves' of the conjuror. What can be said against Wilde's plays except that they lack depth and that he was impertinent in taking up a whole scene with mere worldly chatter? The journalists had already found in *Lady Windermere's Fan* echoes of the younger Dumas' *Francillon* and *Le Supplice d'une Femme*; they could not wait to point out in *A Woman of No Importance* a line that would have been more at home in a melodrama: 'Child of my shame, be still the child of my shame!'

When *An Ideal Husband* was produced in January 1895, the public was enthusiastic but the critics severe. Six days after *An Ideal Husband* was first performed, Wilde made clear his views on the critics in an interview with Gilbert Burgess in *The Sketch*: '. . . The result of the vulgar specialisation of criticism is an elaborate scientific knowledge of the stage — almost

* From *Sunset and Twilight* by Bernard Berenson.

as elaborate as that of the stage manager and quite on a par
with the call-boy – combined with an entire incapacity to
realise that a play is a work of art or to receive any artistic
impressions at all. The moment criticism exercises any
influence it ceases to be criticism. The aim of the true critic
is to try to chronicle his own moods, not to try to correct
the masterpieces of others. . . .' and finished by remarking
'You must have a great future in literature before you . . .
because you seem to be such a very bad interviewer . . . I
certainly like the colour of your necktie very much. . . .'
When one of his friends suggested that some of the critics
could be bought, Oscar replied: 'To judge by their appearance, they should not be very expensive.'

Bernard Shaw however had just become dramatic critic
of *The Saturday Review* and wrote these words: 'Mr. Oscar
Wilde's new play at the Haymarket is a dangerous subject,
because he has the property of making his critics dull. They
laugh angrily at his epigrams, like a child who is coaxed
into being amused in the very act of setting up a yell of
rage and agony. They protest that the trick is obvious, and
that such epigrams can be turned out by the score by anyone
light-minded enough to condescend to such frivolity. As
far as I can ascertain I am the only person in London who
cannot sit down and write an Oscar Wilde play at will. . . .
In a certain sense Mr. Wilde is to me our only thorough
playwright. He plays with everything: with wit, with philosophy, with drama, with actors and audiences, with the
whole theatre. . . .'

Before the first night of *The Importance of Being Earnest*, Oscar
gave an interview to Robert Ross (to whom he dedicated
the play) for the *St. James's Gazette* which appeared on the
18th January 1895: 'Do you think the critics will understand your play?' 'I hope not.' 'What sort of play are we to
expect?' 'It is exquisitely trivial, a delicate bubble of fancy,

and it has its philosophy.' 'Its philosophy?' 'That we should treat all the trivial things of life seriously, and all the serious things of life with sincere and studied triviality. . . . The first act is ingenious, the second beautiful, the third abominably clever.'

This play followed Henry James' *Guy Domville* which had been a flop. It was a triumph. The critics themselves laughed at it heartily and admitted to doing so. In a spirit of contradiction, Shaw had reservations about it: 'It amused me of course,' he wrote in *The Saturday Review*, 'but unless comedy touches me as well as amuses me, it leaves me with a sense of having wasted my evening. I go to the theatre to be moved to laughter, not to be tickled or bustled into it. . . .' Shaw, no less than the French, failed to understand the love of the English for the nonsensical. The characters of *The Importance of Being Earnest* live, like those of Lewis Carroll, in a world of make-believe, and their universe takes on the dimensions of *Alice Through the Looking Glass*. The most popular play in England at that time was *Charley's Aunt* by Brandon Thomas, which was a masterpiece: translated it becomes an absurdity.

20 Cottages with all the Trimmings

From the very beginning of their attachment, Lord Alfred Douglas and Oscar Wilde knew that they would figure in the gallery of famous lovers, such as Orestes and Pylades, Hadrian and Antinous. Now that he held in his arms one of the handsomest and most intelligent young men, and from one of the oldest families in England, Oscar, over-excited by applause, showed his happiness in a way which appeared cynical to strangers and cruel to his ex-favourites. He wrote to Ross: 'Royal Palace Hotel, Kensington. . . . Bosie has insisted on stopping here for sandwiches. He is quite like a narcissus – so white and gold. . . . Bosie is so tired: he lies like a hyacinth on the sofa, and I worship him. . . .' Yes, Oscar certainly must have worshipped him to use such florid, banal comparisons.

The author fascinated the undergraduate just as the over-ripe Madame de Staël fascinated the handsome young man from Geneva, of whom she said: 'Speech is not his language.' As Oscar talked, Bosie forgot that he was with a gentleman of forty, rather overdressed and very well-nourished. Wilde in his rôle of Scheherazade spun the web of his improvisations round his hero, and his dialectic reached great imaginative heights. Much later Lord Alfred was to write: 'Even before I met Wilde, I had persuaded myself that the "sins of the flesh" were not wrong and my opinion was of course vastly strengthened and confirmed by his brilliantly reasoned defence of them, which may be said almost to have been the Bible of his life. He went through life preach-

ing the gospel which he puts into the mouth of Lord Henry
Wotton in *Dorian Gray*. . . . He preached that it was the duty
of every man "to live his life to the utmost", to "be always
seeking for new sensations", and to have what he called
"the courage" to commit "what are called sins" . . . the
difference between us was this: that I was at that time a
frank and natural pagan, and that he was a man who
believed in sin and yet deliberately committed it, thereby
obtaining a doubly perverse pleasure.' But the great difference was the fifteen years which separated them and the self-
indulgence which had begun to leave its mark on the poet.
The elder wanted to make himself indispensable, first by
being always amusing and secondly by rendering useful
services. Also he laid the laurels of his triumph at the feet
of his beloved, and the young man was as proud of them
as a girl would have been with jewellery.

One day, with a rare glimmer of good sense, as they met in
the Savoy, the poet went to a table at the far end of the
restaurant through the little door which led from the inside
of the hotel. 'And when he saw me come in by this little
door, Bosie – who was waiting for me made a scene – Oh!
a terrible, frightful scene. "I won't have you come in by the
side door," he said, "I won't tolerate it. I insist on your
coming in by the main entrance with me; I want everyone
to say 'There goes Oscar Wilde and his minion'." '*

However Bosie had to continue his studies at Oxford and
they could not meet very often. Wilde led Bosie into bad
company, not that he needed much leading. Wilde realised
this only too well when he said: 'In this world there are
only two tragedies, one is not getting what one wants, and
the other is getting it. The last is much the worst, the last is
a real tragedy.'

To keep Lord Alfred busy, Oscar encouraged him to edit

* From *If It Die* by André Gide.

the undergraduate magazine *The Spirit Lamp*, and even wrote *The New Remorse* for the number which came out on 6th December 1892. Six months later there appeared a French sonnet by Pierre Louÿs, an adaptation of a letter from Oscar to Bosie, which must be quoted as it was to pass through many hands before reaching those of the judge: 'My Own Boy, Your sonnet is quite lovely, and it is a marvel that those red rose-petal lips of yours should have been made no less for music of song than for madness of kisses. Your slim gilt soul walks between passion and poetry. I know Hyacinthus, whom Apollo loved so madly, was you in Greek days.

'Why are you alone in London, and when do you go to Salisbury? Do go there to cool your hands in the grey twilight of Gothic things, and come here whenever you like. It is a lovely place – it only lacks you; but go to Salisbury first. Always, with undying love, yours, Oscar.'

And how good were Bosie's poems? Some were not at all bad. To be sure there were too many of them and too much was sacrificed to the taste of the period, but they were worthy of at least some of the praise Oscar gave them. He entrusted the translation of *Salome* to Bosie, but prudently kept a close eye on his work, and this caused a certain amount of friction. In the end Oscar dedicated the English-language edition of *Salome* to Bosie. Some of Beardsley's illustrations for the book were thought to be indecent and he wrote in some irritation to Ross in November 1893: 'I suppose you've heard all about the *Salome* row. I can tell you I had a warm time of it between Lane and Oscar and Co. For one week the numbers of telegraph and messenger boys who came to the door was simply scandalous. I really don't quite know how the matter really stands now. Anyhow, Bosie's name is not to turn up on the title. The book will be out soon after Xmas. I have withdrawn three of the illustrations and supplied their places with three new ones (simply beautiful and quite irrelevant).'

Oscar neglected Tite Street, though he still put in an appearance at his wife's 'Day', but Constance realised that it was not for her that he went. He petted the children, who were always with her, and from time to time he went up to the nursery and told them some wonderful story. Dame Nellie Melba remembered Oscar saying: 'I was telling them stories last night of little boys who were naughty and who made their mother cry and what dreadful things would happen to them unless they became better; and do you know what one of them answered? He asked me what punishment could be reserved for naughty papas who did not come home till the early morning and made mother cry far more?'* Wilde pretended to Bosie to be indifferent to his family and wrote, '. . . A horrid ugly Swiss governess has, I find, been looking after Cyril and Vyvyan for a year. She is quite impossible. Also children at meals are tedious. Also, you, the gilt and graceful boy, would be bored. Don't come here. I will come to you. . . .'

Oscar frequently took houses in the country for his family; Bosie was invited to them† and wrote in his *Autobiography*: 'During the three years which elapsed between my first meeting with Oscar and his conviction in 1895 I stayed with him as his guest . . . in every single case Mrs. Wilde was with him, though at Goring she was absent for some weeks.'

Bosie was sent down for a term as he had failed an examination. Another cause of the anxiety to his parents can be guessed from Queensberry's letters to his son Percy, in which he alludes to its having been necessary to hush up

* Life of Oscar Wilde by Hesketh Pearson.
† Translator's addition.

a story about a boy. Wilde was asked to help and in *De Profundis* he twice mentions this: 'Our friendship really begins with your begging me in a most pathetic and charming letter to assist you in a position appalling to anyone, doubly so to a young man at Oxford: I do so, and ultimately through your using my name as your friend with Sir George Lewis, I begin to lose his esteem and friendship. . . . When I was deprived of his advice and help and regard I was deprived of the one great safeguard of my life.' Wilde when he wrote this was to forget two things, first, that he had always been only too happy to help Lord Alfred and secondly that he had frequently led the undergraduate astray. Sometimes they went to the public house called 'The Crown' near Charing Cross. Oscar was proud to show off his friend to the decadent poets and the out-of-work actors and sailors on leave. In this jungle they were introduced to low-class pederasts by Maurice Schwabe, a boy who was well versed in the customs of these people although elsewhere he kept up the appearance of respectability. He was accompanied by Alfred Taylor, a young man of good family who at the age of thirty had already run through £45,000. Taylor lived in a little house not far from Westminster, open not only to friends who reminded him of his prosperous days, but also to those whom the dark days had brought. The old friends appear to have got on well with the new.* Oscar found this house fascinating for reasons of which pleasure was not the most important. There, he would hold forth in a little sitting-room where the curtains were always drawn, surrounded by newspaper boys and messenger boys to whom he offered fairy stories and cigarette cases. Their cockney

---

* Later Taylor's honourable refusal to turn Queen's Evidence against Wilde meant that he too stood trial, and by doing so he certainly prejudiced Oscar's chances of acquittal. After his release, Taylor lived in Canada and the U.S.A.—Translator's note.

animation amused him, and their underworld activities had
all the attraction of danger.

All the boys knew who he was, some therefore did not
hesitate to importune him in his own home, or to encourage
the flower-sellers to insult him when he crossed Piccadilly
with their rival Alfred Douglas. Neither they nor the street-
walkers minced their words because they complained that
homosexuals took the bread out of their mouths. Sighing
at the vulgarity of the lower orders, Oscar hailed a cab to
take him to Taylor's house where a fancy-dress party was
being held to celebrate the burlesque marriage of the master
of the house with Charles Mason. Pierre Louÿs was also
present, but he did not relate who wore the skirt and who
the trousers. This all took place in a neighbourhood of long
streets of little houses which extended from Pimlico to
Westminster. The hotels sheltered adventurers who had
arrived from the Continent, the barracks of the Brigade of
Guards were close by and the bars in the district were frequented by grooms from Belgrave Square. This semi-rabble,
for all their sporting pretensions, fell back on blackmail
when their compliance did not provide them with enough
to live on. It would be superfluous to enter into the details
of Oscar's adventures there; they emerged at the time of the
trials, but none had any importance in itself. All the boys
were as impersonal as girls in a bordello, but, unhappily,
much less well guarded.

On the first night of *A Woman of No Importance*, a blackmailer named Allen caught Oscar at the stage door of the
Haymarket Theatre and offered him the original of his letter
('My Own Boy') for £10. 'Ten pounds,' said Wilde. 'You
have no appreciation of literature. If you had asked me for
fifty pounds, I might have given it to you . . . besides, I have
a copy of that letter and the original is of no use to me. I

look upon it as a work of art. I should have desired to
possess it; but as you were good enough to send a copy to
Mr. Tree . . . I no longer want the original.' Wilde was able
to keep cool because he had already been warned by
Beerbohm Tree and by a telegram from Lord Alfred. The
letter had been found with others in the pocket of an over-
coat belonging to Bosie which had either been given to, or
stolen by his friend Wood, a large fair youth aged seventeen
whom he had met at Taylor's house. Oscar must have found
him pleasant because he took him to dinner at the Café
Royal, where the boy admitted to having entrusted the
letters to other blackmailers. There was nothing to do but
to await their visits and to console Wood for having fallen
so low.

In his *Life of Oscar Wilde*, Hesketh Pearson records that some
days later another man called on Wilde at Tite Street, 'and in
view of his usual attitude to blackmailers there is no reason
to doubt his description of what took place which he gave
to Tree and which Tree gave to me.

"'Would you like to have all those letters you wrote to
Lord Alfred I've got them here.' 'If they are as perfect as the
one of which some kind person sent a copy to Mr. Tree, I
should certainly like to have them. But why not continue
your admirable practice of sending copies? Then I should
not need the originals.' 'How much will you give?' 'One
cannot estimate their value in money. The price of beauty
is above rubies.' 'Well, you can have them for thirty
pounds.' 'Why do you want thirty pounds?' 'I want to go
to America and make a fresh start.' 'A strange design, but
not – if you will pardon the reflection – not original –
Columbus thought of it before you. I hope you will be
more fortunate than he, and miss the continent on your
way.' 'Here they are,' said the man, producing the letters,
which Oscar glanced at casually, and then wrote a cheque,

handing it to him with the words, 'You are willing to give me the letters, and I am willing to pay for your journey to America. That is a pleasant and amicable arrangement. Good-bye; and the best advice I can give you for the new life you propose to lead is that on the day you land in America – you sail for England.'

After he left, Oscar saw that the letter of which a copy had been sent to Tree was not among them; a few days later Allen came back again with the original and said, 'A curious construction could be put on that letter.' 'Art is seldom intelligible to the working classes,' said Oscar. 'A man offered me £60 for it.' 'If you take my advice you will go to him at once and sell it for £60. I myself have never received so large a sum for any prose work of that length But I am glad to find there is someone in England who will pay such a high price for any letter of mine.' Allen then appealed for help, saying he was penniless. 'Well, I can't guarantee your cab expenses,' said Wilde, but kindly gave him ten shillings and saw him out. An hour or so later another member of the gang called Clibborn was shown in; Wilde became irritable. 'I can't be bothered any more about that letter, I don't care twopence for it.' But the newcomer said he had come to give the letter back. 'Give it back? Why does he give it back to me?' 'Well, he says you were kind to him, and that there is no use trying to rent you as you only laugh at us.' Wilde glanced at the letter which had become very dirty from its passage from hand to hand. 'I think it quite unpardonable that better care was not taken of an original work of mine.' Then, giving Clibborn ten shillings, he remarked, 'I am afraid you are leading a wonderfully wicked life.' 'There's good and bad in every one of us,' replied the man." In spite of these transactions, several more of Wilde's letters to Douglas, as well as copies of the ones he had bought back, found their way into Queensberry's hands, and copies of them circulated among actors and journalists, who said that Oscar had paid enormous sums for the originals.

It does not appear, according to the few letters from Oscar to Bosie that have survived, that these experiences had worn out his passion or exhausted his patience. Oscar took houses in the country with the idea of being able to work more peacefully than in London, no doubt with the under-lying wish of having Bosie by his side. The first of these was Babbacombe, the Pre-Raphaelite house near Torquay, belonging to Lady Mount-Temple, to which he took his family in November 1892. In January 1893 while Constance was away in Florence, Bosie and his tutor stayed there with him. Bosie had come from Salisbury where his mother had a house called St. Ann's Gate in the Close; Campbell Dodgson, who was coaching Bosie for Greats at Oxford, spent a day there with Lady Queensberry, wandering about the cathedral and the close; 'In the evening Bosie appeared with a flutter of telegrams about him,' and the next day announced that he and Campbell Dodgson were going to Torquay to stay with Oscar Wilde. The young tutor, resigned, or perhaps fascinated by Bosie, followed him in a turmoil of luggage amidst which was a scarlet morocco despatch case – a gorgeous and beautiful gift from Oscar, a fox-terrier and a number of lexicons. From Torquay Camp-bell Dodgson wrote: 'Oscar implores me, with outstretched arms and tears in his eyes, to let my soul alone and cultivate my body for six weeks.'* Oscar laid down the following rules for the Babbacombe School: 'Headmaster: Mr. Oscar Wilde, second master: Mr. Campbell Dodgson, Boys: Lord Alfred Douglas, Rules: Tea for boys at 9.30 a.m., Breakfast

* From a letter from Campbell Dodgson to Lionel Johnson quoted in *The Letters of Oscar Wilde* – Rupert Hart-Davis.

at 10.30, Work 11.30–12.30. At 12.30 Sherry and biscuits
for headmaster and boys (the second master objects to this).
12.40–1.30 work. 1.30 Lunch. 2.30–4.30 Compulsory
hide-and-seek for headmaster. 5 Tea for headmaster and
second master, brandy and sodas (not to exceed seven) for
boys. 6–7 work. 7.30 dinner, with compulsory champagne.
8.30–12 Ecarté, limited to five-guinea points. 12–1.30
Compulsory reading in bed. Any boy found disobeying
this rule will be immediately woken up. . . .'

Oscar found time to finish his play *A Woman of No
Importance* which had been begun in the preceding months of
August and September, and Lord Alfred acquired some idea
of the world of Plato, perhaps because he was told that he
belonged to it. But soon his bad temper and capricious
nature disturbed the happy scene, and doors began to slam.
The Parthian shots made Oscar into a positive Saint
Sebastian. Did they become estranged? No, because Bosie
was bored away from Oscar and wrote to the poet, who
was weak enough to reply: 'March 1893. Savoy Hotel,
London. Dearest of all Boys, Your letter was delightful, red
and yellow wine to me; but I am sad and out of sorts.
Bosie, you must not make scenes with me. They kill me,
they wreck the loveliness of life. I cannot see you, so Greek
and gracious, distorted with passion. I cannot listen to your
curved lips saying hideous things to me. I would sooner be
blackmailed by every renter in London than have you bitter,
unjust, hating. I must see you soon. You are the divine thing
I want, the thing of grace and beauty; but I don't know how
to do it. Shall I come to Salisbury? My bill here is £49 for
a week. I have also got a new sitting-room over the Thames.
Why are you not here, my dear, my wonderful boy? I fear
I must leave; no money, no credit, and a heart of lead. Your
own Oscar.'

These agitations did not stop Oscar from writing delicious

letters to the Sphinx, boasting of the intelligence of his beloved, and to Miss Adela Schuster praising the loftiness of his soul. Soon Bosie arrived at the Savoy. A French visitor (the incident is reported by Henri de Régnier to Edmond de Goncourt) was received in the room the two friends shared and saw Mrs. Wilde, in tears, bringing Oscar his letters. Unluckily Bosie did not accept the following invitation of John Addington Symonds: '30 March 1893. . . . You can't be always pampered in the Savoy. It was very pleasant for Oscar pampering you, I doubt not. I wish you would come and see how I can make you comfortable, and feed your soul on honey of sweet-bitter thoughts – in Italy – in Switzerland – it is all the same. . . .' Alas, jealousy had no part in the drama, but spitefulness had. It started by teasing. Oscar who was vain and thought himself handsome, could not stand the smallest unflattering personal remark about his appearance, and was really furious when Bosie did not admire the length of his legs, or if he referred to the heaviness of his jaw. The younger man also commented tactlessly – Bosie never had any tact – on how Oscar, on returning from some smart party, assumed the airs of a débutante who had been to her first ball. Bosie, the aristocrat, pitilessly laughed at some of Oscar's ideas of the manners of the great world. In one of the comedies a Duchess is described as leaving the room 'in a marked manner'. 'Really, my dear Oscar,' criticised Bosie scornfully, 'whenever have you seen people do such a thing?'

London was both tiring and expensive, so Oscar rented a cottage at Goring-on-Thames in June 1893 for a few months to which he took his family and Bosie; but this country holiday proved no less enervating and expensive than London, in fact Oscar found that '. . . life in meadow and stream is far more complex than life in streets and salons . . .'. Men-servants were essential to wait on the numerous friends from Oxford who came for the Henley Regatta, champagne buffets were needed to restore the young men, masses of flowers to convince the London ladies that they really were in the country. The lawn and the moored boats, the clumps of hydrangeas and rhododendrons, the white house with its striped awning, became the background for sordid scenes and reverberated with irretrievable words. Bosie worked at the translation of *Salome*, carefully supervised by Oscar, during the brief times when they were not quarrelling.

After twelve weeks of the terrible strain of Bosie's companionship, Oscar felt he needed rest and freedom, so, on leaving Goring, he went alone for a fortnight to Dinard. Telegrams followed him, alternately despairing and insulting. Oscar decided to break off the friendship completely, but on his return to London, once he saw Bosie again, he could not bring himself to do so. So their futile way of life was resumed; by dint of brilliant conversation and large dinners and supper parties at restaurants, Oscar succeeded in surrounding Bosie and himself with an aura of glamour of the kind that journalists create round famous theatrical figures. As the result of Bosie's unbalanced behaviour – he once shot at a chandelier in the Berkeley Hotel with a pistol he always carried against the event of his father meeting him and becoming violent – Oscar lost a little of his customary elegant charm of manner. His appearance had coarsened, but no one could have remained unscathed by such a life. In search of quiet to enable him to finish *The Importance of Being Earnest*, Oscar took a small house at Worthing for himself and his family to which he invited Bosie. Oscar tells of the events that followed in *De Profundis*: 'Bored with Worthing, and still more, I have no doubt, with my fruitless efforts to concentrate my attention on my play, the only thing that really interested me at the moment, you insist on being taken to the Grand Hotel at Brighton. The night we arrive you fall ill with that dreadful low fever that is foolishly called influenza. . . .' Oscar nursed him and then became ill himself. Bosie recovered, and visited Oscar only to demand money and to insult him. Some of the most celebrated pages of De Profundis are derived from the dreadful scenes which ensued. By then Oscar was quite determined to break, when tragedy plunged the Douglas family into mourning. Francis Drumlanrig, the eldest son, was found dead from an accidental explosion of his own gun. Oscar, by now virtually a member of the clan, wrote a letter of sympathy and in no time at all he and Bosie were to fall into each other's arms.

However hard Oscar tried to break with Bosie, even with the help of Lady Queensberry, they always came together again. In November of 1893 he wrote urging her to remove her son as far away as possible: 'You have on more than one occasion consulted me about Bosie. Let me write to you about him. Bosie seems to me to be in a very bad state of health. He is sleepless, nervous, and rather hysterical. He seems to me quite altered. . . . He does absolutely nothing, and is quite astray in life, and may, unless you do something, come to grief of some kind. His life seems to me aimless, unhappy and absurd. . . . Why not try and make arrangements of some kind for him to go abroad for four or five months, to the Cromers in Egypt if that could be managed, where he would have new surroundings, proper friends, and a different atmosphere? I think that if he stays in London he will not come to any good, and may spoil his young life irretrievably, quite irretrievably. . . .'

While waiting for an answer to this letter, Oscar took rooms in St. James's Place wherein to work. Bosie never left his side. Every morning he arrived to tempt Oscar out to luncheon and to drink champagne. At about five, after

having been to his club or to a race-meeting, Bosie would
turn up and start an evening of pleasure. To a rehearsal
perhaps, to dine either at Tite Street or the Savoy, or to go
to a dinner party – neither was invited without the other,
and the evening invariably ending at Willis' Rooms. All
this cost time and money. On one occasion Oscar wrote:
'I am overwhelmed by the wings of Vulture creditors, and
out of sorts, but I am happy in the knowledge that we are
friends again, and that our love has passed through the
shadow and the night of estrangement and sorrow and
come out rose-crowned as of old . . .'.

From this period, date the reflections on money such as:
'Young people nowadays imagine that money is everything
– and when they grow older, they know it.' After cynicism
came poetry; when Oscar sent a cheque to William Rothenstein to pay for a portrait of Bosie, he wrote: 'The lovely
drawing is complete in itself. It is a great delight to me to
have so exquisite a portrait of a friend done by a friend
also, and I thank you very much for letting me have it.
Enclosed is an absurdly coloured thing, which foolish
bankers take in exchange and for which they give, in reckless moments, gold, both yellow and red.'

Off and on Oscar made quite a lot of money. He was said
to earn about £2,000 a year and in 1894 as much as
£8,000; this enabled him to spend lavishly. Had he been
'keeping' an actress or a demi-mondaine rather than a well-
born young man, jewels and furs would have been demanded and no doubt the expenses would have been
greater. But although Bosie never gave a thought to money
– he took it for granted – life with him cost as much as if
he had been a gold-digger.

Lord Alfred did go to Egypt but not for long, and when
he returned to Paris, Oscar joined him. Later his mother
sent him to Florence, again Oscar joined him and they met

André Gide on the terrace of a café; the Frenchman was embarrassed, found Wilde changed, and scrutinised Bosie prudishly. They would have been wiser to have remained in Tuscany where the blue-stockings cultivated their gardens, but Oscar had to return to London in order to make money, and to resume his absurd and ruinous way of life.

Irishman that he was, Oscar always kept on good terms with the 'Other World'. From time to time he visited Mrs. Robinson, a fortune-teller whom he called 'the Sibyl of Mortimer Street'. When Oscar, harassed by success and scenes, consulted her in July 1894, she said: 'I see a very brilliant life for you up to a certain point. Then I see a wall. Beyond the wall I see nothing.' No one is ever deflected from folly by prophecy but it gives to foolish people the feeling that they are in league with Destiny.

Nothing is more monotonous than the annals of the weak-willed, consisting as they do largely of resolutions quickly forgotten, and final scenes endlessly repeated. But in Wilde's case it was more than this; he seemed to need scenes, to need to suffer. Bosie was the cause of emotions that were not very different from those that a masochist gets from a whip. The recollection of the insults was cruel, but disturbing in the way that bruises are when received from the hand of a loved one. They were basically well matched if it can be certain that the insult earned a caress. Bosie, for his part, wished to make Oscar pay for the fact that he could not help but admire him. He had probably, as Mr. Cyril Connolly has pointed out,* substituted Oscar's image for that of his hated father, hence his excesses of loathing when the two images got confused. One of his most unpleasant phrases in his letters to Wilde is revealing: 'When you are not on your pedestal you are not interesting'.

* *Previous Convictions* by Cyril Connolly.

21 Yellow book and green carnation

Wilde's life during those eighteen months from the autumn of 1893 to February 1895 had the quality of a speeded-up film: scenes, reconciliations, first nights, journeys, all succeeded each other with incredible rapidity. He met new people, made many friends and almost as many enemies. Appropriately, it was a visiting-card which put an end to this worldly life, to the works paradoxically applauded on the stage by those whom the writer had ceaselessly mocked in his essays. The theatre and life with Lord Alfred had lured Oscar from his rôle of sage. His essay *Intentions*, which had appeared in May 1891, was not taken as seriously as it deserved, because Oscar from that moment was to be at the head of the *avant-garde* of the theatre rather than of literature, as he had been ten years earlier. He must have taken this to heart because he did not at all like a publication that brought together many of the advanced writers of that time – largely, perhaps, because his advice was not sought about its contents. In 1894, John Lane, the publisher of *Salome*, brought out a new review bound in yellow linen on which the lettering was black, called *The Yellow Book*. It is '. . . dull and loathsome, a great failure. I am so glad', Oscar wrote to Bosie. It is astonishing to read that short stories by Henry James, Ada Leverson and Arnold Bennett were considered *avant-garde*; there were poems by Maurice Baring and by a lovely young girl called Olive Custance, who was later to marry Bosie, the first story by Baron Corvo, and essays by George Moore and J. A.

292

Symonds. Oscar declared that it was all frightfully boring with the exception of Max Beerbohm's essay *A Defence of Cosmetics*. The great difference between the contributors to *The Yellow Book* and the writer's of Wilde's generation was the taste of the former for the eighteenth century; the modern young people were mad about Pope. Max and Beardsley had a dry, sparkling style, quite unlike the unctuous elaboration of Oscar's stories.

The restraint of this *avant-garde* was to force Bosie into publishing in a new magazine two poems which did not shrink from over-statement. Oscar referred to this magazine when writing to Ada Leverson: 'Dear Sphinx, Your aphorisms must appear in the second number of the *Chameleon*: they are exquisite. *The Priest and the Acolyte* is not by Dorian: though you were right in discerning by internal evidence that the author has a profile. He is an under-graduate of strange beauty. The story is, to my ears, too direct: there is no nuance: it profanes a little by revelation: God and other artists are always a little obscure. Still, it has interesting qualities, and is at moments poisonous: which is something.' To the first, and only, number, Oscar had contributed thirty-five aphorisms entitled *Phrases and Philosophies for the Use of the Young*. 'The first duty in life is to be as artificial as possible. What the second duty is no one has as yet discovered.' 'Those who see any difference between soul and body have neither.' 'Ambition is the last refuge of the failure.'

At the end of the Victorian era the *avant-garde* was less literary than artistic, and it was the drawings of Aubrey Beardsley that caused the scandal of *The Yellow Book*. Some-times he invented strange scenes of his own, sometimes he drew inspiration from what he read. But no matter whether he depicted the heroes of Wagner, of Pope or of Wilde, they were always disquieting – half naked, fringed with lace,

U

beplumed or bewigged. The recent revival of interest in his pictures has been considerable. Brünnhilde, Mademoiselle de Maupin and Salome were the three sisters in this *fin-de-siècle* mythology, a mixture between the stars of the music-halls and those of the pavements of Piccadilly. Here and there, too, we find a black taper, provocative symbol of an esoteric cult. Equivocal and decorative charms were not enough in that mauve decade, the scandalous orchid became the mark of all that was most up-to-date. The walls of London were covered with them; and in posters even the most innocent of goods were thereby given a note of perversity. In the nineties, Queen Victoria's capital regarded itself as the New Babylon and, in Piccadilly Circus, an Art Nouveau statue of Eros rose out of the fountain. Artists with long hair flying in the wind scoured Soho in search of very young models, eager for every eccentricity suggested by the drawings of the diabolical Aubrey. It was the mauve decade, the Beardsley craze.

Beardsley wrote nearly as well as he drew. In an unusual story called Under the Hill he added to the many caricatures of Wilde, which he had already concealed in his drawings, this portrait of Priapusa the manicurist: 'Priapusa's voice was full of salacious unction; she had terrible little gestures with the hands, strange movements with the shoulders, a short respiration that made surprising wrinkles in her bodice, a corrupt skin, large horny eyes, a parrot's nose, a small loose mouth, great flaccid cheeks and chin after chin.'* In this pen-portrait can be recognised the salacious side of Wilde, the man who has been suspected of collaboration in Teleny, a side which his disciples tried to tone down.

At the Café Royal, in John Lane's office, in the corridors

* Under the Hill or the story of Venus and Tannhäuser by Aubrey Beardsley, completed by John Glascoe.

Priapusa by Aubrey Beardsley

of the Haymarket Theatre, in Dieppe, the public was made aware of the laughter and the rows, the raptures and the whispers. Notwithstanding his heavy figure, Wilde dominated a buzzing little world, regaled it with stories and champagne, amused it with his adventures and his quarrels. A dozen young men, led by the indispensable Ross, increased the scandals provoked by their Master. It was not enough that they were looked on askance, for them it was necessary to be recognised from afar, spotted before they opened their mouths. For that reason they chose an emblem: a green carnation. It will be remembered that such a flower had been worn by the leading man in *Lady Windermere's Fan* and also by some of Oscar's friends in the audience at the first night, such as Dodo Benson,* Max Beerbohm and Reggie Turner.

Max's letters, frequently thanking Reggie Turner for presents (Reggie was a generous and frequent giver of recherché presents to his friends), are excellent chronicles of that particular circle, a circle which was not unlike that which revolved round Robert de Montesquiou at the same period with Marcel Proust, Reynaldo Hahn and Lucien Daudet. In London, Oscar's friends would rush round to share the latest joke with Mrs. Leverson, or would hope to get invited by Lady de Grey to hear either Jean de Reszke singing Lohengrin, or the Duke of Cambridge snoring during the performance or Oscar getting rid of a bore with the words: 'Oh, I'm so glad you've come, there are a hundred things I don't want to say to you.' Music-halls were much frequented and thought 'divinely vulgar'. Oscar's new disciples were given lessons in frivolity: 'To win back my

---

* Edward Frederick Benson (1867–1940), third son of the Archbishop of Canterbury, successful novelist, was known as 'Dodo' after the title of one of his books, in which the central character was thought to be modelled on Margot Asquith.

youth there is nothing I would not do – nothing – except take exercise, get up early, or be a useful member of the community.' 'I never put off till tomorrow what I can possibly do – the day after.' 'Young men want to be faithful and are not; old men want to be faithless and cannot.' 'Each time one loves is the only time one has ever loved. Difference of object does not alter singleness of passion. It merely intensifies it.'

In a letter Max reveals that he was no disciple of the master: '. . . Oscar was at the last night of the Haymarket of a *Woman of No Importance*, with him Bosie and Robbie and Aubrey Beardsley. The last of these had forgotten to put vine leaves in his hair, but the other three wore rich clusters – especially poor Robbie. Nor have I ever seen Oscar so fatuous, he called Mrs. Beere "Juno-like" and Kemble "Olympian quite" and waved his cigarette round and round his head. . . . I have just been reading *Salome* again – terribly corrupt but there is much that is beautiful in it, much lovely writing: I almost wonder Oscar doesn't dramatise it.' The whiff of scandal can be smelt in the following letter: '19th December 1893. . . . Bobbie Ross has returned to this country for a few days and of him there have been very great and intimate scandals and almost, if not quite, warrants. Slowly he is recovering but has to remain at Davos during his convalescence for fear of a social relapse. I must not disclose anything (nor must you), but I may tell you that a schoolboy with wonderful eyes, Bosie, Robbie, a furious father, George Lewis, a headmaster (who is now blackmailing Robbie), St. John Wontner, Calais, Dover, Oscar Browning, Oscar, Dover, Calais, intercepted letters, private detectives, Calais, Dover and returned cigarette-cases were some of the ingredients of the dreadful episode. . . . The "*garçon entretenu*", the schoolboy Helen "for whom those horned ships were launched, those beautiful mailed men laid low" was the same as him of whom I told you that he had been stolen from Bobbie by Bosie and kept at Albemarle Hotel: how well I remember passing this place one night with Bobbie and his looking sadly at the lighted windows and wondering to me behind which of the red curtains lay the desire of his soul.'

'12th March – Oxford. . . . Dear Bosie is with us. . . . Is it you who have made him so amusing? Never in the summer did he make me laugh so much, but now he is nearly brilliant. Also is it you who have made him so abnormally, damnably, touchingly conceited about his poetry? Never was he so in the summer. The dons objected to his coming up, so he took his name off the books and wrote to Warren at the time saying that it would one day be Magdalen's proudest boast that she for a time harboured him within her walls, her greatest shame that she had driven him forth – or something to that effect. . . .'

'7th August 1894. . . . Oscar and Bosie dined with me today in the Royal Coffee House and were very charming. Oscar was just in the mood that I like him – very 1880 and withal brimful of intellectual theories and anecdotes of dear Lady Dorothy Nevill and other whores. Bosie came in in a Homburg hat – dove-coloured – and wearing a very sweet present from you in his shirt-cuffs. . . . Oscar also was all admiration and said he supposed that "dear Reg's present to him was in some way delayed . . .".' Finally a premonitory letter which alludes to a raid on a transvestite club in Fitzroy Street and continues jokingly: 'Oscar has at length been arrested for certain kinds of crime. He was taken in the Café Royal (lower room). Bosie escaped, being an excellent runner, but Oscar was less nimble. . . .'

Extraordinary though it may seem, many of Wilde's friends, Harris, Sherard and Shaw, never suspected him, the husband of a pretty woman, of liking boys. They thought his circle of friends was merely part of the general Byzantine rôle he had adopted. It was an innocent era. Ellen Terry was mystified when she heard Oscar say to the young actress Aimée Lowther: 'If only you were a boy, how I would adore you.' An American dramatist heard strange rumours which worried him, and implored Oscar to tell him if they were true. 'Leave the room!' was the reply. 'No gentleman would ask such a question.' Constance Wilde believed that her husband had been mad for those three years but attributed this to the influence of the theatre. Yet Oscar appeared determined to do all he could to enlighten the public.

In 1894, a novel was published anonymously in which the principal characters were obviously taken from Oscar and Bosie, under the names of Esmé Amarinth and Lord Reginald Hastings. The character of Madame Valtesi was thought, mistakenly and only by those who did not know her, to have been based on Mrs. Leverson. At first she was suspected of being the author of the book, but the falseness of this suspicion and Oscar's words to her on the subject have already been quoted. The Green Carnation was written by Robert Hichens, a young man to whom no one had paid any attention, but who had met Bosie and Dodo Benson earlier in the year in Egypt. Bosie had become bored staying with Lord Cromer, in spite of the pleasure of parading with Lady Cromer in fabulous palaces wearing shantung suits and making eyes at that confirmed misogynist Lord Kitchener, who had just returned from India. Bosie went to Luxor, where he met Dodo Benson and Robert Hichens: they went to stay on the dahabeeyah belonging to Frank Lawson, Reggie's half-brother, and on this gilded barge they sailed up the Nile together. On board they talked of Oscar during the sunsets which recalled so many 'purple passages', if only he were there, how short the evenings would seem! What stories he would invent in this magic and equivocal country. The young men recited passages from The Sphinx, which seemed so applicable to their adventures in the moonlight. 'To meet your swarthy Ethiop whose body was of polished jet', or 'That young God the Tyrian, who was more amorous than the dove of Ashtaroth . . .'.

Bosie wrote long letters to his mother, two of which were very revealing of his feelings for Oscar and, by implication, of his mother's attitude to his friendship with Wilde, if not of her knowledge of its nature; it is obvious from one letter that she had said she would like to 'murder' Oscar, and that he was leading Bosie astray, but Bosie defended him and went into raptures about their great love which was like that of Plato and Socrates, Shakespeare and Mr. W.H. Lady Queensberry hoped her son would stay away as long as possible in the East. But there are no Thousand and One Nights without Scheherazade.

Robert Hichens did not miss much and directly he returned to London he made it his business to meet Oscar and his friends, including Mrs. Leverson. In a few weeks he wrote his novel, Oscar's voice can be recognised on every page: 'Dear Lady! . . . intelligence is the demon of our age. Mine bores me horribly, I am always trying to find a remedy for it. I have experimented with absinthe, but gained no result. I have read the collected works of Walter Besant. They are said to sap the mental powers. They did not sap mine. Opium has proved useless, and green tea cigarettes leave me positively brilliant. What am I to do? I so long for the lethargy, the sweet peace of stupidity.'

'To get drunk deliberately is as foolish as to get sober by accident. Do you know my brother? When he is not tipsy, he is invariably blind sober. I often wonder the police do not run him in.'

The descriptions were vivid: 'Madame Valtesi . . . had

travelled down from London in a shady straw hat trimmed
with pink roses. A white veil swept loosely round her face;
she carried in her hand an attenuated mottled cane with an
elaborate silver top. A black fan hung from her waist by a
thin silver chain and, as usual, she was peering through her
eyeglasses at her surroundings. Mr. Amarinth and Lord
Reggie were dressed very much alike in loosely fitting very
light suits with high, turn-down collars, all-round collars
that somehow suggested babyhood and innocence, and
loosely knitted ties. They wore straw hats, suède gloves, and
brown boots and in their button-holes large green carnations
bloomed savagely.' Reggie goes into ecstasies over the marmalade, 'Is not this marmalade God-like? This marvellous
clear, amber glow, amber with a touch of red in it, almost
makes me believe in an after-life. Surely marmalade can
never die', and recites the Song of Solomon to the heiress,
laying himself open, however, to her disapproval by saying,
'How I hate that word natural . . . to me it means all that is
middle-class, all that is of the essence of jingoism, all that is
colourless and without form and void.'

The satire in the Green Carnation was not as innocuous as that
of Patience ten years earlier; in the former it was vices that
were ridiculed, whereas in Patience it was only absurdities.
By then the friendship of Lord Alfred and Oscar had become
public knowledge. Society still invited them, but they were
pointed at in the streets. Allusion to the quarrel between
Lord Queensberry and his son is made in the first chapter of
The Green Carnation when the young hero drives down Piccadilly: 'Presently he passed an elderly gentleman with a red
face and small side-whiskers. The elderly gentleman stared
him in the the face and sniffed ostentatiously. "What a pity
my poor father is so plain", Reggie said to himself with a
quiet smile. Only that morning he had received a long and
vehement diatribe from his parent, showering abuse on him,

and exhorting him to lead a more reputable life. He had replied by wire "What a funny little man you are".'

This telegram had in reality been sent by Lord Alfred after he had received a particularly insulting letter from his father. The success of the book was to Lord Queensberry as the scarlet cape of the matador to the bull. The Marquess was in fact very like an Aberdeen Angus bull, ready to charge the fragile and delightful world of the young men with green carnations – a perfect illustration of a bull in a china shop. Oscar, whose vocation was not that of a matador, did not know what to do to divert such rage. He felt he needed a change of environment. He had been quite amused by the novel despite his comments to Ada Leverson that it was unworthy of her pen.

Wilde and Douglas arrived in Algeria about the 16th January 1895. They pressed on into the desert to the oasis of Blidah where they found the only comfortable hotel and plenty to amuse them. André Gide, already installed in it, was none too pleased to find his solitude disturbed; however he soon fell under Wilde's charm again. Gide often referred to that meeting, which was to be of such importance in his life, and he gave two versions of it; one in In Memoriam, published in 1901, was fairly severe about Wilde's works, the other in Si le grain ne meurt was more severe about the man. On the publication of the latter, Wilde's friends, for once in agreement, were indignant at the misrepresentations, and, as they wished the pederastic proselytism which Oscar had practised since 1885 to be forgotten, they tried to make a martyr of their master. This character, cynical and a familiar of the lowest slums, who is shown to us by the young Puritan, perhaps with a little too much complaisance for his own integrity, had no place in their legend.

Gide did indeed fall once again under the influence of

the poet: 'Always trying to instil into you a sanction for
evil', he trembled at what he rediscovered. Knowing that
Oscar professed not to like Dickens, Gide, when asked what
he was reading, feeling cantankerous, took pleasure in saying
how much he liked Dickens;* Oscar immediately changed
around and started talking of the 'divine Boz' and showed
that under his affected contempt he had considerable esteem
for that author. Oscar then went on to complain that it was
raining: 'I no longer want to adore anything but the sun. . . .
Have you noticed that the sun detests thought?' Nietszche
can be recognised in another exclamation of Wilde's: 'Not
happiness! Above all, not happiness! Pleasure. We must
always want the most tragic. . . .' Luckily Wilde's advice was
sometimes practical: he expounded his theory of guides
which was that it was important to choose the vilest, who
was invariably the cleverest. This Wilde was to be found later,
but more sumptuous and less amusing, as Menalque in
Gide's *Les Nourritures Terrestres*, in the same way as certain
characters of Abel Hermant suggest the Wilde of *The Green
Carnation*.

Already in Blidah the great scene of Faust was being prepared which was to be enacted in Algiers. Wilde-Mephisto-
pheles was to tempt Gide, who in turn played the parts
of Marguerite and of Faust, by offering him youth,
the youth of others. Through an unconscious taste for the
sacrilegious, it was to his mother that Gide related the
various stages of this encounter. He pretended to be horrified
but he was fascinated as well: 'Impossible to evaluate the
young Lord whom Wilde seems to have depraved to the
marrow in the manner of an even more terrible Vautrin. . . .
I hope to be able to understand what is sincere and what
affected in this madness of depravity.' Blidah was a small
town, Lord Alfred was negotiating to carry off an Arab

* Translator's addition.

youth, everyone would therefore be better off in Algiers.
'This Scotsman of twenty-five, branded, ruined, devoured by
a morbid thirst for infamies, who searches for shame and
finds it, such types are to be found in the historical tragedies
of Shakespeare. And Wilde, what more tragic life is there
than his; if he were capable of making an effort he would be
a genius; "I have put all my genius into my life, I have put
only my talent into my works". This is why those who
know him well have that shiver of fear of something very
great and very fine. If Wilde's plays in London did not run
for three hundred performances and if the Prince of Wales
did not go to the first nights, he would be in prison and Lord
Alfred also.'

Prison: everyone was thinking of it, Gide as well as Max.
Perhaps Wilde already knew that he couldn't escape it and,
besides, it would be the best way of putting an end to the
rows and the debts. This romantic vision fitted in with the
rôle of Satan which Wilde acted with enthusiasm, but not
without the shade of melancholy appropriate to a fallen
angel.

The evening when the fall of Gide was decided, the friends
went from bar to bar. Pierre Loti, another frequenter of the
Casbah, may serve as a guide: 'Sometimes it was the deafen-
ing music, great drums struck with all their might by sweat-
ing men, squalling pipes blown hard enough to burst them,
the yells of madmen. And from time to time, led by a little
flute which spun sweet sweet sounds and plaintive melodies,
men danced together with a rose stuck behind their ears,
striking the graceful and lascivious attitudes of dancing
girls. . . . It was a Moorish bath of ill-repute. The bathers had
left and men with nowhere to lay their heads, indeterminate
half-breeds, echos of chance vice, came to sleep for two *sous*
on mats covered in vermin which had been used for
massage. . . . A half Arab haunt, four Negroes quite naked

playing castanets and beating the drum in a Nubian rhythm. And, to the music of this orchestra, ten or more couples of Zouaves and sailors danced together, gravely holding each other by the waist.*

Oscar and Gide were together on this expedition, when Oscar pronounced the ludicrous and fateful sentence: 'Dear, do you want the little musician!', which Gide recorded in *If it Die. . . .* When Gide had agreed and they had returned to their carriage, Wilde started laughing, 'enjoying himself like a child and like a devil'. Satan had triumphed over that virtue which he thought had challenged him for five years; he triumphed and mocked at the same time. But Wilde was also kindly, the great master receiving what he thought was a distinguished novice. Oscar had to return to London to supervise the rehearsals of *The Importance of Being Earnest.* Bosie went to Biskra with the boy (soon to deceive him with a woman), whom he had bought from his family and who immediately took on the airs of a prince; Gide followed in their wake, fascinated by the extravagance of this curious way of life.

* Fleurs d'ennui by Pierre Loti.

22 Scandal

In England a great name excused ill-judged conduct for which a mere gentleman would be asked to resign from his clubs. But from time to time a more than usually scandalous court case would vouchsafe to a public, more amused than shocked, a glimpse of dirty linen marked with coronets. Queensberry, believing that his family was illustrious enough to bear one more stain upon its honour, could not be restrained in his persecution of Bosie. As a sportsman, he warned him of this: '. . . If I catch you with that man (Wilde) I will make a public scandal in a way you little dream of. It is already a suppressed one; I prefer an open one. . . .' Sometimes the Marquess bombarded his family with insulting letters, even obscene ones when they were addressed to his wife or to his daughter-in-law. Sometimes he acted the part of King Lear; his eldest son had killed himself, his children turned their backs upon him. He had married, as his second wife, a lady of indifferent reputation, but after a fortnight she left him and in 1894 she obtained an annulment. Every grief, every humiliation was a banderilla to provoke the old bull further. He had hated Oscar ever since the latter had rescued Alfred from the scandal at Oxford. That the poet compromised Bosie by his morals was only a pretext, to him what was worse was that Oscar had allied himself with Bosie's mother, but the moral question enabled him to play the part of a noble father. Nevertheless his first meeting with Oscar had been a success; one day Queensberry was lunching at the Café

306

Royal and happened to sit near Bosie and Oscar. Bosie asked
him to join them, at first he refused and then reluctantly
accepted. Within ten minutes he was laughing with delight
and by the end of luncheon he was charmed. They talked
animatedly and poor Bosie was quite left out. Soon after
this meeting Queensberry wrote impetuously to Bosie with-
drawing everything he had said about Wilde and adding
that Lord de Grey had said that Oscar was a friend of his and
his wife, and that he was 'perfectly all right', a man of
genius and a marvellous talker.

This armistice was short-lived. A few months later, insulting letters about Wilde were addressed to all the Douglas
family and soon after the publication of The Green Carnation
Lord Queensberry presented himself at Tite Street accompanied by an ex-boxer who looked more like a gorilla. They
were shown in by 'Ginger' the seventeen-year-old servant,
who was small and terrified. Wilde stood up to greet them.
'Sit down,' barked the Marquess. 'I do not allow anyone to
talk to me like that in my own house or anywhere else,' said
Wilde, 'I suppose you have come to apologise for the state-
ment you made about my wife and myself in letters you
wrote to your son. I should have the right any day to prose-
cute you for writing such a letter.' (Lord Queensberry had
written to Bosie that he had heard on good authority that
Constance was petitioning to divorce her husband for his
unnatural practices.) 'It was privileged, as it was written to
my son,' replied the Marquess. 'But how dare you say such
things about your son and me?' 'You were kicked out of the
Savoy Hotel at a moment's notice for your disgusting
conduct.' 'That is a lie.' 'And you have taken furnished rooms
for him in Piccadilly.' 'Somebody has been telling you an
absurd set of lies about your son and me. I have not done
anything of the kind.' Finally Oscar said, 'Lord Queensberry,
do you seriously accuse your son and me of improper

conduct?' 'I don't say you are it, but you look it and you
pose it, which is just as bad. If I catch you and my son
together again in any public restaurant, I will thrash you.'
'I don't know what the Queensberry Rules are, but the Oscar
Wilde rule is to shoot at sight. Leave my house at once.'
'It's a disgusting scandal!' yelled the Marquess. 'If it is so,
you are the author of the scandal and no one else.' Wilde
rang for his servant and said, 'This is the Marquess of
Queensberry, the most infamous brute in London. You are
never to allow him to enter my house again. Now,' and he
went and opened the door, 'get out.'

From that day onward 'the screaming scarlet Marquess', as
Wilde used to speak of him, accompanied by his faithful
bruiser, did the rounds of the restaurants where he was
most likely to run into the two friends. Although Bosie used
to inform his father of the time and place and date when
he and Oscar could be found in public together, no meeting
took place. However, Queensberry warned the head waiters
that if it did there would be a brawl. Oscar was no longer
warmly welcomed, no matter how generous a customer he
had been in the past. Instead he was led to some discreet
out-of-the-way table in a corner.

This persecution brought Oscar and the Marquess's two
sons together, and the implications of Bosie's relationship
with the poet were ignored. Their defence of Oscar was
evinced by a loyalty which was to cost him dear. The
Douglas family put at Oscar's disposal letters from Queensberry in which his name had been brought into disrepute,
and there was more than enough to enable him to win an
action for defamation of character, or even for threats of
murder. For example, Queensberry had written to Bosie on
the 1st April 1894, signing himself 'your disgusted so-
called father'. In this letter he wrote that he had heard that
Wilde was being divorced for sodomy and other crimes and

Lord Queensberry by Max Beerbohm

went on: '. . . If I thought the actual thing was true, and it became public property, I should be quite justified in shooting him at sight. . . .' Marquess or not, such threats as these lead to prison. It was to this letter that Bosie had sent the famous telegram: 'What a funny little man you are.' In the same letter Queensberry wrote, '. . . With my own eyes I saw you both in the most loathsome and disgusting relationship as expressed by your manner and expression. Never in my life have I seen such a sight as that in your horrible features. . . .' To make public such a letter as this would be damaging to Bosie for the rest of his life. So Oscar and the Douglas's decided to do nothing. In De Profundis, Oscar was unfair in his criticism of Lady Queensberry: '. . . Surely, when she heard of your father coming down to my house to make a loathsome scene and create a public scandal, she might then have seen that a serious crisis was impending, and taken some serious steps to try and avoid it? But all she could think of doing was to send down plausible George Wyndham* with his pliant tongue to propose to me – what? That I should "gradually drop you"!'

Nor was anything decided about Bosie's future. The attitude of the literary anarchist was a conventional one. Wilde remained on the side of the family and the law, and it can be seen that, as Richard Ellman said, 'he always played a part of a sinner without however wishing to be taken seriously'. In short, he played the part of a generous uncle or an indulgent godfather. But the spoilt child did not make this part any easier to play when for instance Bosie published the following poem:

* (1863–1913) Grandson of the first Lord Leconfield, M.P. for Dover since 1889 and private secretary to Mr. Balfour 1887–92. Became Chief Secretary for Ireland. Kinsman to Lord Alfred Douglas through Lady Queensberry.

'Here's short life to the man I hate
(Never a shroud or a coffin board)
Wait and watch and watch and wait
He shall pay the half and the whole,
Now or then, or soon or late,
Steel or lead or hempen cord,
And the devil take his soul!'

Oscar had returned to London from Algiers early in
February to supervise the rehearsals of The Importance of Being
Earnest, due to open at the St. James's Theatre on the 14th.
On the 10th February Mrs. Leverson received the following
letter from him: '. . . You were kind enough to say I might
bring someone to dinner tonight, so, after carefully going
over the list, I have selected a young man, tall as a young
palm tree, (I mean "tall as two young palm trees"). His
Christian name is "Tom" – a very rare name in an age of
Algies and Berties – and he is the son of Colonel Kennion
and lives at Oxford in the hopes of escaping the taint of
modern education. I met him on Tuesday, so he is quite an
old friend. . . .' The Sphinx's light touch and amused
readiness to be interested in a new disciple helped to dissipate his worries. Oscar always inspired and charmed her.
It was only after the disgrace and tragedy that she understood the dangers that had lain submerged in his way of
life. 'He was a good, kind and brilliant man, ruined by
follies and a fatal weakness in his character', was her verdict
later.

One can but wonder if Oscar was aware of the imprudence
of making yet another conquest or whether he was so sure
that he could not escape catastrophe that he seized upon
every diversion. More champagne, more applause, more
boys! Wilde arrived from Algiers for the first night like a
galley laden with spices and flowers, in full sail, but with
dynamite in the hold. Some of the actors in his plays dis-

liked him, in particular, as has been said, Charles Brookfield, who had written a parody of *Lady Windermere's Fan* called
The Poet and the Puppets; it was very feeble and Wilde showed
no resentment. Journalists detested Oscar, the public
supported him. He felt slightly anxious when he was told
that Lord Queensberry intended to provoke a scandal at
the first night but what matter, it was fun to introduce a
new friend to the Sphinx.

On the 14th February, everyone in London who could get
in flocked to the St. James's Theatre. Outside the weather was
cold and forbidding, snow was falling and the horses
trampled it to slush. Yet there were many to stand and gawk
at the beauties half-smothered in ermine who hurried into
the theatre. The young men in the audience wore button-
holes of lilies-of-the-valley, and inside the theatre the
atmosphere was warm and scented. At least two of Oscar's
friends, Mrs. Leverson and Miss Schuster, must have felt
their hearts beating faster – apprehension alternating with
an intoxicating elation as the brilliant success of the play
became more and more apparent. Queensberry had booked
a seat for the opening, but George Alexander, hearing of it
in time, had cancelled the booking. However, the Marquess
arrived for the performance carrying what Sherard called 'a
phallic bouquet' of carrots and turnips which he intended
to hurl at the author of the play. He was refused admittance
and every door was guarded by the police. Wilde wisely
remained backstage throughout the performance.

'Well, what did you think of it?' said Alexander after the
play was over. 'My dear Alec, it was charming, quite
charming,' replied Wilde nodding his head in the ponderous
manner peculiar to him. 'And do you know from time to
time I was reminded of a play I once wrote myself called
The Importance of Being Earnest.' This was reported to Hesketh
Pearson by one of the actors, Alan Aynsworth. The Press

was as enthusiastic as the public. Never had Oscar had such good reviews, but the praise exasperated Lord Queensberry as much as it went to Oscar's head.

Soon after this Bosie arrived from Algiers, where the abduction of the young Arab had brought him more expense than pleasure. He installed himself at the Avondale Hotel with Oscar, and brought a companion with him. Thus the idiotic life of extravagance and champagne started all over again. After ten days Bosie left to join his mother in the country; Oscar wanted to go to Paris but he could not pay his bill, which was nearly £140 and the hotel would not release his baggage. Was it the manager's wish to humiliate a scandalous client by this procedure, or had Lord Queensberry put him up to it? Oscar did not leave, indeed he could not.

To be reminded of the atmosphere of former days, to forget money and emotional problems, he called at the studio of the artists Shannon and Ricketts whom he had once launched and who were, by then, well-known. In Charles Ricketts' book *Recollections of Oscar Wilde* he gives a moving description of this visit of the 28th February 1895: 'That evening in Beaufort Street, when we met for the last time before the trial, was cold and dank. I was alone in the empty house at work in a long, low, gloomy room lit only by a lamp and the glass reflector needed to increase the light upon my wood block and tools. In response to loud knocking I opened the front door. . . . Wilde stood in the mist which flooded the street . . . for a little while we exchanged those commonplace enquiries which preface conversation. I then spoke about his plays, "Yes I live in a world of puppets who do not understand, and yet would play with the strings. . . . But why this darkness? This place is like a tomb!" I lit two candles; "My dear fellow, how could you leave the Vale for this dull, dark house? Tell me

about yourself, why this change?" I explained that I was
about to become a printer and publisher with a shop of
my own. "You must print my *Portrait of Mr. W.H.*" There was
a short pause; I hesitated to explain that my scheme included
classics only, the meagre finances at my disposal forbade the
risk that accompanied the issuing of modern works. I dared
not say that if his plays enchanted the public, his books
were far from being successful. . . . Wilde seemed not to
hear, becoming more and more absorbed, while smoking
silently. "I see my dear Ricketts, even your charming picture
of Willie Hughes has not convinced you! – I must work on
the thing again, it is still short for book form. But why do
I say this, as if size meant anything – think of the ocean, how
dull! and of a pearl which can be perfect!" He laughed
silently, then said, "Have you noticed how annoyed pigs
become if you do not cast pearls before them?" . . . In the
street, as his form receded into the gathering mist, he seemed
to me to have aged and to grow older still as he walked
away. . . . A few minutes later Shannon returned and
exclaimed: ". . . . I have just met Oscar in the King's Road.
He stopped me and said charming things about you and
about your publishing his Mr. *W. H.* I thought he looked
tired and preoccupied. We waited in the fog for a hansom
to pass, near a shop with sausage rolls and pork pies lit by
gas. Wilde became quite funny and said suddenly,'What
curious things people will sometimes eat—I suppose they
must be hungry!' A cab passed and, hailing it, he named a
club near Piccadilly." '

'Mr. Wilde, a gentleman left this for you ten days
ago,' the hall porter of the Albemarle Club handed Oscar an
envelope which contained a card on which was written 'To
Oscar Wilde, posing as a somdomite'. (sic). In his rage the
Marquess had mis-spelt the word. 'Who else has seen this

card?' 'No one, Sir, it was I who put it in the envelope and I
don't understand what is written on it.' Thus began the
series of 'if only's' which could have avoided the scandal. If
only Oscar had torn up the card which had not left the
hands of the porter; but, very upset, he had run to the
Avondale Hotel (if only he had been able to leave it ten
days earlier), and asked Robbie to come to the hotel at
11.30 that night: '. . . I don't see anything now but a
criminal prosecution. My whole life seems ruined by
this man. The tower of ivory is assailed by the foul thing.
On the sand is my life spilt. I don't know what to do. . . .'
If only Ross had been sensible he would have advised Oscar
to keep quiet. But no, it was through him that Oscar was
introduced to Humphreys, Ross's solicitor, who asked if
there was any truth in the libel. Wilde assured him that
there was not, whereupon Humphreys agreed to act for
him saying: 'If you are innocent you should succeed.' On
1st March Oscar applied for a warrant, the Marquess was
arrested and charged at Marlborough Street Police Court on
2nd March, the case being adjourned for a week. Then
Humphreys went to the Temple to persuade Sir Edward
Clarke* to lead for the prosecution, he asked Humphreys to
bring Oscar to see him and said, 'I can only accept this brief
Mr. Wilde, if you can assure me on your honour as an
English gentleman that there is not, and never has been, any
foundation for the charges that are made against you.'
Wilde solemnly swore that the charges were absolutely false
and groundless. Was he lying or was he quibbling about
the exact meaning of the word sodomite? If only he had
admitted the truth to the barrister matters would have
rested there, but he was a prisoner of the very prejudices at
which he mocked. 'The one disgraceful, unpardonable and

---

* Sir Edward George Clarke (1841–1931) late Solicitor-General. Was
leading Counsel throughout the three trials.

to all time contemptible action of my life was my allowing
myself to be forced into appealing to Society for help and
protection . . .' (De Profundis).

It is perhaps worth looking at Oscar in terms of the
central figure of an allegory, first provoked by the Furies
who spoke in the name of Respectability, then for a time
upheld by the blind Virtues of Friendship and Courage, only
to be finally pushed over the edge of the precipice by his
sordid loves. The background contains the two dominant
mother-figures: on the one side Speranza, to whom the idea
of a fight against English justice brought back the glorious
days of 1848: (her Oscar was a genius, he would be a hero,
he would avenge Parnell, whom England had got rid of by
underhand means and false evidence). On the other side
was the wronged Lady Queensberry, who at last had found
the instrument of her vengeance. Ever since she had understood the nature of the links between Oscar and her son,
she no longer wished to see Wilde, but she had no scruples
about using him against her husband. These much-loved
mothers threw oil on the flames. In this picture the absurd
was mixed with the tragic. Of pleasure only blemishes were
left, of generosity only blackmail.

The details of the trials have been admirably reported by
Mr. Montgomery Hyde,* and it would be idle to repeat them.
The acrobat had fallen, no longer did the sequins scintillate,
all that remained of his glory was a nine days' wonder
which gripped the man in the street and disgusted the
fastidious. With the adroitness of dustmen raking through
a heap of garbage, Lord Queensberry and his detectives set
about obtaining witnesses to justify the accusation on the
visiting card. The dregs of the racecourse world were enlisted
and it was actually through a prostitute in Piccadilly that
they learned of the boys who went to Taylor's house. Taylor

* The Trials of Oscar Wilde by H. Montgomery Hyde.

and some of the gigolos had been arrested for procuring, and Queensberry's detectives put pressure on them to turn Queen's Evidence. While Queensberry was following this feverish course, uncertain of success, Charles Brookfield offered to sail under his flag, and suborned a commission-aire at the Haymarket Theatre to give the names and addresses of the blackmailers who two years earlier had tried to sell the incriminating letters found in Bosie's over-coat pocket to the manager of the theatre and to Oscar.

In London no one talked of anything but the case; Oscar thought that it would create a good effect if he were to be seen in public with his wife, so, two nights before the trial, he, Constance and Bosie dined together and went on to the St. James's Theatre. Bosie said of her, 'She was very much agitated and when I said goodnight to her at the door of the theatre she had tears in her eyes.' Between the acts Oscar went to see Alexander, who reported their conversation years later to Pearson; 'I don't think you should come to the theatre at such a time,' said Alexander, 'People will think it in bad taste.' 'Are you going to accuse everyone in the theatre of bad taste for seeing my play at such a time?' said Oscar, 'I would consider it in bad taste if they went to anyone else's play.' 'Do be serious.' 'Then you mustn't be funny.' 'Will you take a bit of advice?' 'Certainly, if it is advice I wish to take.' 'Why don't you withdraw from the case and go abroad.' 'Everyone wants me to go abroad. I have just been abroad, and now I have come home again. One can't keep going abroad unless one is a missionary or, what comes to the same thing, a commercial traveller. . . .'

Oscar asked Frank Harris in his position as editor of the *Fortnightly Review* to give evidence that *Dorian Gray* was not immoral, and Harris agreed.* He and Shaw were to lunch together at the Café Royal, and Harris asked Oscar to join

* Translator's addition.

them there after luncheon. Oscar asked if he could bring
Bosie and Harris said 'No'. When Oscar arrived, Shaw got
up to go, but Oscar said: 'Do stay, don't go on my account.'

They both implored him to give up the case, pointing
out that he could not possibly win.* Bosie suddenly
appeared and was furious at their suggestion, 'Such advice
shows you are no friend of Oscar's.' He turned and left the
room; Oscar, muttering, 'It's not friendly of you, Frank,'
went after him.

By this time Oscar believed himself to be playing the
greatest rôle of his career – the artist triumphing over the
brute. He was not pleased with those who wished to deprive
him of this part. Was he not being supported by the two
sons of his noble adversary? Surely he must have envisaged
defeat, but as a dazzling catastrophe. He expected 'the purple
shroud of dead Gods' and he was offered the dirty sheets of
a house of assignation. What was most demoralising from
Oscar's point of view was the inartistic way in which justice
took its course. In after years Wilde was to remember the
horror of the interminable visits to Humphreys when, in
the ghastly glare of a bleak room, he would sit with a serious
face 'telling serious lies to a bald man, till I really groaned
and yawned with ennui'. But when, to give himself courage
and to amuse his friends in the Court, he made brilliant
repartees reminiscent of Whistler's tirades against Ruskin,
he found that he had to deal with a severe judge and a
scandalised, bourgeois jury.

On the 9th March Oscar, accompanied by the
Douglas brothers, went to Marlborough Street Police Court
for the case against Lord Queensberry, who was committed
for trial but released on bail. An entry in Laura Hope's
diary for that day runs: 'To the new Oscar Wilde play The

* Translator's addition.

Importance of Being Ernest (sic) in a box with Constance and Cyril, laughed much and went back behind the scenes.'

Oscar and Bosie, finding London too painful for their nerves, went to spend two weeks in Monte Carlo. Oscar had borrowed £500 from Ernest Leverson and Bosie had scraped together £360 from his family, for the costs of the case. Instead of using the money to suborn witnesses, as Queensberry had done, they spent most of it on a pointless holiday – pointless, as Oscar hated the place. It was thronged with *demi-mondaines* and expatriates of many countries, but at least there was Princess Alice of Monaco for Oscar and baccarat for Bosie. Oscar spent sleepless nights waiting for him to return, and when he did so he had always lost all the money with which he had set out.

Their stay on the Riviera, which became one of the first stations of Oscar's Calvary, was an interval before the great performance. With a grain of commonsense Oscar would have understood that public opinion was solidly against him. Already tourists pointed at him and sneered from afar, but Bosie was indispensable to him. Even if he was no longer sure of freeing him of his father's persecution by the case, he imagined a happiness in shame which would bring them nearer together than prosperity had done. And in that he was not entirely wrong in the light of what was to happen for a short time two years later.

To his great surprise the poet observed that the French newspapers wrote about the case in their own way, and that it was unfavourable to him. They had got their information as the result of an extraordinary coincidence. In those days a criminal charge had to be considered by a Grand Jury to see if the prosecution warranted a True Bill. In error a French journalist had been empanelled. He had lived in England for many years, and went to excuse himself on the grounds of his nationality but, finding the Wilde case was down for hearing, he allowed his professional rather than his civic conscience to triumph and decided to stay. The Grand Jury's hearings were not reported in the Press, but the French papers got all the facts and soon they reached England. Queensberry's letters had included libels on others besides Wilde – Lord Rosebery, then Prime Minister, was also libelled, but with little evidence. The indiscretion of the French Press was harmful to Wilde, as the lawyers argued that if they were indulgent, the public would think that it was to spare the Prime Minister, while if they were severe it would show that Lord Rosebery had nothing to fear from the law. There was therefore as much patriotism as prudery in the atmosphere in which the case was heard.

Instead of returning to Tite Street after his sojourn in Monaco, Oscar went to the Holborn Viaduct Hotel. On the second day of the trial, Oscar met a friend of his called Charles Goodhard in Piccadilly Circus. Oscar was in high spirits, and Goodhard did not like to touch on the subject and so talked about the weather but Oscar said, 'You've heard of my case I suppose?' 'Oh – er – yes, 'replied Good-hard nervously, 'I'm sure I wish you the best of luck – er,' Wilde spared his feelings, 'Don't distress yourself. All is well. The working classes are with me – to a boy.'

The cross-examination did not worry Oscar, who was never at a loss for a reply, but his adversary was Sir Edward Carson, a contemporary at Trinity College, an upright and subtle barrister who had never been able to stand Oscar, and whose professional zeal therefore was reinforced by personal antipathy. A battle of wits which is famous in the annals of the English bar, took place between them. At first the case proceeded like that against Baudelaire and his Les Fleurs du Mal – the defence wished to show Wilde as a corrupter of youth. Everything that had ever been said against Dorian Gray was brought up. Wilde answered with the same kind of paradoxes as those which prefaced the novel. Then Carson quoted the still more cynical paradoxes which had been published in The Chameleon. This review, in which The Priest and the Acolyte and Lord Alfred's poem The Two Loves had been published, he maintained showed Oscar's fatal influence on the young; the Court adopted the attitude of a censor. The stupid vanity of Oscar in mis-stating his age, making out that he was two years younger than he was, increased the bad impression.

Carson, after having cleverly put the jury against the poet, was able, thanks to Brookfield's help, to produce the letters, the originals of which Wilde had bought back from Wood and the other blackmailers, who had kept copies. The impression made by these was disastrous. Finally Carson, with the coolness of a poker player, produced his trump card; he said that he would call as witnesses the boys who had been procured for Wilde. Oscar was thereby forced on to the defensive and Carson had the upper hand. 'What enjoyment was it to you to entertain grooms and coachmen?' 'The pleasure for me was being with those who are young, bright, happy, careless and free. I do not like the sensible and I do not like the old.' From this moment he was no longer believed when he posed as the champion of youth. Besides he had just shocked the Victorians by something far more important than his attachment to Lord Alfred, he had transgressed the social code: a gentleman does not sit at table with people of the lower orders; he can give them tips, but not cigarette-cases. He had betrayed his class and for that he would not be forgiven. With simulated innocence, Carson led him on to say the words that were to damn Oscar irrevocably; referring to a young man who had been Lord Alfred's servant at Oxford, the relentless lawyer asked: 'Did you ever kiss him?' 'Oh dear, no. He was a peculiarly plain boy. He was, unfortunately, extremely

ugly. I pitied him for it.' 'Was that why you did not kiss
him?' Oscar could not find an immediate answer, lost control
and was on the verge of tears.

Oscar's lawyers thought it wiser not to produce Lord
Alfred as a witness, both because they feared Bosie's impulsive nature would be aggravated by Counsel's insults, and
because a son giving evidence against his father would be
sure to antagonise the jury. Bosie chafed under this restraint
and saw with fury that he would not have the opportunity,
to which he had been looking forward, of abusing his
father in public. The Court was also not told of Maurice
Schwabe (with whom Oscar sometimes went to Paris),
because he was the nephew of the Solicitor-General. In view
of Carson's willingness to bring forward his witnesses, Sir
Edward Clarke felt that the only thing to do was to withdraw
the prosecution, on the lines that it was impossible in
certain criminal cases to convict a father who had acted in
the belief that he was helping his son. The jury was
instructed to give a verdict of 'not guilty'; thus it was not
the jury's finding, but the fact of the prosecution being
withdrawn, that won Queensberry the day.

Laura Hope commented thus in her diary: 'April 5th. A
most trying visit from Mrs. William Napier in a most
frantic state about her poor niece Constance Wilde as the
verdict has gone against her monstrous husband – the whole
episode most terrible.'

After this triumph for Lord Queensberry, the two actors,
Brookfield and Hawtrey, took him out to a celebration
dinner. Then Queensberry sent the following message to
Oscar: 'If the country allows you to leave, all the better
for the country; but if you take my son with you I will
follow you, wherever you go, and shoot you!'

Wilde left the Old Bailey about noon and went to lunch
at the Holborn Viaduct Hotel with Bosie. The application

for a warrant for his arrest was made about 3.30 p.m., but the Magistrate delayed granting it for about one and a half hours, and it was not signed until 5 p.m. Whether this was to enable Oscar to get the boat-train for the Continent or not is not certain. Meanwhile Oscar had gone to Bosie's rooms at the Cadogan Hotel. Robbie and all his other friends urged him to leave the country, and when Constance was told what had happened at the Old Bailey she too said she hoped he'd go, but he remained in a state of indecision, although he had half-packed a bag and had drawn a lot of money out of the bank. Oscar sat on with Robbie and Reggie in the Cadogan Hotel while Bosie went to the House of Commons to find George Wyndham to see if a prosecution was inevitable. Wyndham was told by the Solicitor-General that it was. Oscar drank hock and selzer endlessly. At 6.30 p.m. there was a knock on the door, two men entered; 'Mr. Wilde, I believe?' 'Yes, yes,' said Wilde. He was plainly drunk when he got up to go with the police officers. The book under his arm was not The Yellow Book as is so often said, but Aphrodite by Pierre Louÿs, which happened to have a yellow cover.

23 The vengeance of the pharisees

The Wilde affair was a turning-point in the literary and social life of England, as the Dreyfus affair had been in France. Certainly England was not divided politically and there was not the slightest doubt about the guilt of the culprit, but in both cases the conservative elements felt themselves threatened. In the uneasiness felt at the turn of the century with its anarchists and socialists, the people with a position to uphold needed a scapegoat. In France it was the Jews who filled this rôle, in England the aesthetes. A purge seemed necessary to both countries, passing as they were through a crisis of imperialism. After Panama the French patriots decided to have done with financiers, whereas in England the middle-class feared that artists would sap the energy of the Empire and so decided to do away with yellow books and green carnations.

As soon as the newspapers reported Queensberry's triumph, some of Oscar's friends, and some others who might have been his friends, or who otherwise did not have clear consciences, hurried off to Victoria to catch the 5.30 boat-train. Within twenty-four hours, some dozens of gentlemen, young and old, were scattered over the various beaches of northern France. Some felt the urge to visit Florence, others, hoping to be forgotten, went as far as Egypt. Black lists were drawn up in the clubs. The House of Lords was decimated, there was trembling in the City and even at Court. In the country, bachelors gave up painting watercolours and started to play cricket, and ferocious

324

moustaches sprouted on beautiful profiles. The Press, so
often mocked by Oscar, clamoured for his head and Jerome
K. Jerome demanded 'the heads of the five hundred noblemen and men-of-the-world who share his turpitude and
corrupt youth'. It was indeed a far cry from the galley of
Antinous to the boat of the 'three men'. Even the greatest of
families trembled, and Lord Ronald Gower installed himself
with a friend in the South of France.

The Prince of Wales, who had figured in minor scandals,
was in no position to defend his favourite dramatist. There
was a conspiracy of silence in the social world. Gleeson
White, an art critic, friend and contemporary of Oscar, said
shrewdly: 'He will never lift his head again, for he has
against him all men of infamous life.' Later, good-hearted
people began to be indignant, including the Bishop of
London, Dr. Winnington Ingram, who said, 'I knew Wilde,
and, in spite of his one great vice – which was surely pathological – I never met a man who united in himself so many
lovable Christian virtues.'* Henry James gives the best
example of a 'humane' attitude, in a letter to Edmund Gosse:
'April 8th 1895. Yes, too, it has been, it is, hideously,
atrociously dramatic and really interesting – so far as one
can say of a thing of which the interest is qualified by such
sickening horribility. It is the squalid gratuitousness of it
all – of the mere exposure – that blurs the spectacle. But
the fall from nearly twenty years of a really unique kind of
"brilliant" conspicuity (wit, "art", conversation – one of
our two or three dramatists etc.) to that sordid prison cell
and this gulf of obscenity over which the ghoulish public
hangs and gloats – it is beyond any utterance of irony or
any pang of compassion! He was never in the smallest
degree interesting to me – but this hideous human history
has made him so – in a manner.' On a less serious note, Mrs.

* Quoted in *Previous Convictions* by Cyril Connolly.

Y

Patrick Campbell made the unforgettable observation: 'I don't care what they do as long as they don't do it in the street and frighten the horses.'

The collaborators in *The Yellow Book* demanded the dismissal of Beardsley. William Watson said to Lane the publisher, and Henry Harland, the editor of *The Yellow Book*, that they must choose between his poems and Beardsley's illustrations – they chose Watson and respectability. Hounded, and already dying of consumption, the artist turned for refuge to Raffalovich who was very generous to him. John Lane, Wilde's publisher, returned to Oscar's house the manuscript of *The Duchess of Padua* and withdrew copies of his books from the booksellers. He was particularly afraid of being mixed up in the affair since one of his employees, Shelley, was said to have been one of Wilde's minions. George Alexander had Wilde's name blanked out on the board outside his theatre, but claimed that he did so in order that Oscar should receive the very necessary royalties. As Beerbohm Tree was returning from the United States of America and wanted the Haymarket Theatre, it had been arranged that *An Ideal Husband* should be transferred to the Criterion. Wyndham refused to follow Alexander's example and Oscar's name appeared on the boards and the programme for the length of its run, from 13th to 27th April.

After Oscar's arrest, Bosie asked both Alexander and Waller to put up bail in case it should be allowed but both refused. That he tried others is shown in an entry in Laura Hope's diary: 'April 6th. Adrian had a most painful interview with Lord Alfred Douglas, who came to implore him to go bail for that fiend O.W. which was of course impossible.'

Oscar was taken from the Cadogan Hotel to Bow Street Police Court, where he was charged and where he spent the night in the cells. Bail was refused. The next day he was

removed to Holloway Prison and remained there on remand
until his trial. Bosie went to see him every day. There was so
much noise in the room where they met that they could
only exchange a few words, and they turned away their
heads to hide their tears; never before had they felt so close.
Bosie only left England on the eve of Oscar's trial at the
urgent insistence of Wilde's advisers, who thought that his
continued presence would be prejudicial to their client's
chances. 'I don't know what to do,' wrote Oscar to the
Sphinx, 'My life seems to have gone from me. I feel caught
in a terrible net. I don't know where to turn. I care less
when I think that he is thinking of me. I think of nothing
else.' Each day he wrote impassioned letters to Bosie, calling
him poetic names, Prince Fleur de Lys, or Jonquil. As he
was to write later in *De Profundis*: 'I said to myself *"At all
costs I must keep love in my heart. If I go into prison without Love what
will become of my Soul"?'*

Laura Hope's diary contains the following entry for
9th April. 'To the Napiers where I sat with poor Constance,
the most miserable woman in London, I should think.' By
the 19th April Constance was staying at Babbacombe with
Lady Mount Temple.

On the 26th April, Wilde appeared at the Old Bailey, this
time in the dock, side by side with Taylor. For three days,
all the evidence produced or threatened by the defence at
the earlier trial, was repeated and there followed a hideous
procession of witnesses – gigolos, procurers and chamber-
maids. *Dorian Gray* and the poems were attacked once more
and Max Beerbohm reported the events in a letter to Reggie
Turner: '3rd May 1895. My dearest Reg. . . . Ever since I
arrived I have been all day at the Old Bailey and dining out
in the evening – and coming home very tired. . . . Oscar has
been quite superb. His speech about the Love that dares not
tell its name was simply wonderful, and carried the whole

court right away, quite a tremendous burst of applause.
Here was this man who had been for a month in prison and
loaded with insults and crushed and buffeted, perfectly self-
possessed, dominating the Old Bailey with his fine presence
and musical voice. He has never had so great a triumph I
am sure, as when the gallery burst into applause – I am
sure it affected the jury. Public opinion too has undergone
a very great revulsion, so everyone seems to think – nine
out of the twelve jurors were for him. Today they renew
application for bail, but I don't think they can get it. . . .
Oscar stood very straight when he was brought up to hear
the verdict and looked most leonine and Sphinx-like. I
pitied poor little Alfred Taylor – nobody remembered his
existence. Oscar is thinner and consequently finer to look
at . . . it was horrible leaving the court day after day and
having to pass through a knot of renters (the younger Parker
wearing Her Majesty's uniform – another form of female
attire) who were allowed to hang around after giving their
evidence and to wink at likely persons. . . .'

After having argued all sides of the case the jury could
not reach a unanimous decision. If Wilde had not been
associated with Taylor it is possible that he would have
been found 'not guilty'. But the fact that he appeared with a
procurer aggravated a case about which the Court took a
bad view and which had already been condemned by
public opinion.

Fundamentally the man in the street adjusts himself to
morality and patriotism if these virtues allow him to get on
with his own business and to decry anything he does not
understand; French political troubles in the past have been
an excellent example of this. Sensible England was stupefied
by the passions which were aroused by the Wilde case. A
shock of horror made even those still well-disposed towards
Oscar shy away from him. Young men were called 'Oscars'

if they carried obvious bunches of flowers in the streets or were too smartly dressed. Blackmailers reaped a golden harvest. Prostitutes danced in triumph outside the Old Bailey.

The worst moment was when Oscar's creditors, who saw him in prison, his plays taken off and his books removed from libraries, panicked and forced a sale of his possessions at Tite Street. The auctioneer arrived, the house was open to the crowds, invaded by a jovial and dissolute medley of small shopkeepers and the like. Suburban money-lenders, tailors and dressmakers walked about protesting indignantly at the haunt of vice, others laughing loudly at the white furniture and the silk hangings. Everything went for a song. The sale was a disaster, although Oscar's friends did what they could to save one or two of his treasures; thus William Rothenstein bought the Monticelli (and later sold it for Oscar's benefit after his release from prison), and Ernest Leverson bought three pictures which he kept for Oscar. But all the books, inscribed by Huysmans, Verlaine, Hugo and Carlyle, carefully bound, were sold for a few pounds, and the children's toys went for thirty shillings the lot. Constance had only been able to take away her dresses, her fitted dressing-case and some of Oscar's cuff-links. Tite Street was invaded by girls brandishing Mrs. Wilde's umbrellas or Oscar's fine walking-sticks. Chelsea closed its windows so as not to hear the celebrations at the fall of its Prince.

Lord Alfred, as has been said, had left England at Wilde's insistence and went first to Calais, then to Rouen and finally to Paris. Sherard, at Oscar's request, offered *Salome* to Sarah Bernhardt for £400. Although she wept tears over Oscar's plight, she said that she could neither buy nor produce *Salome* but offered a loan: 'What I can do I will – the utmost – out of friendship for a great artist, who is also a man of

good heart, and who, I am sure, is suffering most unjustly.'
But although Sherard called daily at her request, she proved
elusive and never in the end paid a penny. The downfall
of the acrobat led to the collapse of the aesthetic circus and
the greater number went into hiding. Mrs. Bernard Beere,
one of Oscar's favourite actresses, and Mrs. Leverson, tried
to use their influence in political circles: the 'Souls' were
then in power. People would have pardoned Oscar his
pleasures, but his choice of companions in pleasure they
would never forgive. When Harris said that he would give
a dinner party for Oscar on his release, only Lady Dorothy
Nevill had the courage to say, 'I hope you will ask me, I
should be glad to come. I have always liked and admired
him and I feel dreadfully sorry for him now.' Few people
other than Lady Mount Temple and the Adrian Hopes
bothered about Constance, who in her bewilderment
appealed to the 'Sibyl of Mortimer Street': 'You told me
that after the shock, my life would become easier, but will
there be any happiness in it, or is that dead for me?' She
sent the children to Glion in Switzerland in the care of an
appalling governess and joined them there soon after the trial.

When the jury disagreed Oscar was finally allowed bail.
Lord Douglas of Hawick and the Reverend Stewart Headlam*
had put up bail for him which, together with his own
security for £2,500, amounted in all to £5,500. Oscar
immediately left prison and, accompanied by Lord Douglas,
drove to the Midland Hotel where rooms had been reserved.
They had been there only a few hours before the manager
came in and insisted on their leaving. Queensberry had
organised a gang to follow Oscar from hotel to hotel so
that he would be accepted nowhere. They even pursued him
as far as Kilburn and Notting Hill.

* Although he scarcely knew Wilde, he went bail for him as he thought
the case was being prejudged.

About midnight Percy and Oscar shook off the pursuers, no doubt because the latter had taken too much drink at the various stops; Oscar, deadbeat, knocked on his mother's door, Willie opened it, 'Give me shelter Willie,' he gasped, 'Let me lie on the floor or I shall die in the streets.' With these words, as Willie said, he collapsed 'like a wounded stag'. Willie was living with his mother in Oakley Street and kept saying 'Oscar was not a man of bad character, you could trust him with a woman anywhere" To Yeats, Oscar said: 'My poor brother writes to me that he is defending me all over London. My poor dear brother, he could compromise a steamroller.'

In the depths of his humiliation Oscar might have seen in his brother, to judge by Max's sketch, a likeness to himself: 'Cruel monster! Dark, oily, suspect yet awfully like Oscar; he has Oscar's esprit. But he is so awful; a veritable tragedy of family-likeness.'

Yeats called at Oakley Street while Oscar was out on bail with letters of sympathy from people in Ireland; Willie was terrified that the letters were to urge Oscar to run away and kept saying, 'Oscar is an Irish gentleman, he will stay and face the music'. He and Lady Wilde believed that he should stay. Not for nothing had Speranza been the heroine of two cases in Dublin; for her the great days had returned and woe betide anyone who thought to deprive her of them: 'If you stay, even if you go to prison, you will always be my son, it will make no difference to my affection, but if you leave, I will never speak to you again.'

Sherard, who had come over from Paris, was horrified to find Oscar in a dusty little room, a fading arum lily in a glass and a bunch of violets which Ellen Terry had brought with a note saying 'To bring you good luck', among all the disorder. Oscar immediately greeted him with the words, 'Why have you brought me no poison from Paris?' The sound of the phrase pleased him and he kept repeating 'poison from Paris, poison from Paris'. Sherard eventually told him impatiently how to make Prussic acid. At this time Oscar drank lemonade endlessly, no doubt a symptom of shock, and Sherard was always having to go out to buy more soda-water and more lemons. In his opinion, Oscar was making the most of a great tragic rôle.

Guessing Oscar's misery at Oakley Street, Ada Leverson came to fetch him in her little pill-box brougham to take him to stay with her and her husband until the next trial. Ernest Leverson had summoned the servants and offered each of them a month's wages if they did not want to wait upon Mr. Wilde. For the affair was now such a scandal as had rarely been known, little else was talked of in London, the papers were full of it, America, Germany, and all the Continent joined in the controversy, the Europeans saying 'This is how you behave to your poets', and the Americans saying 'This is how your poets behave'. Each servant in turn refused to leave, they appeared proud to wait upon 'poor Mr. Wilde' to whom indeed they had been devoted ever since he had started coming to the house. The coachman was sent away for fear he might talk in public houses. While staying with the Leversons at 2 Courtfield Gardens, South Kensington, Oscar made certain rules in order to avoid any embarrassments for his hosts. He never left the nursery floor, which was put at his disposal like a flat, before 6 o'clock, when he would come down dressed for dinner and talk to his hosts for a couple of hours in the drawing-room. 'When we were alone, he would walk up and down the room smoking a cigarette, talking in the most enchanting way about everything except his trouble.' One evening Frank Harris arrived to tell Oscar of a yacht he had been lent to use as he liked and which was waiting to take him away, and to her surprise asked the Sphinx if she could row; she hastily said she could and immediately saw herself as a 'fine ferryman'. Frank turned to Oscar: " 'Do you happen to know where Erith is?' 'No Frank.' 'It is a little landing place on the Thames,' I went on, 'not many miles away; it can be reached by a fast pair of horses and a brougham in a very short time. There at Erith is a steam yacht ready to start at a moment's notice; she has steam up now, one hundred pounds pressure to the square inch in her boilers, her captain's waiting, her crew ready – a greyhound in leash, she can do fifteen knots an hour without being pressed. In one hour she would be free of the Thames and on the high seas – (delightful phrase eh?) – high seas indeed where there is freedom uncontrolled. If one started now one could break-fast in France, at Boulogne or St. Enogat or any place you like on the coast of Normandy, and one could dine com-fortably at the Sables d'Olonne where there is not an Englishman to be found and where sunshine reigns even in May from morning light. . . .' 'Oh Frank,' he cried, 'how wonderful, but how impossible.' 'Impossible? Don't be absurd, do you see the lights yonder?', and I showed him some lights at the Park gate on the top of the hill in front of us, 'Yes, Frank', 'That's a brougham,' I said, 'with a pair of fast horses.' 'It will take us for a midnight visit to the steam yacht in double quick time. There's a little library on the yacht of French books and English, I've ordered supper in the cabin: lobster à l'americaine and a bottle of Pom-mery. You've never seen the mouth of the Thames at night, have you? It's a scene from wonderland; houses like blobs of indigo fencing you in, ships drifting past like black ghosts in the misty air, and the purple sky above never so dark as the river, the river with its shining lights of ruby and emerald and topaz, like an oily, opaque serpent gliding with a weird life of its own. . . . Come, you must visit the yacht,' I turned to him but he was no longer by my side . . .

he was leaning against the railing hung up with his head on his arm shaking. 'What's the matter, Oscar?' I cried, 'What on earth's the matter?' 'Oh Frank, I can't go, I can't. It would be wonderful, but it's impossible. I should be seized by the police. You don't know the police.' 'Take it that I offer you a holiday in France for ten days. Surely it is better to spend a week with me than in that dismal house in Oakley Street, where the very door gives me the creeps.' 'Oh, Frank, I'd love to, I see everything you say, but I can't. I dare not. I'm caught, Frank, in a trap. I can only wait for the end . . . I could not go about France feeling that the policeman's hand might fall on my shoulder at any moment. I could not live a life of fear and doubt, it would kill me in a month . . . Frank, if I were not in Oakley Street tonight, Willie would tell the police.' 'Your brother?' 'Yes,' he replied, 'Willie . . . you don't know Willie,' he continued, 'he has made my solicitors buy letters of mine, he has blackmailed me.' 'But in that case you'll have no compunction about leaving him. without saying goodbye. Let's go and get into the brougham.' 'No, no,' he repeated, 'you don't understand, I can't go'. Something of the despair and desolation in his voice touched me, I looked at him; tears were pouring down his face, he was the picture of misery, yet I could not move him.'"

One day Constance came to see Oscar at the Leversons' house; she had avoided doing so while he was still at Oakley Street, but now she had come with an urgent message from her lawyer imploring him to go away without fail before the next trial. She was in tears when she left.

In Oscar's refusal to leave there was a variety of different elements: a certain weakness, a fatalism, maternal domination and an ulterior motive – now that he had become *par excellence* a man of the theatre, Oscar felt that punishment, even if he had not faced up to the reality of prison, would, by an admirable contrast, put a stop to a career which in any case was broken, and he preferred opprobrium to an enforced exile in a watering place.

Toulouse-Lautrec happened to be in London at the time, with his friend Conder, who acted as his guide to music-halls and bars. The painter, after having spent the best part of the night which preceded the case in painting a study of Oscar in oils, was amazed at his apparently unconcerned manner. He told stories and could not keep still, but Toulouse-Lautrec was not taken in by his verve. He painted a man with the wan and anxious expression of an actor ill at ease in a part too young for him, and the sadness of Oscar's expression in the picture gives the lie to the heart-shaped mouth and dyed hair.

At the third trial, the prosecution was led by the Solicitor-General, Sir Frank Lockwood; Wilde and Taylor had the same counsel as before. They successfully applied to be tried separately; Taylor was tried first and found 'guilty'. On his way to his club to celebrate the good news, the Marquess of Queensberry ran into his son Percy, and they came to blows, and were only stopped by a policeman. (The 3rd Lord Leconfield, who died in 1952, well remembered his shaken astonishment, when, driving down Bond Street, he came upon his kinsmen 'going at it hammer and tongs'.) Undeterred, they crossed the road and started again until they were stopped by another policeman. They were eventually bound over to keep the peace at Great Marlborough Street Police Station.

Wilde came before the Court on the 22nd May, harassed after lengthy conversations with his lawyers. He was much changed, with tired eyes and a haggard anxious look. The foreman of the jury asked the judge whether 'in view of the intimacy between Lord Alfred Douglas and Wilde' a warrant for the arrest of Lord Alfred had ever been issued, the judge replied that he had not heard this suggested, adding that although they were not concerned with the question of the younger man and his guilt, it would be 'utterly hopeless and impossible' to suppose that Lord Alfred Douglas would be spared just because he was Lord Alfred Douglas. It was necessary once again to listen to the accusations of the witnesses, although Oscar's counsel had very cleverly succeeded at the earlier trial in proving one to have perjured himself, another had refused to give evidence and the judge directed the jury to discount the evidence of a third. Those present in the Court began to ask themselves if the condemnation of Wilde would not amount to a blackmailer's charter. The Solicitor-General had public opinion on his side and was very forceful. Oscar later wrote: 'I remember as I was sitting in the dock on the occasion of my last trial listening to Lockwood's appalling denunciation of me – like a thing out of Tacitus, like a passage in Dante, like one of Savonarola's indictments of the Popes at Rome – and being sickened with horror at what I heard. Suddenly it occurred to me "How *splendid it would be, if I was saying all this about myself!*" I saw then at once that what is said of a man is nothing. The point is who says it.'* When sordid details of the dirty linen at the Savoy were brought up the judge said, 'It is a condition of things one shudders to contemplate in a first-class hotel,' that the housekeeper had not reported the matter. All this was to Oscar, at the same time interminable and distressing, but of vital importance.

The jury retired at 3.30 p.m. on the 25th May; after three hours they returned and found Oscar 'guilty' on all counts, except that referring to Shelley on which the judge had already told them to acquit. The judge said: 'That you Wilde have been the centre of a circle of extensive corruption of the most hideous kind among young men, it is . . .

* *De Profundis*

impossible to doubt. I shall, under the circumstances, be expected to pass the severest sentence that the law allows. In my judgement it is totally inadequate for such a case as this. The sentence of the Court is that you be imprisoned and kept to hard labour for two years.' Some cries of 'Oh! Oh!' and 'Shame!' were heard in the Court. Oscar said, 'And I? May I say nothing my Lord?' The judge made no reply beyond a wave of the hand to the warders who hurried the prisoner out of sight. Sherard was at the trial and recorded that men and women and prostitutes danced in the street, and one of them shouted out, ' 'E'll 'ave 'is 'air cut reg'lar now!'

After these ordeals, the disciples could talk of Calvary. From there it was only one step to make a saint of him. The poet himself was happy to take that step and was to work on his own hagiography in *De Profundis*. The excessively hard sentence had blotted out of people's minds the incredibly irresponsible way in which Oscar had thrown himself into the case, and the obstinacy he had shown when his friends had tried to persuade him to get away in time. There had been a certain amount of hypocrisy in the conduct of the trial, though less than one would expect if one looks back on the Victorian era in general. How could the ordinary man in the street who made up the jury have failed to be deeply shocked by the revelations of homosexual life, and by the fact that the little clerk Shelley had in reality been corrupted by Wilde? When thinking about the case, Sartre wrote in his book on Genêt: 'When Wilde writes "It is better to be beautiful than to be good, but it is better to be good than to be ugly" . . . his "Beautiful" is an engine of war with which he intends to destroy the Good: and his sole aim is to infect others with a very subtle defeatism. . . .'*
In fact Oscar, in a generally very moral epoch, had never

* *Saint Genêt, actor and martyr* by J. P. Sartre.

ceased to profess the absurdity of principles to young men
who, not having his intellectual powers, were ready for
any foolishness. By his conversations and his books he had
excused tendencies that the law of his country considered
criminal, and this as a game. The sneering that Gide heard
after his downfall had already been heard in London and
Oxford. One of the most dreadful things about the verdict
was that Wilde had been convicted of crimes for which he
himself had not the slightest feeling of guilt. Had the verdict
resulted from his relations with Lord Alfred he might by
some have been regarded as a martyr, but as it was a judgement on those pleasures which had brought him to the
dock in company with a procurer, the best he could hope
for was to be regarded as a victim.

24   Prison

Wilde had precipitated himself towards disaster in a way that suggests he had a profound need for it, but he visualised a sombre apotheosis, the end of Satan, prisons like those of Piranesi, a successful suicide. His prison, on the contrary, was like an unsuccessful suicide, with all the vomiting and all the humiliation that a body can give when it is no longer wanted. Two years would pass, grey, dirty, interminable. The shame did not come from the severity of the verdict, but from that body, yesterday so pampered, today plunged into a bath of filth, the fetid air smelling of sinks, skilly and excrement. Total despair accompanied his horror until he realised that a masterpiece could be made out of it. For a long time his imagination was a blank, deprived as it was of enough books and conversation. Sometimes the prisoner was stupefied and dazed, sometimes he feared madness. If the judge was guilty of having inflicted too severe a sentence upon him, the prison authorities were even more at fault for having drawn up the prison regulations: solitary confinement, a badly ventilated cell, not enough food, pointless work, complete silence. Great progress was thought to have been made since the prisons of the eighteenth century, but then at least the rabble suffered together. Although the Governor, the Chaplain and the Doctor agreed that the rules should be strictly followed, the warders were sometimes more humane. For Oscar, who always thought in literary terms, the situation was atrocious because there were no artistic examples of such horror.

Today he could have found certain references in the pages
of Genêt, in the pictures of Francis Bacon, in the world of
concentration camps. In 1895, the idea of misfortune was
still a romantic one. If one is drawn to Wilde one is ashamed
to follow him through these prisons; it is indiscreet, like
reporting the stammering of a great mind become senile.*

As the verdict on Oscar was given so late in the day, he
was kept at Newgate Gaol adjacent to the Old Bailey for
two days, then handcuffed and taken to Pentonville. It took
him many weeks to get used to the food and the plank bed;
he never got used to the loneliness. For the first three months
no prisoner might have any book except the Bible, a Prayer
Book and a hymn book. Prisoners were allowed one visit
(from two people at the same time) and one letter every
three months. The chaplain and the doctor visited the
prisoners, and they could also always ask to see the
Governor. The chaplain at Pentonville is said to have asked
Oscar on his first visit: 'Did you have morning prayers in
your house?' 'I'm sorry, I fear not,' replied Oscar, to which
the chaplain replied, 'You see where you are now.' The
doctor was hardly more consoling, and Oscar's physical
state, with diarrhoea and insomnia, did not surprise him
as it was common to most of the prisoners. '. . . The dreadful
dress that makes sorrow grotesque to look at, the silence,
the solitude – each and all of these things I had to transform
into a spiritual experience. . . .'

About three weeks after Oscar had been sent to prison he
received his first visitor, the politician, R. B. Haldane,
afterwards Lord Chancellor, whom he had met in the days
of his success. It was probably Asquith who encouraged the
visit. Oscar must have been reminded of a particularly

---

* Mr. Montgomery Hyde, author of the admirable account of the trials,
followed step by step the stages of the disaster in another volume
The Aftermath.

brilliant luncheon party given by Mr. and Mrs. Asquith and recorded by Wilfrid Scawen Blunt in his *Diaries* . . . 'the other guests were Mrs. Grenfell, Mrs. Daisy White, Ribblesdale, his brother Reggie Lister and Oscar Wilde, all immensely talkative so that it was almost like a breakfast in France. Asquith alone rather out of it. I sat next to him and was rather sorry for him, though he was probably happy enough. Afterwards, when the rest had gone away, Oscar remained, telling stories to me and Margot.' Blunt goes on to say that, '. . . of all those present, and they were most of them brilliant talkers, he (Wilde) was without comparison the most brilliant, the most ready, the most witty, the most audacious and, in a perverse mood, chose to cross swords with one after the other of them, overpowering them each in turn with his wit, and making shrewd fun of Asquith his host that day who only a few months later, as Home Secretary, was prosecuting him on the notorious criminal charge which sent him to hard labour in prison.' Haldane shared with the 'Souls' a horror of cruelty, and in his own words he was 'haunted by the idea of what this highly sensitive man was probably suffering under ordinary prison treatment'. So this humane Member of Parliament said that he would try to obtain for Oscar the privileges of books and writing materials; Wilde was so overcome by this that he burst into tears; for books he asked eagerly, saying that he only had *Pilgrim's Progress* to read and 'this did not satisfy' him. He asked for *Madame Bovary* among others which, as Haldane pointed out, was unlikely to be sanctioned as the dedication was by the author to his advocate who had successfully defended him on a charge of obscene publication. At this remark Oscar immediately began to laugh and became cheerful. They eventually hit on the work of St. Augustine, several books by Cardinal Newman, Mommsen's *History of Rome*, Pascal's *Pensées*, and Walter Pater's *Renaissance*.

z

Haldane promised to get in touch with Oscar's family; and he went to see Lady Wilde, as Constance and the children, who had changed their name to Holland in the summer of 1895, were in Italy. The children went to school near Heidelberg in 1896, where Cyril remained throughout his school life, but Vyvyan was unhappy there and was sent, at Princess Alice of Monaco's suggestion, to the Jesuit School in Monte Carlo, where she could keep an eye on him.

Soon after Haldane's visit, Wilde received a less welcome one – from Queensberry's solicitor, who came to tell him that the Marquess claimed £677 costs for the case brought against him by Wilde. Misfortune did not save Oscar from what he particularly detested: the law and money affairs.

In July 1895, Oscar was moved to Wandsworth Prison and there in September, while his own solicitor was discussing his affairs with him, the clerk leaned across the table and said to Wilde in a low voice: 'Prince Fleur de Lys wishes to be remembered to you.' Wilde stared at him. The clerk added mysteriously, 'The gentleman is abroad at present.' Suddenly Oscar understood and laughed bitterly. He wrote in his famous letter to Bosie, De Profundis, 'You were, no doubt, quite right to communicate with me under an assumed name. I myself, at that time, had no name at all.' Poor Bosie, tactless as always, should have realised that such poetic expressions were out of place in a prison. In the prisoner's mind this futile gesture became an insult, a provocation. During his bankruptcy hearing Wilde sat in an adjoining room. Luckily friends were giving money and it was hoped that the debts could be paid off. There were many people in the corridor as Wilde passed through with two policemen, '. . . . Robbie waited . . . that before the whole crowd, whom an action so sweet and simple hushed into silence, he might gravely raise his hat to me, as handcuffed and with bowed head I passed him by. Men have gone to heaven for smaller things than that.'

After this experience Wilde was approaching a complete breakdown. He had fits of giddiness and had lost a stone and a half in weight; he felt so ill one morning that he could not get up, but was forced to do so, with the result that he fainted in Chapel, hurting his ear as he fell; he was then taken to an infirmary cell and after some time transferred to the general infirmary ward with other prisoners. The Home Office, alarmed by the publicity his ill-health was getting in the papers, sent two mental specialists from Broadmoor to visit him. When they arrived, they saw him through the door 'smiling and conversing apparently in a friendly and cheerful way with the other inmates of the ward'. The doctors advised that he should be removed to a country prison and allowed books, association with other prisoners under strict supervision, more food and a larger cell. Oscar was much touched when one of his fellow prisoners at Wandsworth whispered to him: 'I'm sorry for you, it is harder for the likes of you than it is for the likes of us.' This kindness brought tears to Oscar's eyes and he replied, 'No, my friend, we all suffer alike.' As he had not learned how to speak without moving his lips they were caught, and since Oscar insisted that he was the first speaker, he got double punishment.

He was visited by Constance and also by Sherard, who informed him that Bosie was about to publish some letters written by Oscar to him, in an article in the Mercure de France. Bosie could not understand why Oscar refused to allow this evidence of his affection to become public. Oscar was in fact very annoyed indeed at the idea and begged Sherard to put a stop to it. The Mercure de France agreed to omit the letters, but Bosie refused the article without them, so finally nothing was published at all. That he was kept in the dark

about Oscar's feelings over this article by Sherard can be
seen in the following letter from Bosie to the Sphinx:
'Villa Tarnasse, Sorrento. September 13th 1895. . . . I have
been made very miserable by receiving the enclosed letter
from the Governor of Wandsworth prison to whom I wrote
asking if I might write to Oscar. I can't make it out at all as
it appears from this letter that Oscar *had* the power to correspond with me but that he deliberately preferred not to.
Can you throw any light on the question? My anxiety has
been added to by the fact that Robert Sherard has not written
to me, and although I have had letters from you and Bobbie
and More Adey* since Sherard's interview, you have none
of you said a single word about what Oscar said at the
interview . . . surely Oscar must have sent me some message.
I am so upset and perplexed by it all . . . I am so afraid that
some secret influence has been brought to bear on Oscar,
or that he has been told some lies about me. It seems to me
quite inconceivable that he should prefer to correspond with
his "family" than with me without some very strong reason
of which I know nothing. . . . I really wish Oscar and I
were both dead. I have taken a little villa at Capri . . . my
address there is Villa Caso, Strada, Pastana, Capri.'†

In November 1895, after his stay in the infirmary,
Oscar was sent to Reading, a red-brick fortress bristling with
battlements and watch-towers. The episode of his transfer
ranks with the forced sale of his possessions as among the
most awful in his history. In *De Profundis* he wrote, '. . . I was
brought down here from London. From two o'clock till
half-past two on that day I had to stand on the centre plat-

---

* Writer and art connoisseur, was Robert Ross's literary executor and
thereby took over the management of the Wilde Literary Estate.
† Letter from Lord Alfred Douglas to Ada Leverson quoted in *The
Sphinx and Her Circle* by Violet Wyndham.

form at Clapham Junction in convict dress and handcuffed, for the world to look at. I had been taken out of the Hospital Ward without a moment's notice being given to me. Of all possible objects I was the most grotesque. When people saw me they laughed. Each train as it came up swelled the audience. Nothing could exceed their amusement. That was of course before they knew who I was. As soon as they had been informed, they laughed still more. For half an hour I stood there in the grey November rain surrounded by a jeering mob.' According to Sherard, Wilde's recognition was accompanied by a peculiarly revolting exhibition of cruelty, when a man who had been staring at the handcuffed figure explained for the benefit of other onlookers, 'By God, that's Oscar Wilde', he then stepped up to him and spat in his face. Wilde had plumbed the depths, but he had found himself a new rôle – the outraged victim – and the disciples would join the drama with incomparable ease.

Then the two faithful, the two pillars of the church of Wilde, Sherard and Ross, went to announce that Bosie intended to dedicate a book of poems to him. Oscar later wrote to Ross saying that the idea was revolting and grotesque, and at the same time he instructed him to make Bosie return a number of Oscar's letters, as well as books and jewellery that he had given him. Bosie replied: 'When he comes out of prison if he chooses to say he does not want my friendship and that he wants his letters back, he can do so with his own mouth.' Bernard Shaw now prepared, for submission to the Queen, a petition, similar to the one drafted without success by Stuart Merrill and mentioned earlier, on the grounds that if Wilde's health broke down he would not be able to earn his living on his release. Nothing came of this either.

On the 3rd February 1896 Oscar had a curious dream. His mother appeared to him, in out-door clothes, but when he asked her to take off her hat and coat and sit down she shook her head sadly and vanished. It was then, he said, that he knew that she was dead. Speranza had caught a chill and it developed into bronchitis and complications. When she realised she was very ill she asked that her son Oscar should be allowed to come and see her. Naturally this was refused as it was against prison regulations. 'May prison help him,' she said when they brought her the news in bed, turning her face to the wall. These, her last recorded words, expressed an eminently Victorian sentiment.

A fortnight later the prisoner was told that his wife was to visit him. She had travelled from Genoa, where she lived near the Ranee of Sarawak, so that he should not hear of his mother's death from a stranger. In this Constance was really noble. She had been deserted and her life ruined, her health was very delicate, she was to die three years later, yet she found the strength to make the journey of forty-eight hours in mid-winter to endure seeing him in front of all the other visiting wives. With her Victorian education and after all she had suffered through him, that she should have been prepared to have come so far to try to spare him some of the pain of hearing of his mother's death, was heroic.

Constance wanted legal control over the children, although her advisors did not insist on a divorce, and there were endless arguments and contention over the money of the Marriage Settlement. When Oscar heard from Sherard that his wife and children had changed their name, the latter afterwards wrote: 'It interested me as a point of psychology to observe with what anxiety he asked what the new name was. In his prisoner's dress, in a shameful cage, his pride remained such that he was keenly desirous to be assured that his people had not assumed a name plebeian or ill-sounding. He approved when I conveyed to him what the name was.' Sherard, admirable in his devotion if not in tact, put himself out to get *Salome* produced in France, and Lugné-Poe finally put it on at the *Théâtre de l'Oeuvre* on the 11th February 1896. In spite of good reviews its success was mitigated because the production was lacking in splendour.

The Governor of Reading Gaol, Major Isaacson, was an ineffectual but vindictive man, who appears to have revenged himself on the prisoners for his own failures, but realising that Oscar was still an important personage he seldom confiscated his books and even allowed him French novels. In June 1897 in a letter to Bosie, Oscar wrote: 'The production of *Salome* was the thing that turned the scales in my favour as far as my treatment in prison was concerned. . . .' After Wandsworth, Reading was at first even more awful, but Wilde ended by discovering a new beauty which was also to be exploited by Genêt half a century later. Sartre stresses in *Saint Genêt, Actor and Martyr* the analogies between them: '. . . the beauties of both men are equally venomous, but Wilde's wants to insinuate itself into men's souls and Genêt's wants to do violence: the former is as easy and pleasant as the latter is difficult and repellent. Wilde's beauty exercises its demoralising action only on objects whose matter gratifies the senses, Genêt's is less concerned with pleasing than with manifesting its magical power . . . for both Wilde and Genêt the final term of the metamorphosis seems the same: one must enter the enchanted world where handsome young men wearing precious clothes play with gems . . . the ignoble reality which Wilde made a point of not seeing and which, at Reading, unexpectedly pounced upon him and broke his back is that which Genêt takes as the matter of his art. . . .'

From cell C.3.3., by standing on a bench, Oscar could see the tops of two trees. If the Governor was a brute, the warders were sometimes more sympathetic. Just before

his release, one of them, called Martin by name, surreptiti-
ously gave him newspapers and small delicacies. It entertained Oscar to talk of literature to a warder who was eager
to educate himself: 'Excuse me, sir, but Marie Corelli, would
she be considered a great writer, sir?' This, admitted Wilde
in telling the story later to William Rothenstein, was more
than he could bear. Putting his hand on the man's shoulder,
he said to him gravely, 'Now don't think I've got anything
against her moral character, but from the way she writes
she ought to be here.' Another warder had married and
Oscar got him a silver tea-service by winning a newspaper
competition; he actually won a piano for another warder in
the same way.

A year after his imprisonment, his friends, headed by
More Adey, again took up the idea of a petition to obtain a
remission of the sentence. Shaw told Willie Wilde that
although he and the Rev. Stewart Headlam were ready to
sign the petition, 'that would be no use, as we were two
notorious cranks, and our names would by themselves
reduce the petition to absurdity'. The fear of public opinion
and the memory of Wilde's insolence were stronger than
pity, and very few signatures were collected. It is ironical
that Holman-Hunt, celebrated for his religious pictures,
especially the *Light of the World* and *The Scapegoat*, refused to
sign saying, 'I must repeat my opinion that the law treated
him with exceeding leniency.'

Frank Harris, crook though he was, behaved very well;
he went to see Oscar twice at Reading, and the second time,
in April 1897, Oscar said: 'It's you Frank, always original!
You come back to prison of your own free will.' Harris had
been to see Sir Evelyn Ruggles-Brise (Chairman of the
Prison Commission) who suggested that he should see
Oscar and report back to him. This he did and it certainly
resulted in better conditions for Oscar; he was given

writing materials, and a new Governor, Major Nelson, was
sent to take over at Reading. Oscar had put in a petition
on the 2nd July 1896, begging for remission of his sentence,
on the grounds that he was terrified of going mad; unfortunately the petition was so lucid and beautifully
written that it defeated its purpose and showed that he was
in perfect mental control. Frank Harris in an effort to get
remission of the last few months of Oscar's imprisonment
went again to the Prison Commissioner who said if he
could get big names it might help – but no one would
sign.

During the last six months of his sentence Oscar was
neither doing oakum picking nor any other form of
manual work. When Arthur Humphreys, the publisher and
bookseller, heard that Wilde was allowed as much to
read as he wished, subject only to Home Office approval,
he arranged for a really lavish consignment to be despatched
to him as a free gift. Wilde was very touched by this
spontaneous act of kindness and wrote: '. . . I see that
romantic surroundings are the worst surroundings possible
for a romantic writer. In Gower Street Stevenson could have
written a new *Trois Mousquetaires*. In Samoa he wrote letters to
The Times about the Germans. . . .' About Huysmans' latest
book, Oscar wrote: 'En Route is most overrated. It is sheer
journalism. It never makes one hear a note of the music it
describes. The subject is delightful, but the style is of course
worthless, slipshod, flaccid. It is worse French than Ohnet's.
Ohnet tries to be commonplace and succeeds. Huysmans
tries not to be, and is. . . .'

At the beginning of the summer of 1896 a young trooper
in the Royal Horse Guards named Woolridge was taken to
Reading Gaol from Windsor. He had 'cut his wife's throat
in a most determined manner, she having excited his
jealousy and (so far as the evidence went) greatly annoyed

him'. It is strange to find the author of the Sphinx giving the following description of the doomed man in the Ballad of Reading Gaol:

> 'He walked amongst the Trial Men
> In a suit of shabby grey;
> A cricket cap was on his head . . .'

Oscar had learned simplicity at the same time as suffering. He was better at depicting it than were the new masters of this style, Kipling and A. E. Housman. He read this poet's A Shropshire Lad when he left prison, and these lines:

> 'There sleeps in Shrewsbury jail tonight,
> Or wakes, as may betide,
> A better lad, if things went right,
> Than most that sleep outside.'

found an echo in his ballad. The rhythm of Oscar's poem recalls the tread of the prisoner's feet during exercise round and round the courtyard. He had said the lines to himself when he was unable to sleep or to ward off nightmares. 'Yet each man kills the thing he loves' he repeated thousands of times. Had he not killed Constance's love, and he was not going to do his utmost to kill his love for Bosie?

To write the famous letter to Lord Alfred was ethically the wrong thing to do, nor was it particularly good as literature. Many intrigues were to result from this venomous dossier when Ross published extracts under the title De Profundis. But with that humour that was always his saving grace at his most high-flown moments, Oscar wrote: 'I think the only thing to do is to be thoroughly modern, and to have it typewritten. Of course the manuscript should not pass out of your control, but could you not get Mrs. Marshall to send down one of her type-writing girls – women are the most reliable, as they have no memory for the important. . . . I assure you that the type-writing machine, when played with expression, is not more annoying than the piano when played by a a sister or near relation . . . the lady type-writer might be fed through a lattice in the door like the Cardinals when they elect a Pope, till she comes out on the balcony and can say to the world "Habet Mundus Epistolam", for indeed it is an Encyclical Letter, and as the Bulls of the Holy Father are named from their opening words, it may be spoken of as the Epistola: In Carcere et Vinculis. . . .'

Drama makes many demands on truth, and for four months before he left prison Oscar worked at transforming his tragedy into a work of art.* Shame, ruin, pain, can be wonderful experiences when they happen to artists such as Oscar. He confessed his faults with joy, in order to enhance the value of the newly discovered virtue of humility. Sometimes the marvellous derivative writer took on the tone of St. Augustine, sometimes he must have reminded himself

* The letter was written on twenty folio sheets (each of four pages) on ruled prison paper. It was handed to Ross when Oscar left prison, and he had two typed copies made. Ross sent Douglas not, as instructed, the original manuscript, but a copy. Bosie always denied receiving it. Ross published extracts amounting to less than half the letter under the title De Profundis in 1905 and a slightly fuller version in 1908. In neither was there any reference to Douglas. In 1909, Ross presented the original manuscript to the British Museum on condition that no-one was allowed to see it for fifty years. The second typescript, kept by Ross and eventually bequeathed by him to Vyvyan Holland, supplied the text for the 'first complete and accurate version' which Mr. Holland published in 1949. This however was found to be incomplete and inaccurate, more than a thousand words had been removed by Ross, almost all of them fiercely critical of Douglas. In 1961 the letter was published in its entirety by Rupert Hart-Davis.

that he was of the same family as Dante, and drew sombre caricatures, like that of the Marquess in Court. The phrase: 'You demanded without grace and received without thanks.' is Wilde at his best. In order to crush Douglas, the poet drew a larger than life portrait of himself: 'I was a man who stood in symbolic relations to the art and culture of my age. I had realised this for myself at the very dawn of my manhood, and had forced my age to realise it afterwards. . . . Byron was a symbolic figure, but his relations were to the passion of his age and its weariness of passion. Mine were to something more noble, more permanent, of more vital issue, of larger scope. . . . I summed up all systems in a phrase, and all existence in an epigram.' Oscar was confident that he was in the right, he wanted to combine publicity and humility.

That Lord Alfred had been odious, and his behaviour mad, is true but he had loved Oscar, he had proved this during the trials, he was to prove it again during Oscar's exile. Oscar only wrote about Bosie's faults, never once mentioning that beauty which had made him forget at the time all the quarrels: real human kindness would have been to say: 'Unhappily I was neither as young nor as good-looking as you.' The well-known critic, Cyril Connolly, Anglo-Irish like the poet, judges severely: 'Certainly De Profundis is an obsessive piece of writing, a quicksand of self-pity and recriminations in which the reader is soon up to the neck.'* Oscar was such a wonderful actor that he brought self-pity to a fine art, finding in shame, on the platform of Clapham Junction, a sublime rôle.

In a letter to Ross Oscar saw things more clearly than in De Profundis. Constance had been advised to demand a divorce, but she would not agree. She did however get a Court Order appointing herself and Adrian Hope guardians of the children. Oscar's friends wanted him to fight this

* Previous Convictions by Cyril Connolly.

directly he got out of prison, but this would mean more
lawyers, more papers; he preferred to give in, to abandon
his rights to the children. '. . . really my friends must face
the fact that (setting aside such details in my indictment
as belonged to my bosom-friend, three in number) I am
not in prison as an innocent man. On the contrary, my
record of perversities of passion and distorted romances
would fill many scarlet volumes. I think it right to mention
this—however surprising and no doubt shocking, it will
sound to many – because More Adey in his letter tells me that
the the opposite side will be obliged to furnish strict details
of the dates and places and exact circumstances of the terrible
charges to be brought against me. Does he seriously imagine
that if I submitted to more cross-examination I would be
believed? . . . It is the case that the charges are not true. But
that is a mere detail. If a man gets drunk, whether he does
so on white wine or red is of no importance. If a man has
perverse passions, their particular mode of manifestation is
of no importance either. . . .'

De Profundis is one of the great rôles of a repertoire
now out-of-date, the interminable plaint of a man condemned to silence for two years. But despite this letter,
it should not be forgotten that the celebrated actor was
really a kind man, who could not bear injustice or cruelty.
To him they were the worst forms of stupidity – his greatest
enemy. While he was writing this indictment, the hideous
prison routine went on round the poet – at night the cries
of men going mad, in the courtyard the warders dragging
away a poor simpleton to be whipped. One day Oscar saw
three children in the main entrance, just after they had been
convicted of snaring rabbits. There was a very humane
warder, newly arrived at Reading, called Martin, who had
become friendly with Oscar. He gave some biscuits to the

youngest child as it was crying from hunger, and was dismissed because the child told another warder of this kindness. The first thing the poet did when he arrived in France after his release was to write a letter to the *Daily Chronicle*, which was published on 28th May 1897, which should really be quoted in its entirety. In it no fine writing, but a condemnation of a society in which such terrible things could happen every day: '. . . Ordinary cruelty is simply stupidity. It is the entire want of imagination. It is the result in our days of stereotyped systems of hard-and-fast rules, and of stupidity. . . . What is inhuman in modern life is officialism. Authority is as destructive to those who exercise it as it is to those on whom it is exercised. . . . A child can understand a punishment inflicted by an individual, such as a parent or guardian, and bear it with a certain amount of acquiescence. What it cannot understand is a punishment inflicted by society. It cannot realise what society is. . . . The child consequently, being taken away from its parents by people whom it has never seen, and of whom it knows nothing, and finding itself in a lonely and unfamiliar cell, waited on by strange faces, and ordered about and punished by the representatives of a system that it cannot understand, becomes an immediate prey to the first and most prominent emotion produced by modern prison life – the emotion of terror. The terror of a child in prison is quite limitless. . . . This terror that seizes and dominates the child, as it seizes the grown man also, is of course intensified beyond power of expression by the solitary cellular system of our prisons. Every child is confined to its cell for twenty-three hours out of twenty-four. This is the appalling thing. To shut up a child in a dimly lit cell, for twenty-three hours out of the twenty-four is an example of the cruelty of stupidity. . . .' This letter, together with another one about Penal Reform, and the publication a year later of the *Ballad of Reading Gaol*, must have helped towards the abolishment by Asquith's government in 1908 of the imprisonment of children. Sixty years later the sufferings of Wilde in prison were specifically recalled when the Wolfenden Committee examined the law on homosexuality.

Shortly before Oscar's release his friends began to make plans for him. They got together a wardrobe for him and Reggie Turner presented him with a dressing-case which, together with its silver contents, was marked with the initials S.M. – Oscar had chosen the pseudonym Sebastian Melmoth. Harris and Ross gave clothes, More Adey gave £25, which he expended on hats, gloves, collars, socks, handkerchiefs, mother-of-pearl studs, French soap, tooth powder, toilet water and a lotion for Oscar's hair which had become very grey. Oscar had begun to think about his appearance again: 'I am under the impression that it is quite white, but I believe that is an exaggeration: there is a wonderful thing called Koko Marikopas, to be got at 233 Regent Street, which is a wonderful hair-tonic: the name alone seems worth the money, so please get a large bottle.'

Ten days before Oscar's release, Adey and Ross went to Reading with Ricketts, who had to wait half an hour while they talked business: when he joined them, Oscar greeted him as if they had just met in Bond Street: 'Both my dear friends would wish me to retire to a monastery,' he exclaimed laughingly, 'why not La Trappe? . . . or worse still, to some dim country place in England: I believe it was Twyford. They speak of Venice later with its silence and dead waterways. No, I have had enough silence.' 'But Oscar,' Ricketts murmured, 'is not Venice, with its beauty and stillness, the very place for work and privacy? There you can see your friends if . . .' 'No!' Oscar exclaimed. 'Privacy! Work! My dear Ricketts, I wish to look at life, not to become a monument for tourists! The French have produced *Salome* during my stay here and it was reviewed in the English Press. France understands the value of an artist for what he is, not for what he has done. Privacy! I have had two years of it ... save for that other self – the man I once was.'

But Oscar's affairs were still in a pitiable state, and he was down-hearted. Constance's advisers had agreed that if Wilde's interest in the Marriage Settlement were surrendered, she would pay him £150 a year, but this would be forfeited if he kept bad company. She also agreed never to institute divorce proceedings based on misconduct by Wilde previous to the trials. As to where he would go, Oscar was not keen to go to Dieppe on the grounds that he was so well-known there; the idea of Boulogne was also unacceptable as Bosie was a frequent visitor, and Brussels was too expensive. Eventually Dieppe was decided upon: Oscar said he could always move on.

On the eve of his release Wilde's solicitor, Hansell, went to Reading for him to sign the Deed of Arrangement. Constance accompanied the solicitor but did not wish her husband to see her. According to the warder, the interview took place in the 'solicitor's room', while outside in the corridor, with the warder, stood Constance, who turned to him and begged 'Let me have one glimpse of my husband'. The kindly warder, himself touched by the occasion, could not refuse her and stepped back silently so that she could look through the glass peep-hole in the door. In the warder's words, 'Mrs. Wilde cast one long, lingering glance inside and saw the convict-poet who, in deep mental distress himself, was totally unconscious that any eyes save those of the stern lawyers and myself witnessed his degradation.' At that moment Wilde was in the act of putting his signature to the deed depriving him of the children. She drew back 'apparently labouring under deep emotion', and a few moments later left the prison with the solicitor.

Oscar had learned that newspaper reporters would be waiting to see him leave prison, and so was suffering badly from nerves, but the Governor reassured him that everything would be done to help him to leave without their knowledge. Saying goodbye to Major Nelson, he left accompanied by two warders for Pentonville, where the next morning his friends went to fetch him.

25 Melmoth the Vagabond

'Sphinx, how marvellous of you to know exactly the right hat to wear at seven o'clock in the morning to meet a friend who has been away! You can't have got up, you must have sat up.' All embarrassment, all apprehensions vanished; Oscar welcomed his friends, including Mrs. Leverson, who recalled that, 'He came in, and at once put us at our ease. He came in with the dignity of a king returning from exile. He came in talking, laughing, smoking a cigarette, with waved hair and a flower in his button-hole and he looked markedly better, slighter and younger than he had two years previously.' The meeting took place at the house of the Rev. Stewart Headlam, 'full of Burne-Jones and Rossetti pictures, Morris wallpaper and curtains, in fact an example of the decoration of the early eighties, very beautiful in its way, and very like the aesthetic rooms Oscar had once loved.' Among the little group there to welcome him, was a beautiful red-haired, violet-eyed young woman called Marjorie Clifton (thought by Oscar to resemble Elizabeth Siddal). Her husband, a young solicitor, had in the past told Oscar that he was madly in love but could not afford to marry. 'How much would you actually need in order to marry Marjorie?' asked Oscar. 'A hundred and fifty pounds, then I could take a tiny flat and work.' Oscar had just received a large sum for *Lady Windermere's Fan*. He wrote a cheque for a hundred and sixty pounds, saying peremptorily, 'Go at once and marry her, boy, and bring her to our house at Worthing for your honeymoon.'

358

Oscar wrote a letter and sent a cab with it to the Jesuit priests at Farm Street, asking if he might go into Retreat for six months. While waiting for a reply he walked up and down talking charmingly until the man returned with the reply, which was that they could not accept him on his impulse of the moment, it must be thought over: in fact, they refused him, and he broke down and sobbed bitterly. However, he soon cheered up, and talked so much that he and More Adey missed the train and only left in the afternoon. As he had been recognised at Hatchard's bookshop in Piccadilly, they went by cab to West Croydon where they caught the Newhaven train. Once there he sent a long telegram to Ross in Dieppe announcing his arrival and thanking him and Reggie for all the friendship they had shown him, signed 'Sebastian Melmoth'; Sebastian, in memory of the martyr, and Melmoth after the sinister hero of a novel written by his great-uncle Maturin. The need for malediction is revealed in the choice of the name of Melmoth, which was the name of a demon. Hugo von Hofmannsthal wrote that it was the mask behind which Oscar Wilde hid a face ravaged by prison and by the approach of death, as if to live his last years in the shadows. It was in fact the last of three masks, Oscar Wilde, C.3.3. and finally Sebastian Melmoth. The sound of the first suggested splendour, pride and charm. The sound of the second was frightening, as if branded by a red hot iron on the shoulder of a criminal. The third was the name of a half-forgotten ghost. The first had a fine forehead, sensual lips, cynical and tearful eyes – a mask of Bacchus. The second, an iron mask with slits to look out from in despair. The third, a pitiful domino hired to hide a lingering agony.

'If he had then begun a decent life, people would have forgotten him, but he returned to Paris and to his dog's vomit. . . .' Wilfrid Blunt who wrote this, did not understand that Melmoth expected nothing more from a society which he had had the folly to defy. Often his disciples tried to reform him, tried to have a good influence on him, not realising that he was dedicated to his own destruction since the Church did not want him, since his children had been taken from him and since his wife imposed so many conditions before they could resume family life. Sebastian Melmoth would be a gentle anarchist who would laugh and squander his talent in conversation, a cynic who would give rein to his weaknesses – alcohol and boys – in order to make life bearable.

One should not be moved to pity because he sank so low; he sought abjection and through it attained exaltation. During the first months of liberty, agreeable disciples retarded his downfall by their kindness, and Oscar was so weak that he could even be tempted by virtue. The return of Lord Alfred was to precipitate the fall, to accomplish the sombre vocation of Melmoth.

The stay in Dieppe was charming, Reggie and Robbie were delightful. Oscar wrote to the Sphinx: 'To find you just as wonderful and dear as ever was no surprise, the beautiful are always beautiful. I am staying here as Sebastian Melmoth – not Esquire, but Monsieur Sebastien Melmoth. I have thought it better that Robbie should stay here under the name of Reginald Turner, and Reggie under the name of R. B. Ross. It is better that they should not have their own names.' Oscar took walks on the jetty arm in arm with Ross, and it must be admitted that it needed courage to greet this tragic and conspicuous figure, surrounded by questionable young men – a courage which Jacques-Emile Blanche lacked, as did Aubrey Beardsley, who went up a side street to avoid him, his skeletal outline bent double, a Morocco-leather portfolio under his arm, on his way to drink a glass of milk at the Casino. He had been converted to Catholicism and murmured 'Vade retro' on meeting one in whose downfall he had been involved. Tourists ostentatiously left the terrace where this little group sipped their absinthe. But there were some remarkable people to whom public opinion was unimportant, notably Fritz Thaulow, a Norwegian landscape painter, who was much respected in Dieppe. In a café, he made a point of inviting Oscar to dinner with him and his family. There Oscar found Conder, consumptive like Beardsley, but unlike him not a convert. Both Wilde and Conder recovered something of their former gaiety in the charming atmosphere of the Thaulow home filled with golden-haired children.

During his first few days of liberty Oscar was indefatigable, he hired a light carriage to drive to Arques-la-Bataille, where he sat on the ramparts of the old castle, or to a beach in the neighbourhood. The sight of the sea and country filled him with exaltation and he began to speak about prison. Reading became an enchanted castle – the warders kindly Mamelukes and Major Nelson the presiding fairy. Wilde's friends noticed when he came out of prison that he had developed a nervous habit of arranging objects symmetrically in front of him, 'I had to keep everything in my cell in its exact place,' he said, 'and if I neglected this even in the slightest, I was punished. The punishment was so horrible to me that I often started up in my sleep to feel if each thing was where the regulations would have it, and not an inch either to the right or to the left.'

He was pleased when he heard that his letter on cruelty in prison, published under his own name in the Daily Chronicle, had created a sensation in England. He sent a postal order for £5 to Martin who had been dismissed, it will be remembered, for giving food to a child, and other sums of money via Ross or Turner to Reading to help prisoners on their release, accompanied by letters which were written in a simple style that could easily be understood. Oscar had arrived in France with about £800, doled out to him by Ross, and he at once resumed his habits of generosity.

After a fortnight the atmosphere at Dieppe became less pleasant; too many backs were turned, the waiters of the cafés were hostile and also there were too many distractions. Oscar decided to install himself in a family *pension* at Berneval-sur-Mer. A week after his arrival in Dieppe, Reggie and More Adey returned to London and Ross remained to see Oscar settled. Oscar wrote that he had asked a fellow prisoner, recently released, to come and stay for a week; he reassured Reggie by writing that he had no doubt that the ex-prisoner was a confirmed mulierast.

During the first weeks at Berneval, Oscar bathed every day. On the beach a man was to be seen prowling about, and Sherard, who was staying at Berneval, wanted to know what he was doing. Oscar replied: 'I fancy he is a detective in the pay of Queensberry, I am sorry for him. It must be tedious work. I have sometimes thought of talking to him and trying to cheer him up, for he has a sad countenance; but then, you see, the romance of secrecy would be gone, and I am sure he has nothing else to live for. *Chacun son métier*. Poor fellow.' He received visitors, Ernest Dowson and the actor-manager Charles Wyndham, Lugné-Poe and William Rothenstein, to whom he afterward wrote preaching his new gospel: 'I am not really ashamed for having been in prison: I often was in more shameful places: but I *am* really ashamed of having led a life unworthy of an artist. I don't say that Messalina is a better companion than Sporus, or that the one is all right and the other all wrong: I know simply that a life of definite and studied materialism, and a philosophy of appetite and cynicism, and a cult of sensual and senseless ease, are bad things for an artist: they narrow the imagination, and dull the more delicate sensibilities. I was all wrong, my dear boy, in my life. I was not getting the best out of me. Now I think that with good health and the friendship of a few good, simple, nice fellows like yourself, and a quiet mode of living, with isolation for thought, and freedom from the endless hunger for pleasures that wreck the body and imprison the soul – well, I think I may do things yet that you all may like. . . .' In fact, he did begin to write, with great care and trouble, the ballad about which he had been thinking for many months.

Very soon M. Melmoth was adored in the village, he gave sticks of barley-sugar to the schoolchildren, bought *The Three Musketeers* for the lighthouse keeper, drank with the fishermen. On the day of Queen Victoria's Diamond Jubilee he gave a tea party for the village children. There were about fifteen of them crushed into his small house and he gave them strawberries and cream, a beautifully decorated cake, and *sirop de grenadine* and they all had presents – each had chosen a musical instrument. They left after toasting the Queen, the French President and Oscar; for days after, the greeting in Berneval was 'Vive la Reine d'Angleterre, Vive M. Melmoth'. As Oscar said: 'I tremble at my position!' Never had he enjoyed himself more. 'Dear Queen,' he said looking at the reproduction of William Nicholson's famous woodcut of the Queen which he had hung on the wall of the dining-room: 'The three women I have most admired are Queen Victoria, Sarah Bernhardt and Lily Langtry. I would have married any one of them with pleasure,' he told Vincent O'Sullivan.

Without a doubt Berneval provided the isolation which suited the new hermit. He thought of building a villa there, and in the meantime he rented a châlet on the edge of a wood looking out to sea: 'Now I can invite my friends –

'But what expense!', said Robbie. Oscar replied: 'I have many irons and a huge fire. But to work I must be isolated here. . . . Overhead there is a lady with two children, perfect darlings, and their racket is appalling . . . as regards people living on me in the extra bedrooms, dear boy, there is no one who would stay with me but you, and you will pay your own bill at the hotel for meals, and as for your room, the charge will be nominally 2fr. 50 a night, but there will be lots of extras, such as *bougies, bain*, and hot water: all cigarettes smoked in the bedrooms are charged extra . . . and if anyone does not take the extras, of course he is charged more. *Bain* 25c. *Pas de bain* 50c. *Cigarette dans la chambre à coucher*, 10c. *pour chaque cigarette, Pas de cigarette dans la chambre à coucher*, 20c. *chaque cigarette*. This is the *système* in all good hotels. . . .'

Installing himself in the Normandy village, Oscar must certainly have thought of the mysterious Englishman who, according to Maupassant, had lived twenty years earlier in those parts in the company of a bejewelled hag and a pretty boy, and who had christened his house *Chaumière de Dolmancé* in memory of *La Philosophie dans le Boudoir*. He frequently appears in the works of Goncourt and Jean Lorrain.

Oscar's first visitor at his châlet was Dalhousie Young, composer and pianist, pupil of Paderewski, who had published a pamphlet entitled *Apologia Pro Oscar Wilde* in 1895, and who was later to advance him £100 for the libretto of an opera to be called *Daphnis & Chloe*; Oscar accepted this but the libretto was never written. However, he refused to accept £700 to build himself a house because he thought it was too generous and quixotic a gesture. Another visitor was Ernest Dowson who had visited him in Oakley Street between the trials and now lived, rather miserably, not far from Dieppe; Oscar lent him £20 when he was in straits; to show his gratitude the decadent

poet tried to help Oscar to become normal: it is alleged by
Yeats, though with no evidence, that Dowson took Wilde
to a brothel. This expedition was said to have been under-
taken without discretion, several friends waited outside the
door and when he emerged Oscar is supposed to have said:
'the first time these ten years and the last – it was like dining
on cold mutton.'

Oscar's generosity drew spongers to Berneval; for them
he played the part of the ruined genius, of the fisherman who
had discovered the truth. It was simpler when André Gide,
not without apprehension, came to spend twenty-four
hours with him. He arrived in the middle of the day to
find that Melmoth was out and not expected back until the
evening – he did not in fact return until the middle of the
night. Gide asked him whether he had known at Algiers
what would happen and he replied: 'Oh, naturally, of
course I knew that there would be a catastrophe, either that
or something else: I was expecting it . . . to go any further
was impossible, and that state of things could not last . . .
there had to be some end to it. . . . Prison has completely
changed me. I was relying on it for that. . . . My life is like
a work of art. . . . My life before prison was as successful as
possible. Now all that is finished and done with.'*

Gide was curious to see Wilde after having written
l'Immoraliste because the character of Menalque owed a lot
to him, and perhaps this was why Wilde did not like the
book. Under the good influence of Ross, Oscar said of
Bosie: '. . . we cannot follow the same path; he has his,
it's very beautiful, I have mine. His is that of Alcibiades,
mine is that of St. Francis of Assisi.' Then Wilde told Gide
about the dramas he wanted to write, one on Pharaoh and
the other on Ahab and Jezebel. These dramas can be imagined,
and that they were never written need not be regretted.

* The Life of Oscar Wilde by Hesketh Pearson.

There had been a plan, instigated by Frank Harris, to drive
Wilde to the Pyrenees in Harris's new motor-car. It was
abandoned however because he and Oscar had had a misunderstanding about money before Wilde left prison, and
Oscar refused his suggestion of visiting him at Berneval.
Later Oscar gave his opinion on the subject of motor-cars.
He had enjoyed a drive in Switzerland in one which constantly broke down: 'They, like all machines, are more
wilful than animals – nervous, irritable, strange things.'

With Beardsley, he met a minor literary adventurer, the
publisher Leonard Smithers. His appearance was unfortunate: fat, puffy, pallid and flaxen-haired. He was always
accompanied by Junoesque mistresses, as well as by a wife
or two, all of them dressed in cycling costumes. Oscar
wrote of him to Reggie Turner on the 10th August 1897:
'. . . I do not know if you know Smithers: he is usually in
a large straw hat, has a blue tie delicately fastened with a
diamond brooch of the impurest water – or perhaps wine,
as he never touches water: it goes to his head at once. His
face, clean-shaven as befits a priest who serves at the altar
whose God is literature, is wasted and pale – not with
poetry, but with poets, who he says, have wrecked his life
by insisting on publishing with him. He loves first editions,
especially of women: little girls are his passion. He is the
most learned erotomaniac in Europe. He is also a delightful
companion, and a dear fellow, very kind to me. . . .' He
also said of Smithers: 'He is rather dreadful, I suppose many
of us are rather dreadful now and do not realise to what we
have come.' After a few weeks of intoxication, this latest
arrival appeared to the exiled poet like a whiff of Soho and
Piccadilly. Smithers wanted to publish the Ballad without
the author's name, and Oscar accepted a small sum of
money and promised to finish the poem before winter
came. But his inclination to write lessened as the days

shortened; Robbie and Reggie had left for London, and he
began to realise that the climate of Normandy was very
much like that of England.

Lord Alfred, who had written to him from the moment of
his release, became ever more pressing. Ross had succeeded
in separating Oscar from Bosie and from Constance during
the first months of liberty, but it was careless of him to have
left the great man alone, a prey to temptation. Oscar began
by resisting the siren-call of Bosie and wrote thus: '. . . Of
course I love you more than anyone else. But our lives are
irreparably severed, as far as meeting goes. What is left to
us is the knowledge that we love each other, and every day
I think of you, and I know you are a poet, and that makes
you doubly dear and wonderful. . . .' In the last days of
August, Oscar was so bored that he wrote of committing
suicide. The agreement between Oscar and Constance had
been that they should not meet for a year, but Oscar wrote
to ask if it couldn't be shortened as he couldn't bear the
thought of winter alone at Berneval without seeing the
children. Her answer, obviously dictated by her advisers,
was unpleasant and attached a list of conditions. On the
6th September he wrote to Carlos Blacker, an old friend of
them both, regretting that Constance had not invited him
to go and see the children. In July she was with the
Blackers and already being affected by the creeping spinal
paralysis which was to kill her. Oscar suggested that as
obviously she could not come to him he should go to her.
On the 2nd September in another letter to Blacker he wrote
'I will come and see Constance in October'. At the beginning
of October he wrote to Smithers, 'My wife's letter came too
late. I had waited four months in vain and it was only when
the children had gone back to school that she asked me to
come to her – whereas what I want is the love of my
children. . . . She sends me photographs of the boys . . .

such lovely little fellows in Eton collars, but makes no
promises to allow me to see them. She says she will see me,
twice a year, but I want my boys. It is a terrible punishment,
dear Robbie, and oh! how well I deserve it.' This was
written to Ross soon after Wilde came out of prison.

On the 28th August Oscar went to Rouen to meet
Bosie, and they stayed at the Hôtel de la Poste. 'Poor Oscar
cried when I met him at the station. We walked about all
day arm-in-arm or hand-in-hand and were perfectly happy.'
Prudently Oscar did not ask if he had read the letter (De
Profundis) that Ross was supposed to have sent him. Instead
they were full of plans; they would leave sinister Normandy
as soon as possible, go to live in Naples among masterpieces,
not only of marble but also of flesh and blood, to create new
works of art. Oscar returned to Berneval, planning to join
Bosie six weeks later. On the 31st August he wrote to him:
'. . . I feel that my only hope of again doing beautiful work
in art is being with you. It was not so in old days, but now
it is different, and you can really create in me that energy
and sense of joyous power on which art depends. . . . Do
remake my ruined life for me, and then our friendship and
love will have a different meaning to the world. . . .' In
order to explain his decision to his shocked friends, he
wrote to Reggie Turner on 23rd September from Naples:
'. . . Much that you say in your letter is right, but still you
leave out of consideration the great love I have for Bosie. I
love him, and have always loved him. He ruined my life,
and for that very reason I seem forced to love him more:
and I think that now I shall do lovely work. Bosie is himself
a poet, far the first of all the young poets in England, an
exquisite artist in lyric and ballad. It is to a poet that I am
going back. So when people say how dreadful of me to
return to Bosie, do say no – say that I love him, that he is a

poet, and that, after all, whatever my life may have been ethically, it has always been romantic, and Bosie is my romance. My romance is a tragedy of course, but it is none the less a romance, and he loves me very dearly, more than he loves or can love anyone else, and without him my life was dreary. So stick up for us, Reggie, and be nice.'

The two friends made their separate ways to the south; Bosie was already at Aix-les-Bains when he was joined by Oscar. In Naples they stayed for two weeks at the Hôtel Royal des Etrangers where they made arrangements to rent the Villa Giudice at Posilippo, a lovely place with marble steps plunging down into the waters of the gulf, with its view of Capri and Vesuvius shaded by umbrella pines; serenades in the neighbouring inn, ancient Thermae frequented by living Greek bronzes – in short, a dream. Good resolutions, wrangles, actions threated by Queens-berry and Constance in the event of their taking up their lives together again, all was forgotten. But the dream was an expensive one, Lord Alfred had as much to lose as Oscar, since Lady Queensberry as well as Constance was bound to cut off supplies from the moment they heard of the reunion. Meanwhile they lived on what money Bosie had left, and worked on the Ballad; Oscar wrote to Ross asking him for his critical advice as the poem progressed, apologising in one letter for one stanza being 'in the romantic vein that you don't quite approve of. . . . With much of your critic-isms I agree. The poem suffers under the difficulty of a divided aim in style. Some is realistic, some is romantic: some poetry, some propaganda. I feel it keenly, but as a whole I think the production interesting: that it is interest-ing from more points of view than one is artistically to be regretted . . . the difficulty is that the objects in prison have no shape or form . . . the horror of prison is that everything is so simple and commonplace in itself, and so degrading, and hideous, and revolting in its effect. . . .' This poem had to be written, perhaps it would free him from the memories of prison. It was certainly a painful exorcism.

Were Oscar and Bosie happy at Posilippo? One doubts it on the evidence of the photographs of them under the vine trellis of a *trattoria*, each looking very proper, with a white bow-tie and boater, but a trifle sour. Bosie's nose had lengthened, spoiling the harmony of his appearance, and Oscar looked less well than when he first came out of prison. There was a lack of ease in their relationship; thus Bosie one day asked Oscar what exactly he meant by 'all men kill the thing they love', to which Oscar replied 'You should know'. (Lord Alfred knew his Shakespeare, and remembered that the famous line had been taken, and inverted, from *The Merchant of Venice*, when Bassanio asks Shylock 'Do all men kill the thing they do not love?')

After a few weeks they went to Capri for a couple of days. At the end of December the friends had not a penny left between them. Constance refused to send Oscar his allowance: 'Women are petty and Constance has no imagination', was his comment. Constance wrote indignant letters: 'I forbid you to see Lord Alfred Douglas. I forbid you to return to your filthy, insane life. I forbid you to live in Naples. I will not allow you to come to Genoa.' In a letter to Carlos Blacker, Constance wrote: '. . . No words will describe my horror of the BEAST, for I will call him nothing else, A.D.' In December Lady Queensberry wrote to say she would cut off Bosie's allowance if he did not leave Oscar. Both friends recognised this as final. Bosie wrote to his mother agreeing not to live with Oscar again and asked her to let him have £200 in order to give to Oscar. He also paid three months rent of the villa in advance.

The separation between the friends had taken place without drama, but it did not efface the bad effect of their having lived together again. Oscar, categorised as incorrigible, wished once more to see himself as a victim. Hardly was he alone again than he wrote to Ross that Bosie was a monster who had abandoned him the moment he had no more money, and never would he see him again.

With the money given him by Bosie, Oscar went to Taormina to stay with Baron von Gloeder, whose photographs of Sicilian youths 'noble and nude and antique' as Theocritan goatherds or shepherds, were reminiscent of Simeon Solomon. Then alone in Naples in winter, the architecture bespattered with mud, and the bronzes hidden by rags and tatters, he went to the melancholy public gardens often frequented by suicides. He became the prey of dark thoughts. He told O'Sullivan: 'I thought of suicide.' 'You?' 'Yes.' O'Sullivan asked why he had not done so before if he was going to do it at all. 'I was never really tempted to kill myself. I never thought seriously of that as a way out. What I felt was that I must drain the chalice of my Passion to the dregs. But one night when there were no stars, I went down to that garden. As I sat there absolutely alone in the darkness, I heard a rustling noise and sighing and a misty cloud-like thing around me. And I realised that they were the little souls of those who had killed themselves in that place, condemned to linger there ever after. They had killed themselves in vain.'

The Irish are always ready to enter into communication with the 'Other World'. Soon after Oscar had returned to Paris, he dreamed that Constance came to see him and that he kept on saying: 'Go away, go away, leave me in peace.' Next day he heard that she had died alone in a clinic after an operation for the creeping paralysis in her back and arms. A Victorian heroine lost in a drama of the fin-de-siècle, her heart had been broken like a character in a novel by Ouida or Marie Corelli. Laura Hope's Journal has the following entry:

'1898 April 8th. A telegram from Genoa with the news of poor Constance Wilde's death – asking Adrian to break it to the Napiers – so we went there after lunch and sad it was for they loved her dearly. Then we walked across Kensington Gardens and saw the lawyer, for Adrian is trustee and executor – so this means much business.' Constance, after Oscar's return to Lord Alfred, was intensely irritated, and had revealed to Carlos Blacker: 'Oscar is so pathetic and such a born actor . . . the boys' expenses will go on increasing until they are grown up and I will educate them and give them what they require. . . .' Constance still had debts to pay while Oscar pestered her for money. These importunings reminded her of Willie Wilde's 'cruelty in forcing his mother to give him money'. There can unfortunately be no doubt that Oscar hoped to live on his wife. Melmoth no longer cared about being a gentleman. But a year later when the poet was passing through Genoa, he stopped to put a bouquet of red roses on her tomb.

The publication of the Ballad drew Oscar to Paris. It was published on Sunday, 13th February. The first edition was of 800 copies at 2/6, with another thirty numbered copies on vellum at 21/-. Oscar regretted the golden peonies and the white peacocks of better days. He would have liked a design by Aubrey Beardsley, with whom Smithers had discussed the poem in August 1897, and who had seemed much struck and had promised to draw a frontispiece for it. Oscar had written on the 4th September 1897: '. . . As regards Aubrey, I wish you could get him to make a definite reply: there is no use in his hedging. If he will do it, it will be a great thing; if not, why not try some of the jeunes Belges – Khnoppf for example. I want something curious – a design of Death and Sin walking hand in hand, very severe, and mediaeval. . . .' By now, poor Beardsley was dying at Mentone, and implored one of his friends to destroy all of his drawings that were pernicious or obscene. He died of consumption on the 16th March 1898 at the age of twenty-five.

Oscar wrote to Smithers on the 20th.* 'Hôtel de Nice, rue des Beaux-Arts. Paris. My dear Smithers. I quite understand how you feel about poor Aubrey. Still you, and you alone, recreated his art for him and gave him a new and greater position – and for such generous and enthusiastic service to art and to an artist you will have your reward in Heaven: at least you will never have it in this world. I have not yet seen Vallette [founder of the *Mercure de France*] – I simply wanted to know the cost of an edition with a French translation – by you and the Chiswick Press – as the type is set up: can you give me an idea – an edition of 500 copies. Also, do you not think that, if the cost be not too great, we might "*Stereotype*"? Have Smith's bookstalls taken the poem? If not, do work it – and supply them with a placard. Could you have a leaflet, with criticisms, put into the leaves of a good magazine? like Pear's soap, and other more useful things. I think it would be profitable – in any case it would irritate the reader. The Athenaeum advertisement is admirable, I feel like Lipton's tea. Yours, O.W.'

The second edition of the *Ballad* was of a thousand copies, printed on the 24th February and issued before the end of the month. The third edition consisted of 99 copies signed by the author appearing under the name of C.3.3. The poem had a great success, and Smithers was astonished. Oscar complained that Smithers was so fond of suppressed books that he tried to suppress his own. It was not published in Germany until after Wilde's death, but it was certainly

* An incomplete copy of this letter is published in The Letters of Oscar Wilde edited by Rupert Hart-Davis; the remaining portion is hitherto unpublished.

2B

the beginning of the great fame of the author in that country and of his influence on Stephan Georg and Hugo von Hofmannsthal.

Soon after this, Frank Harris tried to encourage Oscar to write a play in collaboration with him. Harris had sold the *Saturday Review* and had bought a hotel in Monaco. He invited Oscar to spend the winter with him, the poet accepted and lived for three weeks at Harris's expense in Paris. Then he travelled down to La Napoule, but only to find no sign of Harris. According to the following letter to Robbie, he did not mind too much about this: '27th December 1898. My dear Bobbie, would you kindly send me my January allowance through *Cook's* agency at Cannes? I can then get it cashed at once and if possible send it soon. Frank Harris has, I hear, gone away. He did not come to Napoule after all, nor have I heard from him, though I wrote twice. The weather is charming. Napoule is nice and dull. I take walks in the pine-woods. Yesterday I was by the sea and suddenly George Alexander appeared on a bicycle. He gave me a crooked, sickly smile, and hurried on without stopping. How absurd and mean of him! A nice fellow called Harold Mellor, who is staying at Cannes, comes over constantly to see me. He is a nephew of Mrs. Jacob Bright's. He has a pretty Italian boy with him. They stayed last night at Napoule, and we had plum pudding and Mellor ordered Pommery-Greno, so I kept Christmas pleasantly, and Christmas improves by being kept a day. On the real Christmas I dined alone. The fishing population of the Riviera have the same freedom from morals as the Neapolitans have. They are very nice . . . .'.

Meanwhile Oscar was not idle, and was indeed preparing his plays for publication. At Nice, Sarah was playing *Tosca*, Oscar went to see her in her dressing-room. 'Divine – Oscar my love!' Embraces, crocodile tears, in short a wonderful evening. Oscar cultivated his rich compatriots who found the atmosphere in England uncomfortable. He repaid dinners and several loans with marvellous stories. Mr. Mellor thought that the company of the poet would be the best possible cure for his neurasthenia, and persuaded Oscar to visit him in Gland, near Geneva. Unfortunately, Mr. Mellor was very mean in small ways and only gave Oscar Swiss wine to drink. The poet stated in a letter to Frank Harris: '. . . however I regard the place as a Swiss *pension*, where there is no weekly bill'. He complained that Switzerland had produced nothing but theologians and waiters. On 1st April 1899, he left his host, amicably on his side and with protestations of admiration and remorse from Mellor.

Despite this, a year later Oscar went to Sicily with Mellor and returned with him to Gland for ten days. Oscar would have been the ideal companion in Sicily, erudite and libertine, if he hadn't been recognised by the tourists. At every stage of his travels the poet lost a small part of his heart; at Naples it was to a 'triton', at Palermo, to a Seminarist with beautiful eyes, 'every day I kissed him behind the High Altar'. In Rome, where he stayed on his return journey, he struck up an acquaintance with one Armando whose requests for clothes and neckties were incessant. 'He really bayed for books, as a dog, moonwards.' He was rivalled by Omero but, 'He is so absurdly like the Apollo Belvedere that I feel always as if I was Winckelmann when I am with him. His lips are the same, his hair, his somewhat vulgar, because quite obvious, pride; and he also represents that decadence of the triumph of the face over the body, never seen in great Greek art.' Then there was Dario who went with him to see the Pope. Oscar had predicted this part of his life when he wrote: 'It is nothing to grow old, but the terrible thing is that one remains young.' He was only forty-five, but he looked ten years older and had no illusions about the way in which he spent what energy remained to him, and on the 14th May 1900 he wrote to Ross: '. . . In the mortal sphere, I have fallen in and out of love, and fluttered hawks and doves alike. How evil it is to buy Love, and how evil to sell it! And yet what purple hours one can snatch from that grey slowly-moving thing we call Time! My mouth is twisted with kissing, and I feed on fevers. The Cloister or the Café – there is my future. I tried the Hearth, but it was a failure. . . .'

In Italy the poet divided his time between museums and churches, and on the side he found distractions which enabled him to bear the cares of culture and the pains of religion. This large gentleman, who easily deciphered inscriptions and who always had cigarettes to offer boys, was a forerunner of the characters who enlivened the novels of Norman Douglas, and of Baron Corvo himself.

It brought back his youth to visit the Vatican and he joined a pilgrimage to receive the blessing of Leo XIII on Easter Day 1900. In a letter to Robbie on the 16th April he wrote: '. . . to the terror of Grissell* and all the Papal Court, I appeared in the front rank of the pilgrims in the Vatican, and got the blessing of the Holy Father . . . I was deeply impressed and my walking-stick showed signs of budding. . . .' Oscar was thinking of Tannhäuser's pilgrimage. Later he wrote: '. . . I do nothing but see the Pope: I have already been blessed many times, once in the private Chapel of the Vatican. He, as I wrote to Robbie, is no longer of flesh and blood: he has no taint of mortality: he is like a white soul robed in white. I spend all my money in getting tickets: for, now, as in the old days, men rob the pilgrims in Rome. . . . My position is curious: I am not a Catholic: I am simply a violent Papist. No one could be more "black"

* Hartwell de la Garde Grissell, Chamberlain of honour to the Pope since 1869. Wilde had met him in Rome in 1877.

than I am. I have given up bowing to the King. I need say no more.' Yet he could not resist teasing Robbie, the convinced Catholic, after Grissell had protested to Robbie at his having been blessed by the Pope: '. . . It is a curious, and therefore natural thing, but I cannot stand Christians because they are never Catholics, and I cannot stand Catholics because they are never Christians. . . . He who seven times sought and seven times received the blessing of the Holy Father is not to be excommunicated on postcards by the withered eunuch of the Vatican Latrines. (By "He" I mean myself). . . .'

Pleasures were easily come by which restored and enhanced his innate love of beautiful things. Oscar regained all his sensibility, and he wrote to Robbie: 'On the afternoon of Easter Day I heard Vespers at the Lateran: music quite lovely: at the close a Bishop in red, and with red gloves – such as Pater talks of in *Gaston de Latour* – came out on the balcony and showed us the relics. He was swarthy, and wore a yellow mitre. A sinister mediaeval man, but superbly Gothic, just like the Bishops carved on stalls or on portals. . . . The sight of this Bishop, whom I watched with fascination, filled me with the sense of the great realism of Gothic Art. . . .' '. . . I have not seen the Holy Father since Thursday, but am bearing up wonderfully well. I am sorry to say he has approved of a dreadful handkerchief, with a portrait of himself in the middle, and basilicas at the corners. It is very curious the connection between Faith and bad art: I feel it myself. Where I see the Pope I admire Bernini: but Bernini had a certain dash and life and assertion – theatrical life, but life for all that: the handkerchief is a dead thing . . . – I have been three times to see the great Velasquez of the Pamfili (sic) Pope: it is quite the grandest portrait in the world. The entire man is there.' This portrait of Innocent X hangs in Prince Doria Pamphili's Palace in Rome.

Oscar during his wanderings had discovered photography:
'... By the way, can you photograph cows well? I did one of
cows in the Borghese so marvellously that I destroyed it:
I was afraid of being called the modern Paul Potter. Cows are
very fond of being photographed, and, unlike architecture,
don't move. . . .' It amused Oscar to give his ephemeral
friends an address in London that sounded a little like
Robbie's. He advised Omero that Ross's name was Edmundo
Goss and that his address was the Savile Club.

How right Oscar would have been to have stayed in
Rome, occupying his old age with scholarly works (it
should not be forgotten that he was one of the best scholars
in the humanities of his generation) and by the delicate
problems which arise from alternating the practices of
sodomy and religion. Alas, the great actor missed his
audience. Rome was not an intellectual city and he had no
wish to go to Florence to cultivate lilies among the Botticelli
lesbians; he preferred conversation to conversion, so
returned to Paris. The other reason for his return was more
imperative – his friends, upon whom he depended, wished
to have him near at hand; Robbie could easily get to Paris
from London; in Rome Oscar would escape his influence.
Beneficent as was Robbie's advice on finance and other
matters, he vied with Oscar in his emotional problems. As
Oscar wrote to More Adey from Rome: 'Robbie left me a
legacy of a youthful guide. . . . Omero is his name, and I am
showing him Rome.'

Oscar felt that misfortune awaited him in Paris, where
Bosie had settled, soon to inherit a little money from
his father (the 'scarlet Marquess' died in 1900, a convert to
Catholicism, though he retained to the end his bellicose
character, and spat at his eldest son who was with him at his
death). Bosie bought a racing stable at Chantilly. He and
Oscar met frequently and were on light and easy-going

terms. Harris was full of new projects, there were many young poets in the cafés who adored the *Ballad* and *Salome*, Marcel Schwob and André Gide were in Paris – so much the worse for the Pope. Oscar left Rome to return to France in June 1900.

26   A kind of suicide

Oscar Wilde made his home in Paris from the time of his first return from Italy in 1898 until his death in 1900, though there were long absences, including the trips to Switzerland, Sicily and Rome in 1899 and 1900. His arrival in February had coincided with the publication of the *Ballad* and he remained until December of that year. He chose to live on the Left Bank, in the Rue des Beaux-Arts, a fairly inexpensive neighbourhood which reminded him of his first visit to Paris; to begin with, he settled in the Hôtel de Nice and afterwards in the Hôtel d'Alsace to which he returned frequently, as the proprietors, the Dupoirier family, showed an exemplary patience in waiting for their account to be paid: 'Dear M. Melmoth, he tells such wonderful stories—and always has a pleasant word.' Visits to inns on the Marne or the Seine made welcome breaks in summer: to Nogent-sur-Marne in June 1898, to Chennevières-sur-Marne in August 1898 and July 1899, where he joined the painters Conder and Rothenstein with whom he bathed and went rowing; this was part of the cure to set him up and, according to them, Oscar enjoyed himself – he was not alone and that was the principal thing.

In May 1899 Oscar installed himself at the Hôtel de la Neva, to be nearer the Boulevards, and then moved to the Hôtel Marsollier. There the management theatened to seize his baggage because he could not pay the bill; however the kind Dupoiriers settled the account and took him back to their hotel. Apart from visits to Chennevières, Sicily, Rome and Switzerland, he never again left the Hôtel d'Alsace.

Wilde retained a romantic idea of Paris as the following letter to Harris shows: 'The most wonderful city in the world, the only civilised capital; the only place on earth where you find absolute toleration for all human frailties, with passionate admiration for all human virtues and capacities. Do you remember Verlaine, Frank? His life was nameless and terrible . . . yet there he would sit in a café on the Boul.' Mich', and everyone who came in would bow to him and call him *maître* . . . in England they would have murdered Verlaine and men who call themselves gentlemen would have gone out of their way to insult him in public.' The Paris in which he had taken refuge, however, was very different to the Paris he had known in 1883. The Dreyfus affair had totally absorbed the French people, and the last three years of the century were conspicuous by the recon-sideration of the case, the imprisonment of Zola and the death of the President Felix Faure. Although divided on 'The Affair' the French had also become more and more patriotic since the Fashoda incident, in which the English had regained part of the Sudan occupied by the French in 1898. They hated the English, and the Boer War started just in time to lend this hatred the apparent excuse of indignation. The newspapers published vulgar caricatures of the old Queen and the cartoonist Caran d'Ache represented English soldiers as torturers. Oscar was indignant because in this matter he was violently imperialistic, and Kitchener was his hero. One would have expected that a victim of England like Oscar would have been pleased to hear expressions of pity for the Boers, but quite the contrary: 'English prisons must be very comfortable,' murmured a journalist whom Oscar had just snubbed. An anarchist where morals were concerned, in politics Oscar had suddenly become an extreme Conservative. These right-wing con-

victions were to him a mark of the respectability which he
had not the courage to renounce once and for all. So the
exile was thrilled when he met Esterhazy* with whom he
dined twice, once in the company of his mistress, a *demi-
mondaine* of the lowest grade whom Oscar thought charming.
Not for a minute did Wilde pity Dreyfus: 'Esterhazy is the
author of the *bordereau*, he has admitted it to me. He is much
more interesting than Dreyfus who is innocent. One is always
wrong to be innocent. To be a criminal requires imagination and courage. . . . But it is annoying that Esterhazy
has never been to prison,' he said to Davray, his translator.
The cafés in which Oscar spent his time reverberated more
loudly with political discussions than with literary polemics.

Byzantium, which had already shown a recession in
1895, was then in full flight. Jean Lorrain, drowning the
pain of a terrible illness in ether, lived mostly in Nice;
Schwob, ill and drugged, never left his library on the Ile
Saint Louis; Maeterlinck was beginning to be thought a bore
and Péladan was laughed at; Gustave Moreau was dead,
Rostand triumphed by delving into the romantic wardrobe
for his ideas and inspiration; Huysmans, after *Là-bas*, had
renounced horrors, and Octave Mirbeau in his *Journal d'une
femme de chambre* now made fun of aestheticism. Although he
had proposed Oscar for membership of the *Académie Goncourt*,
he introduced a character in this book, based on Oscar,
called Sir Harry Kimberley, 'symbolist musician, fervent
pederast', and his friend Satorys, 'Beautiful as a woman,
supple as a suède glove'. They are represented as talking in a
characteristic salon of the time, and Wilde's voice can be
recognised, '. . . hardly had one distinguished on the mauve
walls the long, supple, undulating golden sea-weed, which
seemed to move under the vibration of one knew not what

* The forger of the famous document for which Dreyfus was imprisoned
on Devil's Island.

deep and magical water. . . .' To these deliquescences Mirbeau showed a very French reaction: 'Oh, my dear, I would
like to shout obscenities at the top of my voice at those
people. I have had enough of their souls and their green and
perverted love-affairs.' Of his *Jardin des Supplices* Wilde wrote:
'. . . it is very revolting to me, but, for all that, wonderful'.

Yes, people had had enough of the aesthetes and of their
painters: the Impressionists had come to the fore. Decidedly
the poet had never liked them, and he had written from
Rome, but about Palermo, to Ross: '. . . The lemon-groves
and the orange-gardens were so entirely perfect that I became again a Pre-Raphaelite, and loathed the ordinary
Impressionists, whose muddy souls and blurred intelli-
gences would have rendered but by mud and blur those
"golden lamps hung in a green light", that filled me with
such joy. The elaborate and exquisite detail of the true Pre-
Raphaelites is the compensation they offer us for the
absence of motion; Literature and Music being the only
arts that are not immobile. . . .'

Oscar was to pass his last three years in the showy vulgarity
of the Boulevards or in the semi-crapulous shabbiness of the
Left Bank, and that for him was the most distressing aspect,
once the edge had worn off the joy of liberty. With a
simple or a bohemian environment he would not have
regretted great ladies, so much as their houses. Aesthetes
may well have had grand ideas and exciting vices, but
nothing was as important to them as their surroundings.
Oscar sometimes thought of debauchery and sordidness as
an ascent which led to a sublime darkness but he had not
the strength of character to resist good advice and to sink
quietly into misery. He looked back towards the drawing-
rooms and the palaces and yielded to sensible influences. It
took him three long years to die.

Wilde, imposing and dishonoured, stood alone in a

world which swarmed around him as though round a
monument of another era. He had no friends left of his
own age; had he ever had any since Oxford? For the young
Englishmen who came as pilgrims, he acted the grand old
man in the bars near the Madeleine or at the Café Pousset
in the Boulevard des Italiens. The Plato of Chelsea took up
his teaching again beneath a poster of the Belle Otero and
never had he talked better, because he seasoned his parables
with a disillusioned humour. By a kind of conjuring trick –
which always came off, the magician made a blessing of
misfortune and gleaned the benefits with the applause.
'The artist's mission is to live the complete life: success, as
an episode (which is all it can be); failure, as the real, the
final end. Death, analysed to its resultant atoms – what is it
but the vindication of failure: the getting rid for ever of
powers, desires, appetites, which have been a lifelong embarrassment? The poet's noblest verse, the dramatist's greatest
scene, deal always with death; because the highest function
of the artist is to make perceived the beauty of failure.'

This meditation was noted by a young friend, Laurence
Housman* in his book Echos de Paris, which includes other
interesting anecdotes: one day Oscar arrived at a restaurant
with Davray, and Housman wanted to order ortolans: 'So
young, and already so eager for disappointment? Why give
up imagination? "Ortolan", the word, is far more beautiful
than when it is made flesh. If you were wise you would
learn life only by inexperience. This is what makes it
always unexpected and delightful. Never to realise—that is
the true ideal.' Housman: 'Still, one goes on liking plover's
eggs after eating them: at least I do.' Oscar: 'Ah! Yes, an
egg is always an adventure: it may be different. But you are
right; there are a few things – like the Nocturnes of Chopin
– which can repeat themselves without repetition. The

* Younger brother of A. E. Housman, author and artist.

genius of the artist preserves them from ever being quite realised. But it has to be done carelessly.' Another day he returned to his favourite subject: 'I have come to see that St. Helena is, for a world which follows Caesar and not Christ, the greatest place on earth next to Calvary. . . . You smile at me, Robbie, but believe me, in my own ruin I have found out this truth. . . . Great success, great failure – only so shall the artist see himself as he is, and through himself see others – only so shall he learn (as the artist must learn) the true meaning behind the appearance of things material, of life in general, and – more terrible still – the meaning of his own soul.' If the text appears a little feeble, it must not be forgotten that the intonations were inimitable.

Still on the same theme, he went on to speak of Carlyle: 'In his prime he wrote his greatest work – the history of failure – the French Revolution. The time came when, with all his powers matured, he stood equipped for the writing of his supreme masterpiece. There was no need to look far afield for a subject: it stood obvious awaiting him. After his French Revolution he should have written the life of Napoleon – the greatest success, the greatest failure that the world has ever known. He would have done it magnificently. What a spectacle for the world: the Man of Destiny receiving from the son of Scottish peasants his right measure of immortality! But because Carlyle was a Scotsman, he would not take for his hero the man whose life ended in failure; he could not bring himself to face the débâcle of Waterloo, the enduring ignominy and defeat of St. Helena. Had he been true to his art, he would have realised that St. Helena was the greatest theme of all – for an artist the most completely significant in the whole of modern history. But because he had the soul of a Scotsman, because he worshipped success, he looked for his hero and found him in that most mean and despicable character, Frederick the

Great. . . .' The coffee and brandy after luncheon would continue until l'heure verte, unless Oscar was interrupted from his day-dreams by the sudden appearance of a good-looking boy in the distance.

Wilde told Harris about such a meeting: 'I was just getting out of the victoria when a little soldier passed, and our eyes met. My heart stood still, he had great dark eyes and an exquisite olive-dark face – a Florentine bronze, Frank, by a great master. He looked like Napoleon when he was first Consul, only less imperious, more beautiful. . . . I overtook the boy in a short time and asked him to come and have a drink, and he said to me in his quaint French way: "C'est pas de refus . . .". He began by telling me all about his mother, Frank, yes his mother. . . . I found out that the thing he desired most in the world was a bicycle, he talked of nickel-plated handle-bars and chains. . . . Do you remember how Socrates says he felt when the chlamys blew aside and showed him the limbs of Charmides? Don't you remember how the blood throbbed in his veins and how he grew blind with desire? A scene more magical than the passionate love-lines of Sappho?'*

Unfortunately it was difficult to bring back his conquests to the hotel. Robbie refused to understand that he would be better off in an unfurnished flat where he couldn't be asked to leave. Ross, Stuart Merrill and Sherard were dismayed – they feared it would all turn out badly. The latter met Oscar one evening by chance and decided to teach the incorrigible man a lesson. First he became sentimental over their past friendship and then went on to abuse Wilde's friends in unprintable language; Oscar checked him firmly and they parted in anger. Sherard however felt he had a mission to perform and followed Wilde. Another explosion

* *Oscar Wilde* by Frank Harris.

on his part ended in another parting. He made a third attempt the same evening when Wilde accused him of egotism, of thinking only of his own pleasure. 'Were those dreadful journeys to Reading and Wandsworth pleasant?' Sherard burst out, 'My God! Robert! and do you think it was pleasant for me to be in those places?' countered Wilde. Oscar wrote to Ross: 'May 1898, Robert Sherard is here. On Wednesday he created a horrible scene in Campbell's Bar by bawling out "A bas les juifs", and insulting and assaulting someone whom he said was a Jew. The fight continued in the street, and Robert tried to create an Anti-Semite, Anti-Dreyfusard demonstration. He succeeded, and was ultimately felled to the ground by the Jew!'

Happily, Bosie was there, he understood only too well the probable culmination of the sort of life described by Oscar in the following letter to Reggie Turner: '. . . A kind friend took me to the Folies-Bergères last night. . . . The acrobats were more wonderful than ever, but the audience was dreadfully mulierastic, and aged women covered with diamonds of the worst water came up and begged for bocks. On being refused they left with horrible imprecations.

'Bosie has a charming flat in the Avenue Kléber, but has spent all his money and so lives at Nogent, where it rains all day. He comes up every afternoon to look at his apartment, for his "bed is green". I chose it for him at Maple's. He is devoted to a dreadful little ruffian aged fourteen, whom he loves because at night, in the scanty intervals he can steal from an arduous criminal profession, he sells bunches of purple violets in front of the Café de la Paix. Also every time he goes home with Bosie he tries to rent him. This, of course, adds to his terrible fascination. We call him "Florifer," a lovely name. He also keeps another boy, aged twelve! whom Bosie wishes to know, but the wise "Florifer" declines. . . .

'Rodin's statue of Balzac is an astonishing masterpiece, a

gorgeous leonine head, stuck on the top of a cone-shaped dressing-gown. The Philistines are mad with rage about it. I have suggested that the statue to Alphonse Daudet should consist merely of a dressing-gown without any head at all.

'How is my golden Maurice? I suppose he is widely loved. His upper lip is more like a rose-leaf than any rose-leaf I ever saw. I fear he would not be a good secretary; his writing is not clear enough, and his eyelashes are too long, but he would be a sweet theatrophone, and an entrancing phonograph.

'I should go and see my doctor today, but I don't like to, as I am not feeling very well. I only care to see doctors when I am in perfect health; then they comfort one, but when one is ill they are most depressing.'

Maurice Gilbert, alluded to above, was one of Oscar's most devoted friends in the last years. His father was English and his mother French. He had much more to recommend him than the violet-seller or than a certain American painter who was said to have stayed with Oscar in an inn on the banks of the Marne and to have gone off with his dressing-case. All that is known of 'sweet Maurice' is that he divided his affections between all of Oscar's friends; when the poet was ill he visited him and brought him flowers.

Oscar and Bosie very sensibly did not attempt to live together again, but still from time to time there were scenes which in the past would have left Oscar shattered, but by now it was generally the case that Oscar was in the wrong. Bosie once said: 'I thought when he kept asking me for that money tonight, he was like an old prostitute.' When Bosie won at the races, he gave a handful of money to his friend, but most of the time he was so poor that he was reduced to preying on his landlady, who paid for everything including his cigars. Philosophically, as he did not bet himself, Oscar wrote: 'Bosie . . . goes to races every day, and loses of course.

As I wrote to Maurice today, he has a faculty of spotting the loser which, considering that he knows nothing at all about horses, is perfectly astounding.'

Lack of money rendered Oscar's life unbearable, and would have made him unbearable to his friends had he not always saved the situation by his charm of manner. He was unable to keep a penny, he was incapable of passing a restaurant without inviting his companion to a meal, nor in a bar could he resist offering champagne to a delighted audience. Ross patiently forwarded his small income and obtained from rich friends money with which to pay Oscar's debts. At one moment it looked as if prosperity might return; Oscar had sold a splendid plot to Harris who had suggested that they should collaborate in making it into a play. Harris, however, later found that it had already been sold to five other people; Frank gave Wilde £25 only, although he had originally promised £175, because he had to buy off some if not all of the other people who had already bought the same plot from Oscar for £100 each.

In Paris, Oscar became a 'Dubliner' as his father had been before him, going from bar to bar, always ready to engage anyone in conversation, to tell a story, to pay for a round of drinks and only returning home in the small hours. What a relief after the strain of being a man of the world for nearly twenty-five years. Oscar sighed like a fat woman who relaxes after loosening her stays, while remembering nostalgically her former successes. Wilde's new admirers had no interest in 'a gentleman', they were not little dandies like Louÿs, nor well-bred young men like Gide, but bohemians with anarchistic tendencies. Sometimes, to resemble them, Oscar would sport a loosely tied bow at his neck and a velvet suit. It was a gnome-like, would-be poet, called La Jeunesse who introduced him into this circle, and

2C

who observed Oscar, stooping, 'a distended ghost, over a Manhattan'. Sometimes they met in a café in the Latin Quarter or with the staff of the *Mercure de France* led by Rachilde. On one occasion, at the end of a banquet given in honour of Verhaeren, the Belgian poet was completely forgotten and a young Dutch-Jewish painter called Sarluis, whom La Jeunesse and Oscar had forced to stand on the table, had become the centre of attention.

To all those who reacted against the rise of nationalism, the exiled aesthete appeared as a martyr. They applied to Oscar the saying of Tristan Corbière in *Renégat*, 'Pure by dint of having been purged of all disgust.' As for Oscar, he thought anarchists simply charming. He invited the poets to whom Ravachol was a hero to the Kalisaya Bar in the Boulevard des Italiens; with them, it is said, he was present at the execution of an anarchist. He was deeply moved by the suicide of Maurice Léon, the nineteen-year-old author of *Le Livre d'un Petit Gendelettre*. Oscar wrote to Ross: '. . . we went to Montmartre to the Café where Jehan Rictus,* the poet, recites. I was received with great honour and everyone was presented to me. I was not allowed to pay for my *bocks* and the *chasseur*, a lad of singular beauty, begged for my autograph in his album, which contained, he told me, the autographs of *cinquante-trois poètes, et deux meurtriers!* I graciously acceded.' One of Oscar's stories which particularly amused the boulevardiers was about the 'dear Queen' (by then no one doubted that he had been an intimate at Windsor): 'If the Prince Consort could enter the Queen's private apartments, a dish full of oranges would be left in the ante-chamber. If the Queen wished to sleep alone, there would be no oranges – there were always oranges.'

* Jehan Rictus, pseudonym of the anarchist poet Gabriel Randon de Saint-Arnaud (1867–1933) whom Oscar admired and to whom he gave an inscribed copy of the *Ballad*.

Those who had known Wilde in the good days dreaded finding him in low company. Thus Gide, who had twice sent him quite considerable sums of money (he was only mean about small things), reproached himself for having been ashamed to sit at a table with him. He felt indebted to Wilde because he frequently retold Oscar's fables to young provincials, brilliantly imitating the master's voice. Wilde was full of praise for Gide's *Saül*, whose madness Gide ascribed to his hopeless love for David, and his wild jealousy of Jonathan.

In July 1898, Oscar '. . . dined with Maeterlinck and his wonderful mistress, Georgette Leblanc, the prima-donna of the Opera Comique, a woman very like Sarah Bernhardt. They have a lovely little house near the Bois de Boulogne – all white walls, and green furniture, and Burne-Jones photographs, heaps of books, and Dutch brass candlesticks, and copper things. He is *bon garçon*. Of course he has quite given up art. He only thinks of making life sane and healthy, and freeing the soul from the trammels of culture. Art seems to him now a malady. And the *Princess Maleine* an absurdity of his youth. He rests his hope of humanity on the Bicycle. . . .'

Among those whom Oscar repaid for their good dinners with equally good stories were several Americans: Ada Rehan, the actress, Stuart Merrill, and also a journalist, Vincent O'Sullivan, who wrote his own memorial in *Aspects of Wilde*. In it, he describes the exile as being always well-dressed and shaven, passing a trembling hand over his face as if to brush aside a nightmare, and he noted one of Oscar's unpublished stories: 'You know, Nero was obliged to do something. They were making him ridiculous. What he thought was; "Here everything was going on very well, when one day two incredible creatures arrived from somewhere in the provinces. They are called Peter and Paul or some unheard-of names like that. Since their arrival life in

Rome has become impossible. They collect crowds and block the traffic with their miracles. It really is intolerable. I, the Emperor, have no peace. When I get up in the morning and look out of the window, the first thing I see is a miracle going on in the back garden.' Wilde also talked wonderfully about French novels. He made the heroes live as if they had been friends of his: 'When I was a boy two of my favourite characters were Lucien de Rubempré and Julien Sorel. Lucien hanged himself, Julien died on the scaffold, and I died in prison.'

Sometimes Oscar arranged that his current gigolo was invited out to dinner as well and would be critical of his table manners. He once rebuked a French boy for the way he ate oysters. The boy was upset and, as Vincent O'Sullivan writes, when Oscar had gone, 'the boy, almost in tears, explained that his mother had taught him to eat oysters in the way he did: "*Ma mère n'est pas une princesse, c'est entendu, mais elle a du monde*". We tried to assure him that his mother was right and Wilde wrong, which was indeed the case, but he could not be comforted.' Oscar acted the part of the aristocrat in an airy manner which was disconcerting to those whom an hour or two later he would touch for a loan, saying: 'Once I was a king, now I want to be a beggar.' It is, however, necessary to refute those memoirs which show Wilde on the boulevards, shabby, holding out his hand to Englishmen whom he had known in the past. Among those who were pleased to treat him royally was Serge Diaghilev, a rich and handsome young Russian, who was to bring the Russian Ballet to Europe and who wanted to buy some of Aubrey Beardsley's drawings to reproduce in his review *Le Monde de l'art*. Alas, no one has recorded the conversation between those two great aesthetes, each of whom did so much to make the world a little more beautiful and a little less boring.

'I have made an important discovery – that alcohol taken in sufficient quantities produces all the effects of intoxication.' But so large a man must have needed to drink a great deal to obtain that result. One day, when talking of the consequences of drinking absinthe, he announced: 'After the first glass, you see things as you wish they were. After the second, you see them as they are not – finally, you see things as they really are, and that is the most horrible thing in the world. . . . Take a top-hat. You think you see it as it really is. But you don't, because you associate it with other things and ideas. If you had never heard of one before, suddenly saw it alone, you'd be frightened or laugh. That is the effect absinthe has, and that is why it drives men mad.'

After his return from staying in Switzerland with Harold Mellor in May 1900, Oscar possibly realised that there was nothing more to be expected from life, and that it would be tactless to prolong it. There was a final unpleasant evening with Bosie, but as it occurred in the Café de la Paix, Oscar refused to make a scene. The fear of being without money had become an obsession. The play that Oscar had meant to write with Harris, who had finally written it alone, was about to be put on in England. Oscar, who it will be remembered had already been paid for the plot, wrote long letters claiming considerable sums, letters which were to be his last literary efforts. Ross and Turner were less often in Paris, and Bosie, the racing season being over, was planning to go to England for the 12th of August to stay with his brother Percy for the shooting. It was not very long before a charming young lady was to come into his life – Olive Custance, a poetess who fell romantically in love with him and called him Prince Charming. Before Bosie left Paris he and Oscar dined together happily at the Grand Café, except that towards the end of dinner Oscar became very depressed; he said that he had a presentiment that he had not long to live and went on: 'if another century began and I was still alive, it would really be more than the English could stand'. It was their last meeting, and the terrible lovers parted good friends.

Oscar consequently went out less during the hot summer

Il ne faut regarder ni les choses ni les personnes. Il ne faut regarder que dans les miroirs

Car les miroirs ne nous montrent que des masques.

Oscar Wilde

One of Wilde's last epigrams

of 1900, he had his meals brought up to his room, and spent his evenings re-reading Balzac and sipping brandy and soda. One day on a steamer going up the Seine to St. Cloud, he met the Comtesse de Brémont, who asked him why he no longer wrote: 'Because I have written all that I was to write, I wrote when I did not know life; now that I do know the meaning of life, I have no more to write. Life cannot be written, life can only be lived – I have lived.' When Sherard visited him and saw writing materials on the table, he congratulated him, but Oscar replied: 'One has to do something. I have no taste for it now. It is a penance for me; but, as was said of torture, it always helps to pass an hour or two.' If he did not write it was less from laziness than from the fear of being out of fashion.

When he did go out it was to visit the Exhibition, which delighted him. He would stroll along the quayside from the Rue Bonaparte, stopping at a little restaurant, 'Nothing is so fattening as a dinner at 1 fr. 50,' as he so rightly remarked. Arriving at the great gateway of the Cours-la-Reine surmounted by a gigantic statue of a Parisienne looking like Sarah Bernhardt: 'that serpent of the old Nile, older than the pyramids'; one can imagine him repelled by the dust and the crowds, but soon allowing himself to be jostled from one pavilion to another. The Byzantine halls of ingenius machines, the mediaeval bars, the rococo kiosks with bulbous turrets climbing to the sky, domes like spider's webs which defied the laws of gravity, banners in Liberty colours. The art which he had pioneered was displayed all over Europe. Beardsley's flora unfurled themselves in plaster creepers round pillars, the designs of William Morris covered walls and chairs like moss. Fanciful conceptions, objects of apparent fragility, disguised the most utilitarian sections. It was the triumph of fate: at last the Blue Bird was ready to fly from plaster cages to tell of marvellous things which should, but did not, exist. No doubt he stopped at the section devoted to painting; to him, 'the most beautiful modern picture is Shannon's portrait of himself'. This would have reminded him of his friend Charles Ricketts, of the studio he shared with Shannon, of the Greek vase, of the portrait of Mr. W.H. painted on worm-eaten wood.

A little further on, there was the Egyptian café; as he wrote in a letter: 'A slim brown Egyptian, rather like a handsome bamboo walking-stick, occasionally serves me drinks at the Café d'Egypte. . . .' Then, the Rodin pavilion, a rotunda fronted by a portico, near to the Pont d'Alma. 'Rodin has a pavilion to himself and showed me anew all his great dreams in marble. He is by far the greatest poet in France, and has, as I was glad to tell myself, completely outshone Victor Hugo.' 'A lady who gazed with horror at Rodin's statue of Balzac had her attention directed to Rodin himself who was passing by. She was greatly surprised at his appearance, "Et, pourtant il n'a pas l'air méchant" was her remark,' wrote Oscar.

Oscar would have returned to the Rue des Beaux Arts, very dignified, leaning on his walking-stick, and climbed the spiral staircase to his room on the first floor, facing the courtyard. The bed was some inches too short for him, the furniture consisted of a rickety table, a faded threadbare sofa and a few book-shelves. Over the mantlepiece hung a tawdry mirror, into which he would never look, nor would he seek the time from the massive clock of metal and marble supported by a crouching lion which stood upon it. The wallpaper was a horror of large magenta flowers: 'Decidedly one of us will have to go,' he said once, as he looked at it.

On the 10th October his headaches became so bad that Oscar had to have an operation on his ear; he had suffered ever since his fall at Wandsworth, but the operation was expensive and did no good. Robbie Ross came to him at the time of the operation, to find Oscar worried about money, but seeming well and in high spirits. The Embassy doctor attended him. On All Souls' Day Robbie went to Père Lachaise with a friend; when he returned Oscar was thinking about epitaphs and asked if he had chosen a place for his tomb: 'When the Last Trumpet sounds, and we are crouched in our porphyry tombs, I shall turn and whisper to you "Robbie, Robbie, let us pretend we do not hear it".'

Although no doubt Robbie would have liked Oscar to be converted to Catholicism, he never pressed the point. The afternoon before Robbie left Paris with his mother, Reggie Turner saw him in Oscar's room. Robbie wrote of this to More Adey: 'Oscar told us that he had had a horrible dream the previous night – that he had been supping with the dead. Reggie made a very typical response: "My dear Oscar, you were probably the life and soul of the party".' Reggie hardly dared to take the invalid out because when he did Oscar always insisted on stopping at every café to drink a glass of absinthe. Reggie finally installed himself in the hotel, and held himself responsible for all expenses. Maurice Gilbert frequently visited the poet and brought him flowers. The doctor said that worry about money was delaying his patient's recovery, and when Ross wrote to Bosie about this, although he had already sent cheques, he immediately sent £10 and promised more. He also wrote to Harris, who turned a deaf ear. Happily the proprietors of the hotel demanded nothing and provided Oscar with delicacies and champagne right to the end.

Oscar was improving so Ross returned to London, but according to the doctor it was then his drinking that was killing him. The pain in his head became very bad and he was given injections of morphia, but on 26th November the doctor said he could not give him any more. Ice-packs were applied to the sick man's head; he was delirious most of the time. Turner, exhausted, sent for Ross who arrived on 28th November. He immediately went to fetch an English priest, Father Cuthbert Dunne, of the Passionists. The priest administered conditional Baptism and Extreme Unction. He could not administer the Viaticum as Oscar was semicomatose, but he was roused from this and tried to talk and the priest was satisfied that he understood what was being done. On 30th November 1900, in the afternoon, Oscar Wilde died. He was washed and laid out by his two friends. They went through his papers and burned a lot of them, but what was done with Bosie's letters? In the event they were not returned to him.

When it was discovered that Melmoth's name was in reality Wilde, the officials asked whether he had committed suicide or had been murdered. They threatened to take Oscar's body to the Morgue. Eventually, after a fee and a few drinks, the officials signed the certificate for burial, and left before mourners began to arrive – Jehan Rictus, Raymond de la Tailhade, Tardieu, Charles Sibleigh, d'Humières, George Sinclair, and various English people who gave assumed names, and two veiled women who prayed at the foot of the bed.

The funeral took place on the 3rd December at Saint-Germain-des-Prés. Bosie arrived from Scotland in time to be present, and he paid for the ceremony and was the chief mourner. Ross has been blamed for not telling Bosie in time for him to see Oscar before he died, but he himself had not known the seriousness of Oscar's condition until 28th November.

There were many flowers and the Dupoiriers sent a wreath made of beads, on which were the words 'To my tenant'. About fifty people were at the funeral; an icy rain was falling, and the intimate friends crowded into four carriages, to go to Bagneux cemetery. On the way, they discussed the epitaph, and they chose the words from the 29th Chapter of the Book of Job: 'Verbis meis addere nihil audebant et super illos stillabat eloquium meum.' ('To my words they durst add nothing and my speech dropped upon them.')

27   Epitaphs

Wilde, creator of myths, soon became a legend. The zeal of disciples like Ross, of friends such as Sherard, have made his life the subject of gospels, some maledictory, others merely obscure. His rehabilitation in France came about through excellent translations of his works, while in Germany and Russia the success of *Salome* (with the help of the music of Strauss) paved the way for a qualified approval in England. For a long time the French saw him as the mauve and bloated Mephistopheles painted by Lautrec, mocking at Gide's fall; and his name remained the synonym of a proclivity which could not be mentioned in respectable circles. As the society which condemned him disappears, so the tragic and obscene significance of his name is slowly being effaced. The case which in the words of Max Beerbohm 'made the unmentionable mentionable', dealt the first blow to the Victorian taboos; after Wilde came Freud and Lawrence. Wilde's reputation now rests on the memory of a cultivated and charming intelligence, of a prodigiously good comedian unfortunately tempted by tragedy, and on the echo of the supreme dialogue in his plays.

But for more than thirty years, Wilde was a *bête noire* to the conventional, and for poets a magician, the last prince of Byzantine romanticism, overthrown by materialism, in the midst of his pearls and velvet. This is the interpretation of Hugo von Hofmannsthal in an article which appeared soon after his death: 'Oscar Wilde walked towards catastrophe like Oedipus, blind and clear-sighted. His destiny

and his character were inextricable. . . . Oscar Wilde, an
unseemly personage of a tragic unseemliness. His aestheticism had something hysterical about it. All the jewels among
which he pretended to live so voluptuously were like eyes
petrified in death by the threat directed against him by life.
Ceaselessly he challenged life and insulted reality, but he
felt that life was lying in wait for him in the shadows,
always ready to pounce.'

The English, who after all had known Oscar, were more
reasonable. Max Beerbohm, in his obituary in The Saturday
Review on 8th December 1900, was reticent: 'Despite the
number of his books and plays, Mr. Wilde was not, I think,
what one calls a born writer. His writing seemed always to
be rather an overflow of intellectual energy than an inevitable, absorbing function. That he never concentrated himself
on any one form of literature is a proof that the art of
writing never really took hold of him.' To this very day, in
England, distinguished writers take the attitude that the
tragedy of Oscar is the last word in bad taste. Lord David
Cecil, Sir Kenneth Clark and even Cyril Connolly treat poor
Oscar with little respect. When the collection of his letters,
edited by Rupert Hart-Davis, appeared, Cyril Connolly
wrote in Previous Convictions: 'My three days with Wilde's
letters are no proof of his genius. On the whole they are
viscous, even oppressive, they adhere rather than delight
and one is left with the impression of having escaped at
last the clutches of some great, greedy beetle.' While the
opinion of Yeats was that the decision to make a martyr of
Wilde accounted for half his fame.

The most generous judgement is that of Jorge Luis Borges
(Enquêtes, 1946): 'By reading and re-reading Wilde in the
course of the years, I have noticed a fact which his pane-
gyrists seems not to have suspected: the simple, easy-to-
verify fact that Wilde was nearly always right. The Soul of

Man Under Socialism is not only eloquent but fair. His diverse articles in the *Pall Mall Gazette* and the *Speaker* were full of perspicacious observations which went beyond the possibilities of Leslie Stephen and Saintsbury in their best days. He offered to the age that which it craved, emotional comedies for the many, verbal arabesques for the few, and he accomplished these dissimilar tasks with a kind of careless happiness. . . . Wilde, a man who despite being used to evil and misfortune, retained an invulnerable innocence.'

Yet the sinister side cannot be concealed. Oscar brought bad luck to all those whom he loved, as well as to his immediate family. Condemned by laws which came from the Bible, the curse extended like that of God: 'Visiting the iniquities of the fathers upon the children until the third and fourth generation of them that hate me.' The eldest son Cyril, old enough at the time of the scandal to understand its nature, grew up into a handsome and melancholy young man; after having done well in his studies in Germany, he travelled in the Far East and was killed at the beginning of the First World War; the younger son, Vyvyan, surmounted the horror with which he was surrounded during childhood and wrote an excellent book about his parents.

Before the last war, Oscar's niece (by Willie's second marriage) was sometimes to be seen in the literary and feminine circles of Paris. Dorothy Ierne Wilde resembled Oscar in his youth, talked like him and lived elegantly but in great confusion. 'She did not dramatise anything, but drama revolved round her like ravens round a belfry.'* She took drugs but kept her looks till her death in 1941.

Ross and Douglas were also to have their lives poisoned by a quarrel which prolonged itself for years until Ross died

* Germaine Beaumont.

in 1918. This quarrel split the faithful into partisans of
Robbie and defenders of Bosie, of which the former were
the more numerous. Ross had been admirably patient and
generous, it is true; he had dedicated his life to the poet of
whom he was the literary executor, but he had wished to
impose his views of Oscar on others, to be alone at his side
like a guardian angel. Ross was amusing, insinuating, dis-
simulating; in short, what would once have been called
jesuitical. On his side he had the beautiful Souls, and also
all those who had been onlookers of the drama of Wilde,
and wished to be taken for Souls.

Douglas, impossible as always, was more frank. A year
after Oscar's death he published a fine poem:

> 'I dreamed of him last night, I saw his face
> All radiant and unshadowed of distress,
> And as of old, in music measureless,
> I heard his golden voice and marked him trace
> Wonders that might have been inarticulate
> And voiceless thoughts like murdered singing birds.
> And so I woke and knew that he was dead.'

Then he tried to re-make his life. The parents of Olive
Custance were determined that she should make a good
match, which he could not be considered to be, so Bosie
went to the United States in the hope of finding an heiress.
In Washington there was a question of marriage, in name
only, with a friend of Olive's, Miss Barney. While in
Washington he was made a member of a smart club, but
unfortunately another member insulted him about his
friendship with Oscar Wilde and the club demanded to
know from Bosie's cousin, Percy Wyndham, why he had ever
put him up for membership. Despite the efforts of the staff of
the British Embassy and of some New Yorkers to put the

matter right, Bosie, hurt and shocked, returned to England. Then he learned that Olive was about to marry a friend of his: this decided him, he took her out to luncheon, persuaded her that they must marry, and they eloped together. The marriage as such did not last, but they remained on affectionate and friendly terms, although living separately. The prestige of having been loved by the notorious decadent gained him conquests, which the rapid decline of his beauty could no longer assure: at one time he had seduced Romaine Brooks away from both d'Annunzio and a princess.

In 1905, the first version of De Profundis appeared, and a slightly fuller version in 1908. This dramatic letter, expurgated of all the attacks on Bosie, caused a great sensation, and Lord Alfred wrote a cautious review of it. In 1913, Arthur Ransome's book on Wilde was published in which he libelled Bosie; the latter, having inherited his father's mania for litigation, sued for defamation of character. Ross, to support Ransome, produced the allegedly integral version of the letter; cruelly wounded, Bosie attacked Ross. At the same time he became a convert to Catholicism and, published Oscar Wilde and Myself, in which, among other fictions, he denied having shared Wilde's pederastic tastes. Gide was the first to protest at this, however he had himself been rapped over the knuckles on the publication of In Memoriam. Ross was in effect the butt of Bosie's persecutions. When Robbie's manservant tried to blackmail him, his weak heart was unable to stand up to the threats and he was found dead in his flat. This mattered little to Bosie, who at the time was involved in a libel case, having accused Winston Churchill of having, when First Lord of the Admiralty, caused the death of Bosie's old admirer, Lord Kitchener. For this Lord Alfred got six months. At the end of his life, dividing his time between religious retreats and shady cinemas in Brighton, Lord Alfred wrote a more honest book than his first ones. Those who knew him then retain the memory of a courteous and very cultivated man. That most perspicacious critic, Sir Desmond MacCarthy, wrote of him: 'Alfred Douglas was not in the least mad. He was one of the most charming people I have met – super-ficially – and charming in the way some boys are – even when he was well over forty. But, on provocation, he might become a festering mass of spite; and like all deeply vindictive natures, he loved a fight. And true to his type, the outlaw aristocrat, he was a very dirty fighter, not caring what weapons he used; and also caring precious little what means he took to get his way when in a tight place or wanting money.'* Lord Alfred died in 1945.

Up to the last war, the memory of Wilde aroused passions. Sherard, faithful but obtuse, wrote a book called *Bernard Shaw, Frank Harris and Oscar Wilde*, with a preface by Shaw. As Sherard had been reconciled with Lord Alfred, Ross appears in it as a sinister plotter; the key to this work is a conversation with Monsieur Chiappe in the archives of the Prefecture of Police about a search for Wilde's dossier which was not to be found: incontrovertible proof, no doubt, that Oscar lived like a saint in Paris.

What became of the victims of the case, such as the little office clerk Shelley, is not known; but the real friends also had their share of troubles; Harris spent a short term of imprisonment for contempt of court, when he was publish-ing *Modern Society*. In 1914 there was a warrant for his arrest: he escaped to France, but soon had to return and went into hiding in England in a house belonging to Lady Warwick (the former Lady Brooke). It is said that he repaid her kind-ness by stealing a number of the letters King Edward VII had written to her but the circumstances of the case, even after the publication in 1966 of a book called *My Darling*

* *Memories* by Desmond MacCarthy.

Daisy by Theo Lang, still remain unclear. He finished his days on the Riviera writing a book modelled on Casanova: *My Life and Loves*. This well-informed liar helped to dissipate the legend of Wilde the martyr, even though his book was more vivid than truthful. Bernard Shaw's preface to this book was very fair to Oscar, but the moment one is reasonable one automatically becomes unfair to him. The elegant Lord Ronald Gower also came near to public scandal, as he was one of the admirers of the handsome Captain Shackleton (brother of the explorer) who was involved in the theft of the jewels of the Order of St. Patrick. The details of this Irish *Affaire du collier* are to be found in a fascinating pederastic book by Francis Bamford and Viola Bankes called *Vicious Circle*.

Reggie and Max both lived in Italy for many years, one in Florence, the other in Rapallo. Having returned to London in the last war, Max spoke on the B.B.C. three times a week and often frequent echoes of the laughter of the old days in the Café Royal helped Londoners to get through the nights of bombardment.

Mrs. Leverson kept alive the memory of an Oscar more delicious and more delightful than tragic, and transmitted it to a new generation of aesthetes, the Sitwells. After her husband had lost a lot of money, she set herself to work, and the result was six novels whose wit recalls her Wildean days. The Sphinx, who died in 1933, remained to the end an enthusiast for gaiety.

For Lady Archie Campbell, a particularly gifted medium, good relations with the 'Other World' appear to have continued until after her death in 1923, if a family story worthy of Wilde himself can be believed; on the morning of her funeral, it was noticed that the rope of the bell-tower was broken, but as the cortège was preparing to drive from the castle to the cemetery, her fairy-friends made the bells play magical music until she was buried.

2D

The Importance of Being Earnest and Lady Windermere's Fan, typically Edwardian plays, were bought by the actor-manager George Alexander from the Official Receiver soon after Oscar's death, and in 1905 parts of De Profundis were put on sale and translated into all languages; from then on the rapid revival of Wilde's work began, helped by the lack of writers of that particular kind of charm in England at the time. In July 1909, when all debts had been discharged, thanks to Ross's efforts, Oscar's remains were transferred to a place of honour in the Père Lachaise cemetery and the statue was the work of Jacob Epstein. Carved in stone are Oscar's own lines:

> 'And alien tears will fill for him
> Pity's long-broken urn
> For his mourners will be outcast men
> And outcasts always mourn.'

The scandal provoked by this sculpture was the last associated with Oscar. A sphinx, crowned with a tiara, and remarkably virile, emerges from a mass of stone. A generation after Oscar's death, Hesketh Pearson recorded that ten people asked to see his grave to every one who showed interest in the graves of Balzac, Chopin or de Musset. Nearby is to be found the admirable recumbent figure of Victor Noir by Dalou, which resembles the young anarchists who surrounded the poet in his last years.

Naturally, apocryphal stories grew up round the legend. Immediately after Wilde's death, there appeared under, the name of Sebastian Melmoth, translations from the Satyricon and of Ce qui ne meurt pas of Barbey d'Aurevilly. Then there appeared in America a rather scandalous correspondence with Sarah Bernhardt. Finally, a Mrs. Chon Toon, later arrested for fraud, sold to a publisher the manuscript of a

Siamese entertainment *For the Love of the King*. She pretended
that she had been brought up at Speranza's knee, had been
engaged to Willie and had been an intimate friend of Oscar.
Certainly she was worthy of that family, whom she had
known slightly from being a Dubliner herself. She was also
an inexhaustible chatter-box, to whom a pink parrot from
which she was inseparable would chatter back.

In 1905 a man called J. M. Stuart Young, pretending to
have been a friend of Wilde's, wrote a book about him called
Ostrac the self-sufficient filled with apocryphal correspondence.
And who was Dorian Hope, who passed himself off alternately as the son of Oscar or of Bosie and who sold a variety
of forged letters? Finally, a medium published *Psychic
Messages from Oscar Wilde*. (H. T. Smith) and Guillot de Saix
translated a doubtful *Jezebel*. Ross gave his permission, in a
much too flattering preface, to a young American poet to
complete and publish *The Florentine Tragedy*. Other forgeries
revived the interest of the faithful. Davray, his friend and
translator, the guardian of the Wilde cult in France, fulmin-
ated in *Le Mercure de France* against André Maurois and Edmund
Gosse.

After 1920, the pernicious bad taste of the stories, and of
Salome, saved Wilde from the oblivion into which his more
fastidious contemporaries had fallen. Everyone knows the
Dorian Grays of the Spas, surrounding their fragile beauty
with what they had been able to pick up cheaply. The plays,
for a time eclipsed by those of Somerset Maugham and Noël
Coward, have been constantly put on in London. *Lady
Windermere's Fan* and *The Ideal Husband* have been made into
excellent films, with designs by Cecil Beaton and a version
of *The Importance of Being Earnest* was directed by Anthony
Asquith. An Irish actor, Micheál MacLiámmóir, from time
to time gives a one-man show, occupying the stage for two
hours with a monologue which he calls *The Importance of*

Being Oscar, without ever being boring, and his voice is said
to be very like that of his compatriot. There have been two
fairly accurate films about Wilde; several films of *Dorian
Gray*; several *Salomes*, since that of Strauss the best-known is
The Tragedy of Salome written by Florent Schmitt for Ida
Rubenstein. Today the revival of Art Nouveau has exhumed
Wilde the critic, better but less remembered than Wilde the
writer and poet, as much the friend of the Pre-Raphaelites
and of Beardsley as of the architects such as Godwin and
Mackmurdo who heralded the style.

But the person is always more important than his works,
if he is to become like Wilde a symbol of his era. The same
can be said of Jean Cocteau between the two wars of Cubism
and Surrealism. Those who knew Wilde got their idea of
his prestige more from his improvisations and from
his incredible verbal generosity than from his published
works. But Cocteau's charm was dry and did not have the
disturbing orientalism of Wilde, his voice was nasal and
light, without the modulations of the great actor. In an age
when authority had become suspect, Cocteau wanted to be
more friend than master like the magician of Chelsea. Their
teaching was more or less the same: 'I am a lie which always
tells the truth.' wrote Cocteau; Wilde had said, 'An artistic
truth is one of which the contrary is also true,' and 'I live
in terror of not being misunderstood.' Unfortunately for
Cocteau, he finished as a prisoner of millionaires on the
Riviera, which is, after all, less good for a legend than
Reading; he aged, loaded with honours, repeating that he
was a decadent poet. This academic end shows what that of
Wilde would have been, without his instinct for self-
destruction, his flair for the dramatic, without his taste for
horror which sets into relief all the rôles of this great actor.
Indeed, with Sarah Bernhardt, he was perhaps the greatest
actor of his time.

Appendix

Mr. Brian Reade, an expert on this kind of literature, gives the facts about *Teleny* thus: 'Charles Hirsch, a Parisian bookseller, came to London in 1889 and opened a shop in Coventry Street where he sold Continental books and newspapers. Wilde was a frequent customer of his, and Hirsch used to obtain for him *Alcibiades enfant à l'Ecole* and *The Sins of the Cities of the Plain*. Many of these were reprints of well-known works of this character. Towards the end of 1890 Wilde brought into the shop a thin paper commercial-style notebook, wrapped up and sealed. This he instructed Hirsch to hand over to a friend who would present his card. Shortly afterwards, one of Wilde's young friends whose name Hirsch had forgotten by the time he recorded the incident called at the shop and after showing Wilde's card took away the packed up notebook. A few days later the young man came back and handed the manuscript to Hirsch, saying another man would call and collect it in a similar manner. In all, four men seem to have taken away and returned the manuscript, and the last left the wrapper undone. Succumbing to temptation, Hirsch opened the parcel and read the contents of the notebook, the leaves of which were loose. On the cover there was a single word TELENY; inside about 200 pages of a novel which appeared to be a collaborative effort. No author's name was given. The handwritings were various; there were conspicuous erasures, cuttings-out and corrections. Hirsch believed that some of the writing was Wilde's. In due course Hirsch gave the manuscript back to Wilde. He next came across *Teleny* when he found it had been printed by Leonard Smithers in an edition privately issued and limited to 200 copies, with only the imprint "Cosmopoli" at the bottom of the title page, and the date 1893. In this printed version, Paris had been substituted for London as the scene of some of the action, and there were certain differences of detail. There was an added sub-title *Or the reverse* of the *Medal*, and the Prologue had been cut out. When Hirsch got to know Smithers in 1900, he asked about the book, and was told that Smithers had wished not to upset the self-respect of clients by leaving the story with a London background. There was also *Des Grieux. A Prelude to Teleny* which was announced for publication by the Erotica Biblion Society in 1908. One can go over the names and literary mannerisms of some of the better-remembered persons in his circle in 1890, but to associate any of them with the authorship of *Teleny* would be difficult. Copies of *Teleny* in the 1893 edition are very rare indeed. The British Museum has one, but those in private possession have been reduced in number no doubt by executors and others who considered them unfit for anything else than fire. A new edition was brought out by the Olympia Press of Paris, and in it Wilde was definitely, but mistakenly, credited with the authorship; and an expurgated version was produced in paperback form by Icon in 1966, with an introduction by Montgomery Hyde.'

Bibliography

(Books with an asterisk have been quoted from in the translation)

ENGLISH

Amico, Tomaso d': *Wilde's Aesthetics*
Bamford, Francis and Bankes, Viola: *Vicious Circle.* 1965.
* Beardsley, Aubrey: *Under the Hill.* 1966.
Beerbohm, Max: *Works.*
* Beerbohm, Max: *Letters to Reggie Turner.* 1964.
* Behrman, Samuel: *Conversations with Max.* 1960.
Benson, E. F.: *As We Were.* 1930.
* Berenson, Bernard: *Sunset and Twilight.* 1964.
Berenson, Bernard: *Sketches for an autobiography.*
Birnbaum, Martin: *Beardsley and Wilde.*
* Birnbaum, Martin: *Oscar Wilde, Fragments and Memories.* 1920.
* Blanche, Jacques-Emile: *Portraits of a Life-Time.* 1937.
* Blunt, Wilfrid Scawen: *My Diaries.* 1921.
Bremont, Comtesse de: *Oscar Wilde and His Mother.* 1911.
* Brasol, Boris: *Oscar Wilde.* 1938.
* Cecil, Lord David: *Max.* 1964.
* Connolly, Cyril: *Previous Convictions.* 1963.
* Croft-Cooke, Rupert: *Bosie.* 1963.
Cruse, Amy: *The Victorians and their Books.* 1967.
Douglas, Lord Alfred: *Oscar Wilde and Myself.* 1914.
* Douglas, Lord Alfred: *Autobiography.* 1931.
* Douglas, Lord Alfred: *Poems.* 1928.
Ellis, S. M.: *Wilkie Collins, Le Fanu and others.* 1951.
Ervine, St. John: *Oscar Wilde, a present time appraisal.* 1951.
* Evans, B. Ifor: *English Poetry in the late 19th Century.* 1933.
Freeman, William: *Life of Lord Alfred Douglas.* 1948.
Gaunt, William: *Aesthetic Adventure.* 1945.
* Gide, André: *If it Die . . .* 1951.
* Gide, André: *Journal.* 1947.
* Gide, André: *In Memoriam.* 1951.
Grosskurth, Phyllis: *John Addington Symonds.* 1964.
Gunn, Peter: *Vernon Lee.* 1964.

411

Green, Julien: Journal. 1961.

Hare, Humphrey: Swinburne. 1949.

* Harris, Frank: Oscar Wilde. New edition. 1965.

Harris, Frank: My Life and Loves. 1964.

* Hart-Davis, Rupert (ed.): Letters of Oscar Wilde. 1962.

* Hichens, Robert: Green Carnation. 1894.

Hofmannsthal, Hugo von: Sebastian Melmoth.

* Holland, Vyvyan: Son of Oscar Wilde. 1954.

Holland, Vyvyan: Pictorial Biography of Oscar Wilde. 1960.

Holmes, C. J.: Self and Partners. 1936.

* Hope-Nicholson, Jaqueline: Life amongst the Troubridges. 1968.

* Housman, Laurence: Echos de Paris. 1923.

* Housman, A. E.: A Shropshire Lad. 1914.

Hutchinson, Horace: Portraits of the Eighties. 1920.

* Hyde, H. Montgomery: The Trials of Oscar Wilde. 1948.

* Hyde, H. Montgomery: Oscar Wilde, The Aftermath. 1963.

* James, Henry: Selected Letters. 1956.

James, Henry: Notebooks. 1947.

Jullian, Philippe: Edward and the Edwardians. 1967.

Jullian, Philippe: Robert de Montesquiou, a fin de siècle Prince. 1967.

Lambert, Eric: Mad with much heart. 1967.

Langtry, Lily: The Days I knew. 1925.

* Leverson, Ada: Letters to the Sphinx from Oscar Wilde. 1930.

* Lewes and Justin Smith: Oscar Wilde Discovers America.

* MacCarthy, Sir Desmond: Memories. 1953.

Mahaffy, John Pentland: Rambles in Greece. 1876.

Masefield, Muriel: Disraeli, Peacocks and Primroses. 1953.

May, J. Lewis: John Lane and the Nineties. 1936.

Moore, George: Confessions of a Young Man. 1904.

Nordau, Max: Degeneration. 1895.

* O'Sullivan, Vincent: Aspects of Oscar Wilde. 1936.

Painter, George: Marcel Proust, 2 vols. 1959, 1965.

* Pearson, Hesketh: Life of Oscar Wilde. 1946.

* Pearson, Hesketh: Bernard Shaw. 1942.

Pearson, Hesketh: Gilbert. 1957.

* Pennell, Life of James McNeil Whistler. 1908.

* Poe, Edgar Allan: Works. 1927.

Praz, Mario: The Romantic Agony. 1951.

Prichard, Cooper: Conversations with Oscar Wilde.

Queensberry and Colson: Oscar Wilde and the Black Douglas. 1949.

Quennell, Peter: Ruskin. 1949.

* Raffalovich, André: Cyril and Lionel. 1884.

Renier, G. J.: Oscar Wilde. 1938.

Redesdale, Lord: *Memories*. 1915.
* Ricketts, Charles: *Recollections of Oscar Wilde*. 1932.
* Robertson, W. Graham: *Time Was*. 1931.
Rodd, Sir Rennell: *Social and Diplomatic Memories*. 1922.
Rothenstein, Sir John: *Life and Death of Conder*. 1938.
Rothenstein, Sir William: *Men and Memories*. 1931.
Russell, Leonard: *English Wits*. 1940.
* Sartre, Jean Paul: *St. Genet, Actor and Martyr*. 1964.
* Sherard, Robert: *Life of Oscar Wilde*. 1906.
* Sherard, Robert: *The Real Oscar Wilde*. 1911.
* Sitwell, Sir Osbert: *Noble Essences*. 1950.
Sitwell, Sir Osbert: *Right Hand Left Hand*. 1945, 1949.
Starkie, Enid: *From Gautier to Eliot*. 1960.
Steen, Marguerite: *Pride of Terrys*. 1961.
Symons, A. J. A.: *Aubrey Beardsley*. 1966.
Symons, A. J. A.: *Quest for Corvo*. 1955.
Sutton, Denys: *The Art of Whistler*. 1966.
White, Terence de Vere: *The Parents of Oscar Wilde*. 1967.
* Whistler, James McNeill: *The Gentle Art of Making Enemies*. 1890, 1968.
* Wilde, Oscar: *Collected Works*. 1948.
Wyndham, Horace: *Speranza*. 1951.
* Wyndham, Violet: *The Sphinx and her Circle*. 1963.

FRENCH
Barney, Nathalie: *Pensées d'une Amazone*. 1921.
Blanche, Jacques-Emile: *La Pêche aux Souvenirs*. 1949.
Bourget, Paul: *Notes d'esthétique*.
Bourget, Paul: *Etudes Anglaises*.
Brada: *Notes sur Londres*.
Cazamian, M.: *Romans et idées en Angleterre*. 1923.
Champion, Pierre: *Marcel Schwob et son temps*. 1927.
Delay, Jean: *La Jeunesse de Gide*. 1963.
Eekhoud, Georges: *Le Cycle Patibulaire*.
* Goncourt, Edmond de: *Journal*. 1915.
Jaloux, Edmond: *Saisons Littéraires*. 1942.
Joyant, Maurice: *Henri de Toulouse-Lautrec*. 1927.
La Jeunesse, Ernest: *Nos Contemporains*.
La Jeunesse, Ernest: *Introduction à Salomé*.
Lebois, André: *Jarry l'irremplacable*. 1950.
Lemonnier, Léon: *Vie d'Oscar Wilde*. 1931.
Lorrain, Jean: *La Petite Classe*.
Lorrain, Jean: *Modernités*.
Lorrain, Jean: *Monsieur de Phocas*. 1901.
Merle, Robert: *Oscar Wilde, Thèse*. 1948.

Merle, Robert: *Oscar Wilde ou la destinée de l'homosexuel*. 1955.
Mirbeau, Octave: *Critiques d'Art*.
Mirbeau, Octave: *Journal d'une femme de chambre*. 1900.
* Raffalovich, André: *Uranisme et unisexualité*.
Renard, Jules: *Journal*. 1887.
Roditi, Edouard: *Oscar Wilde*.
Schwob, Marcel: *Roi au Masque d'or*. 1893.
Schwob, Marcel: *Vies imaginaires*. 1896.
Thomas, Louis: *L'Esprit de Wilde*.

Index

415